Blue-Collar Pop Culture

Blue-Collar Pop Culture

From NASCAR to *Jersey Shore*

Volume 1: Film, Music, and Sports

M. Keith Booker, Editor

 PRAEGER

AN IMPRINT OF ABC-CLIO, LLC
Santa Barbara, California • Denver, Colorado • Oxford, England

Library of Congress Cataloging-in-Publication Data

Blue-collar pop culture : from NASCAR to Jersey Shore / M. Keith Booker, editor.
    p. cm.
  Includes index.
  ISBN 978-0-313-39198-9 (hardback) — ISBN 978-0-313-39199-6 (ebook)
  1. Blue collar workers—Social life and customs. 2. Popular culture. I. Booker, M. Keith.
  HD4901.B59   2012
  305.5'620973—dc23   2011035380

ISBN: 978-0-313-39198-9
EISBN: 978-0-313-39199-6

16 15 14 13 12   1 2 3 4 5

This book is also available on the World Wide Web as an eBook.
Visit www.abc-clio.com for details.

Praeger
An Imprint of ABC-CLIO, LLC

ABC-CLIO, LLC
130 Cremona Drive, P.O. Box 1911
Santa Barbara, California 93116-1911

This book is printed on acid-free paper (∞)

Manufactured in the United States of America

For my three sons, Adam, Skylor, and Benjamin.

Contents

Set Introduction

M. Keith Booker

"Culture," as Raymond Williams has famously noted, "is one of the two or three most complicated words in the English language," largely because the same word is used to encompass a wide variety of concepts and practices (87). Moreover, in the context of academic studies, the word *culture* is used differently in different disciplines. The word *popular* has a complex etymology and usage as well, meaning that the term *popular culture* has a wide range of possible meanings. The term is quite widely taken to encompass specific "artistic" forms, such as film and television, that are specifically produced for consumption by large audiences. This sense of the term *popular culture* also generally applies to music, though music as a cultural practice also includes a variety of forms that are more informal (and less corporate) than film and television production generally are. However, following the pioneering work of Williams himself, *culture* is now also commonly taken to encompass a variety of ordinary practices of everyday life. In some cases, this broader sense of popular culture, like the film and television industries, is still dominated by large corporate producers. For example, sports have long been a crucial part of working-class culture in the United States, and a variety of sports is played by working-class individuals on a daily basis. But it is also the case that, in the United States, sports can be big business, with major professional leagues dominated by teams that are themselves lucrative enterprises, valued in the hundreds of millions of dollars. The essays in this collection discuss a number of aspects of American popular culture, including not only film, television, music, and sports, but also a variety of other cultural practices, from religion, to food, to tourism. Whatever the form of culture, however, the focus in this collection is on the relevance of this culture to the lives of working-class individuals in the United States.

Class, of course, is a notoriously vexed category in the United States. Constance Coiner, in her introduction to the 1997 republication of Alexander Saxton's 1948 novel *The Great Midland* (an introduction tragically cut short by Coiner's untimely death aboard TWA Flight 800 in July 1996), praises the book for its sophisticated handling of the issue of class in modern American society. For Coiner, Saxton, who published a total of three novels from 1943 to 1959, thus differs from most of his contemporaries among American writers. He also offers an important object lesson to American literary scholars, who, Coiner suggests, continued even in the supposedly politicized teaching and criticism of the 1990s, to treat class as "the last taboo, the Great Unmentionable" (xi). Coiner was right, of course, and the situation remains largely unchanged more than a decade after her comments. The specter of the New Criticism, with its subtext of Cold War anticommunist hysteria, continues to haunt English departments all over America, typically in the guise (sometimes naïvely sincere, sometimes simply disingenuous) of rescuing the beauties of art from the ugly clutches of (leftist) politics. While American literary critics have, in recent years, begun to surmount the ostensibly complete rejection of politics (which really amounted to a rejection of *leftist* politics) that marked the criticism of the decades immediately after World War II, they have continued to avoid class as an analytical focus, preferring to concentrate instead on the more fashionable categories of race and gender, which critics have not been so conditioned to abhor by a half century of Cold War propaganda.

Of course, the effacement of class in American literature amounts primarily to an absence of the *working* class in American literature. With this in mind, one might argue that the effacement of class in American literature and American literary studies is not particularly surprising. After all, within the broader context of modern culture, literature is typically a rather elite pursuit indulged in primarily by a relatively privileged and highly educated minority, even though there have been moments in modern American cultural history when, locally, this was not necessarily the case—as with the proletarian literature movement of the 1930s. This movement has received considerable critical attention from scholars such as Barbara Foley and Alan Wald in recent years, while I myself have attempted to document a broader tradition of left-leaning worker-oriented novels in *The Modern American Novel of the Left*.

Such studies have demonstrated that there is a somewhat richer tradition of working-class representations in American literature than has generally been recognized, those this tradition is strongly rooted in the special moment of the Depression years of the 1930s. Still, despite such revelations, the American working class has historically had relatively few opportunities to generate a culture of its own—partly because of historical denial of the existence of class in the United States leaves no space for the development of a specifically working-class culture. One might contrast here the situation in Great Britain, where class consciousness has long been more highly developed than in the United States and where there is a stronger tradition of working-class culture. For example, E. P. Thompson's magisterial *The Making of the English Working Class* outlines the rise of a vibrant English working-class culture in the early nineteenth century, emphasizing that this culture is not merely a product of the contemporary industrial revolution, but of hundreds of years of class-based resistance to agrarian capitalism and political oppression. Such traditions are essentially nonexistent in the United States, making the development of working-class cultural traditions far more difficult.

Other aspects of American culture, of course, are ostensibly less elitist, and indeed many of the products of American *popular* culture have been disparaged by critics as lacking artistic merit by adopting a least common denominator approach in an attempt to appeal to the largest possible audience. Such works of culture have often been labeled as "mass" culture to indicate this search for broad appeal, with the pejorative implication that any attempt to appeal to a "mass" audience is inimical to genuine aesthetic achievement. This attitude, of course, suggests an elitist contempt for the masses themselves. On the other hand, it should be remembered that "mass" culture is produced *for* the masses, not by them, and that the bulk of this production is carried out by the large and powerful corporate entities that make up the American Culture Industry.

This Culture Industry has been famously seen by Max Horkheimer and Theodor Adorno as a crucial support for the capitalist power structure in the United States. In their seminal essay "The Culture Industry: Enlightenment as Mass Deception" (published in their 1947 book *Dialectic of Enlightenment*), Horkheimer and Adorno critiqued the operations of the Culture Industry in ways that have remained strongly influential in cultural studies ever since. Befitting the Marxist perspective of the Frankfurt School of whom they were central members, Horkheimer and Adorno place particular emphasis on the functioning of the Culture Industry as a key element of a capitalist system that maintains its power through the ideological manipulation of the general population. As a result of this manipulation, most individuals endorse and support the capitalist system, even though the majority of them are disadvantaged by it. In particular, Horkheimer and Adorno argue that the products of Western popular culture are designed to provide an entertaining diversion from the realities of day-to-day capitalist exploitation. This entertainment helps to make the daily lives of individuals more bearable despite the true conditions of their existence. As a result, they are less likely to take action to change those conditions or even to recognize that they need to be changed. Indeed, the latter element of this phenomenon is crucial to the Horkheimer and Adorno discussion of the Culture Industry. For them, the products of Western popular culture immerse consumers in a never-ending stream of mind-numbing images that dull the faculties and essentially act to stupefy the general population, rendering them largely incapable of the kind of critical thought that is needed to understand the workings of capitalism or to envision alternatives to it.

This analysis emphasizes that the "official" popular culture of the United States is not an expression of the point of view of the working class so much as an attempt to manipulate and control that point of view to the advantage of America's corporate masters. Thus, far from the organic working-class culture described by Thompson as arising in early nineteenth-century Britain, American popular culture might be seen as a powerful force that interferes with the development of anything like a genuine working-class culture in the United States. On the other hand, in order to work its effects on a working-class audience, popular culture must surely appeal to working-class sensibilities. Thus, while it is surely the case that the tastes and values of individuals are to a large extent a product of their interaction with the products of the Culture Industry, it is also surely the case that the ideological domination of the masses by official culture can never be complete, especially in a capitalist society in which the official ideology is itself inherently complex and multiple.

Thus, whatever the power of the American Culture Industry (and however dominated it might be by large corporations with little or no interest in stimulating vital and independent working-class identities), one would expect that there might be cracks and fissures through which working-class perspectives might shine through. In fact, the representation of class in American culture is a highly complex and vexed category in general. Still, it is clearly the case that the working class has generally been underrepresented and misrepresented in American popular culture. Except for certain kinds of workers (such as cowboys or hard-boiled detectives) who can easily be romanticized as individualist heroes, American film and television have typically been much more interested in representing the experience of professionals such as scientists, artists, doctors, and lawyers than in telling the stories of ordinary working people. Such workers have traditionally either been absent altogether, present merely as background (essentially part of the scenery), or, in some cases, present as degenerate villains. When blue-collar workers have been major characters, they have quite often been represented as louts or buffoons, especially when they are male. Indeed, it is probably no accident that so many of the most successful blue-collar protagonists have appeared in animated television comedies (one thinks of Fred Flintstone, Homer Simpson, and Peter Griffin), where their representation can literally be cartoonish. Working-class women have received somewhat better treatment in lead roles on film and television, though examples such as *Norma Rae* in film or television's *Roseanne* are made all the more striking because they are so rare.

Even in film and television, however, working-class characters and concerns might be more prominent than is generally realized, class itself being such a forbidden category in American political and cultural discourse that most film and television critics don't even think in terms of class. As a result, such critics don't typically look at films from a working-class point of view, making working-class issues virtually invisible to them. One premise of this two-volume collection is that the working class is, to an extent, underrepresented in American popular culture making it all the more important for critics to focus on working-class themes when studying popular culture. Another premise, however, is that the working class might well have a more prominent presence in American popular culture than has generally been realized, if only critics (and popular audiences) would focus their attention on that presence.

The first volume of this collection contains 20 essays on American film, music, and sports written by critics who are, for a change, focused on class (and particularly the working class) as a central concern. They do indeed find a range of works and practices that focus on working-class characters and working-class experience, though the representation of workers and their lives in American film is often highly problematic. Similarly, the second volume contains essays on American television, again demonstrating that a fairly wide range of American television series has dealt with working-class life, though again in ways that sometimes descend into stereotyping or condescension toward workers. This volume also includes a section of essays that addresses aspects of everyday life such as religion, food, and tourist attractions.

Together, the 38 essays in these two volumes suggest that the relationship between the American working class and American popular culture is in fact quite complex. Indeed, while it is true that American popular culture foregrounds working-class concerns less than it should and that the working class is as often misrepresented as represented in that culture, it is also the case that close and careful reading of American popular culture can reveal more instances of positive engagement with working-class issues than might be evident on the surface.

Works Cited

Booker, M. Keith. *The Modern American Novel of the Left.* Westport, CT: Greenwood Press, 1999.

Coiner, Constance. "The Old Left and Cross-Gendered Writing." Introduction to *The Great Midland,* by Alexander Saxton, xi–xxviii. Urbana: University of Illinois Press, 1997.

Foley, Barbara. *Radical Representations: Politics and Form in U. S. Proletarian Fiction, 1929–1941.* Durham, NC: Duke University Press, 1993.

Horkheimer, Max, and Theodor W. Adorno. *Dialectic of Enlightenment.* Translated by John Cumming. New York: Seabury Press, 1972.

Thompson, E. P. *The Making of the English Working Class.* 1963. New York: Vintage-Random House, 1966.

Wald, Alan. *Exiles from a Future Time: The Forging of the Mid-Twentieth-Century Literary Left.* Chapel Hill: University of North Carolina Press, 2001.

Wald, Alan. *Writing from the Left: New Essays on Radical Culture and Politics.* London: Verso, 1994.

Williams, Raymond. *Keywords: A Vocabulary of Culture and Society.* Rev. ed. New York: Oxford University Press, 1983.

Introduction

Blue-Collar Culture Industry: Film, Music, Sport, and the American Working Class

M. Keith Booker

Film as a medium rose to popularity in the United States in the early years of the twentieth century, running slightly ahead of radio in its development. It was thus the first modern "mass" medium. Importantly, film was also quite widely viewed, in its earliest years, as a medium best suited for working-class audiences. As Steven Ross has argued in his important book *Working-Class Hollywood* (1998), film became a crucial part of the culture of American organized labor as early as the first decade of the century and continued so until the political repression associated with World War I put a virtual halt to the making of such prolabor films (and to radical organized labor activity in general). Even pioneer silent filmmaker D. W. Griffith, although often remembered for his racist politics in films such as *The Birth of a Nation,* had certain working-class loyalties and made numerous early films of protest against the exploitation of workers by emergent American capitalism. And, of course, Charlie Chaplin (essentially exiled from America in the 1950s because of his leftist politics) consistently lampooned the rich and showed sympathy for the poor, even in his earliest films, though it was not until the sequence of films beginning with *Modern Times* (1936) and extending through *The Great Dictator* (1940) and *A King in New York* (1957) that his leftist political position became overt in his films. Given the participation of such important figures as Griffith and Chaplin, it is clear that early working-class film was central to the evolution of the cinema itself.

Indeed, it is important to recognize that film as a popular medium historically arose very much at the same time that a genuine American working class began to form with the dramatic growth in industrialization in the United States around the beginning of the twentieth century. Thus, Robert Sklar points out in *Movie-Made America,* his important cultural history of American film, that the movies emerged as an important force in American culture "from the bottom up, receiving their principal support from the lowest and most invisible classes in American society" (3). Further, Sklar points out that the American film industry emerged during a crucial turning point in American history, as the explosive growth of consumer capitalism at the turn of the century led to a radical restructuring of American society and in particular the rapid growth of an urban working class that included unprecedented numbers of immigrant workers, newly arrived (mostly from Europe) to feed the ever-expanding demands of burgeoning American capitalism for more (and, preferably, cheaper) labor.

The growth of this new class of American workers understandably led to considerable tensions and anxieties; even as these new workers provided the principal fuel for the growth of what we now think of as the American way of life, these newcomers were at the time widely regarded as a dangerous threat to established American values. Among other things, the prominence of immigrants among the early twentieth-century working class established a close connection between class and ethnicity that has remained an important part of the American cultural landscape ever since. Where film is concerned, anxieties over the association between the new medium and immigrant workers established a tendency to suspect that film was exercising a negative influence on American society that remains in place in America as well: if immigrants threatened American values, then so did film.

The 1920s saw the beginnings of the reemergence of working-class film, though this phenomenon was quickly cut short by the rise to dominance of Hollywood and the Hollywood style in American film. Nevertheless, films with working-class themes continued to be made and even experienced something of a resurgence in the 1930s, as can be seen by the fact that left-leaning documentaries, such as Pare Lorentz's *The Plow That Broke the Plains* (1936) and *The River* (1937), were made under the sponsorship of the U.S. government as part of the New Deal. Independent leftist film companies produced a number of important prolabor documentaries in the 1930s as well, and even commercial Hollywood films were forced to pay attention to the social and economic conditions brought about by the Depression of that decade.

The Depression also played a central role in the dramatic increase in production of proletarian novels in the 1930s, and many of these novels were eventually made into films, though often in diluted form. John Ford's 1940 adaptation of John Steinbeck's *The Grapes of Wrath* was probably the most successful of these films, and its depiction of the tribulations of the working-class Joad family remains one of the classics of American cinema. And, certainly, the down-home, Everyman protagonists who populated many of the early films of Frank Capra—from *It Happened One Night* (1934) to *Meet John Doe* (1941)—could be considered blue-collar characters because of their seeming working-class values, even if they do not actively engage in typical working-class jobs.

With the entry of the United States into World War II, progressive filmmakers who might formerly have been concerned with working-class issues turned their attention to the making of antifascist films, including a few films (made at the behest of the U.S. government) designed to drum up sympathy and support for the Soviet Union, allied with the United States and Great Britain against Nazi Germany and the Axis powers. Political films through the 1940s were dominated by such themes, and the war years brought leftist filmmakers, with their strong antifascist experience and credentials, to the forefront in Hollywood. After the war, the anticommunist purges that swept Hollywood ended the prominence of left-leaning filmmakers, many of whom were blacklisted or (as in the case of the Hollywood Ten) even imprisoned for their supposedly procommunist points of view.

In this climate, any return to working-class themes in American film became a near impossibility. Exceptions such as the union-sponsored *Salt of the Earth* (1954), made outside the Hollywood system by blacklisted filmmakers, only served to highlight the virtual absence of overtly working-class themes in American film of the 1950s, even if the cowboys who populated Westerns and the private detectives of film noir had obliquely blue-collar associations. With the coming of the 1960s, the situation began to change, and the blacklist was broken with films such as *Spartacus* (1960, written by Dalton Trumbo, one of the Hollywood Ten), the slave rebellion at the center of which can clearly be taken as a displaced allegory of collective working-class resistance to exploitation.

Meanwhile, the general social climate of the 1960s was conducive to the making of politically engaged films that often critiqued mainstream

American social values, though class issues were largely overshadowed by concerns related to race and gender, thanks to the prominence of the civil rights and women's movements of the decade. Still, films that sympathetically addressed the plight of American workers did return to Hollywood in the 1960s, with the work of the formerly blacklisted Martin Ritt deserving special mention in this regard. Ritt made a number of films treating working-class concerns in the 1960s and 1970s, culminating in the mainstream success of *Norma Rae* (1979), an avowedly prolabor film that gained a Best Picture Oscar nomination and won two Oscars, including Best Actress for star Sally Field. More than 30 years later, *Norma Rae* remains one of the key classics of working-class cinema, though it is also clear that the success of the film came partly because its treatment of class and labor issues was combined with a treatment, more popular in Hollywood, of gender issues.

Coming along slightly later, the films of John Sayles also deserve special mention for their sympathy with the downtrodden and disenfranchised, and often in ways that foreground class inequality as the crucial element in the oppression of these groups. Indeed, Sayles's *Matewan* (1987) is a far more politically radical examination of American labor activism than is *Norma Rae*, while its greater pessimism merely makes it more representative of the true history of labor in America. Very much a work in the tradition of the proletarian culture of the 1930s, *Matewan* is based on the bitter and bloody labor battles that tore through the West Virginia coal fields in the early 1920s. In particular, the film focuses on a conflict between the Stone Mountain Coal Company of Matewan, West Virginia, and the coal miners who work for the company. When hired goons are sent in to put down a strike, the miners meet force with force, and even win a temporary victory, but it is clear that this is a war they cannot ultimately win under the social, political, and economic conditions that prevailed at that time (or in ours). The film, however, is not utterly pessimistic; its sympathetic treatment of the striking miners is nothing short of inspirational, while the movement of the film clearly suggests that workers could have tremendous political power if they would only stick together and stand firm.

Sayles has continued to make thoughtful films that show compassion for social and economic outsiders to this day, though he would never again focus on organized labor in the way he did in *Matewan*. However, his small independent films have had little impact on the mainstream Hollywood film industry, which has continued to focus on action, special effects, and personal drama/comedy rather than larger social concerns, especially if those concerns involve the working class. Still, the essays in this volume indicate that the working class has continued to play an important role in Hollywood film, almost in spite of the industry's efforts.

The first essay in this volume, by Jan Goggans, deals with the depiction of office workers (mostly female) in silent film and Golden Age Hollywood film. Among other things, this essay demonstrates that the focus on women workers in more recent films from *Norma Rae* to *North Country* (2005) has extensive roots in the Hollywood tradition, even if women workers in film were initially situated largely in office environments. On the other hand, especially with the coming of the Hollywood Production Code in the 1930s, the honest depiction of the experience of working women became more and more difficult. Golden Age Hollywood struggled to mirror the situation of real women in a political and cultural climate that discouraged women from working and a labor economy that could not support their attempts to build on the previous decade's expansion of the female workforce. Goggans concludes that representations of working-class women in Golden Age film often sought to represent their real experience, but more often, films inadvertently represented the complicated and often impossible subjectivity of a woman in the working world.

Catherine Chaput follows with a discussion of a number of films, including *Salt of the Earth, Norma Rae,* and *North Country,* among others that focus on the role of women in labor activism. These films are based on actual historical union activity in the United States and thus serve as important reminders of important moments in labor history. Tracing a common "structure of feeling" among these films, Chaput concludes that they are most important not for their depiction of unionization efforts but for their understanding of the way class, race, gender, and sexuality are all mutually involved in an ongoing struggle for justice.

In this same vein, Lisa Hinrichsen examines the history of films about working-class lives, paying special attention to the relationship between race and class in these films. In addition to offering a brief history of cinematic representation of these categories of identity, her essays offers a close reading of Courtney Hunt's 2008 independent film *Frozen River.* Highlighting the racial, sexual, and class-based crossroads of power, this film tells the story of two working-class women of different races who uneasily collaborate together to smuggle illegal immigrants from Canada to the United States in the North Country area of upstate New York. Rather than crossing the "official" border, a bridge full of police surveillance and border control measures, they drive across an unguarded frozen river on the Mohawk Territory of Akwesasne, which stretches across national borders. Together these three different legal, cultural, and economic spaces intersect to form what Mary Louise Pratt terms a "contact zone," which allows the intermingling of two or more cultures. Thus, the film, by almost exclusively portraying working-class characters within this complex contact zone, seeks to place working-class identity within a global, multiracial, and multicultural framework. As *Frozen River* evinces, the future of working-class identity is one in which cultural hybridity comes to play an important role, and the film, which powerfully destabilizes assumptions about white privilege, ultimately portrays the border as a zone where the disenfranchised must negotiate with one another and manufacture new relations, hybrid cultures, and, ultimately, multicultural communities and families.

Meanwhile, though Hinrichsen's work focuses on the far north, her essay leads into a series of essays that focus on working-class identities, especially among poor whites in the South. Lorie Watkins Fulton begins this section with a discussion of Dorothy Allison's novel *Bastard out of Carolina*, with special reference to its film adaptation. Fulton finds that this novel/film combination effective challenges a number of stereotypes about poor whites (especially poor white women) in the South. Katie Sullivan Barak and Justin Philpot next examine the portrayal of "rednecks" in American film, while at the same time considering the larger constellation of cultural stereotypes that define poor southern whites in American film. Barak and Philpot also investigate the differences and similarities among the portrayals of the "redneck," "white trash," and "hillbilly" over the past 40 years. Of particular concern is the role of generic conventions and expectations, the narrative force that often predetermines which we see in a given film: the redneck, white trash, or hillbilly character. Next, Andy Johnson's essay continues this "southern" arc of the volume by discussing how the southerners in the 1977 film *Smokey and the Bandit* combine both progressive southern culture and the spirit of the Old West using the genre of the trucker film. Johnson traces the history of the trucker film and shows how the genre reveals popular culture's interest in the blue-collar professional drivers, leading to an elevation of the long-haul trucker into working-class folk heroes. Finally, Daniel Cross Turner's essay discusses a number of films that ostensibly focus on the topic of "Southernness," including Elia Kazan's *A Streetcar Named Desire* (1951), John Boorman's *Deliverance* (1972), the Coen brothers' *O Brother, Where Art Thou?* (2000), and John Hillcoat's *The Road* (2009). Turner argues that, while indeed focusing on the South, these films are centrally concerned with the topic of work and, by extension, the working class.

Iris Shepard's essay on the limited representation of working-class children in contemporary American children's film is the first of several essays in this volume that deal with working-class children and young adults. Shepard argues that the imaginary relationships that children's films have been building between children and the issue of class over the past three decades seem to be more ideologically conservative and reactionary than in previous decades. It is followed by Jennifer Dutch's discussion of the films *The Last Starfighter, Explorers,* and *Space Camp,* all of which feature young protagonists, and all of which seem to present positive images of the accessibility of the American dream to such protagonists. Dutch, notes, however, that these images might, in fact, make this dream seem more accessible than it really is. Finally, Richard Mora and Mary Christianakis look at a number of high school genre films featuring urban working-class youth and argue that these films promulgate both the myth of meritocracy and the culture of poverty narrative by the students as either unsalvageable or as having the potential to becoming law-abiding, contributing members of society if they set aside their deviant lifestyles and cultural ways and accept mainstream values.

The final segment of this section looks at two examples of genre film, beginning with Marcus Schulzke's discussion of the representation of working-class characters in war movies. Schulzke notes that these representations are often quite positive, but that the figuration of blue-collar characters in these films is heavily dependent upon the overall perception of the conflict in which they are involved.

Concluding the coverage of film in this volume, Brian Granger looks at representation (and devaluation) of working-class labor in Hollywood musicals, and how a general misunderstanding of film musical form has masked the productive ways labor can be read in these films. Working from Rick Altman's theory of the film musical as a conceptual structure of social values in opposition, Granger offers an adjustment to this theory and demonstrates how its application to working-class musicals like Walt Disney's *Newsies* (1992) is useful in developing a critical appreciation for the ways in which Hollywood addresses and avoids its own problematic representations of labor.

Granger's essay on the musical provides a transition into this volume's coverage of the topic of music in blue-collar culture. The four essays in this section deal with a variety of ways in which American popular music intersects with working-class life. Music has a special place in any discussion of "blue-collar" popular culture because popular music, as a cultural form, often has more authentic working-class roots than do forms such as film and television. For example, there is a strong tradition of the use of music to support the cause of organized labor. Perhaps the best-known American labor song is the ballad "Which Side Are You On?" written by Florence Reece in 1931 to support the attempts of coal miners in Harlan County, Kentucky, to organize to resist exploitation and violent intimidation by the mine owners. That song, which has been something of an anthem of organized labor ever since, stands out for its open understanding of labor struggles as a matter of class conflict. It has been recorded many times, perhaps most memorably by folk music icon Pete Seeger in 1967. In addition, Seeger and Woody Guthrie, probably the two most prominent figures in American folk music, frequently sang in support of workers battling for justice, while also often directly critiquing the capitalist system that enables (even depends upon) the unfair treatment of workers.

On the other hand, as the songs of such "protest" singers gained a wider audience amid the political movements of the 1960s, they also began to lose some of their working-class specificity, highlighting the failure of those movements (based in demands for racial and gender equality and strongly built upon a sense of generational differences, especially with regard to the Vietnam War) to understand the fundamental importance of class or to mobilize working people in support of their causes. Emblematic of this phenomenon (and of so many other phenomena in American cultural history of the past half century) is the music of Bob Dylan, the most prominent heir to the folk tradition embodied in the work of Guthrie and Seeger. While Dylan's music expresses a consistent sympathy for the downtrodden and the misunderstood, it seldom figures this sympathy in class terms, signaling the decline of worker-oriented folk music in America. Several of Dylan's compositions, such as the early "Song to Woody" (included on Dylan's self-titled inaugural album in 1962), openly acknowledge his debt to his folk predecessors, especially Guthrie. Dylan even directly quotes the title line of "Which Side Are You On?" in his own "Desolation Row" (*Highway 61 Revisited*, released in 1965); however, he does so amid a stream of surreal and apocalyptic images that express a strong sense of social crisis but that do not identify class struggle as a key element of this crisis. Meanwhile, Dylan's accumulation of influences over the course of his career (from the Roman poet Ovid to Humphrey Bogart movies to the television series *Star Trek*) gradually diluted his folk origins and made him instead a sort of compendium of American pop culture, trying on one identity after another. Even a late song such as the suggestively titled "Workingman's Blues #2" (on the 2006 album *Modern Times*) is aimed more at the downtrodden in general than specifically at workers, and certainly seems less situated within working-class culture than had Merle Haggard's more roughly hewn "Workin' Man's Blues" from 1969, which it updates with a reflection on the changing place of workers within evolving global economic conditions. Still, Haggard's version, with its repeated declaration that "I'll be working long as my two hands are fit to use," is far more obviously blue collar in its orientation than is Dylan's update, which is more of a general lament for hard times; it is certainly not the kind of workers' rallying cry that made "Which Side Are You On?" so special.

Of course, music is a broad category that involves not only the products of large recording companies, but also a wide variety of more informal means for the recording and distribution of music. Moreover, new digital means for reproduction of music have led to dramatic changes in the way music is distributed among listeners. Live performances also constitute an important element of musical culture, and, while such performances may also involve big-money corporate-sponsored tours by high-profile performers, they more frequently involve smaller performances by local amateur or semiprofessional performers, some of whom may even be performing more for their own entertainment than for consumption by audiences.

Music thus inherently contains certain "grassroots" elements that cannot be found to the same extent in film and television. In addition, if folk music proper seems to have drifted away from its working-class roots, other forms of American music with folk connections have maintained a stronger sense of affiliation with the working class. For example, the first essay in this volume involves a discussion of the blues, one of the forms of American music that has the most authentic roots in working-class or "folk" culture. On the other hand, blues music has become increasingly commercialized in recent years, at the same time exercising a strong influence on the evolution of rock and roll music, which itself has achieved even more commercial success, while sometimes still striving to maintain its own connections with working-class life. Moreover, as the essay by Terrence Tucker emphasizes, blues music, rooted in the work of African American performers, is also one of the forms of American popular culture that speaks most directly to the history of race relations in America.

If blues music has exercised a strong influence on the evolution of American rock and roll music, the same can be said of folk music (especially in the work of Dylan himself). However, of all of the major American forms of popular music, rock music is the most cosmopolitan in the extent to which it has been directly influenced by contemporary forces outside the United States. Thus, though rock had arisen as an important form from sources in indigenous country, folk, and (especially) rhythm and blues music, the course of American popular music was changed radically in the early 1960s with the arrival of the so-called British Invasion, as a number of British rock groups (headlined by the Beatles) gained tremendous popularity in the United States. These British groups, of course, had themselves been heavily influenced by earlier developments in American rock music, but they also brought significant new elements, not the least of which was the fact that many of these new British performers strongly identified with their own working-class roots, in keeping with the much stronger working-class cultural traditions in Great Britain, as opposed to the United States. The next essay in this volume, by Sandra Dawson, deals with this phenomenon, focusing specifically on the ways in which the American reception of the British invasion touches on the issue of class and on the ways in which class is figured differently in the United States and in Great Britain.

The next essay in this volume, by Ryan Poll, focuses on one specific performer, Bruce Springsteen, whose tremendous critical and commercial success have not prevented a strong and ongoing identification with the working class. However, Poll argues, Springsteen's status goes well beyond the performer's own blue-collar image and the fact that so many of his songs express sympathies for workers. Springsteen's music, Poll argues, is especially important for the way it relates narratives of working-class experience within the specific framework of the past few decades, a difficult and changing historical context that has continually posed new challenges to working-class people in America. Springsteen's lyrics, Poll argues, evolve from articulating working-class alienation in an industrialized economy into a progressive art that recognizes and critiques the structural violences constitutive of global capitalism. As Springsteen's class consciousness develops, his music moves away from hopeless, frustrated, and alienated individual workers and focuses more on imagining emerging collectivities grounded in compassion, care, and a sense of social justice.

Finally, the section on music in this volume ends with an essay by William DeGenaro on musical reactions to the 9/11 bombings in New York and Washington, DC. DeGenaro notes that 9/11 changed virtually every facet of American culture, including popular music. In particular, these responses were often designed to promote a specifically working-class brand of patriotism. Moreover, DeGenaro notes that this music was part of a larger phenomenon in which the media were uncharacteristically flooded with working-class iconography and heroic images of working-class individuals (especially police and firefighters). Popular music stars downplayed their elite backgrounds in an effort to establish legitimacy during a cultural moment when "working class" became associated with "patriotic."

Some donned working-class uniforms; some reached into their catalogue for songs (such as "Salt of the Earth" by the Rolling Stones) that spoke to the cultural imperatives to align with workers/patriots. Country stars like Toby Keith crafted jingoistic, blue-collar, post-9/11 anthems. Some singer-songwriters like Springsteen, meanwhile, took a more humanistic approach and wrote 9/11 anthems that focused on working-class individuals instead of abstractions. Finally, some punk and folk acts like Green Day and Ani Difranco crafted musical responses that expressed political and class-based disenfranchisement during the post-9/11 moment. What all these 9/11 representations have in common is they allow us to meditate on existential and material realities, in particular the realities of American working-class mythology. Among other things, DeGenaro argues that this phenomenon suggests that class in America, while a material reality, is also a matter of performance.

The final section of this volume contains our essays that deal with some of the ways in which sports intersects with working-class life in the United States, though the first two essays actually focus on films about sports. First, Derek Maus looks at the representation of blue-collar athletes and blue-collar values in American sports movies, with a special emphasis on baseball and boxing. Among other things, the prominence of such films suggests the extent to which sports and blue-collar values are intertwined in the popular imagination. Maus maintains that sports movies tend to locate athletes among the relatively powerless in opposition to a greedy and corrupt ownership class that threatens not only the sanctity of whatever game is being depicted but also the meritocratic ideal of the American Dream. However, he argues that sports films rarely cross over into revolutionary rhetoric of class conflict in depicting this opposition, preferring to argue for an equitable "playing field" on which the quintessentially blue-collar values of hard work, honesty, and humble use of talent lead to just rewards.

While Maus's essay deals with mainstream sports, the next essay, by Rebecca Tolley-Stokes, deals with the much more marginal sport of roller derby, and particularly with films about roller derby. Tracing the cinematic representation of roller derby from *The Fireball* (1950) to *Whip It!* (2009), Tolley-Stokes examines the changing social role of roller derby (and, to an extent, of roller skating in general) over that period, noting in particular the working-class resonances of the sport, which have recently taken on a particularly feminist intonation as well, with the sport now dominated by player-owned, women-only leagues.

Bob Batchelor follows with an essay on NASCAR stock-car racing, perhaps the single sports phenomenon that is most closely associated with the working class in the popular mind. Focusing particularly on the Earnhardts, Dale and Dale Jr., Batchelor argues that the Earnhardts symbolize the transition from "classic" to "corporate" NASCAR. While the older Earnhardt represented "classic" racing by winning and crafting an on-track tough-guy image, Dale Jr. is embraced by fans based on his family name and by being thrust on fans through multiple sponsorships and celebrity status. The schism is between Dale Sr. "earning" his iconic status, while his son was "handed" the mantle without deserving it based on his performance. Yet, from a business perspective, any division between the two is blurry. The Earnhardt family symbolizes both the traditional, blue-collar roots of early NASCAR and today's big business appeal of the sport.

For Batchelor, consumerism is essentially at the heart of the new "corporate" NASCAR and the way the sport as a product is marketed today. And, while Dale Jr. symbolizes the way the sport is sold on the contemporary corporate stage, Dale Sr. actually began this move by growing in stature beyond the sport itself, becoming universally iconic, rather than just a star within the parameters of his individual sport. It is as if Dale Earnhardt Sr. and NASCAR rocketed in popularity and importance concurrently, riding the wave of increasing popularity through televised races and multichannel marketing opportunities that gave them both virtually unlimited platforms.

Eoin F. Cannon closes this volume with a discussion of mixed martial arts (MMA), which—in a little more than a decade of legal legitimacy—has come to rival boxing as the leading commercial combat sport, and has transformed the popular cultural imaginary surrounding fighting. Unlike boxing, whose social practice and cultural symbolism are both firmly working-class, MMA does not have a clear social valence. In its promotional rhetoric and event spectacle it is intensely individualistic, but its training practices and social structures are much more complicated. Its fighters come from a widening zone where the working and middle classes share financial instability and employment uncertainty, and MMA's own labor practices often reflect the worst of this world. The fighters' training networks and fighting methods, however, exemplify the best of the values needed to survive this new landscape, in often tense combinations of self-reliance and collectivity, submission and autonomy, flexibility and resilience, and creativity and fatalism.

Together, the essays in this volume indicate a number of ways in which various aspects of American popular culture, despite the dominance of large, corporate forces, often address issues of special concern to the working class. At the same time, these essays suggest many of the complexities of class in America, including a growing ambiguity in the boundary between working-class and middle-class positions in contemporary American society.

Works Cited

Ross, Steven J. *Working-Class Hollywood: Silent Film and the Shaping of Class in America.* Princeton, NJ: Princeton UP, 1998.

Sklar, Robert. *Movie-Made America: A Cultural History of American Movies.* Rev. ed. New York: Vintage-Random House, 1994.

PART I

Blue-Collar Film

Chapter 1

Blue Collars and Pink Skirts: Female Office Workers in Early and Golden Age Cinema

Jan Goggans

The less skill and exertion of strength implied in manual labor, in other words, the more modern industry becomes developed, the more is the labor of men superseded by that of women.

—Karl Marx

King Vidor's *The Crowd* (1928) tells the story of a young man, born on the Fourth of July, who is slowly engulfed in New York's hostile and uncaring world of business. As John's birth date suggests, he is an all-American boy, the pride of his father and the hope of his mother. Yet, despite his buoyant dreams of success, he becomes part of the crowd, swallowed up by the city, his talent and enterprise unwelcomed and unnoticed by those who could help him rise up in society and life. In a telling scene, he sits at desk number 137, and the camera's slow pull back, drawing progressively farther and farther away from John, reveals countless numbered desks at which similarly anonymous young men sit. While John's struggles to set himself apart from the crowd seem resolved by the film's final shot of a laughing crowd at the cinema, the happy ending is ambiguous, for the crowd's laughter has been foreshadowed by the film's earlier directive: "The crowd laughs with you always but it will only cry for a day." This commentary, inserted via title card into the mostly silent film,[1] forewarns audiences of the dangers inherent to the struggle for individuality: "We do not know how big the crowd is and how great its opposition until we get out of step with it." For John, the youthful desire he once expressed to "be something big" is overturned and tarnished by the heedless crowd that ignores both his triumphs and his tragedies. His working-class status threatens far more than his financial well-being; it threatens to make him inconsequential, one of many, all of whom will turn away from him if he gets "out of step."

Vidor's film highlights a number of crucial characteristics of early cinema, from the silent films of the early twentieth century to the beginnings of Hollywood's rich Golden Age. During this time, the country's troubled response to shifting attitudes toward class and money, increasing tension over labor markets, and ongoing differences in economic and cultural status for men and women were themes movies explored in a variety of narratives that sought both to articulate and antagonize blue-collar culture in the United States.[2] As work and the working class changed, the office became a place that bespoke men's struggles with individuality. Ultimately, as in Vidor's film, the office served to signify masculine failure to achieve success and autonomy. Working class was, such films suggest, a decent enough starting point, and carried with it honest American values such as filial love and the desire to do some good in the world. Only when men found themselves swallowed by the increasing automations of an impersonal workforce did their status become a liability; workers, films suggested, were good men, who deserved to get ahead in life, if only they could.

But working-class life (and the working world it included) was a different place for women, as was demonstrated by a Paramount Pictures silent film released just a few years before *The Crowd*. In *Manhandled* (1924), a young Gloria Swanson plays Tessie McGuire who, like John, is "one of the crowd."[3] But Tessie's life in the crowd is vastly different than John's, as the opening words warn: "The world lets a girl believe that its pleasures and luxuries may be hers without cost . . . that's chivalry. But if she claims them on this basis it sends her a bill in full, with no discount . . . that's reality." In this way, women are set up immediately to be "manhandled" in a variety of ways, their chronic and constant commodification within culture and society a simple fact of life, and their opportunities to get ahead or rise up through hard work and individualism, nonexistent. The film makes Tessie's status as a female worker clear. Its title card tells audiences: "In Thorndyke's Dept. store at the end of the day. Tired feet. Tired hands. All women." In this world, working-class girls see little of the chivalry the title card mentions, and no discounts. On the way to work, Tessie is splashed with mud by a car speeding by her, and on the subway train, the larger, taller men overrun her: she is crushed between them and her hat repeatedly knocked off, she is inadvertently prodded, and more than one man winks lasciviously at her. But her return home from work makes clear that marriage offers little escape in Tessie's eyes; longing to go out and dance, she suffers her boyfriend Jimmy's unwillingness to do so, and watches unhappy couples fight in the windows across from hers. One wife looks hot and harassed; the other struggles with a baby. Tessie is convinced that married life "ain't any good—not for people like us!"

To reinforce the working-class tenor of Tessie's woes, the film opposes blue-collar workers to the artists and intellectuals of the era. Tessie fascinates a novelist who thinks "a shop girl was a strange but interesting human being," and the temper she displays in an argument that leads to her dismissal from Thorndyke's urges him to call her "that little Bolshevik." In a reflection of the era's worry over increased strife caused by labor unions and "red" organizations, the novelist decides "to cultivate" this "rebel," his immediate desire to reform Tessie drawing a firm line between the two classes. And the film does not encourage audiences to root for female laborers. The novelist's high-handed attitude and elitist demeanor are not presented as decidedly worse than Tessie's own approach to life. Her manners at a high society party, including a slapstick scene in which an impromptu and tipsy dance causes her undergarments to fall off and trip her, would be amusing to theater audiences but painful to think of in reality. When she is offered a lucrative position posing as Russian royalty, she is tempted by the promise of higher social standing and increased contact with high society types, and she accepts the offer gladly. "So," the movie's title card intones, "Tessie climbed out of Thorndyke's basement, happy in the thought that she was keeping pace with Jimmy in his struggle to rise in the world." But the film has already made clear that her struggle is far less noble than that of Jimmy, who is hard at work trying to develop a marketable patent. No matter where she is in society, the film insists on her commodification; whether by force or choice, she is no less hunted and pawed over than the goods she once sold, but the film refuses to truly address the trap that reality created for many women workers. While Tessie is at first frustrated by her limited choices, she will consistently make incorrect choices in her limited world and openly regret them. Ultimately, when Jimmy charges that she is "like the goods you hated to sell in Thorndyke's basement—rumpled—soiled—pawed over—Manhandled!" she can only tearfully look away, accepting the charge. And while the film provides an escape route through Jimmy and Tessie's ultimate reconciliation and marriage, the world that the film inadvertently recounts is a damned if you do, damned if you don't scenario that provides no escape for actual female workers.

Because working women were rapidly becoming both a fixed economic reality and a troubled cultural locus, representations of the female labor force occurred in a richly varied site, one in which women's roles developed in response to the American economy as well as its changing attitudes toward women and their role in culture and society. As Dorothy Brown writes, "Women *had* always worked, but the nature of the work and the work site . . . radically shifted" (77). As a result, blue-collar girls in early cinema were a variety of things—harlots, helpmates, harried, and harassed—but they were never boring.

As the nineteenth century drew to a close, labor practices changed dramatically. In much of the United States (and Europe), workers had become a class, and labor had become a collective political front. Unions, seeking to protect workers and wages, grew increasingly powerful and brash in their confrontation of capitalism's discontents. For a variety of reasons, female labor was slow to unionize and despite the relative success of garment workers and the ILGWU, even a quadrupling of unionized women that occurred after 1920 found only 1 in every 15 female workers in a trade union, compared to 1 in every 5 males (Kessler-Harris 22). Most unions advocated exclusively for a living wage for male workers, who served as heads of the family. In assuming that a male wage was sufficient to support women and children, the working-class political movement removed the necessity of employment for women and "the notion of the worker became more intricately tied to masculinity" (Enstad 4). This idea was articulated in art, literature, and, as the genre developed, films such as King Vidor's *The Crowd*.

Despite this wide-ranging ideal of the masculine worker, women entered the workforce in increasing numbers. As the postbellum exodus from farm to factory raged, and immigration proceeded unimpeded, cities swelled with cheap labor. Between 1880 and 1920, immigrants to U.S. cities doubled their populations and, in coinciding with the growing consumer industries, they took over the production of food and clothing. Both, formerly the province of women, responded easily to the idea of a female labor force, if not an actual female working class, and the proportion of all women who held jobs jumped from 20.4 percent to 25.2 percent, "the sharpest upturn of any [period] prior to 1940" (Chafe 55).

In tandem with the new working woman who lived and labored more publically than even her mother had, images of the "New Woman," social and political demands for women's vote, and, via the growing culture of consumerism, advertisements that promoted everything from beauty products to "efficient" housekeeping gradually eroded the nineteenth-century construct of separate spheres and created a "preoccupation with the emotional and sexual bonds between women and men" (Peiss 7). While labor conditions themselves, including strikes, perpetuated a separate sphere existence for working-class men and women, leisure, a broadly defined category that included everything from amusement parks to theaters, focused consistently on male and female interaction, producing distinct ideas about both. With 60 percent of the vaudeville theater made up of the working class by 1910, the new film industry geared itself to this same audience. Indeed, motion pictures were shown primarily to vaudeville audiences, with a short film acting as a signal to audiences to leave the theater (Peiss 143–45). "Cheap theater," penny arcade kinetoscopes, and nickelodeons all created a symbiotic relationship between the new "moving pictures" and the relatively new working class: films sought to capture the working class, both in the theater and on the screen. The moment coincided with vast changes women faced not only in society but in the labor force.

Thomas Edison's early short, *Why Jones Discharged His Clerks* (1900), provides a starting point for this key change in American labor. The film opens with two male clerks seated in a broker's office playing cards. When their boss enters, they hide the cards, and watch blandly when he disappears behind a screen with a woman; when both clerks get up on chairs to look over the screen, the chair tips and the screen crashes down. One clerk jumps out the window and the other, as the title indicates, is discharged. The entire scenario is apparent to the audience, from the fondling couple that is initially out of the clerks' range of vision to the chair as it is about to tip, and theater patrons likely laughed in delight at the send-up of the white-collar boss's "work" that day, and the exposure of the two male clerks as clumsy dilettantes, since the typical clerk in the late nineteenth century was an aspiring businessman apprenticed to the petite bourgeoisie (Davies 5). Their decided lack of inspiration on the job was both an antagonism of the class structures in the clerical reality of the time and a foreshadowing of changes in the making. For, as Davies writes, by the 1930s clerks were no longer apprentice capitalists looking for a promotion, and most were likely to remain clerical workers all of their lives, promoted perhaps to "supervisor of a typing pool or head of bookkeeping department" (5). They were, in short, women.

By as early as 1918, the female clerical worker had become familiar enough to audiences that James Montgomery Flagg's *Girls You Know* film series included in its compilation of "popular images of young women" a short titled *The Steno* (Harvey 307). Such a film articulated the shift in women's labor that occurred when women found themselves as valuable in the office as they had proven themselves to be in the factory. *The*

Stenographer's Friend, or, What Was Accomplished by an Edison Business Phonograph (1910) indicates the shift the clerical world made, moving in only 10 years from the male clerks who were the focus of the comedic short film to a female workforce at the center of a propaganda film. Here, an overwhelmed and exhausted female stenographer is unable to keep up with her male superiors until an Edison salesman arrives and demonstrates his company's new "voice writing" system. With the new technology in place, the stenographer sits madly typing up the recordings her bosses have dictated, and at the end of the day, both men hold up empty work baskets. The 5:00 P.M. quitting time the film extols does not account for the newly filled baskets of cartridges that will greet the stenographer first thing in the morning, and its solution serves only to widen the gap between male and female workers. Yet, even as technology affirms the male/female hierarchy, the film also indicates that in the work world, men were becoming dependent on a number of skills that were rapidly being associated with women.

A number of explanations exist for women's eventual overtaking of clerical work in the U.S. labor force. For one thing, they mastered the typewriter and found jobs as typists. Davies points out that when Mark Twain bought his first typewriter in 1875, the salesman had a "type girl" to demonstrate it; since then, the machine and the role have intertwined. As a new technology, it was not yet sex typed as male, so the dexterity it required soon became a female's purview. Additionally, women easily supplied the literacy such a job required. In the late nineteenth and early twentieth centuries, the number of female high school graduates exceeded male, sometimes by as much as 30 percent. (It would not be until 1970 that the numbers were in line.) But perhaps most of the explanation lay in the reality of wages. Women's labor was cheaper than was men's, and they generally received one-third to one-half of men's wages (Kessler-Harris 103). Between 1910 and 1920, the clerical workplace became increasingly feminized, and by 1930, women filled more than 52 percent of clerical positions. As Brown points out, "for the working-class woman, it was a way up, an escape from the manual labor of the factory to clean white-collar respectability" (95).

As Edison's film version of the stenographer's "friend" illustrates, both the nature of work and the devices clerks used changed rapidly during this time. By the 1920s, banks, real estate and insurance offices, publishing houses, and trade and transportation industries all needed clerks to handle "the mounting paperwork required by the demands of modern business and federal taxes and regulation" (Brown 95). The social perception of women as tolerant of routine and manually dexterous made a woman a desirable office worker. Female factory workers' willingness to picket and even strike notwithstanding, women provided a more docile labor force, less apt to complain and, through social expectations that they marry and raise children, a disposable and replaceable labor force. At the same time, social expectations of marriage and maternity complicated the modern stance of the working woman, including the office girl. Kessler-Harris points to the "struggle to contain the tension between certain kinds of labor power" and the dominant idea of a woman's role as nurturer and homemaker (98). Because traditional familial roles were generally easier for middle- and upper-class women to uphold, a growing dichotomy solidified between "highbrow" and "lowbrow" women, but also within the ranks of female workers themselves. Socioeconomic status determined not simply work opportunities, but employment desires, and as vocational educational opportunities opened new doors for some working-class women, office and even department store positions ranked higher than factory and domestic work. And the public perception of female labor was even more volatile than schisms within the ranks. Even those whose ostensible aim was to help working women by writing about their plight often took, inadvertently, the "downward gaze" of Jacob Riis's *How the Other Half Lives*. Additionally, bourgeois women attempting to write about working-class women "were stigmatized as unladylike" (Cook 3). Thus, while working-class women themselves approached office jobs as an avenue to respect, or marriage, or both, society's response was articulated in a bipolar image of the "steno."

In the 1915 Edison silent film *A Sprig of Shamrock,* two Irish sweethearts marry, and move to New York. When the wife must return to Ireland, the lonely husband instigates an affair with his new stenographer. This early version of the immoral steno set a clear path that defied the reality of the hard-working female office clerk depicted only five years earlier, and soon after *A Sprig of Shamrock,* Bluebird Photoplays produced *Scandal Mongers* (1918). While the supposed moral of the story is the deleterious effect of gossip, the action indicts the steno's lack of a moral compass. When a happily married broker gives his injured stenographer a ride to work his companions assume the two are having an affair. The man's wife files for divorce and the stenographer marries a neighborhood suitor and leaves town to live down the disgrace. Thus, the working-class stenographer is not simply unable to rise in society, but punished for attempting to do so. This inescapable trajectory would mark working-class women as the industry moved into the 1930s and beyond. One element of the "fallen women film" was just such punishment for attempting to rise above the working class, and is best demonstrated in films such as *Stella Dallas* (1937), where working-class Stella is punished for her class transgressions by being forced to lose both her husband and daughter.[4]

Many films within the genre highlighted the attractive face, figure, and hair of the stenographer, and also her unabashed desire for clothing—furs and jewels, fashionable gowns and hats. The working woman's move to present herself in upscale modes of clothing began decades earlier, and since the turn of the century, female factory workers had sought to construct their own identities through fashions. Nan Enstad argues that when working-class women freely adlibbed and augmented fashions they read about in dime-store novels, "they staged a carnivalesque class inversion that undermined middle-class efforts to control the definition of 'lady'" (10). Spending money more readily on shirtwaists or hats than new boots, factory girls "played with identity, trying on new images and roles, appropriating the cultural forms around them—clothing, music, language—to push at the boundaries of immigrant, working-class life" (62). Thus, middle-class observers may have categorized these early working-class women as seeking upward mobility, but transgressions of boundaries were just as important within the working class, where proper clothing "traditionally helped to define respectability" (Peiss 63). Film culture's representations for and of the working-class world drew on the expanded visual ubiquity of screen stars, and in a narcissistic turn, films sought to represent working women as Hollywood understood film stars and the film world.

Thus, despite the actual shift in office employment statistics, cinema delighted in suggesting that the most sought-after employment venue for an enterprising woman was not at a typewriter, but in Hollywood, where early versions of the casting couch populated a new type of office. Film after film sent its heroine off to attempt movie stardom, and time and again, in a self-perversion or parody, she was sent home to small-town happiness as wife and mother. That theme was inscribed across a variety of genres, both melodrama and comedy. In Mack Sennett's *The Extra Girl* (1923), hopeful actress Sue wins a contest and arrives at the Golden State Film Company, but when the director sees what she really looks like, he offers her not film work but a position in the costume department. Surrounded by but unable to wear the expensive costumes of film stars, her days are long and the work is drudgery, but throughout, she retains her hope for a breakthrough. Yet the movie cannot condone such female hopes permanently, and after her fling with Hollywood, Sue returns home to marriage and family. A far darker scenario unfolds in *A Girl's Folly* (1917), when young Mary follows a dashing actor, hoping to become a star but settling for a life as his mistress. Her life is filled with beautiful dresses, shallow relationships, and plenty of alcohol, and only when Mary's mother finally arrives on the scene does Mary see the error of her ways and return home to the romance she left behind. But the film world is not fully condemned, for when Mary kisses her former suitor, one train conductor calls it "romantick," but his companion smiles sagely and retorts, "Romantick nothing! That's movin' pictures!" Thus, the film incriminates not the world of "movin' pictures" but the young woman whose folly places her in harm's way. And while both films provide views of the new film industry that are in turn recriminating and boastful, the woman's role is steadfast: she will be happier at home, fulfilling the appropriate role of wife and mother.

While simplistic at surface level, the moralistic plot of such films contains a number of realities within the changing scope of female subjectivity: women did want more than husbands and babies, and the working world was simultaneously seductive and fraught with danger. While the film industry may have seen itself as dispensing morality in such films, it presented an equal measure of narrativized desire, the beautiful clothing and romantic attentions women gained through even temporary stardom creating a puzzle for female audiences. How could one reject such prizes in favor of the old-fashioned role of wife and mother? The screen star's association with modernity and a glamorous life, and the filmed presence of that fulfilled desire, spoke to the reality of women's choices and the dangers those choices forced during this time, when the reality of suffrage and the lure of the flapper and the "new woman" combined with increased opportunities for the more respectable position of clerical work, as opposed to factory work. Presumably asked to look attractive in her new office role, the female typist and clerk confronted unforeseen harassment. Vapnek's study cites a typist who wrote into the *Times* about her life working for a millionaire for three dollars a week: "Could I but declare myself and make known the indignities to which I have been subjected the earth might better for them open and swallow up the accursed" (59). Working office women's perceived roles and the conflicted opportunities they provided all insinuated temptations that society both feared and desired. The plethora of films in which temptation in any form played a role speaks to the era's struggle with the changing face of womanhood, and in few places was that face more changed than in the office.

In this time frame, the most complex of all office work for women was born, a position that offered autonomy, success, glamour, and excitement, all in the masculine milieu. Despite the perceived masculine nature of newspaper reportage, and the literary world's unstinting condescension of the female writer, female news reporters were pervasive enough at the turn of the century that society had begun to worry about them. Jean Marie Lutes cites a 1901 *Ladies' Home Journal* article that asks, "Is the Newspaper Office the Place for a Girl?" Yet, as Lutes points out, the question was by then rhetorical at best, for by that time, "women reporters were already a visible subset of the nation's newspaper journalism" (1). Women's entrance into this venue was by no means untroubled. As a female writer, not recorder, a woman reporter faced a host of preconceptions and perceptions about her work. Sentimental and domestic literature of the time provided a stereotype for the woman writer as a sob sister, and Lutes quotes a scathing view of women's reportage in *Good Housekeeping* in the short story "The Sob-Lady." Mulling her work, the young female reporter concludes, "someone else does the news; I go over and write the picture." Supposedly lacking masculine logic and ability, but working in a masculine medium, "front page girls," as a 1936 history called them, were seen as both careless writers and hypocrites whose conjuring up of "emotional extravagance" covered their own unfeminine lack of feeling for those about whom they wrote (Lutes 3).

While later cinema would develop this very theme, the silent film era preferred simply to ignore the front page girl altogether. For example, in *The Final Extra* (1928), the film opens by extolling the virtue of the printed page: "Here shall the Press the People's rights maintain / Unawed by influence and unbribed by gain / Here Patriot, truth her glorious precepts draw / Pledged to Religion, Liberty, and Law" runs the opening scene's Joseph Story quotation. Yet, in this hallowed office, only male reporters are presented to fight the battle for truth and freedom. Indeed, even the society column, "Smart Social Happenings of the Week," clearly a woman's territory, is in the hands of young Pat Riley, whose pen name Cholly Meadowbrook suggests how superficial his writing in this genre must be.

The introduction of sound coincided with far greater changes in the world than Garbo's infamous ability to talk. The crashing ticker tape, ubiquitous enough within cinema to become a cliché, signaled more than economic readjustments. Gender changed, as did class. All three types of office work took on a heightened role during the Great Depression, when social and legal sanctions insisted that a woman with a job prevented a man from supporting his wife and children. Women who had flirted with autonomy in both cinematic and everyday endeavors found themselves pushed out of the workplace and back into the home, where they were encouraged to pick up the domestic economies they had recently put down and to "make it do or do without."[5] Laura Hapke charges that "working women, especially married ones, became the scapegoats of a movement to reassert the separate sphere thinking of past decades" (xv).[6] Along with financing worries within the studio system, there were, additionally, changes in Hollywood's attitude and production once the Motion Picture Producers and Distributors of America (MPPDA) formally adopted a production code in 1930. The Hays Code, as it was known, was in part a response to society's increasing concerns over film content. While it was formally "a set of guidelines for self regulation," by 1931 the West Coast described participation as "mandatory," and in its simplest translation, the code legalized censorship (Jacobs 27–29). The new Hollywood that appeared in 1932 looked problematically at women.

One solution to the dilemma of women who worked was to turn stenographers and secretaries into prostitutes, a complicated sleight of hand that brushed over the "office wife" who threatened the actual wife. While refusing to acknowledge the number of actual wives who needed or wanted to work but were unable to do so, Hollywood portrayed the tarnished "office wife" as obviously out to steal the successful businessman away from his loving wife. This shift provided a fantasy that both elevated women and minimized their actual contributions to society. For example, in *Wife vs. Secretary* (1936), only Van and Linda (Clark Gable and Myrna Loy) seem unaware of the temptation posed by Gable's secretary, Whitey (Jean Harlow). Even Linda's mother-in-law suggests that her son needs no temptation put in his way, but Linda insists her protection against such a threat is "love and trust," and her job is to make his life "pleasant," a "refuge" from his work. As if to ensure that viewers understand that *only* Linda, a sparkling and beloved high society wife, can provide that "refuge," the film moves quickly to Whitey's house, where her dowdily dressed mother criticizes her husband's manners as he sits noisily slurping soup at the dinner table. Whitey's boyfriend Dave (Jimmy Stewart) is there, and has promised a gift; when she teases him about it, he promptly tells her, "if and when you ever trick me into marrying you, I'll wear the pants." And yet, if Whitey seems doomed by this grimly lowbrow life, a call from Van rushes her down to the office, and the audience sees immediately that she is indeed a working girl. Her ability to multitask, not simply to type up documents, but to produce quickly all the necessary documents, to manage multiple business calls and demands, and to work tirelessly with a crew writing and typing up a new contract that will bring in a large account for Van all make it clear that Whitey is actually a key part of his publishing business.

Whitey's combination of clerical skill and feminine ability to decorate the office and anticipate in advance all of Van's needs makes her the perfect "office wife," and when her affection for Van combines with those skills, she becomes a lethal threat that the film must mitigate. Significantly, despite Whitey's obvious allure, the film insists repeatedly on the wealth of Linda and Van, their superior relationship with each other, and their desirable standing in the world. Whitey is, literally, never given a break. When Linda misunderstands her presence in Van's hotel room and threatens divorce, rather than offer apology or explanation, Whitey can only tell Linda that if she leaves Gable now, she'll never get him back: "You're a fool," she smirks, "for which I'm grateful." When Whitey ultimately hands Van over to Linda, she gives up not simply her man, but her pleasure in work, and her chance at success, sinking into a grateful marriage to the man who has insisted he will "wear the pants." The working-class status of Whitey's home, and Dave's mention that their own fight of three days is the longest they've ever had, suggesting a chronic stream of spats, are both clear indications that Whitey and Dave will replicate the unhappy marriage that opened the film. Thus, office girls were not simply tarnished enough to desire married men, their working-class breeding made them undeserving of a good marriage.

The newspaper office continued to provide opportunities for women, more so in films than real life, but Hollywood adamantly frowned at the successful female reporter while simultaneously reflecting some of the professional realities of the newspaper office. While Philip Hanson's reading of the "intersection" of life and film in the Great Depression looks at newspaper reporters as a "comic version of being trapped by economics in a set of power dynamics beyond one's control," it is significant that the two movies he first lists feature female reporters (196). Thus, while Frank Capra would eventually turn to male reporters to effect the downfall of Mr. Smith when he went to Washington, it was first, in *Mr. Deeds Goes to Town,* that the reporter's inability to live up to democratic ideals is put on film. In so doing, films suggested that women reporters, in their inability to effectively sustain the freedoms of the press, served the country more patriotically by going home and getting married. In *His Girl Friday* (1940), Hildy Johnson (Rosalind Russell) tries to quit her job, and announcing she wants to live a "normal life." But she is drawn in to her ex-husband's newspaper when an innocent man is sentenced to hang, and as the political mechanizations of the city slowly come undone, so does Hildy's resolve to marry her insurance-selling beau, move to Albany, and raise a family. Ultimately, Hildy reconciles with her husband and the newspaper editor Walter and sets out both to remarry and keep working at the paper, solidifying Walter's status in Hildy's life as both boss and husband. This masculinization of a woman seems, ironically, to confirm standard codes of heterosexual monogamy and Hanson argues that the fact that Walter and Hildy become "a match only after she has been properly masculinized" nonetheless supports the framework of marital solutions (132). But the fact of the film is that little of the reporter/editor marriage into which Hildy will reenter suggests marital bliss, or even a marriage. Her first honeymoon was delayed by a miner's strike, and the closing scenes make it clear that her second honeymoon will be similarly delayed, a reality she accedes to as she puts on her hat and coat. Hildy and Walter are at best business partners; they are equally excited by the sound of a siren or gunfire and the breaking lead both promise. In this sense, the working girl in the newspaper office is made not simply masculine but, in her childlessness, monstrous. Here, the film says, is the shrew untamed.

Two Frank Capra films are equally troubled by women in the newspaper office, providing personas ultimately less sympathetic than does *His Girl Friday*. In both *Meet John Doe* (1941) and *Mr. Deeds Goes to Town* (1936), female reporters intentionally set out to further their financial status by exploiting the naïveté of a babe-in-the-woods innocent, played in both films by Gary Cooper. Both women have working-class roots and each has a certain rectitude: in the first film, Ann Mitchell (Barbara Stanwyk) angles for a $1,000 bonus for her invention of John Doe so that she can pay off her widowed mother's debt; in the second Babe Bennett (Jean Arthur), already a star reporter, regrets her publications on Deeds enough to resign from the newspaper. Still, neither is spared personal and professional tragedy. Mitchell tastes the bitter success of diamonds and furs, realizing she has driven the man she loves to enact the suicide she has created as a story, and in the process, makes herself seriously ill; Bennett sits distraught and hysterical while Deeds quietly and calmly refuses to defend himself against a society in which he has never found his place. And in the end, both women leave the newspaper office for good, presumably grateful to become wives and mothers. And yet, the films offer little hope for success in either marriage: Deeds has given away his money, and Bennett, a New York urbanite, will somehow have to make her way in Mandrake Falls, becoming as "pixilated" as everyone else the Faulkner sisters indict, and Mitchell can only cling fragilely to Cooper's Long John Willoughby as a small band of stalwarts promises to re-form their John Doe club.

Just as Hollywood rearticulated the front page girl of the decade before, the era did not turn its back on the dream of Hollywood stardom, but instead rearticulated it as little more than an office job. *Stage Door* (1937) reworks an Edna Ferber play about blue-collar theater hopefuls. Ginger Rogers plays Jean Maitland, one of many young women living in a boarding house for female theater hopefuls, all of whom accept poverty and exploitation while they are seeking a "break" in the industry. Against those working girls, the film posits the pedigreed Terry Randall (Katharine Hepburn), who also seeks theatrical fame, although she does not, like many in the theatrical boarding house, need the money. Maitland and Randall are antagonistic, with Randall's sometimes infuriating lack of understanding of actual poverty a counterpoint to Maitland's equally unlikable willingness to exploit men for money and women for their men. Ultimately, the high society Randall turns out to have a heart of gold, thereby absolving the monied fantasy of anything like class consciousness or responsibility. After the young woman whose hoped-for theater role Randall has taken commits suicide, she gives the performance of a lifetime, her sorrow over the suicide infusing her formerly wooden acting with passion and grief. In her heartfelt closing words she dedicates the performance to the dead young woman, while in the theater's front row all the boarders sob, holding on to each other. After the play's curtain falls, Maitland goes to Randall's dressing room and they shun publicity in order to go visit the morgue and pay their last respects together. Thus, Randall closes the gap between highbrow and lowbrow culture, securing Maitland's affection while simultaneously ensuring a profit for her father's investment in the play.

Less neatly sewn up was *Dance, Girl, Dance* (1940), whose screenplay was cowritten by Tess Slesinger, author of the extraordinary 1934 proletarian novel, *The Unpossessed* (1934). That novel explores in near-savage terms the largely hidden demarcations of class and status within the proletariat and indicts women's often impossible subjectivity within the warring class worlds of the country. *Dance, Girl, Dance* is a gentler narrative, but Slesinger's fierce stance and the direction by Dorothy Arzner, one of few women to survive the studio-era move to virtually all male directors, makes its view of the working girl unapologetic.

The film situates the working girl's office in a bar that fronts a gambling house. When police raid the bar, and move to take the chorines who dance in it down to the station, Judy O'Brien (Maureen O'Sullivan) confronts the uniformed men, saying angrily that the girls there are "just trying to earn our living, just as you are." Her spirited speech inspires one patron to take up a collection on the girls' part, and while his infatuation for O'Brien is clear, Bubbles (Lucille Ball), as the troop harlot, hussy, and seeming entrepreneur, appears and spirits him away. Her role as harlot and gold digger is solidified when she appears later, furious that her efforts that evening have resulted only in a stuffed animal. When she disappears, O'Brien and the rest of the girls are left to try learning the hula, but without Bubbles's sex appeal, the dance falls flat. When Bubbles returns and undulates her hips, she saves the gig, a move that allows O'Brien to apply to a dance school and, she hopes, fulfill her dream of a career in ballet. In this complicated scenario, Bubbles's sex appeal both antagonizes and affirms the working girl's social status, complicating the choice over money or respect and affirming the original social judgment of the working girl. The script insists on this complication as class-based, for when O'Brien auditions for a dance school, she is immediately censured for her attempt to move into elite society: "Your interpretation of a bird is lovely [the teacher tells her] but haven't you ever heard of a typewriter, a telephone?" The working world, the film argues, is open for women, but only as long as they know their place. More than 20 years after Swanson's Tessie McGuire was "manhandled" by artistic types who saw clerical work as a woman's given place, *Dance, Girl, Dance* affirms the retention of that belief.

Soon after O'Brien's audition, Bubbles reenters as a wealthy and glamorously dressed success. Her clothes and her residence near Central Park are all the result of burlesque, where her hula moves and brassy persona have made her a success. She offers O'Brien a job, and while it becomes clear that her chaste appearance on the stage is only to increase the audience's desire for "Lily," Bubbles's burlesque persona, O'Brien keeps the job and enjoys the steady and stable income. Through a series of external romantic entanglements, the relationship between the two women grows from tolerant to tense, and ultimately explodes when Bubbles pushes O'Brien on stage and her costume comes apart. "Go ahead and stare," she says furiously to the audience, "I know you want me to tear my clothes off. . . . What's it for. So you can go home and strut before your wives and play at being the stronger sex." Thus, the movie both confronts and contradicts a number of stereotypes. Ultimately, while relationships and class status factor into many of the film's scenes, O'Brien's angry indictment of the male willingness to commodify the working woman, the woman whom as she said at the film's beginning, is "just trying to earn a living, as you are," is at the heart of the plot.

It is a given that silent films were anything but silent and that the Golden Age of the silver screen was tinged green, but only for a select few. As the moving picture industry developed and moved west, it brought with it a host of concerns about race, gender, and more than is readily apparent, class. Ironically, in the years before films gained a voice, class was addressed openly, in films such as Vidor's *The Crowd* and Frank Capra's *The Younger Generation* (1929), an adaptation of Fannie Hurst's exploration into immigration, capitalism, and class. But the new voice that films gained technologically was soon silenced by MPPDA directives in the production code, and along with sexuality, class issues were communicated only indirectly, through suggestion, allusion, or coding. For women, that coding was doubled, as a movie such as *His Girl Friday* demonstrates. Messages about the appropriate stance of a working-class woman were complicated by the film industry's desire to visually enchant through beauty and clothing unavailable to those whom the characters they put on the screen were representing. The core of desire embodied in a movie star's appearance and the audience's ability to acquire that sought-after desire through its participation in the filmed event provided a conflicted stance on working-class women, one that was troubled in the first half of the century by rapid changes in work, economic shifts, and the changing place of marriage and family in a society that made both increasingly difficult for working women. As Brown wrote, "women had always worked." Nothing in the first half of the twentieth century changed that. But *how* they worked changed rapidly, as did how they were *perceived* at and for their work. Representations of working-class women often sought to represent their experience, but more often, films inadvertently represented the complicated and often impossible subjectivity of a woman in the working world.

Notes

1. Vidor's film, at the very onset of sound in motion pictures, is a hybrid, with some reels silent, and some providing sound.

2. See, for example, Sylvia Cook, *Working Women, Literary Ladies: The Industrial Revolution and Female Aspiration* (Oxford: Oxford University Press, 2008); Jacqueline Ellis, *Silent Witnesses: Representations of Working-Class Women in the United States* (Bowling Green, OH: Bowling Green State University Popular Press, 1998); Gavin Jones, *American Hungers: The Problem of Poverty in U.S. Literature, 1840–1945* (Princeton, NJ: Princeton University Press, 2008); Laura Hapke, *Labor's Text: The Worker in American Fiction* (New Brunswick, NJ: Rutgers University Press, 2001); and Eric Schocket, *Vanishing Moments: Class and American Literature* (Ann Arbor: University of Michigan Press, 2006), among others.

3. Quotes from title cards in *Manhandled*, Famous Players-Lasky Corp., 1924.

4. For more on the genre and its relation to the production code of 1930s Hollywood, see Lea Jacobs, *The Wages of Sin: Censorship and the Fallen Woman Film, 1928–1942* (Madison: University of Wisconsin Press, 1991) and Leanord Jeff and Jerold Simmons, *Dame in the Kimono: Hollywood, Censorship and the Production Code* (Lexington: University of Kentucky Press, 2001).

5. A well-known motto of the time, the phrase served as the title of Jeane Westin's oral history. See Susan Ware, *Holding Their Own: American Women in the 1930s* (Boston: Twayne, 1982), 2.

6. Along with Hapke, see Ware, *Holding Their Own: American Women in the 1930s* and *Beyond Suffrage: Women in the New Deal* (Cambridge, MA: Harvard University Press, 1981).

Works Cited

Brown, Dorothy. *Setting a Course: American Women in the 1920s.* Boston: Twayne, 1987.

Chafe, William H. *The American Woman: Her Changing Social, Economic, and Political Roles, 1920–1970.* Oxford: Oxford University Press, 1972.

Cook, Sylvia. *Working Women, Literary Ladies: The Industrial Revolution and Female Aspiration.* Oxford: Oxford University Press, 2008.

Davies, Margery W. *Woman's Place Is at the Typewriter: Office Work and Office Workers 1870–1930.* Philadelphia: Temple University Press, 1982.

Enstad, Nan. *Ladies of Labor, Girls of Adventure: Working Women, Popular Culture, and Labor Politics at the Turn of the Twentieth Century.* New York: Columbia University Press, 1991.

Hanson, Philip. *This Side of Despair: How the Movies and American Life Intersected during the Great Depression.* Madison, NJ: Fairleigh Dickinson University Press, 2008.

Hapke, Laura. *Daughters of the Great Depression: Women, Work, and Fiction in the American 1930s.* Athens: University of Georgia Press, 1995.

Harvey, Sheridan, et al., eds. *American Women: A Library of Congress Guide for the Study of Women's History and Culture in the United States.* Hanover, NH: University Press of New England, 2001.

Jacobs, Lea. *The Wages of Sin: Censorship and the Fallen Woman Film, 1928–1942.* Madison: University of Wisconsin Press, 1991.

Kessler-Harris, Alice. *Gendering Labor History.* Urbana: University of Illinois Press, 2007.

Lutes, Jean Marie. *Front Page Girls: Women Journalists in American Culture and Fiction, 1880–1930.* Ithaca, NY: Cornell University Press, 2006.

Peiss, Kathy. *Cheap Amusements: Working Women and Leisure in Turn-of-the-Century New York.* Philadelphia: Temple University Press, 1986.

Vapnek, Lara. *Breadwinners: Working Women and Economic Independence, 1865–1920.* Urbana: University of Chicago Press, 2009.

Ware, Susan. *Holding Their Own: American Women in the 1930s.* Boston: Twayne, 1982.

Filmography

When possible, call numbers for silent films held by the Library of Congress are for viewing copies.

The Crowd. Metro-Goldwyn-Mayer; directed by King Vidor; screenplay by King Vidor and John V. A. Weaver, 1928. LOC call number, VBG 0981-0982.

Dance, Girl, Dance. RKO Pictures; directed by Dorothy Arzner; story by Vicki Baum; writing by Tess Slesinger and Frank Davis, 1940.

The Extra Girl. Mack Sennett Productions; directed by F. Richard Jones; produced by Mack Sennett; scenario by Bernard McConville, 1923. LOC call number, VAB 0270.

The Final Extra. Gotham Productions; directed by James P. Hogan; personal supervision of Glenn Belt; titles by Delos Sutherland, 1928. LOC call number, VAA 9156.

A Girl's Folly. Paragon Films; directed by Maurice Tourneur; story and scenario by Frances Marion and Maurice Tourneur, 1917. LOC call number, VAB 1485.

His Girl Friday. Warner Brothers Studio; directed by Howard Hawks; screenplay by Charles Lederer from the play *Front Page* by Ben Hecht and Charles MacArthur, 1940.

Manhandled. Famous Players-Lasky Corp.; directed and produced by Allan Dwain; scenario by Frank Tuttle (a shortened version, reedited for home distribution, of the 1924 feature released by Paramount). LOC call number, FCA 5039-5040.

Meet John Doe. Warner Brothers Studio; directed by Frank Capra; screenplay by Robert Riskin; story by Richard Connell and Robert Presnell Sr., 1941.

Mr. Deeds Goes to Town. Columbia Pictures; directed by Frank Capra; screenplay by Robert Riskin; story by Clarence Budington Kelland, 1936.

Stage Door. RKO Pictures; directed by Gregory La Cava; screenplay by Morrie Ryskind and Anthony Veillor from the play by Edna Ferber and George S. Kaufman, 1937.

Wife vs. Secretary. Metro Goldwyn Mayer; directed by Clarence Brown, screenplay by Faith Baldwin, Alice Duer Miller, Norma Krasna, and John Lee Mahin, 1936.

Chapter 2

Striking Women: Gender, Labor, and Working-Class Politics in Film from *Salt of the Earth* to *North Country*

Catherine Chaput

Men make their own history, but they do not make it as they please; they do not make it under self-selected circumstances, but under circumstances existing already, given and transmitted from the past.
—Karl Marx, *The Eighteenth Brumaire*

An explosion at Upper Big Branch Mine, in Montcoal, West Virginia, claimed 29 lives on April 5, 2010. Six months later, at the Pingyu Coal and Electric Company in central China, another 37 workers died in a similar explosion. While these and other work-related deaths made little news, the 33 miners trapped deep underground, after the copper and gold mine near Copiapó, Chile, collapsed, occupied international headlines on and off for months. In fact, the rescue continued to make news long after the last miner was retrieved. Although the accident and death rate of this one industry might seem surprising in light of contemporary safety regulations and advanced technologies, this surprise is, no doubt, fueled by the continued mismatch between working-class life across the global landscape and popular depictions of that life in newspapers, on television, or in films. Our sense of history, as Marx says, comes to us through the cultural, political, and economic constraints we inherent. Among the constraints limiting our historical consciousness are the cultural representations of workplace tragedies like these mining accidents, creating distance between various labor practices and our daily experiences. Marx goes on to say that important historical events occur twice: "the first time as tragedy, the second as farce" (*The Eighteenth Brumaire* 15). If the historical events of workplace struggle exemplify tragedy, perhaps the cultural representations of them—however well done—provide the farce.

The farce to which I refer is the gaping hole between our stated beliefs about the world, brought to life in films or other cultural products, and our lived experiences in that world. This failure to adequately represent lived experience lies at the heart of many explorations into popular culture. For instance, Raymond Williams, one of the founding theorists of the British cultural studies tradition, laments that "the strongest barrier to the recognition of human cultural activity is the immediate and regular conversion of experience into finished products" (*Marxism and Literature* 128). To communicate specific events, such as working-class labor, to those who do not share this experience requires the representation of lived activities within fixed products—words, images, sounds, and artifacts. No communication, no understanding, and no social change will take place without this transformation of lived experience into product form and yet such cultural production simultaneously connects and distances. It distances because cultural production transforms the complexities of dynamic, lived experiences into stable products, relegating them to the historical past tense. To take my opening example: the mining explosions that kill workers on a nearly daily basis do not circulate in public discussion because such dramatic workplace accidents exist in the historical past tense. If accidents do exist, they must do so within the constraints of our contemporary history. Workers must be saved, as were the Chilean miners; or, if killed, they must exist in an economically less developed country, which metonymically transposes an event into the historical past tense.

To unearth these lived experiences from their cultural graves, analyses need to explore the complexity of labor—both industrial and postindustrial—within its social relations. The task of such criticism, Williams says, is to make represented experiences "present in specifically 'active readings'" (*Marxism and Literature* 129) by exploring "the structure of feeling" associated with lived experience (*Marxism and Literature* 132). A structure of feeling signals the emergent, or preemergent, values that distinguish one experience from other similar experiences. This concept is structural because it tracks interlocking relationships that form the scaffolding on which we build our cultural connections and yet it becomes known not rationally or intellectually as much as through habit, sensation, and intuition. When reanimating a cultural text, breathing contemporary life into its frozen past-tense body, one needs to explore the pattern of relationships within a text but also re-member that "the significance of an activity must be sought in terms of the whole organization, which is more than the sum of its separable parts" (*The Long Revolution* 65). Taking its cue from Raymond Williams, this chapter explores points of intersection among several working-class films focused on union politics and female protagonists as they offer entry into a larger structure of feeling. Because I am interested in the everyday lived experi-ences of working-class populations, I limit the scope of my analysis to films that tell the story of real-world labor struggles.

The chapter seeks to make two contributions. First, it will resurrect indus-trial, blue-collar work—taking place inside factory doors, in underground mine shafts, and throughout a range of nondigitalized, large-scale technolo-gies—from the annals of history. Cultural representations that transform ongoing blue-collar life into the past tense of bygone historical eras prompt many audiences to mistakenly believe that these problems existed "back then" but not "today." Second, the chapter offers insight into this cultural experience by intersecting workplace struggle (a point on the grid of class relations) with lines of gender, race, and sexuality. The crystallized pattern that emerges will not idealize working-class culture nor simply document the many aspects that contribute to such experience. Rather, this reading will explore a structure of feeling—"a sense of the ways in which the par-ticular activities combined into a way of thinking and living" (*The Long Revolution* 63). A structure of feeling is neither imposed nor reactionary. On the contrary, it emerges through a group's active problem solving; it is, says Williams, "social experiences in solution" (*Marxism and Literature* 133). The repeated pattern of the films I discuss, which document the lived ex-perience of different historical moments, different regional locations, and different industries, suggests that this solution has not yet taken hold, even as it erupts in conjunctural moments (to paraphrase Antonio Gramsci) of workplace struggle.[1] In short, the chapter argues that working-class culture, when pushed up against the wall and forced to organize itself within a united framework, provides emergent solutions to the problems of con-temporary life under the aegis of capitalism. These solutions, even though they may exist on the tips of our tongues and constitute part of our deeply held ideological commitments, do not fully manifest in practice and are, therefore, still emergent.

The next section briefly summarizes the seven films under investigation and the historical events that each represents. It is followed by an analysis of the working-class structure of feeling collectively revealed within the films.

This structure of feeling demonstrates the power of solidarity across class, gender, race, and sexual differences and suggests that such power cannot be sustained within workplaces regulated by corporate, union, and government oversight. The chapter ends by speculating about the absence of this sentiment in contemporary Hollywood films.

Representing a Century of Struggle in Film

Labor struggles, on the margin of American society, often spilled onto center stage throughout the turbulent twentieth century. A handful of these stories have become fodder for Hollywood filmmakers. I focus on seven such films, each of which converts specific labor struggles into popular form in order to describe and disseminate blue-collar experiences to a diverse national audience. Each film represents a critical event in American labor history— some depict the formation of a union, others depict a union strike, and one tells the story of a union's failure to protect its female workers. Across their differences, these films reveal a collective story of the crucial role women play in labor struggles, both as workers and as nonworkers, through a structure of feeling that connects race, gender, and sexuality to working-class politics.[2] Listed in chronological order of their real-life antecedents, the following offers a brief summary of the film plots before proceeding to the analysis.

- *Matewan* (1987), written and directed by John Sayles, depicts the efforts to unionize the Phelps-Dodge mine near Matewan, West Virginia. This film, like many of Sayles's projects, offers a fictionalized account of historical events: a 1920 unionizing effort at a Mingo County mine ending in a gunfight in which several workers and company men were killed. These events left a lasting imprint on this small town. In fact, if you travel to Matewan today, you will see a sign welcoming you with the words: "Matewan: Home of the Matewan Massacre." You can even walk up to the historically restored building façades to receive museum-like snapshots of this struggle.
- *Salt of the Earth* (1954) tells the story of a 1951 strike at the Empire Zinc Mine in New Mexico. The workers, primarily Mexican Americans, are not only depicted but also form part of the cast—prefiguring the strategy, made popular by HBO's *The Wire*, of using real-life participants as character actors. Filmed with the cooperation and financial support of the International Union of Mine, Mill, and Smelter Workers, this film was written, directed, and produced by individuals who were blacklisted for refusing to answer Congressional inquiries about the supposed Communist infiltration of the film industry. Largely suppressed when first released, it has since become a classic of labor film history.

- *Harlan County War* (2000), written by Peter Silverman and directed by Tony Bill for Showtime, fictionalizes Barbara Kopple's groundbreaking documentary *Harlan County USA* (1976), which tracks the Brookside Mining strike of 1972–73. While the speech patterns, bluegrass music, and the Kentucky landscape pale in comparison to the original documentary, this made-for-TV film highlights key aspects of the workers' struggle including the role of women on the picket line, the vexed relationship between the national union and the local members, as well as the impoverished living conditions of workers.

- *Norma Rae* (1979), directed by Martin Ritt, dramatizes one woman's efforts to unionize the textile factory in which she works. The film is based on Crystal Lee Sutton who lent her advocacy to the unionizing campaign at the J.P. Stevens towel factory in Roanoke Rapids, North Carolina. In great part due to her hard work, the employees voted to join the Textile Workers of America on August 28, 1974. With an Academy Award performance by Sally Field, *Norma Rae* is arguably the most recognized union film to come out of Hollywood and certainly sets the standard for the representation of strong female union organizers on film.

- *Silkwood* (1983), directed by Mike Nichols, narrates the story of Karen Silkwood, a worker in the Kerr-McGee nuclear plant who spearheads union efforts to expose safety violations at the factory and dies under suspicious circumstances on November 13, 1974. Taking place in rural Oklahoma, the film highlights the role of women in union activism as well as the policing of sexuality in order to undermine such efforts. Among the many supposed breaches of proper sexual conduct, Karen Silkwood was never married, did not have custody of her children, and lived on and off with her boyfriend.

- *North Country* (2005), an adaptation of Clara Bingham and Laura Leedy Gansler's *Class Action,* offers a fictionalized account of one woman's struggle against the sexual harassment she and other women received as the first female workers employed by the Eveleth Mines in northern Minnesota. The struggle culminates in a landmark 1984 class action lawsuit against the company. Directed by Niki Caro, the film illustrates female activism and provides a twist on traditional gender relationships: the men must stand in solidarity with the women workers.

- *Bread and Roses* (2000), written by Paul Laverty and directed by Ken Loach, takes place in Los Angeles and provides a snapshot into the 1990 Justice for Janitors campaign. A social movement organization related to a parent union for service employees, Justice for Janitors draws attention to the salary and benefit issues of the contract employees who clean hotels and office buildings. The film highlights specific workplace injustices while emphasizing the same pattern of female-led union activism as well as the policing of sexual, racial, and national boundaries.

Capturing a Working-Class Structure of Feeling: Gender, Race, and Sexuality

Across a range of locations from the deserts of New Mexico to the harsh climate of northern Minnesota to the hollows of Kentucky and West Virginia, this selection of films brings to light the complexity of working-class struggle, one deeply inflected through gender norms and divergent cultural experiences. These films acknowledge the overwhelmingly masculine landscape of working-class labor: the owners and top management are male; the workers are predominantly male; and the national union infrastructure is similarly populated by men. The women in the films, even the ones who work outside the home, are responsible for maintaining the household and for childcare. In each case, however, the women are critical to workplace organizing efforts. They sustain their working husbands physically and emotionally, step into the picket line when legal sanctions prevent the workers from continuing to do so, and advocate fearlessly on their own behalf.[3] Women not only "hold the line," they spearhead many of the organizing efforts and bring domestic politics to the forefront. In other words, women occupy center stage in these dramas regardless of their relationship to workplace labor.

Workplace and domestic concerns merge throughout these filmic representations, showing how female labor enables and reproduces able-bodied workers and thus functions as an extension of workplace politics. For example, *Salt of the Earth* narrates a labor strike through the eyes of Esperanza Quintero (Rosaura Revueltas), the wife of Ramon Quintero (Juan Chacón), who is one of the more active union men. While Ramon sees the strike as necessary to improve working conditions and to ensure that Mexican workers receive the same safety precautions as their Anglo counterparts, Esperanza insists that the demands include improved living conditions such as running water in the company-owned homes. Without running water, Esperanza and the other wives begin each morning chopping wood and collecting buckets of water to heat for bathing, laundry, and cooking. An endless cycle of chopping wood, stoking the fire, cooking, cleaning, and maintaining the house constitutes the long work day for these women. Eventually these domestic labor conditions do become part of workplace demands, thanks to the company-owned homes, the women's activism, and the raised consciousness of working men.

Perhaps the lack of indoor plumbing in primarily immigrant communities of rural New Mexico of the 1950s isn't surprising. But what should we make of the fact that this same problem persists in the 1970s in the rural spaces of Kentucky decades after the success of such a groundbreaking strike effort? At a time when most of the national news focused on gas prices, rising consumer inflation, and inner-city poverty, many working-class people purchased food at company stores and lived in company homes that still did not provide running water. In the dramatically titled *Harlan County War,* Ruby Kincaid (Holly Hunter)—the main protagonist as well as wife and daughter of striking miners—haggles with a man at the grocery store over additional money her husband is supposedly entitled to because of overtime work. With only company scrip to pay for necessities, the workers have little choice but to accept the limited choices and high prices at these stores. Later in the film, on a union-organized trip to Washington, DC, Ruby marvels at the hotel bathtub. She runs her fingers across the shiny, virtually new, plumbing in a scene that emphasizes the importance of such apparently mundane aspects of domestic life. The following scene depicts a stockholders meeting at which the company representatives announce that they are working to upgrade workers into trailer homes.[4] As proper homes become central to striking demands, the concerns of home life bleed into the workplace, making it difficult to distinguish where working-class labor begins and ends. Shopping, washing, cleaning, cooking, and health care all become labor demands in atmospheres in which companies maintain homes, shops, and doctors, as they do in these films.

Similarly linking *Salt of the Earth* and *Harlan County War* across the more than two decades and 1,300 miles separating them is the role non-employed females play in the unionizing efforts. In both films, the mining population is exclusively male while the women take care of the homes and the children, yet the women must also take over the picket lines after legal injunctions prevent the men from actively striking. The Taft-Hartley Injunction prohibits miners from obstructing the entrance of the Zinc Empire mine depicted in *Salt of the Earth.* However, as the women's auxiliary members astutely point out, this injunction prohibits the miners but not others from walking the picket line. In a community motion passing 103 to 85, they decide that the women will take over the picket line, even against the objections that such physical activities are inappropriate for females and fears that they will fail because of their innate weakness. The women go to the mine, walk the picket line, and do not fail. In fact, the sheriff is forced to arrest them in an effort to break the line. With the women striking or in jail, the men assume responsibility for the home and childcare—raising their consciousness to the difficulty of that work. In the climactic scene, the women and men work together to replace items removed from a home eviction. The futility of this circular situation forces the company to settle with the union demands. Referencing the female-male divide as well as the gap between the Mexican and Anglo workers, Esperanza narrates this scene by stating that "together we can push everything up as we go." With this proclamation, she evokes the underlying collectivity at heart in this and other unionizing efforts.

This struggle repeats itself in quite similar terms in *Harlan County War* as the women decide to take over the picket line after a judge declares that no more than three workers may walk on the picket line at a time. When Ruby and the other wives suggest that they take over the line (as they are not workers), the union organizer replies that women have never served on picket duty before. An understanding of labor history, even as represented in these films, reveals the error of this statement. However, his comment, regardless of its veracity, suggests the degree to which women on the picket line challenge the deeply held link between masculinity and labor struggles. Each time women stand in for male workers, it is as if they are doing so for the first time, pointing out the historical unsustainability of labor interests across gender divides.

The failure of such gender solidarity becomes even clearer as women enter the workplace. Precipitated by the postindustrial turn in the United States that outsourced many working-class jobs as well as the shift in family structures that increased the percentage of single-mother homes, the demographic of men in the workplace and women in the home changes abruptly after the 1970s. Consequently, films such as *Norma Rae, Silkwood, North Country,* and *Bread and Roses* tell the story of women who work in factories, in mines, and as janitors. These women do not support their husbands' union efforts, but fight for their own working rights. Not surprisingly, the protagonists of these films are all unmarried women: Norma Rae (Sally Field) is a single mother with children from different fathers; Karen Silkwood (Meryl Streep) is separated from the father of her children and living with her boyfriend; Josey Aimes (Charlize Theron) is seeking a divorce from her abusive husband; and Maya (Pilar Padilla), an undocumented Mexican immigrant, is single and living with her sister's family. While *Norma Rae, Silkwood,* and *Bread and Roses* take the presence of women in the workplace for granted—even as they depict explicit and implicit sexual harassment throughout those workplaces—*North Country* demonstrates the severe disruption caused by women entering traditionally male-dominated working spaces. Indeed, the entire film exposes the gendered nature of the mining industry as well as working-class identity more generally.

According to this film, working-class gender roles correspond to labor practices and the transgression of those boundaries marks one as a legitimate target for verbal as well as physical derision. In one among many such scenes, a male worker helps himself to a cigarette from the chest pocket of a female coworker, caressing her breasts as he does. When Josie complains, she is told that she has no business working there because her employment takes jobs from deserving men. Her boss summarizes his position in three directives: "work hard, keep your mouth shut, and take it like a man." The women who work at the mine are assumed to be unfeminine and therefore open to whatever abuse they receive: they are simultaneously considered "masculine" and the objects of men's sexual pleasure.

In contrast to the actions of the male mine workers, the film demonstrates idealized male behavior through the character of Bill White (Woody Harrelson). We are introduced to Bill, a local man who has been practicing law in New York and has returned to town to recover from his recent divorce, at a bar where the workers are celebrating their Friday night. Indicative of the crossing of class and gender lines, Bill is assumed to be emasculated because of his white-collar profession as well as the fact that his wife is ending their marriage. Having a beer with his friend, he confesses that his wife offered to pay him alimony, which he refused, explaining "I already feel like half a man. I should wear a mini skirt, too?" Immediately after this discussion he further asserts his masculinity by intervening in a potential fight between his friend and another man. The man dismisses his efforts to stop the fight by mocking him—"what are you gonna do, my taxes?"—but Bill responds with a decisive blow to the man's face that presumably reestablishes his manliness.

Importantly, Bill serves as Josie's lawyer and fights for a class action rather than an individual lawsuit. After a dramatic build-up in court, Bobby (Jeremy Renner)—a male coworker and sexual antagonist of Josie—reveals that their high school teacher, Paul Lattavansky (Brad William Henke), raped Josie. With this revelation, Josie transforms from a promiscuous and therefore unreliable witness to an innocent victim. It is only after this shift that her once-reluctant female coworkers join the suit, which ultimately succeeds. Much like *Salt of the Earth* or *Harlan County War,* the film suggests that individual and collective goals can only be accomplished through gender cooperation. Josie's father (Richard Jenkins), who speaks up for her at a union meeting; Bill, who defends her case; and Bobby, who admits that he failed to protect Josie from their predatory teacher, must stand beside women inside and outside the workplace just as the women have stood beside them.

Besides exploring gender and class relations, this array of labor-oriented films articulates the racial divisions that similarly cut through working-class politics. The overwhelmingly white working-class laborers of these films harbor taken-for-granted racist sentiments that often erupt during workplace struggles. For instance, *Matewan* depicts local white workers who fight against the black workers arriving as "scabs." In the second scene of the film, a train filled with black workers who have been imported to replace the striking white workers stops unexpectedly outside of town. The doors open and the men are asked to step off the train. They are then physically attacked by the white workers who emerge from the woods with sticks and clubs. After a short but intense fight, the black men get back into the train. These racial tensions are clearly driven by a proprietary sense of work. The striking white workers feel that the black workers are stealing their jobs. This notion that white men are entitled to jobs that people of color and women take from them often prevents a fully united working-class identity—a social stumbling block that these films work against.

With the rapidity only available on film, the racial tensions separating Matewan's working classes become muted almost to extinction at a worker's meeting during which they deliberate about the possibility of organizing a union. The meeting begins with only white workers who eventually allow Joe Kenehan (Chris Cooper), the professional organizer, to enter after he has proven his authenticity by correctly answering a string of queries about famous labor struggles. Next enters Few Clothes Johnson (James Earl Jones). Although he has recently endured a surprise beating from these men, his sense of labor injustice (he has to pay for housing, food, equipment, and health care with company scrip without any means of ensuring fair pricing) compels him to seek their solidarity. When he says he has business with the union, one man shouts out, "go home nigger, Goddamn scab." Few Clothes responds forcefully with "I been called a nigger and I can't help that—the way white folks see us—but I ain't never been called no scab." This scene connects racial ignorance to labor struggle and prompts an extensive speech by Joe about the attempts of employers to divide the working class. Joe says that companies position whites against blacks, native against foreign, neighbor against neighbor even though there are only two sides: worker and nonworker. After this speech, the white workers organize with the black and Italian immigrant workers and together they refuse to work at the mine, beginning the strike that occupies the rest of the film. Although the strike is unsuccessful—a violent gunfight sends the workers back into the mine—racial and ethnic unity enable the workers to get much further than they would have otherwise.

While racism, like that depicted in *Matewan,* was vehemently attacked in U.S. culture throughout the 1960s and 1970s, *Norma Rae* suggests that its residual undercurrents remained strong. The campaign to unionize the factory workers, composed of men and women as well as whites and blacks, repeatedly runs up against racism. First, Norma Rae asks Reverend Hubbard (Vernon Weddle) to hold the union meeting at the Baptist church, explaining that there would be blacks sitting beside whites, and is turned down flatly. She then decides to hold the meeting at her house and her husband Sonny Webster (Beau Bridges) tells her with sincere concern that there are black men in their home. Finally, a group of white men attack a single black worker because of a notice posted on the factory bulletin board stating that the black men were trying to unionize so that they can obtain power over the white men. None of this surprises Norma Rae, who understands the racial politics of her small southern town, but she bucks these sentiments at every turn because she knows that racial divisiveness undermines her ultimate organizing goals. Indeed, she says that she's never had any trouble with black men—only white men, she adds, have caused her problems.

Silkwood further demonstrates that race, gender, and working-class identity remain uneasily linked. One early scene, for instance, includes Thelma Rice (Sudie Bond) talking to Karen in the locker room as they get ready for work. In between discussion of hair and makeup, Thelma, whose daughter is dying of cancer, tells Karen indignantly that "They're making my daughter die next to a colored person." This somewhat mundane discussion acknowledges the implicit racism among many working-class individuals and illustrates how racism intersects with both gender and sexuality. The fact that her daughter, taking on the position of unnamed innocence, is dying next to a black patient is amplified by the fact that this is a black male, crossing gender boundaries and implying a potentially inappropriate sexualization of that death. The everyday quality of racism is further underscored by the fact that Drew, the most sympathetic character in the film, owns, among his few possessions, two Confederate flags—a large one over his bed and a smaller one over the window. These flags signify his working-class masculinity in an otherwise female home at the same time that they show how such masculinity stems, in part, from race antagonisms.

Set in New Mexico several decades earlier, the racial tensions of *Salt of the Earth* revolve around the conflicts between Mexican and Anglo workers. In this case, labor disputes connect to shifting national borders. The region in which the mine is located was part of the land acquisition resulting from the 1848 Treaty of Guadalupe Hidalgo in which nearly one-fifth of the contemporary United States, including present-day California, Arizona, and New Mexico as well as parts of Utah, Nevada, and Colorado, was taken from Mexico. According to the treaty, Mexicans living in those regions had the option to move or become U.S. citizens. Many people stayed, but the titles to their land—either nonexistent or written in Spanish-language documents—were not recognized by the U.S. government.[5] Consequently, these repatriotized individuals were at the mercy of whatever work they could find. This was the case for the Mexican workers in *Salt of the Earth,* whose families could be traced back for generations on the land that was now company owned. Regardless of this long historical claim to the land, these workers were treated as foreigners. Company owners indiscriminately called them "Pancho" and described them as "bull-fighters" or "full of chili." The racism that the mine workers endure manifests in an uneven workplace environment in which white workers are afforded more safety precautions than their Mexican counterparts. When Mexican workers complain, they are told simply, "That's no way to talk to a white man."

The inequities of this racism trickle downward into gender relations. As Esperanza correctly observes to her husband, "Anglos look down on you, you look down on me." But this downward spiral stops as Esperanza takes agency for her own entitlement, suggesting too that racial divides will end when subjugated races resist structural inequities just as unions resist workplace inequities. As mentioned earlier, the union successes—propelled to a large degree by women's efforts—bridge gender divides; similarly, such victories begin to heal racial divides as well. Mexican workers achieved parity with Anglo counterparts only by working across gender division. The solution to racial tensions that emerge as workers compete for jobs in an insecure economic environment, as put forth by these films, is the raising of historical consciousness and collective organizing that unionization offers. If workers understood the varying histories and struggles that stem from divergent racial, national, and ethnic differences, those workers would see a common thread among them: the desire to make a living, feed a family, and celebrate life accomplishments.

In addition to the strategy of divide and conquer through gender and racial divisions, resistance to working-class organizing in these films includes apparatuses for policing workers through sexual practices. Sexual conduct among men, while it certainly exists, goes unexplored at the same time that the sexual conduct of women takes on key significances. Commonly, women organizers are undermined because of nontraditional sexual practices. Traditional sexuality in these films can be expressed within the confines of heterosexual marriage and with appropriate deference to one's husband. Nontraditional sexuality includes sexual conduct outside of marriage as well as sexual aggression by women. Highly sexualized women cannot be trusted as this trait indicates an unreliable character. The working-class films discussed here challenge these themes by valorizing female protagonists and allowing them a range of sexual practices.

One of the most prevalent of these sexual expressions is the implicit romantic relationship between the male union organizer and the local female. Nearly all the female protagonists develop strong attachments to the outside organizer. This theme plays out in *Matewan, Harlan County War, Norma Rae, Silkwood,* and *Bread and Roses.* In many of these films, the relationship remains platonic, even as the long hours spent together causes jealousy and suspicion. The appearance of sexual wrong-doing sometimes stems from a highly sexualized representation of the female organizer. Norma Rae, for instance, carried on a relationship with a married man, produced a child from a one-night affair with another man, and has a host of ex-lovers about which her father and everyone else in town knows. Because of this history she is often the recipient of sexual jokes and advances. In one scene, she falls asleep in the hotel room where Reuben Warshovsky (Ron Leibman) works when union management arrives. They tell her and Reuben that her sexual past—real and imagined—undermines the organizing effort. In another scene, she is arrested at work for violating an order to leave the factory. The arresting officer jokes that he's scared to be in the police car alone with her. The one person who doesn't judge Norma Rae for her sexual history is Reuben, whom she has never slept with but admits that he is "in her head." The depth of this relationship comes through in their final good-bye. As they express their feelings for each other, Reuben says, "Norma, what I've had from you has been sumptuous." Although they only shake hands, the lingering scene and Reuben's unusual choice of words suggest a sincere and deep attraction that stems, in large part, from shared labor politics.

In a parallel representation, *Silkwood* depicts Karen as a highly sexualized woman who becomes involved with Paul Stone (Ron Silver), her union organizer. As an elected union member, Karen travels to Washington, DC, with Paul and two coworkers. The pictures of that trip suggest a burgeoning romance between the two that her boyfriend Drew cannot tolerate. Although there is certainly closeness between Paul and Karen, precipitated mostly by shared intellectual and personal commitments to organizing against the company, the exact nature of this relationship remains unclear. More than simple jealousy of Karen's attraction to this other man, Drew is thrown off by her intense desire to advocate on behalf of workers and against the company. From his perspective, a viewpoint with which the film appears to sympathize, it is best to simply perform one's work and not agitate.

Drew, the more stable of this pair, represents the level-headed position and, not uncoincidentally, he has no former relationships, no children, and no infidelities. Karen, on the other hand, appears less stable. She does not have custody of her children who live with their father, often flies off the handle at work (once flashing her breast at a coworker who she finds staring at her), fails to follow the rules, and forgets to do such simple tasks as requesting the day off in order to visit her out-of-town children. Her erratic nature is underscored by constant flirtation and a supposedly extensive sexual history, though this history remains primarily implicit. The final piece of damning sexual behavior associated with Karen's untrustworthy character is the fact that she lives with her lesbian coworker, further undermining her already fragile reputation. Karen does not reciprocate the romantic feelings of her housemate Dolly (Cher) but is clearly tolerant of, if a bit uncomfortable with, this sexual difference. Karen's rather free sexual expression, much like Norma Rae's, leaves her and her organizing activities vulnerable to the harsh judgments of others.

Nevertheless, Karen is the one person who extensively researches the effects of plutonium exposure, makes repeated phone calls to both her coworkers and the union, documents the various safety violations at the plant, blows the whistle on the cover-up of production defects, and risks her job to gather information. She has accumulated enough information to pass along to a *New York Times* reporter (who will apparently run a story about the safety hazards at the plant) when she dies abruptly in a car accident. The cause of the accident and Karen's death remain uncertain, although the film—and reporting of the event—certainly suggest foul play. The focus on sexualized female protagonists, like Norma Rae and Karen, reinforces the perception that loose women, predominant among the working classes, cannot be trusted at the same time that it undermines that representation by valorizing such characters as independent, principled, intelligent, and highly trustworthy. In this way, the film leaves audiences with an ambiguous picture of working-class women, labor, and sexuality—a picture that no doubt mirrors many social contradictions.

There are, of course, representations of female sexuality that fail to live up to this living complexity. In *Matewan*, for instance, the naive Bridey May (Nancy Mette) figures as a pawn used by the company spy, C. E. Lively (Bob Gunton), to turn local workers against Joe Kenehan. After losing her husband in a mining explosion, Bridey May consoles herself by watching people come and go at the train station. As it becomes clear that she has an attraction to Joe, the company men tell her that he has spread sexual rumors about the two. C. E. Lively explains with vivid detail how Joe talked about Bridey May's sexual aggression. This is so humiliating to her that she takes his advice and tells a lie about Joe that almost results in his death. The plan to kill Joe is thwarted at the last minute when Danny (Will Oldham) delivers a sermon that plants seeds of doubt in the minds of his fellow workers. Through no volition of her own, Bridey May escapes complicity in this murder plot and remains socially as well as sexually pure. Representing these working-class women—wives and widows of miners—as sexually virtuous recuperates the image of highly sexualized working-class women, turning this long-standing narrative on its head. The resulting virtuosity, however, belies the original stereotype and leaves little room for developing a complex picture of women, sexuality, and class. Indeed, the fact that Bridey May can be so easily manipulated by rumors of her sexual activities suggests the enduring power of this connection between improper sexuality and working-class femininity, a bond that can be leveraged against working-class politics to this day.

The myth of oversexed working women, for instance, plays an important part of *North Country.* The primary means by which the mining company defended itself against sexual harassment charges is through repeated reference to Josie's promiscuous nature—she had sex with her high school teacher (later revealed as a rape), she had a child out of wedlock (explained by the rape), she left her husband who wanted to continue their marriage (he was physically abusive), and she was the initiator of sexual advances toward her male coworkers (simply untrue). Even though these allegations are proven false, the fact remains that they had to be accounted for before Josie's sexual harassment case could be taken seriously by the union and the local community. According to this logic, a rape victim who has been beaten by her husband is a more reliable worker than a sexually promiscuous woman who leaves her husband without justification.

Among the more recent union-oriented films, *Bread and Roses* offers a complex illustration of the relationship between sexuality, working-class identity, and labor, including prostitution as a key component in this matrix. The film begins with two unnamed coyotes smuggling a group of Mexicans, including Maya, across the border. Once in Los Angeles, the van pulls into a low traffic alley to release the individuals and collect payment, but Maya's sister Rosa doesn't have enough money (she has only $300 of the $800 fee). Consequently, Maya is forced back into the van and the two men toss a coin to see who gets to take her home. Back in his apartment, the winner undresses, enters the shower, and instructs Maya to wash his back.

While he continues to wash, Maya quickly escapes and finds her way to Rosa's house without having to prostitute herself. As this film indicates, the sale of women for sex correlates to class identity as well as to legal status. The labor of prostitution—forced or not—often falls on the shoulders of poor women and especially undocumented immigrants as they are vulnerable to economic need as well as the threat of deportation.[6]

If sex slavery and prostitution occupy an extreme position in the relationship between working-class women and sexuality, then a more moderate position includes a range of feminized jobs wherein a woman's sexuality functions as an implicit component of the work. For instance, Maya initially takes a job as a waitress at a bar where the clients make repeated sexual comments and advances, culminating in her quitting that job. She then gets a job with Rosa cleaning office buildings. At this job, her supervisor, Pérez (George Lopez), tells her to tighten her uniform shirt so as to emphasize her breasts. The workplace, it is clear, becomes an opportunity to sexually exploit women who need the work and have few other options. As the number of families headed by single mothers increase, women, like men, need employed labor in order to house and feed their families. Unlike men, however, they are vulnerable to a range of practices that understand female sexuality as the entitled possession of the men in power over these women.

Women who escape harm are often portrayed as more idealistic than those who are hardened by chronic abuse, whether sexual, physical, or emotional. Revelatory of this dynamic, Maya and Rosa occupy different ends of possibility in this narrative. Rosa, who has been emotionally and physically abused by the system, can no longer imagine collective action beyond the interests of her own family. She trusts no one—neither the company nor the union nor her coworkers. When Sam Shapiro (Adrien Brody), the union organizer, shows up at her house with a pay stub from 1982 to discuss the wages and benefits lost to janitors over the last decades, she throws him out indignantly. "You fat union white boys, college kids, what the hell do you know? I believe in nothing, nobody, nada, nothing but this," screams Rosa as she gestures to herself. Maya, on the other hand, has worked in these spaces relatively unscathed and thus retains hope in the union, in her fellow workers, and in the possibility of just labor practices. She runs after Sam with the stub he accidentally left behind and inquires more about the union, beginning her role as a leader in the organizing struggle.

The political opposition between Rose and Maya extends to their sexual characterization, as well. Maya is often placed in sexually compromising positions because of her working-class and illegal status, but she always manages to avoid serious danger. Her sister, Rosa, however, does not share this same fortune. Rosa, we later find out, slept with her boss, Pérez, in order to get Maya her job. This wasn't the first time that Rosa had to sell sex. In a heated confrontation with Maya, Rosa reveals that she worked as a prostitute in Tijuana in order to send money to her struggling family. Screaming and crying, she tells Maya repeatedly that she had to do this so the rest of the family could survive. Every night for five years, she tells Maya, she was told to "suck their dicks, Rosa . . . fuck, Rosa, fuck." The intensity of this scene, played out in Spanish, the native language of the sisters, demonstrates the naivety of non-working-class people. Maya, the younger and more protected sister, is our protagonist and the eyes through which we explore the unionizing efforts of these janitors. She, just like the audience, is surprised at the depths of abuse and humiliation her sister had to endure. Although Maya develops a romantic interest in Sam Shapiro, a thematic hallmark of unionization films, her relationship remains pure: they hold hands, kiss, and argue about the difference between intellectual and practical labor struggles. In this way, Rosa is forced to carry the scars that link sexual labor (as well as sexual abuse) to working-class women, resulting in a hardened exterior and a drive to protect herself. Because she has not had to compromise her sexual virtuosity, Maya can represent the openness of collective organizing.

Just as they resist sexism and racism, these films suggest that working-class solidarity requires organizing against sexual coercion and toward sexual freedom. If workers are sexually compromised—whether through rumors (Bridey May) or through rape and prostitution (Josie and Rosa)—they cannot organize effectively; however, sexually free women—whether sexually adventurous (Norma Rae and Karen) or more timid (Maya)—energize collective organizing and function well within union efforts. Stated differently, the films don't just advocate for labor rights; they argue for individual rights across a range of intersecting difference both in and out of the workplace.

An Overarching Structure of Feeling and Its Implications: Concluding Thoughts

These films—ones that fictionalize real-life strikes, organizing efforts, and other labor struggles—demonstrate that working-class politics intersect with a range of other identity traits, including gender, race, and sexuality. No defining characteristic takes precedence and there is no simple calculation between work, class, and identity. On the contrary, the films represent a complex structure in which a nascent sentiment emerges, a feeling that appears to be always in process but never quite fully present. Such a structure of feeling, one might conjecture, correlates to a sensibility that erupts in conjunctural moments wherein the contradictions and limitations of capitalism across a range of cultural, political, and economic spaces become highly visible. Through collective organizing, workers—those contracted by corporations as well as those who labor at home—come together across gender, across race, across nationality, across linguistic divides, and across sexual differences to image the possibility of a world in which one's freedom does not depend on someone else's restrictions.

This structure of feeling and the possibilities it imagines reflect Marx's highly debated critique of democracy as political freedom. In his "On the Jewish Question," Marx argues that "*political* emancipation certainly represents great progress. It is not, indeed, the final form of human emancipation, but it is the final form of human emancipation *within* the framework of the prevailing social order" (35). Drawing an analogy between this critique of the democratic state and the role of workplace struggle, one might suggest that workplace rights are not the final form of rights for working-class people. Just as democratic freedom is all that can be achieved by the democratic state, labor unions can only achieve workplace equity. Consequently, the larger emancipation imagined in these films, and representative of a particular working-class structure of feeling, cannot be achieved through traditional unionizing efforts.

Illustrative of this limitation is a 2010 *New York Times* article that reviews the British film *Made in Dagenham* and its dramatization of a 1968 autoworkers strike wherein female workers demanded equal pay. Citing interviews with executives, directors, producers, and academics, the article claims that working-class characters, especially those related to union jobs, are "so last century" (Leah Rozen). Hollywood filmmakers, according to the article, do not foresee profitable representations of working-class individuals because they are, in their words, "losers." In one respect, these characterizations are simply classist, offensive, and dismissive of the immense profits that blue-collar popular culture has produced. In another respect, however, they reveal what Gramsci calls "incurable structural contradictions" (178). Workplace struggles, that is, are symptomatic of larger social and cultural inequities and cannot be resolved without taking into account this larger terrain. Ultimately, the strength of these blue-collar films is not that they depict unionization efforts but that they imagine the relationship among class, race, gender, and sexuality to be mutually imbricated in an ongoing struggle for justice.

Notes

1. Gramsci discusses conjunctural moments as those wherein crucial economic contradictions surface and must be resolved through short-term solutions. A conjuncture, even if it last for years, offers government-based solutions that are not sustainable long-term solutions (*Prison Notebooks* 177–78).

2. The main exception to the list of films I offer is *Hoffa* (1992), which, like these other films, provides a fictionalized account of historical events. It focuses on Jimmy Hoffa's advocacy and leadership on behalf of the Teamsters Union over a 40-year period from the mid-1930s through the mid-1970s, emphasizing the relationship between working-class labor and the construction of American masculinity. The films I track, however, depict specific labor struggles, located in a particular place and time. They follow a narrative format of workers and their families against owners and their allies. The selected films use characters to tell a broader story about working-class struggle rather than using working-class struggle to profile the character of any single person.

3. See Barbara Kingsolver's *Holding the Line* for another illustration of women who take over striking efforts on behalf of their husbands.

4. In the Kopple documentary, *Harlan County USA*, on which this film is loosely based, one woman bathes her child in a metal bucket clearly too small for this young girl. Without either running water or a proper bathtub, the child squeezes into the bucket, with her legs, torso, and arms exceeding its boundaries, as her mother pours water over her.

5. See Richard Griswold del Castillo's *The Treaty of Guadalupe Hidalgo: A Legacy of Conflict* for a history of land, language, and racial struggles.

6. For a range of views on this issue, see Louise Gerdes's edited collection *Prostitution and Sex Trafficking*.

Works Cited

Bread and Roses. Dir. Ken Loach. Parallax Pictures, 2000.

Gerdes, Louise, ed. *Prostitution and Sex Trafficking.* Detroit: Greenhaven Press, 2006.

Gramsci, Antonio. *Selections from the Prison Notebooks.* New York: International Publishers, 1971.

Griswold del Castillo, Richard. *The Treaty of Guadalupe Hidalgo: A Legacy of Conflict.* Norman: University of Oklahoma Press, 1990.

Harlan County USA. Dir. Barbara Kopple. Cabin Creek Films, 1976.

Harlan County War. Dir. Tony Bill. Showtime, 2000.

Kingsolver, Barbara. *Holding the Line: Women in the Great Arizona Mine Strike of 1983.* Ithaca: Cornell University Press, 1996.

Marx, Karl. *The Eighteenth Brumaire of Louis Bonaparte.* New York: International Publishers, 1994.

Marx, Karl. "On the Jewish Question." *The Marx-Engels Reader.* Ed. Robert C. Tucker. New York: Norton, 1977. 26–52.

Matewan. Dir. John Sayles. Cinecom Entertainment Group and Film Gallery, 1987.

Norma Rae. Dir. Martin Ritt. Twentieth Century Fox, 1979.

North Country. Dir. Niki Caro. Warner Brothers Pictures, 2005.

Rozen, Leah. "Hollywood's Vanishing Have-Nots." *New York Times* AR 16. 14 November 2010.

Salt of the Earth. Dir. Herbert J. Biberman. Independent Film Productions with International Union of Mine, Mill, and Smelter Workers, 1954.

Silkwood. Dir. Mike Nichols, ABC Motion Pictures, 1983.

Williams, Raymond. *The Long Revolution.* Peterborough: Broadview Press, 2001.

Williams, Raymond. *Marxism and Literature.* Oxford: Oxford University Press, 1977.

Chapter 3

Canadian Crossings: Exploring the Borders of Race and Class in Courtney Hunt's *Frozen River*

Lisa Hinrichsen

In an age in which Hollywood cinema thrives by churning out popular films such as *Pretty Woman* (1990) that largely present portraits of easy social mobility, reinforcing ideological fantasies about American classlessness, it is no surprise that nuanced cinematic portraits of working-class life—much less racially diverse working-class life—are not given substantial screen time. While, as sociologist Michael Katz argues, pervasive political pressures have moved critical discussions of exploitation and inequality into the discursive realms of identity and morality, long-standing and widespread beliefs in the mutability and indeterminacy of American class structure have also contributed to this critical blindness (8). Mirroring cultural production, scholarly attention to issues of race, gender, and sexuality has flourished, but class has remained a less examined category of identity.[1]

However, film scholars and historians of American working-class life have recently provoked each other to produce important reconsiderations in both fields.[2] This intellectual intersection between social history and film studies has not only altered the narrative of the rise of mass entertainment in the United States, making it far more nuanced and complete, but it has also creatively and productively challenged the lenses through which we envision working-class lives and leisure. In bringing film and labor history together, critics such as Noël Burch have returned to the historical origins of cinematic production, illuminating the way in which movies emerged in the early twentieth century as an affordable working-class pleasure. Working people were simultaneously the primary consumers, producers, and subjects of the early silent films, and many of these films, which were made by eminent directors such as Charlie Chaplin, D. W. Griffith, and William de Mille, addressed working-class interests, desires, and politics (see *The Eviction* [1904]; *A Corner in Wheat* [1909]; *The Sowers* [1916]; among others). Movies like *The Jungle* (1914; based on Upton Sinclair's novel of the same name), *Toil and Tyranny* (1915), and the pro-union film *The Blacklist* (1916) depicted struggles for labor justice and encouraged working-class solidarity.

Despite these auspicious early cinematic appeals to a working-class, racially and ethnically diverse audience, the form and breadth of mainstream cinema quickly altered as Hollywood became defined by conservative production regulations, like the establishment of the Production Code Administration (PCA) in 1934, and the rise of procapitalist sensibilities. Though American cinema, especially during the labor-conscious decade of the Great Depression, has periodically revived cinema that portrays revitalized class-consciousness and offers a populist ethos, Hollywood has also served to bind and realign audiences with bourgeois norms and dominant ideological beliefs, including notions of racial hierarchy. The resulting films affirm business and consumer values, and offer up a myth of a classless America in place of labor-conscious portrayals, ultimately reinforcing what Fredric Jameson describes as the capitalist "cultural logic" that favors the cult of the individual rather than the collective.

As this chapter argues, the coalescence between labor history and cinematic representation has been significantly constrained by commercial interests and market concerns. It has also been constrained by a long-standing lack of accuracy regarding the diversity of *who* the working class are. The overlap between labor history and cinematic representation reveals a history largely confined to working-class *white* identities, resulting in a representational history that neglects trenchant intraclass divisions as gender, ethnicity, and race. As Daniel Bernardi argues, U.S. cinema has consistently constructed whiteness at the heart of its aesthetic project. Critic Jane Gaines makes an even more provocative claim, arguing that "Cinema aesthetics and the aesthetics of racial distinction . . . are one and the same" (3). Indeed, important American films like Griffith's 1915 *Birth of a Nation*, for example, famously sutured aesthetic innovation to mass appeal in order to offer a distinctly whitewashed version of history through which Americans were to understand their collective past and enact their future. By presenting a fantasized screen memory of white racial dominance tied to national belonging, early cinema, despite its appeals to working-class values, set a precedent for functioning as a site where ideology, fantasy, and enjoyment powerfully coincide to have a political power that transcends the site of the cinema itself, for representational exclusion is intimately tied to other forms of exclusion and disenfranchisement.

Similarly, many studies of working-class culture and politics have largely concentrated on white working-class life. If scholarship on American culture tends to evince a pervasive blindness regarding class, then class-focused scholarship reveals an unconscious focus on questions of whiteness. Even remarkable books like David Roediger's *The Wages of Whiteness: Race and the Making of the American Working Class* (1991), a seminal study of the significance of racism in the formation of the nineteenth-century white working class, unconsciously cast working-class studies as preoccupied with questions of whiteness (currently evinced in the surfeit of recent work on "white trash" identities).

In the history of American film, as in the longer history of American literature, representations of class are inextricably interwoven into a complex social fabric in which other determining factors such as gender, ethnicity, religion, education, race, and geography are also at play. As numerous critics have noted, contemporary mainstream cinema reveals, for the most part, a disturbing reliance on narrative structures that foreground fantasy structures, including the elevation of the bourgeois ideal as a symbol of racial egalitarianism. In invoking what critic Houston A. Baker calls, in another context, the idea of "AMERICA as immanent idea of boundless, classless, raceless possibility," mainstream Hollywood cinema frequently evades the frank presentation of class, race, and gender struggles, instead directing the American public on a mass scale to misrecognize the nature of both the racial divide and the class divide within American culture (65). For cinema delivers, as Slavoj Žižek has aptly argued, ideology through enjoyment, and in the process, often transforms lived struggle into aesthetic pleasure.[3] Just as themes of working-class solidarity and collective action often give way to fantastic stories of cross-class romance and upward mobility, cinematic portraits of racial trauma often transform too easily into sketches of racial harmony that evade adequately dealing with lived struggle, offering instead idealizations of inclusiveness. Films like *Trading Places* (1983) and *Brewster's Millions* (1914, 1985) can be seen to bolster widespread beliefs in the mutability and indeterminacy of American class structure at the same time that they subtly deliver racial stereotypes cloaked in comedy, ultimately betraying American anxiety about black social mobility.

Despite mainstream film's proclivity toward elevating bourgeois materialism and erasing or drastically simplifying multicultural identities, the recent rise in independent filmmaking offers hope for thoughtful cinematic representations of both progressive labor issues and racially diverse identities. While avoiding the way in which critical discussions of class frequently become obscured by issues of identity politics, as Michael Katz has argued, this chapter seeks to contribute to both film studies and labor studies by analyzing the representation of class as it coincides and overlaps with the representation of race and gender. I seek to parse out the ambivalent, complex, and conflicted racial dimensions of class—and class-based dimensions of racism—by examining the intersection between race, class, and contemporary culture through a focused analysis of Courtney Hunt's 2008 independent film *Frozen River*. Through revealing how the film portrays class and race (including whiteness) as intersecting categories of identity, often sharing an interlocked material and social network structure, this chapter will also attend to how class produces particular onscreen forms of racialization (and vice versa) that become manifested on the cinematic screen, which itself serves as one of the sources of racial identity formation. Offering a portrait of a multicultural working class increasingly affected by political and economic issues of transnationalism and globalization, *Frozen River* sophisticatedly renders the working-class figure's relationship to national identity, political affiliation, and communal belonging in the age of late capitalism.

Frozen River meditates on the intersection of class, race, and culture through presenting the story of two working-class women of different races who uneasily collaborate together to supplement their meager (legal) wages by smuggling illegal immigrants from Canada to the United States in the North Country area of upstate New York.[4] Ray Eddy (played by Melissa Leo) is an underpaid part-time clerk at the local Yankee Dollar Mart in the small, economically depressed town of Massena, New York. She is visibly struggling to make ends meet and to raise her two sons alone during a bitterly cold winter that shakes the fragile walls of her broken-down trailer. In the days before Christmas, her husband, a compulsive gambler, abandons the family, disappearing with the entirety of the funds she had slowly saved to finance the balloon payment on a new double-wide mobile home.

While searching for her missing husband at the local Native-run bingo hall, Ray meets by chance Lila Littlewolf (played by Misty Upham), a young widowed Mohawk woman. Lila's theft of Ray's husband's abandoned car—an act motivated, we soon learn, by her own economic and moral desperation—brings them together. Situated across ethnic identities but linked by a similar condition of economic need, the two women enter into a fragile partnership smuggling undocumented immigrants over the U.S./Canadian border, relying on Lila's contacts and knowledge of the Mohawk land and Ray's automobile to make the journey. Together, they put their own lives at risk, crossing the treacherous, frozen St. Lawrence River under the cover of night to make $1,200 each per journey.

Though the film focuses a bit more on Ray than it does Lila, it does so in a way that deliberately unsettles whiteness. As the film moves toward presenting us with our first glimpse of Ray, the camera first reveals to us her current trailer home, focusing on its stark exterior and on a decrepit, broken children's carousel abandoned in the snow, underscoring its presence as symbolic of a happier, more prosperous time. Outside in a pink bathrobe, Ray sits in her old car, the door ajar, the glove compartment where the cash for the trailer was kept pulled open, left exposed and barren. The camera traces her body from the ground up, allowing us to see her body first via a faded rose tattoo stretched across her big toe, then giving us a glimpse of her weathered hands holding a pack of cheap cigarettes. Her slumped posture alerts us immediately to her sense of trouble and anxiety. The film lingers on her face, bare of makeup, and etched with lines, as she sucks on a cigarette and looks forlorn, hungry, and fierce.

This opening scene is one of many in the film where we are allowed to see Ray in a private moment and to grasp a sense of her extreme vulnerability despite the tough front she displays to the world. It is also a scene that strategically presents us with familiar tropes of working-class existence, including ways that the body itself comes to signify class. Accordingly, this initial surveying of Ray's body has a double—even paradoxical—function: it instructs viewers to the necessity of reading the body in film that consistently renders emotion through unspoken expression, and, as the film progresses, it also challenges us to surmount merely seeing Ray as a laboring body, a walking "white trash" stereotype, for the rest of the film strives—and admirably succeeds—in delivering a picture of working-class life filled with emotional and intellectual complexity that adds a nuanced interior to the exterior we "read" in this first glimpse. Thus, the film declares a sympathetic allegiance with the working class early on, making clear its intention to offer a rich portrait of the life of working-class women as well as a complicated analysis of the economic, social, racial, and political forces that act on and shape individual identity.

In telling a story of two similarly disenfranchised women of different races that live in a borderland zone between Canada, the United States, and Mohawk territory, Hunt's film examines how the border functions as a site that is not only a paradigm of crossings, intercultural exchanges, and circulations of power, but also as a place of anxieties, resistances, and uneasy negotiations. Rather than crossing the "official" border, a bridge full of police surveillance and border control measures, Ray and Lila drive across an unguarded frozen river on the Mohawk Territory of Akwesasne, which stretches across national borders. By flashing its opening scenes from the lake to the highway and border control, the film immediately makes us aware of the difference between Native-claimed space—the open yet treacherous space of the frozen river—and the "official" space of white culture, demarcated by highways, road signs, and omnipresent border police that come to signify white cultural anxiety about immigration. Yet as the film proceeds, it repeatedly reconfigures our conceptions of racial privilege, reworking stereotypes about what it means to be poor and white, and Native American. Together these three different legal, cultural, and economic spaces intersect to form what Mary Louise Pratt famously termed a "contact zone," a space that allows the intermingling of two or more cultures.

Thus, the film, by almost exclusively portraying working-class characters within this complex contact zone, seeks explicitly to place working-class identity within a global and multicultural framework.[5] Calling to mind Frederick Jackson Turner's 1893 address "The Significance of the American Frontier in American History," which positioned the frontier as a space of promise, progress, and ingenuity, and certainly cognizant of contemporary anti-immigration rhetoric and anxiety, Hunt's *Frozen River* meditates on the American frontier—which is to say, America itself—as an ideologically fraught space. As the camera traces the two women's repeated smuggling trips, *Frozen River* foregrounds the breakdown of national borders—here, literalized as a wide-open, unguarded frozen river—due to the transnational flow of capital, goods, and laboring bodies. The film makes us aware of contemporary culture's simultaneous reliance on and violation of borders in various ways: through situating the film on the border of the United States and Canada, through its nod to the cheap Chinese-made goods sold at the Yankee Dollar Mart, and through the stream of immigrant bodies that uncomfortably squeeze themselves into the trunk of Ray's car. At numerous moments throughout the film, Hunt carefully underscores how the border is a place of discursive discontinuity as well as cultural and legal difference: Ray, for example, initially refuses to recognize Mohawk sovereignty, instead calling it "New York State." Ultimately, the uncertainty here about where the women are, what laws are in effect, and what nation is in power, ends up destabilizing Ray's assumptions about her white privilege, throwing her emotional defenses off balance, and enabling revelations about their shared vulnerabilities and fears.

For we encounter a site of jurisdictional chaos, where the sheer multiplicity of policing forces complicates the smooth working of law, ultimately opening the space for exploitation. At one point, Lila even tells Ray that the police themselves used to be in on the smuggling, "back when it was cigarettes and everyone did it." Her comment here indirectly reminds us that the police also represent the working class in the film and, as *Frozen River* proceeds, we see Hunt strategically remind us of this fact, portraying the police as living parallel lives to Lila and Ray, buying cheap goods at Yankee Dollar and working through the Christmas holidays. The distinction between smuggling and legitimate trading, as well as between police and criminals, is complicated further by Lila's claim that the Mohawk Nation is a "free trade" area exempt from U.S. laws. Thus, space, place, and race complicate questions of law, ethics, and naming. They also complicate the women's strategies for economic survival, adding to their confusion about how to proceed pragmatically and ethically. Earning a living—legally or illegally—becomes an intellectually, ethically, and pragmatically complicated act and we see, via this focused portrait of working-class life on the border, the complexity of "making do" in contemporary capitalism. Rendered as a site of violence, surveillance, discrimination, and danger, the visual landscapes of both the official border and the unofficial border across the frozen river immediately foreshadow what we already know: that these women are in a position of such emotional need and material lack that they willingly take on the danger inherent to an illegal crossing.

The film asks us to think critically about how this fluid crisscrossing of borders challenges, confirms, or corrects ideological notions of class solidarity, national identity, and racial belonging. Against a conservative mainstream media that promotes the idea that there is an ongoing border control crisis due to a flow of undocumented immigrants coming into the United States and threatening American jobs, nurturing nativist anxiety and fostering the militarization of borders, *Frozen River* indicates that Americans themselves take advantage of the porousness of national boundaries, finding a way to profit off of the stream of foreign bodies making their way into the United States. The film portrays the undocumented workers that cross the border as no threat to the American status quo, for, as Lila reveals to Ray, they enter in a state of enslaved dependency, under the watchful eyes of their "snakeheads" who will exact wage bondage for years after their arrival. When Lila tells Ray about these unsettling economics of crossing the border, Ray scoffs, unbelieving: "To get here? No fucking way," a wry comment that, despite its brevity, serves to powerfully deflate the desirability of arriving on American shores.

Indeed, the downtrodden places we see in the film—the Pioneer Inn, the Yankee Dollar, the mobile homes that fail to live up to the "Live the American Dream" message that ads promise—undercut a sense of American possibility. The film thus consciously takes language referencing a historical sense of America as a New World place of promise and ingenuity (and even a little Yankee thriftiness), and repositions it in relation to locales that bear feelings of anxiety, claustrophobia, paranoia, and hopelessness. In the process, *Frozen River* unsettles ideological assumptions about the fluidity and mobility of American class structure, and dramatizes the diminishing of the "American Dream." Even Ray's teenage son T.J. knows the outright impossibility of making a sufficient living through a part-time job at Yankee Dollar: "Bet I can make more than you," he calls out, taunting his mother and foregrounding his own barely suppressed rage at his own helplessness.

Frozen River indicates that such lack, however, can paradoxically foster community, and, in highlighting these allegiances born of necessity, reveals a kind of quiet optimism. For it is Lila and Ray's shared need that sutures their relationship despite deep cultural differences (one of the first things we learn about Lila, for example, is that she does not like "whites"). *Frozen River* aptly portrays that together they are caught in a bind between what their country (and, in the case of Lila, her tribe) cannot or will not provide them with, and what they need—or feel they need, as the film is aptly aware of the power of consumerism to transform want into perceived need.

For the border is also a place where the circuits of commodity production and circulation come into relief: when Ray's youngest son, Ricky, asks what will happen to their old home when their new one arrives, she playfully tells him that their home will be crushed, shipped to China, and made into toys that then will be shipped back to the United States and sold at Yankee Dollar. Ricky asks if she will then buy him these toys—and, in effect, repurchase their own transfigured home. Ray's quick yes nods to the complicated networks of global trade that form the basis of the everyday American citizen's day-to-day life—which, as *Frozen River* portrays it, is full of the desire to trade up but the impossibility of doing so, and that involves a lifestyle reliant upon cheap imports and invisible, exploitable labor. The waste generated by this cycle of consumerism is easily exported abroad, where the entire process is repeated and transmuted back into a kind of collective enjoyment, where the human, economic, and environmental costs can be forgotten (Ray and her son both gleefully giggle at the idea that their junked mobile home will be transformed into toys). The film pairs this and other embedded references to the realities of contemporary global trade with critical reflections on the historical reality of displacement, migration, and immigration in the United States: the displacement of Native Americans, the establishment of America as a nation of immigrants, and the various historical and ideological transformations of "America" through changing geographic and demographic alterations.

The various characters' ongoing preoccupations with configuring, purchasing, and economically sustaining a home underscores how having and maintaining *any* sense of home in our contemporary age depends not only on local politics but also on an ongoing and complicated negotiation with the global community and the formation of transnational solidarity. (As the cover of the DVD case announces: "Desperation has no borders.") *Frozen River* hints at what it might mean for Ray to feel at home: when we see her bathroom, we are given a brief glimpse of a shelf overloaded with bath products that visibly promise to deliver romance, relaxation, and sensuality. However, we never see Ray using the products—we see her only looking at herself in a corroded mirror and poor lighting, frantically trying to assemble a brave face for the day ahead. Later, we see that the small bathtub is filthy with age and the showerhead corroded with rust. When we later see her parked outside the model of the mobile home she wants to buy, we hear her tell Lila that it is not the expanded space that she is after, it is the *insulation*—a word that resonates far beyond the architecture of the home, into the cushioning she needs from the everyday struggles of her life. Lila instantly understands the resonance of this word, for she makes her own makeshift home in a small camper equally subject to the strong winter wind.

The fragility of the protective walls that surround Ray and Lila—literally realized in the shaky, thin metal walls of their trailer homes and figuratively in the lack of a supportive economic cushion—shakes their ability to voice themselves in the world. Lila struggles to reconnect with her baby boy who was taken from her by her mother-in-law, following her husband's death in the cold waters of the frozen lake in the midst of a failed smuggling expedition. Standing in the dark, snowy night outside, Lila looks longingly in through the windows at her mother-in-law's home, watching her baby boy play inside, but does not venture into the home. Instead, she stands silently, unable to even approach the door when she offers up money to help with his care: she tosses her hard-earned money through the darkness in a can. Likewise, night after night, Ray struggles in the privacy of her bedroom to get her voicemail message on her cellphone just right, deleting her voice over and over again, trying to find the right note of confidence and self-reliance. Though the film shies away from sentimentalizing these women, thus avoiding turning them into objects of pity, it does reveal to us the invisibility and voicelessness of the disenfranchised in these scenes where Lila walks in the woods unseen and where Ray's voice goes unheard on her deleted messages. As the film progresses, we are asked to think also about the unseen, silenced, and undocumented immigrants in the trunk, concealed from the public notice and from the eye of the law. *Frozen River*'s concerns about visibility are thus underscored not only through these glimpses into the hidden private worlds of the poor, but in the film's foregrounding of the fear of surveillance that border crossing inherently raises. Here, Hunt spotlights the role of racial difference between Lila and Ray. Terrified of being pulled over as they begin their first smuggling trip, Ray quizzes Lila on how to pass unnoticed by the police car that guards around-the-clock the only road into town. Lila derisively states, "Just remember you are white!" In doing so, she nods to a myth of racial privilege that ultimately fails to materialize in the film, much less to protect Ray, as it is she who will end up in prison, not Lila.

Despite this nod to racial difference, and the ongoing "privileges" of whiteness in the American economic and legal landscape, *Frozen River* ultimately portrays the border as a zone where the disenfranchised must negotiate with one another and manufacture new relations, hybrid cultures, and, ultimately, multicultural communities and families, especially as realized in the reconfigured, multicultural family at the end of the film, where Lila temporarily becomes the mother to Ray's two sons. The film underscores this message by documenting Ray's transition from xenophobic citizen to a woman who, out of both necessity and a deeply cultivated trust, creates her own multicultural family. Ray initially sees the undocumented workers that stuff themselves into her trunk as distinctly "Other," sharing nothing—not even a common language—with her, and certainly not a shared sense of economic disenfranchisement. At numerous points in the film, Ray vilifies the illegal aliens she helps across the border, most notably by seeing the Pakistani family she transports as potential terrorists: "Let's hope they aren't the ones who blow themselves and everyone else up." Midway across the river, she spontaneously ditches their bag for fear that it contains weapons: "Nuclear power, poison gas, who knows what they have in there. I'm not going to be responsible for that." Ray here epitomizes the majority views and nativist ideologies that shape public immigration legislation, such as California's Proposition 187, which, when passed in 1997, prevented undocumented immigrants from making use of U.S. education and health care systems, as well as its historical precedents such as the 1882 Chinese Exclusion Act and the Johnson-Reed Immigration Act of 1924, which established an immigration quota system and created the Border Patrol to uphold this new system.

The film, however, powerfully critiques this racial paranoia, political anxiety, and nativism, instead stressing the need for solidarity and compassion. The cruel irony is that the bag Ray assuredly tosses from the car contains life, not the instruments of death: the Pakistani couple's baby is nestled inside, hidden in blankets, and Ray's attempt to act as border control, protecting the security of her nation by not allowing the bag passage, is exposed as a spectacularly misjudged act. Ray and Lila are ethically forced to return and "be responsible for that." When they drive out onto the frigid, dark ice to locate the lost bag, the baby they find initially appears to be dead, but, pressed against Lila's warm chest, it revives on the journey back across the frozen lake. Whereas Lila believes this to be a miracle wrought by "the Creator," and a moment deeply emblematic of her own desires to revive her relationship with her son, Ray's reaction returns us to the fraught pragmatic territory of the material logistics of motherhood: "All I know is Kmart is closed and I got nothing for under the tree." Motherhood, in addition to their shared class status, forms a link between Ray and Lila, forming the suturing bond of ethical community between them and the unnamed Pakistani woman whom we see sobbing with gratitude to feel her child in her arms again, miraculously alive.

As scenes like this demonstrate, *Frozen River* focuses on the intersection between ethics and emotions of motherhood and its many economic obligations. The film stresses to its viewers that at the very moment when women need to earn the most money—when nuclear families have shattered—they may not be able to via traditional legal means, due to the double disenfranchisement that working-class women face as a result of class and gender discrimination. In scenes like the one in which Ray inquires about the possibility of a full-time position at Yankee Dollar and is bluntly told by her much-younger male boss that "I see you as a short-timer. Not here for long, not really committed," we are asked to think about how women are systematically excluded from positions of power. After working almost two years at Yankee Dollar as a part-time employee, Ray protests, stating that at least she shows up on time, unlike Pat, another female employee that is consistently late. When Pat dashes in a moment later, the camera guides us to study her appearance: she's young, blonde, and more conventionally attractive than Ray. The camera follows Ray's gaze at Pat's lower back, where we see a tattoo that reads "How YOU doin'?" Age, sexuality, and class bias coincide in this scene, for though Pat's body shares the same misguided tattoos as Ray's physique does, her clothes, hair, and casual demeanor code her as belonging to a slightly different class status, with a correspondingly different degree of cultural and sexual desirability. We are left believing that Pat might be made assistant manager, though she does not have Ray's experience or her desperate economic need for the position. Trapped by age, class, and gender bias, and forced into a subservient position that excludes her from legally earning enough to put more than popcorn and Tang on the dinner table (as we see in one crucial scene), Ray thus is constrained to turn to illegal ways of making ends meet. The stability of the family, which is key for the continuity of the nation, is paradoxically dependent on the violation of national and state laws, and the film underscores this irony.

At the end of the film, Ray and Lila decide to make one final run to earn the remainder of the money that Ray needs for the deposit on the double-wide. They are forced to drive up to Montreal to find a smuggler who needs to transport people to the United States. The smuggler tries to cheat them out of their payment, only giving them half the cash they have earned on their previous runs. Ray threatens the smuggler with a gun—a bold move, but as she states, "I'm so tired of people stealing from me"—and receives the rest of the payment. However, he shoots at her as she leaves, grazing the side of her head. Bleeding and in a panic, she drives haphazardly along the highway, speeding away from the scene of the standoff. A police car follows her, its lights flashing, and it proceeds to track her into Mohawk territory and to the boundary of the frozen lake. Despite the black ice on the lake, Ray pushes ahead to cross the river, driving across its dangerous surface in the dead of night. Her wheel plunges beneath the surface of the ice, immovably wedging the car into the lake.

Forced to abandon the car, Lila, Ray, and the two Chinese women they were transporting run across the lake and into the woods, ultimately hiding out at a Mohawk home as they debate what to do next. The police need someone to arrest, and it initially seems that Lila will be that person. Ray runs off into the woods but finds herself turning around, returning to the home and surrendering to the police, for she is unable to let Lila take the blame and be exiled from the Mohawk tribe and from her son's life. Before Ray turns herself in, she gives instructions to Lila about how to take care of her children: what to feed them, their allergies, their likes and dislikes. The final scene of the film portrays Lila outside Ray's mobile home, holding her baby, smiling at Ricky and at T.J., who has finally successfully fixed the children's carousel that we saw at the beginning of the film. We see their new home—a single-wide, not a double-wide—heading down the highway to be delivered. The conclusion of the film has us think about questions of sacrifice and interdependence, and we see the family reconfigured into a multicultural, female-headed household and we have every sense that the bond between Lila and Ray will continue after Ray's release from prison.

As *Frozen River* evinces, the future of working-class identity is one in which cultural hybridity comes to play an important role. Though multicultural alliances are purchased at a high price in the film, triggered by mutual economic need and sealed and solidified by Ray's sacrificial imprisonment, the film delivers to us an ending tinted with optimism. Highlighting the racial, sexual, and class-based crossroads of power, Ray and Lila's journey debunks nativist ideology and illuminates the working-class underbelly of contemporary capitalist America. In doing so, it offers a reconfigured vision of working-class solidarity across ethnic, racial, and national lines, emphasizing that workers of the *world* must unite.

Notes

1. In 2002, Larry Griffin and Maria Tempenis published an analysis of the types of articles that have appeared in *American Quarterly,* a widely regarded scholarly journal, since its inception in 1949. In surveying this vast critical terrain, they concluded that there is a long-standing bias in American studies toward multicultural questions of gender, race, and ethnicity at the expense of critical analyses of social class.

2. See, among others, the pioneering Robert Sklar, *Movie-Made America: A Cultural History of American Movies* (1975) and, more recently, Charles Musser, *The Emergence of Cinema: The American Screen to 1907* (1990); David E. James and Rick Berg, eds., *The Hidden Foundation: Cinema and the Question of Class* (1996); and Harry M. Benshoff and Sean Griffin, *America on Film: Representing Race, Class, Gender, and Sexuality at the Movies* (2004).

3. See, for example, *For They Know Not What They Do: Enjoyment as a Political Factor* (2008).

4. Though an independent film, *Frozen River* was widely seen and well-recognized: it earned 23 awards and 14 nominations, including the Best Feature award from the 2008 Sundance Film Festival. Melissa Leo received a 2008 Best Supporting Actress Academy Award nomination and a 2008 Best Actress Broadcast Film Critics Association nomination. Courtney Hunt garnered a 2008 Best Screenplay Broadcast Critics Association nomination.

5. As Stephen Holden noted in the film's *New York Times* review, *Frozen River* "evokes a perfect storm of present day woes: illegal immigration, ethnic tension, depressed real estate, high gas prices and dire poverty."

555

Works Cited

Baker, Houston A. *Blues, Ideology, and Afro-American Literature: A Vernacular Theory.* Chicago: University of Chicago Press, 1987.

Benshoff, Harry M., and Sean Griffin. *America on Film: Representing Race, Class, Gender, and Sexuality at the Movies.* 2nd ed. Oxford: Wiley-Blackwell, 2009.

Bernardi, Daniel, ed. *The Persistence of Whiteness: Race and Contemporary Hollywood Cinema.* New York: Routledge, 2008.

Burch, Noël. *Life to Those Shadows.* Berkeley: University of California Press, 1990.

Gaines, Jane. "*The Scar of Shame*: Skin Color and Caste in Black Silent Melodrama." *Cinema Journal* 26, no. 4 (1987): 3–21.

Griffin, Larry J., and Maria Tempenis. "Class, Multiculturalism, and the *American Quarterly*." *American Quarterly* 54, no. 1 (2002): 67–99.

Holden, Stephen. "Only a Few More Smuggling Days Left before Christmas." *New York Times,* August 1, 2008, Section E0, Lexis-Nexus Academic.

James, David E., and Rick Berg, eds. *The Hidden Foundation: Cinema and the Question of Class.* Minneapolis: University of Minnesota Press, 1996.

Jameson, Fredric. *Postmodernism, or, The Cultural Logic of Late Capitalism.* Durham, NC: Duke University Press, 1991.

Katz, Michael. *The Undeserving Poor: From the War on Poverty to the War on Welfare.* New York: Pantheon, 1989.

Musser, Charles. *The Emergence of Cinema: The American Screen to 1907.* Berkeley: University of California Press, 1990.

Pratt, Mary Louise. "Arts of the Contact Zone." *Profession* (1991): 33–40.

Pratt, Mary Louise. *Imperial Eyes: Travel Writing and Transculturation.* London: Routledge, 1992.

Roediger, David. *The Wages of Whiteness: Race and the Making of the American Working Class.* London: Verso, 1991.

Sklar, Robert. *Movie-Made America: A Cultural History of American Movies.* New York: Vintage, 1975.

Turner, Frederick Jackson. "The Significance of the American Frontier in American History." *American Historical Association Annual Report for the Year 1893.* Washington, DC: American Historical Association, 1894.

Chapter 4

Challenging White-Trash Stereotypes: The Question of Class in *Bastard out of Carolina*

Lorie Watkins Fulton

Anjelica Huston's directorial debut, *Bastard out of Carolina* (1996), bears a genealogy as complex as that of its main character, Bone. Huston developed the project for TNT, but when Ted Turner and other network executives viewed her graphically violent depiction of Dorothy Allison's novel, they realized, as one spokeswoman put it, "Her vision of the film and what we could air were not the same thing" (Luscombe). Turner offered the project back to Huston, and she tried for a big-screen feature, but the film eventually went to Showtime where it first aired on December 15, 1996.

Closely based on Allison's 1992 novel,[1] the film remains true to its "grit lit" roots.[2] In contrast to the ideology of grit lit stands those ubiquitous white-trash jokes of the Jeff Foxworthy variety: jokes about houses that move (and cars that don't), jokes about folks returning from the dump with more junk than they took, jokes about having the local taxidermist on speed dial, jokes that begin, "You might be a redneck if . . ." These jokes, of course, turn on the stereotype of white trash, a stereotype that *Bastard out of Carolina* seeks to destroy. Dorothy Allison and other white-trash writers deliberately use the term when writing and talking about class issues in an effort to rob the phrase of its power (Reynolds 357). Any reader of Allison's work must, therefore, consider how the inflammatory term *white trash* differs from other, less offensive designations like "poor white" or "working class." While many characteristics describe white trash, the term itself proves quite elusive; consequently, people most often identify white trash as an attitude (364). No one trait, not even poverty, defines the term (362), though scholars persist in their attempts to do so.[3] Allison's terminology resists such distinctions and she refers to herself and her family by using the terms *poor, white trash,* and *working class* interchangeably (*Skin* 33, 18, 20). Allison herself describes the definitions of the poor as "just slippery . . . like mayonnaise on glass" ("Dorothy Allison"), and her broad usage stands as an attempt to defuse the negative connotations of the loaded term by equating it with other designations.

Southern literature defines and chronicles the white-trash caricature that Allison's novel and Huston's film challenge.[4] Most literary and film critics agree that *Bastard out of Carolina* challenges white-trash stereotypes; however, few focus on exactly how the novel issues this challenge. I would argue that Allison undermines class myths through quite specific and deliberate narrative inversions that force readers to look at these familiar white-trash stereotypical characteristics in unfamiliar ways; her stealthy attack on stereotypes of white trash firmly establishes Allison as one of several grit lit writers who "have reclaimed a once-derogatory label for their own empowerment" (Bledsoe 88). Accordingly, the semiautobiographical Bone appears to elude the fate she seemed destined to live out early in the narrative; *Bastard out of Carolina* reconfigures the term *white trash* and its attendant conditions to redefine Bone's life in a way that makes it worthy of a good country song, instead of the butt of a white-trash joke. In bringing the novel to life, Huston does a remarkable job of preserving the spirit of Allison's novel; however, the nature of the genre necessitates certain compromises. Despite these compromises, or perhaps more accurately because of them, Huston's film even more impressively challenges white-trash stereotypes because viewers can identify with Bone as they move beyond her appearance and into her heart.

Most critics cite the realistic portrayal of impoverished characters as the main method by which *Bastard out of Carolina* subverts white-trash stereotypes; however, they do not typically address the details of that characterization.[5] The narrative's characters achieve this reality primarily by eluding objectification, and they do so largely because Bone narrates the tale from her own sympathetic point of view. Bone's narration provides an "insider's view of white-trash experiences" (McDonald 15), one that forces readers to consider the situation through her eyes. Allison has said that she deliberately tried to get readers "inside Bone" so that they could "get a different view" of the white-trash perspective ("Moving" 78). Matthew Guinn rightly observes that the society of the novel objectifies Bone and her family by branding them with the label of white trash (24); however, readers react to Bone differently because we experience the story through the perceptive filter that the immediacy of her narration affords. While Huston's film adaptation attempts to get viewers inside Bone's head in similar fashion, the effect falls somewhat short because the audience can see the dirt on Bone's face and hear the twang in her voice. The novel's narrative remove is more complete and readers can look through Bone's eyes without prejudice in a way that an audience viewing a film cannot.

In focusing on Bone, critics have (for the most part) failed to acknowledge that *Bastard out of Carolina* also inverts stereotypes of white trash via its other characters.[6] Most notably, Anney, Bone's mother, stands out as a character that readers cannot neatly pigeonhole into a convenient category in either the novel or the film. Anney may look and sound like white trash, but she does not fully fit the stereotypical "bad poor" mold that Jillian Sandell references because she expresses quite traditional ideas about morality (213). Allison writes of white trash and morality as they apply to her own life in *Skin* when she observes that her family had fewer problems accepting her lesbianism than they did accepting "the way I thought about work, ambition, and self-respect" (25). Allison infuses Anney's character with just such a conventional sort of virtue. Like Allison's own family, the Boatwrights all see Anney as somehow more moral than themselves, and, again like Allison's relatives, they do not approve of it. Cousin Deedee tells Bone, "Your mama's the kind that gets us all in trouble" and compares her to "something out of one of them stories they tell in Sunday school" (*Bastard* 145). Bone also believes that her mother has "made herself different from all her brothers and sisters" (31), and she is probably right because Anney hates it when people refer to her as trash. Bone observes, "The stamp on that birth certificate [the one that certifies Bone "a bastard by the state of South Carolina"] burned her like the stamp she knew they'd tried to put on her. *No-good, lazy, shiftless*" (3). Anney emphatically rejects the label of trash and tells Bone, "We're not bad people. And we pay our way. We just can't always pay when people want" (82). Until the story's end, Anney epitomizes the "good poor" category that Sandell speaks of and comes across as a valiant, virtuous woman struggling to maintain her morality in the face of extreme poverty. In the end, though, she fails to fit this stereotype as well when Allison offers a final twist on Anney's character and unexpectedly inverts that respectable stereotype when Anney deserts Bone and reconciles with the husband who brutally attacked her child. In doing so, she becomes one of the narrative's most evil characters, arguably worse than even Glen; Bone at least expects him to treat her badly. Her mother's unforeseeable desertion almost certainly hurts far more deeply than Glen's abuse ever could.

While *Bastard out of Carolina* makes Anney come alive by first valorizing her and later revealing her failings, Allison reverses that process with Anney's brother, Earle. He enters the novel as a quintessential redneck, a womanizer who drinks too much and spends quite a bit of time in jail (*Bastard* 12). McDonald points out that, while Earle and the other uncles reinforce some stereotypes, their tenderness with their nieces and nephews defies others (19). In addition to this tenderness, Earle exhibits acute powers of perception. From the beginning, he doubts the wisdom of Anney and Glen's marriage, and repeatedly asks Anney if she is "sure" that she really wants to go through with it (*Bastard* 40); he later ponders deep subjects like the meaning of family and contemplates various aspects of life and the complicated relationships that it entails (89, 126). Allison initially creates Earle in the notorious image of a white-trash male, a standard "Bubba," if you will, and then expands and develops his character by undermining that stereotype and assigning him an uncharacteristic level of emotional perception. This development lends itself well to the screen adaptation because viewers learn to see beyond the stereotype in much the same way that readers do in the novel.

While Allison creates credible individual white-trash characters in *Bastard out of Carolina,* she also questions stereotypes about larger class designations in a way that doesn't transfer to the film version as powerfully. A significant aspect of Allison's analysis concerns the intersection of class and racial attitudes. McDonald asserts, "The few African Americans that appear in the text are 'niggers' . . . and the Boatwrights scorn them, feeling no shame about being racist" (22). The Boatwrights undoubtedly engage in such racist practices; however, Allison uses Bone's reflections about race to undercut the assumption that all white-trash characters are racist. Bone transcends conventional white-trash prejudices against people of color when she first spies Alma's African American neighbor. Even though Bone longs for a connection with the neighbor, she assumes that the girl would not allow this because "Her mama had probably told her all about what to expect from trash like us" (*Bastard* 86). Bone's assumption elevates the neighbor to a level of power, and her resulting feelings of inadequacy weaken myths of white racial superiority while showing how deeply the label of trash hurts Bone. These and other perceptions also elevate African Americans in more general ways. For example, the choir that Bone hears performing impresses her greatly. She instinctively appreciates their talent and upon first hearing them thinks, "This was the real stuff" (169). McDonald shows that the fight that ensues between Bone and Shannon Pearl after Shannon refers to the choir as "niggers" causes Bone to recognize "connections between racial and class oppression" (22). Thus it would seem that while the Boatwright clan as a whole endorses racial prejudice, Bone's perceptive insights undermine the power of that endorsement within the text by showing that it is not absolute. Eliding race from the film adaptation so completely eliminates the nuanced analysis that the text realistically portrays.

In addition to race, *Bastard out of Carolina* also interrogates traditional depictions of poor southern women in both film and print versions. In an interview with Carolyn Megan, Allison discusses how the women of the narrative fail to see female family members as their main source of power. The Boatwright women do value their female community, but they "didn't think it was nearly as important as what a man and woman made together" (77). In spite of all the evidence to the contrary, Anney continues to feel that she needs a man to take care of her (McDonald 19). When the Boatwrights initially discover Glen's abuse of Bone, Anney remarks to Raylene, "Oh God. Raylene, I love him. I know you'll hate me. Sometimes I hate myself, but I love him" (*Bastard* 246). Anney tolerates Glen's behavior, even at the price of her self-respect and her daughter's safety, because she truly believes that she cannot survive without him. She cannot see that Glen weakens her, much less discern that he robs her of that power at its source by removing her from the female familial community upon which it feeds. Allison, though, makes sure that we notice that Glen isolates Anney from her sisters because "the further away from her sisters, the less powerful she becomes" ("Moving" 77).

While Anney does not, perhaps even cannot, value the power she derives from the women in her family, Bone can. She likes "being one of the women with my aunts" and feels pride at their separation from "the whole world of spitting, growling, overbearing males" (*Bastard* 91). In the novel, Bone defies her male cousins by ganging together with the Boatwright girls to play "mean sisters," a game in which the girls assume the personalities of the fictional sisters of various infamous men and "do everything their brothers do. Only they do it first and fastest and meanest" (212). In spite of Anney's betrayal, *Bastard out of Carolina* even concludes by affirming the value of female community in Bone's life. As the novel closes, readers hear Bone declare, "I was who I was going to be, someone like her [Raylene], like Mama, a Boatwright woman." Bone still identifies with and refuses to reject her mother even when Anney chooses to remain with Glen. In retrospect, Bone realizes that Anney gave birth to her far too young and that her "life had folded into mine." And though Bone identifies herself as a Boatwright woman, she does not automatically assume that her life will inevitably become a tragic reflection of her mother's existence. Her identity seems full of possibility as she wonders, "What would I be like when I was fifteen, twenty, thirty?" (309). As does Raylene, Bone possesses the potential to defy expectations and exist as a Boatwright woman on her own terms.

While men confine most of the Boatwright women to lives of hopelessness, Moira Baker observes, "Raylene transforms the domestic space that entraps her sisters into a locus of resistance" (26). This resistance makes Raylene the novel's "most fulfilled character" (McDonald 21), and this fulfillment transfers to the screen nicely when Raylene says that she enjoys the solitary life she's created for herself on the river. In a scene that only appears in the novel, Raylene jokes that trash rises, but by deliberately removing herself from the world that views the Boatwrights as trash, Raylene, McDonald claims, transcends what others think of her (21). Raylene's home literally gives value to another sort of trash. In fact, it even seems made of trash because Raylene's "walls were lined with shelves full of oddities," including trash collected from the river. The trash that rises at the bend of the river near the house has added value in that it "drew the fish in," and made it one of the best places to fish in the county (*Bastard* 181). Furthermore, Bone and Raylene sell different items, or trash, that they rescue from the river, so others must value it as well (182). Deborah Horvitz notes, "Raylene's metaphor (and her actual work) of making beauty out of trash resonates deeply with Bone" (253). Consequently, it also registers deeply with Allison's readers, and her positive alignment of Raylene and her home with trash differentiates Raylene as a unique brand of southern woman, an independent one who possesses the power to define both herself and the world she chooses to live in. And by leaving Bone in Raylene's care at the tale's end, Allison hints that her future holds similar self-fulfillment.

While *Bastard out of Carolina* offers affirmative depictions of African Americans and women, both film and print versions offer another class inversion that paints a decidedly negative portrait of the middle class. The narrative ironically subverts the supposed superiority of the middle class by making Glen, with his middle-class roots and aspirations, "the greatest evil in the book" (Bledsoe 83). J. Brooks Bouson quite rightly describes Glen as an "amalgamation of middle-class refinement and lower-class brutality" (108), but his class-conscious attitudes do seem to evolve as the novel and film progress. He enters the story "embracing a white-trash identity" because he "aspires to be like Earle Boatwright" (McDonald 19). Glen wants to "marry the whole Boatwright legend" in order to "shame his daddy and shock his brothers" (*Bastard* 13). In the family legend that Glen embraces, the Boatwright women consistently treat the men like "overgrown boys" (23), and the novel includes Glen in this category when Ruth describes him as "just a little boy himself" (123). One of the narrative's most damning statements against the middle class lies in the fact that Glen's abuse of Bone escalates only *after* he ceases identifying with the Boatwrights. His refusal to see himself as an overgrown boy foreshadows this upcoming rejection. The first time that Glen verbally blows up he screams at Anney, "Don't give me that mama shit" (69). Allison solidifies his crossing over in terms of class identification when he lashes out at Earle for berating his father, Mr. Waddell (98–99); earlier, when Glen fancied himself white trash, even Earle thought it strange that Glen did not object to his criticism of the Waddell family (38).[7]

Likewise, before Glen rejects his white-trash identity in both print and film versions, he has only molested Bone once, in the car at the hospital (46). After he begins to identify with his middle-class family in chapter seven, however, his abuse of Bone escalates to include the severe beatings found in chapter eight. Bone's white-trash identity seems to legitimize, at least for Glen, this abuse. The first time that Glen severely beats Bone, he does so after he catches her and Reese running in the house (*Bastard* 106). Curiously, of the two sisters, Glen punishes only Bone even though both girls broke his rule. This event marks the beginning of a pattern because later Bone notes, "It was when Reese and I were alone with him that he was dangerous. If I ran from him, he would come after me" (111). He always goes "after" Bone, never Reese. In fact, Glen fails to reprimand Reese for anything during the entire course of the narrative. He chooses to abuse Bone, at least in part, because she presents the easiest target. Bone holds herself apart from Glen even before Anney marries him. She begins narrating chapter three by observing, "Love, at least love for a man not already part of the family, was something I was a little unsure about" (32), and this distance continues to grow even after the marriage. For example, Allison describes a family hug after Anney gives birth to her stillborn baby in which Bone wants to participate, but cannot. Bone reflects, "I wanted him to love us. I wanted to be able to love him" (51–52). Try as she might, though, she cannot muster such feeling.

In addition to emotionally distancing herself from Glen, she refuses to passively accept his mistreatment. Bone observes in both versions, "I had a talent for sassing back and making Daddy Glen mad" (110). While Bone's defiant reserve makes her the target for Glen's rage, it does not fully account for Glen's failure also to harm Reese. One explanation that seems logical in light of Glen's ideas about class is that Glen abuses Bone because he sees her as fundamentally inferior. He does not abuse Reese because in his view, she possesses an inherent respectability that Bone lacks. Lyle Parsons, Reese's father, came from a lower middle-class family, and Anney had married him before she conceived Reese (6). In contrast, the state of South Carolina has legally declared Bone a bastard (3), and she never remembers meeting her father (25). The designation *bastard* apparently carries highly negative connotations for Glen. The first time he strikes Bone, Glen justifies it by saying that she called him a bastard (107). Obviously, he thinks that Bone committed quite a serious offense if it merits the sort of "punishment" he responds with, and she even realizes later that Glen abuses her primarily because of the way he sees her: "Sometimes when I looked up into his red features and blazing eyes, I knew that it was nothing I had done that made him beat me. It was just me, the fact of my life, who I was in his eyes" (110). Glen claims that he beats Bone because he cares "how she turns out" (107). Even as he rapes her, Glen says that he does so to "teach" her to "shut up" and show him respect (284). However, the audience learns that, whatever Glen may say, his actions only illustrate his feelings of entitlement. Glen abuses Bone because he believes he has a right to do so, and that right makes him feel powerful in a world that daily denies him the respect he craves.

In addition to Glen, Allison censures Tyler Highgarden and the Waddell family as representatives of the middle class in a scene from the novel that does not appear in the film. Both Bone and her mother develop an intense dislike for Highgarden when Anney makes Bone turn herself in for shoplifting items from the Woolworth's store that Highgarden manages. After Highgarden delivers his condescending lecture, Bone observes of Anney, "I knew she was never going to . . . let herself stand in the same room with that honey-greased bastard" (*Bastard* 98). By degrading both mother and daughter during the incident, Highgarden issues dual reprimands: he admonishes Bone for shoplifting, and, more important, reproaches Anney for not acting like the thieving white trash that he assumes she is. When Bone later breaks into the store, Guinn observes that she enters from the roof, a space located physically above Highgarden to "destroy the emblems of Highgarden's superiority." Guinn further proposes that Bone destroys the store in an act of "defiance, not theft" (25).[8] While Bone does begin her attack on the store to defy Highgarden, during the destruction, she realizes her truer purpose. As Bone considers smashing the picture frames on display in the store that resemble the ones displayed in the Waddell home, she stands in the aisle "trying to think what it was that I really wanted, who I really wanted to hurt" (*Bastard* 225). She really wants to injure Glen's family and the perfect lives that those photographs chronicle, but she settles for a surrogate in the form of Tyler Highgarden's store. As Bone leaves behind the destruction that she has wrought, she thinks of using her hook to "go all the way over to Uncle James's house and pull up my mama a rosebush or two" (226). Her notion supports reading the attack on the store as a condemnation of all that she thinks the Waddells stand for that also acknowledges her desire, at least for her mother's sake, for their material affluence.

In print form, *Bastard out of Carolina* redefines white-trash stereotypes not only by questioning assumptions about other categories of class but also by validating various lower-class practices and beliefs; most obviously, the novel gives credence to superstitious practices. In one such instance, Bone's Eustis aunts make a love knot for Anney prior to her marriage to Glen. After making the knot, the aunts bury a piece of honeycomb wrapped in lace in the backyard in some sort of connected ritual. Anney, obviously not believing in folk magic, places the knot into the bottom of a flowerpot upon receiving it and then forgets about it (*Bastard* 41–42). Later, Bone finds the knot and "the whole thing [falls] to dust" (104). That same week, the aunts discover that "a dog had dug up the honeycomb and torn right through the lace" in which they had buried it. Both aunts interpret this occurrence as a negative sign (105), and just after their discovery of it, Glen's abuse of Bone escalates. Bone reflects, "I tried to be careful, but something had come apart. Something had gotten loose like the wild strands of Aunt Marvella's hair unraveling in the dust.[9] There was no way I could be careful enough, no way to keep Daddy Glen from exploding into rage" (108). With this reference, Allison links Bone's aunts' dark premonitions to the intensification of her abuse, and, in doing so, validates the practice of folk magic and superstition as a legitimate source of knowledge.

In addition to the practice of folk magic, Allison empowers the language of poor whites with her portrayal of working-class speech. Jennifer Campbell asserts, "Bone records characters' speech in a working-class dialect while her own speech is recorded as 'standard.'" This practice putatively helps to make Bone's stark story more acceptable to readers. Campbell writes that "the subtle but powerful light of middle class speech" dispels "shadows cast by sexual abuse, economic exploitation, [and] psychological hopelessness" (120). Though this likely holds true for some readers, such an interpretation also dangerously misjudges the role of speech in *Bastard out of Carolina* by privileging middle-class speech as somehow more acceptable. Allison intends to glorify the dialect of poor whites, not devalue it by comparison to middle-class speech; she told Minnie Bruce Pratt that, like Alice Walker and Toni Morrison, she tries to produce dialect written "with love and respect." McDonald believes that by writing in the dialect of poor whites, Allison "allows for an acceptance of her characters' dialect and thus its respect" (19). Authorial intentions aside, Campbell's assertion fails to recognize that Allison *does* record Bone's actual speech in dialect. For example, when talking with Granny, Bone says, "Cousin Temple says you a heathen" (*Bastard* 144). In another such instance, Bone lashes out at Shannon Pearl and says, "You so ugly your own mama don't even love you" (172). Later, after she has destroyed Highgarden's store, Bone tells Grey as they leave, "Come on. We an't gonna lock the door, you know" (225). These and other various excerpts record Bone's dialectical speech directly; she only narrates in Standard English, and this usage could indicate a couple of different purposes. Allison could utilize Standard English to emphasize the time elapsed and Bone's educational and cultural advancement between the period of the story and her telling of it. Or Allison could use Standard English as a narrative device to reflect the more formal nature of written speech as opposed to the informality of oral communication. Instead of opting for Standard English narration in the film, Huston wisely chooses to have Laura Dern's voiceover narrative sections of the film employ dialectical speech that is less heavily marked than the dialogic sections of the film. Whatever the reason for Bone's Standard English narration, Allison clearly exalts white-trash dialect through Bone's evaluation. Bone thinks that Earle's speech resembles "the language of gospel music, with its rhythms and intensity" (148); she transfers her love for Earle to include his manner of speech, and thus symbolically creates the dialect of love and respect that Allison wants to exalt. In contrast, Bone thinks Aunt Madeline's middle-class speech a "cold accent" (103), one similarly reflective of her personality, at least as Bone perceives it.

While *Bastard out of Carolina* clearly values working-class dialect, the novel offers a more complex portrayal of another white-trash practice that the film for the most part neglects, fundamentalist religion. In his essay entitled "White Trash Religion," Matt Wray discusses the powerful relationship between white trash and fundamentalist religion and elucidates how this type of religion "brings a sense of spiritual power and righteousness to those who . . . suffer from a fundamental lack of social and economic power" (207). Wray illustrates the centrality of apocalyptic fantasies to fundamentalist beliefs by noting that the Apocalypse represents "total liberation from a fallen world of sin and misery" (194). *Bastard out of Carolina* details a very ambiguous relationship between Bone and religion. In accordance with Wray's observations, Bone does fantasize about the Apocalypse. She likes to read Revelations because "it [promises] vindication" and she takes "comfort in the hope of the apocalypse" (*Bastard* 152). Even as Glen rapes her, Bone thinks to herself, "God will give you to me. Your bones will melt and your blood will catch fire" (285), and her fantasy about some sort of apocalyptic revenge against Glen becomes a significant part of what helps her to survive the attack.

Because Bone relies on religion to carry her through the most violent act of abuse that she experiences in the novel, Allison seems to validate religion as a source of personal power; however, she does not present religion as offering Bone any useful solution to her problems. Bone tries to join 14 different churches, but she cannot commit to the idea of salvation (151). The eventual baptism in which Anney forces Bone to participate seems quite useless in that it contradicts fundamentalist beliefs about salvation. During the baptism Bone thinks, "The magic I knew was supposed to wash over me with Jesus' blood was absent, the moment cold and empty" (152). While Allison's ambivalent portrayal of the role of fundamentalist religion does depict religious belief as a source of comfort for Bone, its lack of any real saving power shows that any tangible salvation will have to come from Bone herself.

Somehow, Bone does save herself. Glen's abuse apparently ceases after he rapes her at age 12, but, as Vincent King observes, Bone narrates the novel from an age of at least 17 (136). In that chapter Bone also reveals that she survived the aftermath of Glen's abuse by constructing a new identity for herself as Ruth Anne, and she begins the novel by making the reader aware of these two identities: "I've been called Bone all my life, but my name's Ruth Anne" (1). The narrator telling this story no longer thinks of herself as Bone. The nickname designates the victim of the story, not the survivor she has become, and the construction of her new identity as Ruth Anne embodies Allison's most powerful challenge of white-trash stereotypes, a challenge that the film fails to issue, though Laura Dern's voiceover narration does identify the sources of all three names.

Before constructing this new identity, though, Bone must first reject the social definitions that label her "white trash." Guinn notes, "Bone is acutely aware of her family's position in the social hierarchy" (23), and she even states that she and Reese "knew what the neighbors called us . . . we knew who we were" (*Bastard* 82). The stamp on Bone's birth certificate legally declaring her a bastard also signifies her label of trash; it substantiates "the expectations society has of Bone's people" (Guinn 24). The birth certificate symbolizes society's definition of Bone as a bastard; therefore, Anney's giving Bone an unstamped birth certificate at the novel's conclusion implies "that Bone herself will be responsible for filling out the blank spaces of her own identity" (King 135). Katrina Irving observes that the unstamped birth certificate allows Bone to occupy an "impossible space" because "she has become 'authorized' despite her absence of a patriarchal name" (101). With this absence, Allison legitimizes Bone *as* a bastard even as she removes the stamp and reconfigures the connotations associated with that label. Instead of using "bastard" as a traditionally negative classification, Allison inverts that meaning to emphasize Bone's potential for creating her own identity, one unconcerned with the name of the father. Significantly, the film removes all ambiguity when Bone instead receives a birth certificate stamped "Certified."

Throughout *Bastard out of Carolina*, Bone tries, in various ways, to redefine herself. Instead of viewing herself as Glen or her family sees her, she tries to characterize herself through "gospel music, her complex sexual fantasies, bizarre tales of violence, and avid reading" (King 124). While none of these outlets provides Bone with the power to change her world, Aunt Raylene ultimately does. When Bone observes the bus full of travelers (in the film they are passengers on a boat) and comments that she "hate[s] them" because she thinks they regard her and Raylene as "something nasty" (*Bastard* 262), Raylene reveals the insight that finally gives Bone the power to transform her life by showing her the impossibility of making assumptions about the travelers, or about anybody else. It "could be they're jealous of you" (*Bastard* 262), she points out. By forcing Bone to consider another point of view, Raylene "teaches her how to create a different kind of story, one based on something more than hate" (King 134). King feels that *Bastard out of Carolina* "ends before Bone can fully integrate this information" by creating a story that allows her to see things from the other side (135), but the conclusion of the novel does show Bone beginning to incorporate at least part of Raylene's lesson. As the sheriff questions Bone after Glen's attack, Bone remembers Raylene's comments and thinks, "What must it be like to be Sheriff Cole? What made him who he was? I'd think about that sometime, but not now" (*Bastard* 297). Clearly, Bone has begun to consider different perspectives, and this practice will ultimately define how she tells her story. By narrating *Bastard out of Carolina*, Bone transforms herself, as King notes, "from the victim of a story into the author of one" (136). Furthermore, Bone teaches Raylene's lesson to readers by using her narrative perspective to force readers to experience *Bastard out of Carolina* through the unfamiliar eyes of a trashy 12-year-old girl that the world looks down on.

Finally, readers and viewers must consider the larger social implications of *Bastard out of Carolina*'s critique of stereotypes and class issues. Allison definitely intends to affect her readers on such a scale; she writes in *Skin*, "When I sit down to make my stories I know very well that I want to take the reader by the throat, break her heart, and heal it again" (180). She believes that "some things must be felt to be understood," and that literature "is the lie that tells the truth, that shows us human beings in pain and makes us love them" (14, 175). Allison has said that she has "life work to do," which involves "learning to love what was not loved" ("Dorothy Allison"). One aspect of this work involves creating characters like Bone and teaching readers to love them, and, by extension, encouraging widespread social tolerance and acceptance of those outside the norm.

Some critics, however, feel that Allison's fiction actually contributes to class prejudice by commercializing marginalized positions. Sandell argues, "participating in the marketplace is often perceived to be a stand-in for collective social change" (226). She claims that keeping issues of class "safely located in books and popular culture" allows society to keep "such issues at arm's length" (216). Moreover, she suggests that writing and reading about class issues makes them a source of entertainment rather than problems requiring corrective action (216). Minrose Gwin similarly questions whether *Bastard out of Carolina*'s tale of abuse contributes "to the ideology that perpetuates the father's violence and power in the first place" (436). The issue transfers to the film in a much more visceral way. Critic Lisa Schwarzbaum says of the "implicit versus explicit visual interpretation" in the novel versus the film:

> "He kicked again, and his boot slipped along the side of my head, cutting my ear so that blood gushed," Allison writes, telling Bone's story in the first person. "Then that boot thudded into my belly and I rolled sideways, retching bile down my right arm." Yes, it's all right there on the page. But we can stand a lot more violence in print than we can when we're watching a real little girl playing a fictional girl with blood, however fake, coming out of her mouth, thrown around by a real adult playing a man who rapes his stepdaughter. When Huston grabs us by the eyeballs and forces us to watch such sickening violence, we become voyeurs—and feel ashamed.

Schwarzbaum concludes, "The agonizing moments that convey what it's like for Bone to feel helpless and afraid of Daddy Glen even when he's not torturing her are where the art is. The pornographic violence is artifice."

While such arguments surely apply to stereotypical white-trash novels and films filled with gratuitous violence, *Bastard out of Carolina* redeems itself as Allison's characters cross the boundaries of their socially assigned roles and cause readers to ponder their potential. Social change can only arise from changing attitudes, and *Bastard out of Carolina* definitely has the power to affect such change. Christopher Renny suggests that teaching "works by working-class writers challenges students in productive and dangerous ways" (55). Renny believes that working-class literature calls for a revolution in thinking and causes students to examine their own attitudes (55). Allison ideally wants her fiction to inspire just this sort of questioning. In *Skin,* she writes that the designations people use to "categorize and dismiss each other" must "be excavated from the inside" (35). Perhaps narratives such as *Bastard out of Carolina* will provide the first step in such excavation.

Notes

1. Though some scenes are rearranged and others are left out, Anne Meredith's teleplay often lifts entire narrative sections from Allison's novel. Page references for quotations in Allison's novel correspond to sections in Huston's film either as direct quotes or closely paraphrased scenes unless noted otherwise.

2. Robert Gingher defines *grit lit* as "facetious shorthand for fiction devoted to the rough edges ('grit') of life." These writers "typically deploy stark, sometimes violent narratives of poor white southerners," and "exploit the full power of the gritty, mundane particular." It is often "proudly insistent on its own cultural distinctiveness" and sometimes features "regional, often self-mocking humor" (319). For a full treatment of the genre, see Matt Wray and Annalee Newitz's *White Trash: Race and Class in America.*

3. Erik Bledsoe identifies the characteristic that defines the essence of the white-trash identity as "excess—excessive alcohol, excessive sex, excessive violence" (68). The authors of *Deep South* define it in terms of morality and describe a 1941 anthropological survey that defines "poor" as an economic designation, but distinguishes the term *trash* as implying "debasement in all categories of life" (Davis, Gardner, and Gardner 65). More recently, John Hartigan has supported that distinction by writing, "poor whites and white trash might look and sound the same, but they are quite different" (50). That differentiation, and thus the definition of white trash, necessarily lies in our perception, the very arena that Allison's adoption of the term targets.

4. The American southern poor white figure first appeared in literature in 1728 when William Byrd II wrote derisively of the North Carolina "lubbers" (McDonald 16). Poor whites subsequently evolved as occupants of negative fictive roles, frequently appearing in literature as comedians, victims, or villains (Bledsoe 70). Allison became acutely aware of clichéd literary depictions of white trash at an early age, and began writing because she realized that her family did not fit traditional literary depictions of the poor (*Skin* 18). She said in an interview with Carolyn Megan, "When I couldn't find my story, I wrote it" (73), and later remarked

to Minnie Bruce Pratt that when she began reading, she "went looking particularly for working-class novels. And Christ, you know what you find—Erskine Caldwell!" Allison elaborates in *Skin* how most literary depictions of the poor resemble "Steven Spielberg movies or Erskine Caldwell novels, the one valorizing and the other caricaturing" (15). Jillian Sandell confirms that Allison's characters do not fit into conventional notions of the "good poor" and the "bad poor" (213), and her observation reverberates throughout discussions of Allison's work.

5. Concerning the novel, Kathlene McDonald observes that Allison will not "keep the reality invisible" in *Bastard*, and remarks that Allison's "refusal to synthesize the contradictions of her characters" adds complexity and interest to the novel (18, 22). David Reynolds states it even more vaguely: "Allison both forces her readers to associate her characters with easy stereotypes and oddly defuses some of those stereotypes" (359). Sandell somewhat more concretely points out, "Allison tempers her portrayal of poverty with the strength and courage of her characters and family members, while also showing their flaws and mistakes" (213).

6. As Caroline Gordon and Allen Tate point out in *The House of Fiction*, "[authority in fiction] is never wholly a technical matter. A given technique is the result of a moral and philosophical attitude, a bias towards experience on the part of the author; and as the author begins to understand what it is in life that interests him most, he also becomes aware of the techniques which enable him to create in language his fullest sense of that interest. Material and technique become in the end the same thing, the one discovering the other" (623).

7. See J. Brooks Bouson's "'You Nothing but Trash': White Trash Shame in Dorothy Allison's *Bastard Out of Carolina*" for an enlightening analysis of the conflicting motives that drive the actions Glen takes (108–12).

8. Bouson similarly speculates that Bone vandalizes the store in an act of revenge for the humiliation she suffered at Highgarden's hands (112).

9. Although Bone does not make this information explicit, the love knot seems made of, among other things, the strands of Aunt Marvella's hair that unravel when it disintegrates into dust.

Works Cited

Allison, Dorothy. *Bastard out of Carolina*. New York: Plume, 1992.

Allison, Dorothy. "Dorothy Allison." Interview with Minnie Bruce Pratt. *Progressive* 59.7 (1995). 20 December 2010 http://findarticles.com/p/articles/mi_m1295/is_n7_v59/ai_17105308/.

Allison, Dorothy. "Moving toward Truth: An Interview with Dorothy Allison." Interview with Carolyn E. Megan. *The Kenyon Review* 16.4 (1994): 71–83.

Allison, Dorothy. *Skin: Talking about Sex, Class, and Literature*. Ithaca, NY: Firebrand Books, 1994.

Baker, Moira. "Dorothy Allison's Topography of Resistance." *Harvard Gay and Lesbian Review* 5.3 (1998): 23–26.

Bastard out of Carolina. Dir. Anjelica Huston. Perf. Jennifer Jason Leigh, Ron Eldard, and Jena Malone. Showtime, 1996. DVD.

Bledsoe, Erik. "The Rise of Southern Redneck and White Trash Writers." *Southern Cultures* 6.1 (2000): 68–90.

Bouson, J. Brooks. "'You Nothing but Trash': White Trash Shame in Dorothy Allison's *Bastard out of Carolina.*" *Southern Literary Journal* 34.1 (2001): 101–23.

Campbell, Jennifer. "Teaching Class: A Pedagogy and Politics for Working-Class Writing." *College Literature* 23.2 (1996): 116–30.

Davis, Allison, Burleigh B. Gardner, and Mary R. Gardner. *Deep South.* Chicago: U of Chicago P, 1941.

Gingher, Robert. "Grit Lit." *The Companion to Southern Literature.* Ed. Joseph M. Flora, Lucinda H. MacKethan, and Todd Taylor. Baton Rouge: Louisiana State UP, 2002. 319–20.

Gordon, Caroline, and Allen Tate. *The House of Fiction: An Anthology of the Short Story.* New York: Scribner, 1960.

Guinn, Matthew. *After Southern Modernism: Fiction of the Contemporary South.* Jackson: UP of Mississippi, 2000.

Gwin, Minrose. "Nonfelicitous Space and Survivor Discourse: Reading the Incest Story in Southern Women's Fiction." *Haunted Bodies: Gender and Southern Texts.* Ed. Anne Goodwyn Jones and Susan V. Donaldson. Charlottesville: UP of Virginia, 1997. 416–40.

Hartigan, John Jr. "Name Calling: Objectifying 'Poor Whites' and 'White Trash' in Detroit." *White Trash: Race and Class in America.* Ed. Matt Wray and Annalee Newitz. New York: Routledge, 1997. 41–56.

Horvitz, Deborah. "'Sadism Demands a Story': Oedipus, Feminism, and Sexuality in Gayl Jones's *Corregidora* and Dorothy Allison's *Bastard out of Carolina.*" *Contemporary Literature* 39.2 (1999): 238–61.

Irving, Katrina. "'Writing It down So That It Would Be Real': Narrative Strategies in Dorothy Allison's *Bastard out of Carolina.*" *College Literature* 25.2 (1998): 94–107.

King, Vincent. "Hopeful Grief: The Prospect of a Postmodernist Feminism in Allison's *Bastard out of Carolina.*" *Southern Literary Journal* 33.1 (2000): 122–40.

Luscombe, Belinda. "Thanks, but No Thanks." *Time* 147.16 (1996). 15 November 2010 http://www.time.com/time/magazine/article/0,9171,984404,00.html.

McDonald, Kathlene. "Talking Trash, Talking Back: Resistance to Stereotypes in Dorothy Allison's *Bastard out of Carolina.*" *Women's Studies Quarterly* 26.1,2 (1988): 15–25.

Renny, Christopher. "Cultural Borders: Working-Class Literature's Challenge to the Canon." *The Canon in the Classroom: The Pedagogical Implications of Canon Revision in American Literature.* Ed. John Alberti. New York: Garland, 1995.

Reynolds, David. "White Trash in Your Face: The Literary Descent of Dorothy Allison." *Appalachian Journal: A Regional Studies Review* 20.4 (1993): 56–66.

Sandell, Jillian. "Telling Stories of 'Queer White Trash': Race, Class, and Sexuality in the Work of Dorothy Allison." *White Trash: Race and Class in America.* Ed. Matt Wray and Annalee Newitz. New York: Routledge, 1997. 211–30.

Schwarzbaum, Lisa. Review of *Bastard out of Carolina. Entertainment Weekly* (13 December 1996). 11 January 2011 http://www.ew.com/ew/article/0,295 431,00.html.

Wray, Matt. "White Trash Religion." *White Trash: Race and Class in America.* Ed. Matt Wray and Annalee Newitz. New York: Routledge, 1997. 193–210.

Chapter 5

Rednecks in Film: Identity and Power from *Deliverance* to *Cars*

Katie Sullivan Barak and Justin Philpot

The term *redneck* is often used as shorthand in popular media, readily summarizing a person's socioeconomic status, beliefs, attitudes, and habits. It is important to note, however, that the term's ubiquity does not necessarily denote a character's role in a particular work nor does it guarantee homogenized deployment across individual films. It is best to consider *redneck* as distinguishing, rather than defining, a particular type of characterization. There are significant differences between portrayals of poor southern whites across films, especially those of different genres, and *redneck,* while still a valuable term, cannot encompass all of them. We propose that existing terms, synonymous though they may be in popular use, can be utilized to describe the difference between, for example, Bo "Bandit" Darville (Burt Reynolds) in *Smokey and the Bandit* (1977) and the hillbilly rapists of *Deliverance* (1972). Though we can place these characters within the lineage of the redneck in American film, it is clear that some distinction must be made between them if scholars want to come to grips with an individual film's meaning. To this end, we offer a rough history of how *redneck,* in all its iterations, has been presented on screen and how these differences can be best expressed.

Contemporary scholarship on the *redneck* is work necessarily rooted in questions of race and socioeconomic class. In their essay "What Is 'White Trash?'" Annalee Newitz and Matthew Wray begin, "White trash is, in many ways, the white Other," (168) embodying a whiteness that "signals something other than privilege and social power" (169). They continue:

> The term *white trash* points up the hatred and fear undergirding the American that discourses of class and racial difference tend to bleed into one another, especially in the way that they pathologize and lay waste to their "others." Indeed, "subordinate white" is such an oxymoron in the dominant culture that this social position is principally spoken about in our slang in terms like *white trash, redneck, cracker,* and *hillbilly.* (169; emphases in original)

That so many terms exist to describe economic disparity between whites is evidence enough that, in American culture, "one of the worst crimes of which one can accuse a person is poverty" (170). Whereas racial epithets directed at minorities often carry with them the implicit understanding that the target is both racially and economically marginalized in society, to denote a subjugated white subject demands that *trash* amend the otherwise normative racial identity. So too, with *redneck;* the term originally described poorly educated, agricultural laborers whose necks were deeply tanned in contrast to their otherwise white complexion. Critics often deploy the term to condemn an inherent racism born of either ignorance or breeding. This, combined with the overtones of lower- and working-class station, placed *redneck* squarely alongside *white trash* as a derogatory term for some time. It is only recently that some Americans—a good number of them men living outside the American South—have sought to reclaim the term, lifting it from its regional context and transforming it into a nationally relevant political and cultural identifier.

This shift from derogatory phrase to reclaimed identifier is both prefigured and reflected in the portrayals of the redneck in American film from the 1970s into the twenty-first century. Unfortunately, it is at this point that the term's usefulness for film studies comes into question. The portrayal of the redneck in popular film does not neatly align with more general understandings of the term, its meaning, or who may self-identify as such. Indeed, there seems to be quite a bit of confusion, even among those who would claim redneck as a critical part of their identity, about what exactly constitutes a redneck. Comedian Jeff Foxworthy's career was made on the term, but it would be difficult to argue that his material, spanning a national comedy tour, a pair of concert films, and several books, is quite the same as Sarah Palin telling a national gathering of the NRA, "You're a redneck if you've ever had dinner on a ping pong table" (*New York Daily News*, May 15, 2010). As we will show throughout this chapter, however, the narrative demands of film, as well as audience expectations, have conspired to provide film and popular culture scholars a practical model for understanding and identifying the redneck in American popular film.

No one would confuse *Smokey and the Bandit* for *Deliverance,* yet both are repeatedly conjured up in American popular culture and called into service to mark the redneck, white trash, or hillbilly character in contemporary film. Such references belie the decades-long development of the redneck character. Indeed, portrayals of the redneck in American film are culturally, and therefore historically, dependent. For simplicity's sake, we have broken down our analysis by decade, choosing examples we feel are indicative of the changes made by producers, directors, writers, and actors in service of narrative and generic demands. While such an approach cannot provide a complete genealogy of the redneck in film, it does provide us the flexibility to impose general categories roomy enough to house and account for the evolving nature of the redneck character and his filmic cousins, the poor white trash and hillbilly characters. These three constructs need to be considered in light of one another, both because they each inform characterizations of the others and because each has been deployed to meet specific ends.

For their part, film audiences would be hard pressed to define precisely what the redneck means, what it represents, in American culture. While films produced during the 1970s and into the 1980s were likely to place rednecks geographically in the South, the figure of the inbred, ill-spoken, God-fearing, and possibly racist poor southern white has become a pop culture standard, most commonly used in contemporary film in one of two ways— as monstrous other or comic relief. As such, rednecks, poor white trash, and hillbillies can exist anywhere the narrative demands them. Indeed it is this flexibility, in league with the demands and expectations of producers of and audiences for narrative film, which helps us understand the differences and similarities of particular portrayals of the redneck.

We suggest there are three overlapping categories of poor southern whites in American film—*rednecks, white trash,* and *hillbillies.* Conceived here these terms are not synonymous. Rather, they describe types of similar, but clearly different, characters often found in films released since *Deliverance.* We acknowledge that these are loaded terms, and the similarities between characters can make clear distinctions difficult. We agree with Newitz and Wray that they share a common connotation, but we advance these terms, in the absence of better, to help film scholars make critical distinctions between characters, their motivations, and their role in shaping any particular film's meaning.

Perhaps no film better illustrates the impact of film on popular conceptions of culture, place, and time than *Deliverance* (1972), and it is just as well that it serves as an example of how ambiguous and contradictory meanings are successfully deployed in support of narrative demands. The film follows four Atlanta businessmen kayaking down the Cahulawassee River before it is dammed and the rural surroundings flooded. The film sets up several distinctions between individuals from Atlanta as opposed to the inhabitants of rural Georgia, but it is not simply a matter of town mouse versus country mouse. Rather than advance a simple opposition, the film reveals the difficulty of applying a single term to characters that fulfill distinctly different roles in a film despite their similarities. Rather, it is their actions, surroundings and implied socioeconomic status that identify them within the bounds of the narrative. As much as we may agree that the nameless rapists in *Deliverance* are hillbillies (Bill McKinney and Herbert "Cowboy" Coward), we are left to decide whether the Griner brothers, or the family that cares for Ed (John Voight) and Bobby (Ned Beatty) at the end of the film, are also hillbillies. As it is presented in the plot, they are clearly *not* the same kind of hillbilly as the rapists encountered up river. There is no decision to make so far as these characters are concerned. They may live in the same area and exhibit some of the same characteristics, but describing them as hillbillies does not offer any indication of their motivations. In fact, their actions, standing in stark contrast to those of the rapists, serve to anchor the film's ambiguous message about the toll of modern civilization on the natural world and the nation's marginalized citizens. They are certainly connected to the rapists, but the conventions of narrative film demand we make a distinction between them in service of the film's theme. The two characterizations are similar, but not the same.

In the wake of the civil rights movement depictions of the redneck were often split, either representing the worst aspects of southern racism and institutional corruption or an honest and hardworking if underprivileged member of the community. In fact, films that portray rednecks, poor white trash, or hillbillies often pit one in opposition to another, or one in opposition to straight middle-class society, in order to mark a particular character as either hero or villain. Consider, for example, *Smokey and the Bandit* (1977), a film whose antagonist, Sheriff Buford T. Justice (Jackie Gleason), is little more than a caricature of the racist southern lawman. As he attempts to thwart Snowman and Bandit (Jerry Reed and Burt Reynolds) in their beer-hauling adventure, he leaves his home-state and jurisdiction of Texas and chases them through Louisiana, Mississippi, Alabama, and Georgia. He is systematically outwitted and outclassed by Bandit as they traverse the South, the two characters juxtaposed, highlighting the difficulty of trying to adequately account for these differences within a single, reductive category like *redneck.*

Focusing on elements of appearance housed within the mise-en-scène provides a physical imagining of how the redneck, white trash, and hillbilly are similar but different. Costumes, props, and make-up adorn and inform the character. Bo "Bandit" Darville wears tight blue jeans, a plaid shirt, and cowboy hat. Similarly, his partner in crime, Cledus "Snowman" Snow, wears the same outfit, but tops it off with a mesh-backed, adjustable baseball cap adorned with the Caterpillar logo. Bandit and Snowman are rugged but clean and Reynolds is projected as a sex symbol. This is in stark contrast to the hillbillies in *Deliverance.* Beyond the generic differences between the films, it is clear that these characters are meant to inspire something different in the audience's understanding and as such are designed to look and feel different. While Snowman and Bandit are aesthetically clean-cut, the nameless hillbillies occupying the land around the river are dirty. Predominantly in army green and wearing overalls, button-up khaki or plaid shirts, work boots, baseball hats, the hillbillies' clothes do not look much different from the river-rafting vacationers they terrorize or the adventurous truck drivers hauling beer across state lines. The major difference lies in the unkempt nature of the rest of their appearance: their clothes are filthy, skin grimy, and they have yellowed or missing teeth.

These differences in appearance are amplified in films that require a specific characterization to meet specific genre demands. To put it another way, contemporary use of the redneck, white trash, and hillbilly in comedy and horror films necessitates a distinction between portrayals, if only because they are utilized to different ends, in different narrative structures, and with different audience expectations. The literary drama of *Deliverance* provides the space for both the redneck and the hillbilly in part because of the type of film it was produced to be and the audience to whom it was sold. *Smokey and the Bandit,* a comedy, relied on characterizations that emphasized the difference between types of redneck. The work-a-day reliability of Snowman calls on the communal and familial relationships seen to be at the heart of redneck culture. Bandit is a living legend, a trickster hero resentful of authority and the arbitrary enforcement of the rule of law. Sheriff Buford T. Justice is the epitome of southern corruption. Each of these conceptions has been incorporated into the larger popular image of the redneck, most often deployed independently depending on context. Echoing the hillbilly rapists of *Deliverance,* the savage clan of *The Hills Have Eyes* (1977) is the redneck as seen in a funhouse mirror. The admirable qualities of the redneck character are twisted and made ugly or else totally inverted. Otherness, not difference, is the hallmark of the horror film, necessarily reliant on characterizations that emphasize a lack of humanity.

In the introduction to his wonderful collection of essays on gender and horror film *The Dread of Difference*, Barry Keith Grant notes that a great deal of work on the horror film has addressed the idea that "the experience of horror in the cinema is almost always grounded in the visual representation of bodily difference" (6). Grant is quick to note, however, that approaches focusing on issues other than gender have been varied, including work that has focused on contemporary social problems such as racism, violence, ecological decay and, of particular interest here, class. Given the focus of the volume, however, Grant is obliged to qualify gender as vital to our understanding of the genre, for "whether one prefers to examine horror films in terms of universal fears or historically determined cultural anxieties, issues of gender remain central to the genre" (7). We agree, but wish to use Grant's work as a jumping-off point for our construction of difference and otherness as it applies to the redneck, white trash, and hillbilly character.

Part of what makes the distinction between difference and otherness so appealing, and so vital to our understanding of the distinction between the redneck, white trash, and hillbilly character, is the overlapping connotations of the terms. Indeed, Grant is reliant on otherness to inform and amplify his definition of difference in much the same way an understanding of the hillbilly is necessary to define the redneck. You need one to understand the other and the distinction will either incorporate fear or appreciation depending on how the characters are constructed. In his brief discussion of 1950s science fiction horror films *Them* (1954), *Invasion of the Body Snatchers* (1956), and *The Blob* (1958), Grant argues that "perhaps the most frightening moment in any of these films—for heterosexual male viewers, at least—is the close-up of Dana Wynter's face in *Invasion of the Body Snatchers* as she responds dispassionately to Kevin McCarthy's ardent kiss" (4). He continues:

> Director Don Siegel has pinpointed the nature of the fear expressed in this scene in his observation that McCarthy tries "to kiss her awake in a delicious non-pod way but she's a limp fish and he knows immediately she is a pod. In my life, I am sorry to say, I have kissed many pods." Here the director, like so much of horror cinema generally, disavows the possibility of his own inadequacy and projects it onto the woman as Other. (4)

Here, the horror comes not from difference but similarity and even the unquestioned sexual power of the male protagonist falls short in reversing this plague. While Wynter argues that the gender binary, otherwise inviolate, has been utterly destroyed by the presence of the pods and their leveling homogeneity, we see this exemplified in the representations of rednecks, white trash, and hillbilly characters. They are the same and yet different from the middle-class population perceived to be in the audience.

Grant posits here that gender difference, social, cultural, and biological, can be amplified into monstrosity, creating an Other. We argue something similar. Despite the interchangeable quality of these portrayals, the redneck, white trash, and hillbilly characters are utilized in contemporary film in distinct ways. Whereas difference and otherness are utilized by Grant as points on a spectrum in understanding gender difference in horror film (we do not think he is using these terms interchangeably), we argue that difference and otherness apply to specific characterizations of southern working-class men and women, and that each of these characterizations is associated with a genre—comedy and horror, respectively.

This is an important distinction for two reasons. First, it highlights the ways in which socioeconomic class in America is recognized and commented on in film. In many ways, the redneck stands in for the working class in contemporary film regardless of geographic or cultural difference. Secondly, it illustrates the ways in which means of film production, in this case the demand to meet the expectations of comedy and horror films placed on both producers and audiences, influences the types of characterizations we see as filmgoers and offers us the chance to see which cultural values are being reinforced, challenged, or even negated. Understanding the difference between portrayals helps us understand why specific characterizations are deployed and how consumption of film and other media shapes our understanding of American culture as a whole.

Our understanding of the redneck is, in a sense, a matter of degree. But whereas the shift between difference and other as embodied by women in horror film described by Grant is advanced as being contained within a single genre, we argue the distinction between redneck, white trash, and hillbilly is necessary, and made possible by, the specific demands of comedy and horror film. This is not to say that the break is complete, even, or immutable. Just as gender difference can be seen as the heart of both horror films and romantic comedies, for example, the same things that make a redneck funny in a comedy are the things amplified and made monstrous in horror films. Despite similarities, there are critical qualitative differences between the two forms, and each speaks to particular cultural anxieties, beliefs, and understandings of privilege and class.

A key example of hillbilly othering in a horror film comes from the nameless clan of murderers in *The Texas Chainsaw Massacre* (1974). Leatherface and his family must be visually different from the group of teenagers who will be murdered on their property. This is achieved through make-up and costuming. Both Leatherface and the members of his family are wearing blue-collar work clothes like coveralls, jeans, khaki pants, and button-up shirts; in addition, they appear greasy and unclean. This is contrasted to the teens who may wear similar items, but the cut, fit, and cleanliness establish separation with which audiences can identify. Additionally, unsettling accessories and bodily difference add to the strangeness of the rural Texans. The hitchhiker (Edwin Neal) wears a fur purse around his neck that has the face and paws of the animal still on it. He has small scabs on his cheek, neck, arms, and hands. A shiny red scar stretches from the side of his nose down across his right cheek. The presence of this blemish on the hitchhiker's face is unsettling, and facial irregularities mark the rest of the hillbilly family as well.

More than aesthetics, the situations, attitudes, and behaviors exhibited by redneck, white trash, and hillbilly characters are meant to highlight difference from the rest of society. While redneck characters reveal the rustic, time-honored values that have gotten lost in the bustle of city living, white trash, and hillbilly characters show the consequences of an uncivilized, uneducated society. Hardworking rednecks may have to operate outside the law like Bandit and Snowman, but there is a connection to the common man. White trash and hillbilly characters, on the other hand, are not contributing members of society but parasitically feed off either the land or the rest of middle-class American society as envisioned through the normal, unsuspecting characters. Both *The Texas Chainsaw Massacre* and *Deliverance*'s nameless hillbillies appear for the most part to be unemployed. The former's hitchhiker suggests the slaughterhouse's new mechanized killing process put many people in the area out of work. Once inside Leatherface's slaughterhouse and taxidermy showcase, one might question whether or not his specific skill set stems from a previous stint at the kill plant. The only working member of the family appears to be Jim Siedow's character, a gas station attendant and human barbecue chef. Later he is mocked for only being the cook rather than participating in any of the actual killing. There is not much information regarding the hillbillies in *Deliverance*, but it is presumed that they are too ignorant or backward to function outside of their rural homes and are just living on the land.

Another difference between the redneck, white trash, and hillbilly is situated in familial relationships. Family values are a key American ideal espoused in most Hollywood film, but they are particularly essential to these characters. The focus on family personifies the salt-of-the-earth, good-at-heart traits of redneck characters, but is warped in white trash or hillbilly portrayals. The redneck can be thought of as representing the mythical

American family, with patriarchal authority central to family governance and held together through work and faith. The white trash or hillbilly family is dysfunctional and violent, with overtones of emotional, physical, and sexual abuse. Incest is often alluded to if not directly addressed, with physical deformity, particularly facial disfigurement, serving as an indicator of inbreeding. Related to the portrayal of these family relationships is the unspoken reliance on community in the traditional family represented by the redneck, and the reclusive, clannish mannerisms of the white trash or hillbilly. In the redneck we have a picture of family and communal responsibility. Selfless, the redneck can be counted on to do the right thing when confronted by a threat to family or community. The white trash or hillbilly character is selfish, acting out of fear and self-interest, willing to sacrifice others, including members of his own family, to maintain his way of life.

The elements discussed above are central to the past four decades of redneck, white trash, and hillbilly characters, but as time progressed elements were added and taken away. Many of the visual cues stayed the same, but in the 1980s the roles for rednecks changed and the trope shifted. In *Planes, Trains, and Automobiles* (1987) and the *National Lampoon's Vacation* series (1983, 1989, 1997) the redneck, white trash, and hillbilly characters play smaller roles, which requires them to be easily recognizable to audiences. Owen (Dylan Baker), the redneck, is sent to pick up Neal Page (Steve Martin) and Del Griffith (John Candy) to take them to the Wichita train station. The audience is introduced to Owen through his muddy rubber boots, work gloves, several layers of dirty-looking clothes yet no winter coat, and a mesh-backed, adjustable baseball cap worn high on his head. When his wife emerges from the car, she also appears dirty, although not as mud-caked, and is layered in the same manner with long underwear, thick socks, and work boots beneath her knee-length skirt. Although never discussed, Owen's occupation appears to be some kind of farming based on his knowledge of the trains for farm animals, his costume, and the pickup truck filled with hay. His expression seems mildly hostile, with piercing eyes, and his mouth slightly open around a wad of chaw. Owen's slow responses seem recalcitrant and untrusting. The redneck couple gives the travelers the information they need and drive out of their way to get the two travelers on a train, but the scene touches upon values, family structure, and work ethic in two minutes with costuming, mannerisms, and limited dialogue.

Cousin Eddie (Randy Quaid) from the *Vacation* films pulls from redneck, white trash, and hillbilly characters. Unlike the hardworking redneck attire or soiled hillbilly costumes, Eddie sports undergarments like dingy long johns, short bathrobes, or sleeveless undershirts in public. When dressing up, he pairs unlikely combinations of clothing like a polyester baby blue leisure suit, boldly patterned shirts, and white vinyl loafers. Frequently his clothing is ill-fitting, either too tight or too short. Eddie's clothing looks out-of-date, as if it were purchased either at a thrift store or when those styles were current. The latter notion fits with the characterization of Eddie as a man who has had a string of bad luck for decades and is the epitome of bad taste in clothing and decorum. The geography is a little unclear as Cousin Eddie moves to suit the narratives. His seemingly nomadic lifestyle is explained by Eddie's inconsistent employment, falling prey to quick money-making schemes, and bad luck, which align him as a white trash character. He works every freeloading angle with the Griswolds, consistently asking them for money, and walks the line between lazy and legitimately hard up. The film's comedy also relies on hillbilly characteristics through undertones of incest. When his daughter, Cousin Vicki (Jane Krakowski), is bragging about French kissing, she exclaims "Daddy says I'm the best at it." This occurs in the first film and is the only time incest is used as a joke. Overall, though, the character cares very much for his family and adores Clark, making Eddie also resemble the redneck.

Although the Cousin Eddie character stretches intact and unevolved from the 1980s through the 1990s, redneck characters as a whole underwent a change during the final decade of the twentieth century. Films like *My Cousin Vinny* (1992), *Kalifornia* (1993), *The Beverly Hillbillies* (1993), *Forrest Gump* (1994), *Sling Blade* (1996), *Black Sheep* (1996), and *Boys Don't Cry* (1999) provide some of the same character traits we have discussed so far. The redneck was on the move both geographically and generically. Within the plots, redneck geography moves out of the South and into any rural area; Washington, Nebraska, and California become places where the redneck or hillbilly could also exist. Genres shifted as well and as the above list shows, the redneck moved into more dramatic genres that required more complex characters, which affected his depiction as a whole. While straight comedy films still predominantly relied on the redneck caricatures developed in the previous decades, the rednecks and hillbillies in dramas had to be more realistic in order to function within more complex narratives.

The prevalence of character complexity is fundamentally different from the caricatures displayed in the previous two decades of film. *The Beverly Hillbillies* (adapted from the 1960s television program) and *Black Sheep* exemplify the straight comedy approach with the former barely modernizing the story of the Clampetts and using "Dueling Banjos," the now iconic instrumental from *Deliverance* in the latter. Similarly, films like *Kalifornia* and *Boys Don't Cry* play on milder, more relatable versions of the monstrous hillbilly, which work to make both plots seem more real and the characters more threatening. Early Grayce (Brad Pitt) looks the part of hillbilly serial killer with his Confederate flag mesh-backed hat, greasy hair, and bad teeth. His backwoods nature is only one aspect of his persona rather than its defining quality. The raping, murdering antagonists, John Lotter (Peter Sarsgaard) and Tom Nissen (Brendan Sexton III), in *Boys Don't Cry* possess the ignorance, drawls, and class portrayals typical of the hillbilly, but, again, these are only aspects to their deeds, not the source of it. These films propose that redneck, white trash, and hillbilly characters are not necessarily inhuman and as such their actions must still be considered against that of the group at large; they are not separate from the rest of society, just a different level. The trope recedes away from the extremes of redneck and hillbilly in 1990s drama, adding depth and realistic depictions of these characters.

This shift to humanization through more moderate representations also makes the redneck appear more sympathetic. *Forrest Gump* and *Sling Blade* have mentally deficient protagonists who complicate the polarized understanding of redneck and hillbilly constructed in decades prior. While Forrest Gump (Tom Hanks) might be from Alabama, named after the originator of the Ku Klux Klan, and dim-witted, his portrayal is not a carbon copy of the ignorant, raping hillbillies from *Deliverance.* The story traipses along dropping Gump into circumstantial good and bad luck; life happens to Gump rather than the other way around. His inserted presence at the historical highlights from the middle and latter half of the twentieth century provides us the perspective of someone without the depth to grasp the culturally significant events. This attitude jives with the 1990s push for a more colorblind society. Similarly, the character of Karl Childers is mentally disabled, but unlike Gump's worldly existence, Childers (Billy Bob Thornton) stays in his small Arkansas town. After murdering his mother and her lover at the age of 12 and rehabilitating in an institution until he is middle aged, Childers attempts to live life on his own, finding a job as a mechanic and making friends with a young boy named Frank (Lucas Black). Both Gump's and Childers's simplistic understanding of the world highlight the difference between right and wrong and the crooked paths that getting to those places sometimes take. Childers is forced to kill again in order to save the family that accepts and takes him in, but rather than pushing him toward the monstrous hillbilly extreme, his actions highlight his dedication to Frank and his mother, shifting the weight of the hillbilly trope to the abusive Doyle Hargraves (Dwight Yoakam). The point in discussing these films at length is that they stand out in their expansion of the unquestioning, simplistic depictions of the redneck. Gump and Childers offer humanized, sympathetic characters, although still othered in their mental disabilities. Lotter and Nissen murder Brandon Teena and Grayce murders at least five people on screen and possibly more off. These dramatic portrayals are still different from horror films like *The Texas Chainsaw Massacre* or *Deliverance* because audiences are expected to connect on some level to the human beings represented instead of disconnecting from the othered caricatures.

The seemingly progressive stance films took toward the poor southern white in the 1990s has not continued into the new millennium. Like the 1990s, the redneck is still occupying more central roles, but, unlike *Smokey and the Bandit,* the films are extensive explorations of the stereotype, amalgams of generalizations and hackneyed jokes possibly stemming from Jeff Foxworthy's enormously popular comedy routines. Even with the return to major roles, the supposedly redneck characters are caricatures. *Joe Dirt* (2001) and *Talladega Nights: The Ballad of Ricky Bobby* (2006) are two examples of this. Set in the millennium, Joe Dirt (David Spade) is still wearing clothing that would have easily fit into films from the 1970s. He is seen wearing both overalls and coveralls, shorter denim cut-offs, and he drives around Los Angeles shirtless. Additionally, Dirt's costuming directly references 1970s popular culture with T-shirts sporting the AC/DC band logo or with "I choked Linda Lovelace" across the chest. The most striking visual characteristics of Dirt are his mullet hairstyle and facial hair. Radio DJ Zander Kelly (Dennis Miller) suggests that Dirt is so inbred that the sideburns and goatee naturally grow into their typical redneck shape.

Like Cousin Eddie, Joe Dirt's geography is muddled. He was abandoned as a child at the Grand Canyon and the search for his parents takes him all over the United States. When the story opens he is living in Los Angeles and working as a janitor, but the small town of Silvertown, Idaho, is his dream place to live. When he finally locates his parents they are living in Louisiana. Dirt is different from his parents; he lands on the more redneck side of the spectrum while they are decidedly white trash. They only agree to meet him for financial reasons while he sought them for the pleasure of connecting to family. Being a comedy, the film does pull from the three character types to create humor. For example, Dirt's potentially incestuous sexual encounter, his proximity to abject materials like feces, and his provincial worldviews are bits of comedy that reference hillbilly, but his overall demeanor and values make him more relatable and redneck. Ultimately, the message of *Joe Dirt* is that if you work hard you will be happy and that home is where you make it, which sometimes means forming family from friends.

Also focused on bringing a family together, *Talladega Nights* uses NAS-CAR as a backdrop to the familiar plot. This film also provides the spectrum of redneck and white trash to create comedy. The only geography mentioned is North Carolina, but not much more is focused on location. Ricky Bobby (Will Ferrell) and Cal Naughton Jr. (John C. Reilly) are both NASCAR drivers and spend most of the film wearing their racing coveralls. While it is not clear if the brands Wonder Bread and Old Spice adorning their costumes are meant to signify lower-class or blue-collar preferences, their disinterest in educating their children, junk food diet, McMansion, and general apathy toward anything beyond their own backyard and experiences clearly mark the family as lower class. Despite his considerable financial success, Ricky Bobby's habits, wants, and interests support, and are the product of, this white-trash utopia.

Reese Bobby, Ricky's father, is of particular interest in this abridged genealogy of rednecks because he seems to be an anachronistic rendition of Reynolds's character from *Smokey and the Bandit.* He consistently has a beer in his hand, sports a moustache, and embodies the kind of rough masculinity brought to the screen by Burt Reynolds. When helping Ricky reacquaint himself with fast driving, Reese uses a series of unconventional teachings like trapping a cougar and putting it in the car to blindfolding Ricky and telling him that driving is in the heart, not with the eyes. His homespun, backward-seeming advice successfully gets Ricky Bobby back on the race track.

While Ricky Bobby and Joe Dirt are the main characters in their films, there are still rednecks that appear in the fringe of other films. Randy (Christopher Meloni), better known as Freakshow, from *Harold and Kumar Go to White Castle* (2004), encapsulates much of the scary hillbilly aesthetic and scenarios made familiar in movies throughout the previous three decades, but is situated in the backwoods of New Jersey. When the two protagonists experience car trouble after sliding off the main road, Freakshow the tow truck driver appears out of nowhere ready to give them a lift. He wears a mesh-backed, adjustable baseball cap worn high on his head and gray coveralls. The music is foreboding and Freakshow's presence is meant to conjure the hillbilly. Dubbed Freakshow because of the hideous boils covering his face and hands, he picks up and drives Harold and Kumar back to his house. The scenario of being lost in an unfamiliar area and being forced to rely on a scary stranger for help combined with his unsettling appearance are contrasted with Freakshow's friendlier redneck attributes. On the ride, they cannot stop focusing on his pulsating, oozing boils and yellow crust-filled ears. Speaking with a drawl, he promises to fix their car and get them cleaned up, questions Harold and Kumar about their relationship with Jesus, and suggests they have sex with his wife. The situation is surreal and uses decades of redneck and white trash/hillbilly characters to create comedic juxtapositions and play with audience expectations.

Most of the films discussed thus far are for a more mature audience, but younger generations may have been acquainted with the redneck trope in the 2006 Disney-Pixar joint production *Cars*. The film is predominantly set in Radiator Springs, a dilapidated town sent to ruin after the transition from Route 66 to interstates. The specific location of Radiator Springs is not made clear, but the landscape is a generalized Southwest setting. With its single blinking stoplight, Radiator Springs is meant to evoke the façade of a very small, hick-filled town. The only character that seems at home within the rural small town is Mater, a rusted-out tow truck. Voiced by Larry the Cable Guy (David Lawrence Whitney) from the Blue Collar Comedy Tour, Mater is the vehicular avatar of the redneck trope. Translating these human characteristics to a car might seem difficult, but with the addition of Whitney's exaggerated twang and aspects of his stand-up routine incorporated into dialogue, the stereotype is evoked. Cementing the representation is Mater's appearance: missing hood, as well as hubcaps and protruding buck teeth through his front grill, as well as his occupation as a tow truck driver. Similar to Reese Bobby, Mater has his own collection of redneck sayings and is the best "backwards driver" in the region. He passes along the power and skill of reverse driving to Lightning McQueen (Owen Wilson) and, along with the rest of the rural population in Radiator Springs, teaches him the importance of friendship.

The millennium also provided several remakes or revivals of 1970s popular film, including *The Texas Chainsaw Massacre* (2003) and *The Hills Have Eyes* (2006). It is clear that the decades between film versions saw a dramatic shift in the horror genre. More gruesome, voyeuristic, and vivid in the slaying, the new version of *The Texas Chainsaw Massacre* provides variations not only to the plot, but the hillbilly representations as well. While the 1974 version had Leatherface's trophy room and kill area in the kitchen on the first floor, he has been moved to the basement. The new damp setting features more space for keeping bodies and elaborate ways of holding victims before and after kills. The old Leatherface had a wall of heads, predominantly of cows and vermin, and a room of bones, but the new Leatherface's trophies are fingers, bathtubs full of blood, and even more faces from previous victims. Whereas the 1974 version made Leatherface into a wild animal content in his rural, homemade slaughterhouse and almost frightened by the arrival of outsiders, the 2003 Leatherface seems like a much more malicious, plotting killer. In 30 years, two versions of the same hillbilly appear drastically different.

One interesting addition to the millennial *Texas Chainsaw Massacre* is the inclusion of hillbilly women within the plot. The hitchhiker is a woman, and not a member of the Leatherface clan but a victim of it. The barbecue/gas station attendant role is now Luda May (Marietta Marich) and that male role shifts to Sheriff Hoyt (R. Lee Ermey). Sheriff Hoyt is a deranged version of Sheriff Buford T. Justice, but adds the fear of hillbillies with more power. There are two more women added to the plot, Henrietta (Heather Kafka) and an unnamed older woman (Kathy Lamkin). When Erin (Jessica Biel), the millennium's version of Sally, stumbles into the women's trailer seeking respite from the chainsaw-wielding killer, she is met by the pale, bathrobe-clad Henrietta. Her cropped hair and freckles give her an androgynous, almost pixie-like appearance, but the mossy teeth, quiet sing-song voice, and hollowed eyes are contrasted with her malicious actions to heighten the creepiness of her character. The addition of women and children to the plot where there were none before adds new elements to the hillbilly woman. The assumed sexual availability of farmers' daughters, the loyal and hardworking redneck family-woman, and women exoticized by their distance from civilization bleeds into threatening and monstrous depictions of obese, uneducated, and murderous backwoods white trash/hillbilly women. We feel a more focused analysis on the redneck and white trash/hillbilly woman is an area ripe for further review.

Admittedly, there is cold comfort in suggesting that the redneck, by virtue of being the characterization most commonly associated with comedy, is positive. Advancing the argument that Cousin Eddie is necessarily a more positive portrayal of the redneck than Leatherface because he doesn't kill anyone is equally unsatisfying. The bar is set too low to be meaningful. Rather, it is in the very simplicity of comedy and horror films that we find the redeeming quality of the redneck. Reliant on the difference between characters for its jokes and gags, the comedy film puts the redneck in a position where his difference from others is equal to the difference of others from him. This is not to say that the redneck is treated equally, or that the audience is not meant to laugh at the redneck character, only that, small concession though it may be, the potential exists for the nonredneck characters to be as much on the hook for their ignorance and their assumptions as the redneck is. No such opportunity exists for the white trash or hillbilly character.

Throughout this chapter we have argued that the figure of the redneck in American film is part of a larger conception of poor, southern whites, a conception that also includes portrayals of white trash and hillbillies in a more or less oppositional position to the redneck. We have also argued that the demands of contemporary genre film have helped create these portrayals, and can in turn be used to discern something of their meaning. The redneck in American film cannot be said to be the American redneck, or even the popular (in a cultural sense) idea of the redneck. We must, of course, consider all of these notions as mutually reliant on one another for their meanings. "Squeal like a pig" has become pop culture shorthand for hillbilly, and the Confederate flag identifies a particular type of redneck quicker than a line of dialogue ever could. Despite all this, we must consider the redneck in American film in the terms of film and genre studies first. This position, we believe, opens up a discussion of the redneck that is reliant upon the text for support, but must also include an understanding of the means of film production, genre theory, and audience expectations. Taken together, we can begin to untangle something as unwieldy as "the meaning of the redneck."

Works Cited

The Beverly Hillbillies. Directed by Penelope Spheeris. DVD. Twentieth Century Fox, 1993.

Black Sheep. Directed by Penelope Spheeris. DVD. Paramount Pictures, 1996.

Boys Don't Cry. Directed by Kimberly Pierce. DVD. Fox SearchLight, 1999.

Cars. Directed by John Lasseter and Joe Ranft. DVD. Walt Disney Pictures, 2006.

Christmas Vacation. Directed by Jeremiah S. Chechik. DVD. Warner Bros. Pictures, 1989.

Deliverance. Directed by John Boorman. DVD. Warner Bros. Pictures, 1972.

Forrest Gump. Directed by Robert Zemeckis. DVD. Paramount Pictures, 1994.

Grant, Barry Keith. "Introduction." In *The Dread of Difference: Gender and the Horror Film,* edited by Barry Keith Grant, 1–12. Austin: University of Texas Press, 1996.

Harold and Kumar Go to White Castle. Directed by Danny Leiner. DVD. New Line Productions, 2004.

The Hills Have Eyes. Directed by Alexandre Aja. DVD. Twentieth Century Fox, 2006.

The Hills Have Eyes. Directed by Wes Craven. DVD. Blood Relations Company, 1977.

Joe Dirt. Directed by Dennie Gordon. DVD. Columbia Pictures Corporation, 2001.

Kalifornia. Directed by Dominic Sena. DVD. PolyGram Filmed Entertainment, 1993.

Molloy, Joanna. "Sarah Palin at National Rifle Association Lobs Laughing Crowd with 'Redneck' Jokes." *New York Daily News,* May 15, 2010, nydailynews.com. Accessed January 13, 2011.

My Cousin Vinny. Directed by Jonathan Lynn. DVD. Twentieth Century Fox, 1992.

Newitz, Annalee, and Matthew Wray. "What Is 'White Trash'? Stereotypes and Economic Conditions of Poor Whites in the United States." In *Whiteness: A*

Critical Reader, edited by Mike Hill, 168–86. New York: New York University Press, 1997.

Planes, Trains, and Automobiles. Directed by John Hughes. DVD. Paramount Pictures, 1987.

Sling Blade. Directed by Billy Bob Thornton. DVD. Miramax, 1996.

Smokey and the Bandit. Directed by Hal Needham. DVD. Universal 8 Films, 1977.

Talladega Nights: The Ballad of Ricky Bobby. Directed by Adam McKay. DVD. Sony Pictures Entertainment, 2006.

The Texas Chain Saw Massacre. Directed by Tobe Hooper. DVD. Bryanston Distributing, 1974.

The Texas Chainsaw Massacre. Directed by Marcus Nispel. DVD. New Line Cinema, 2003.

Vacation. Directed by Harold Ramis. DVD. Warner Bros. Pictures, 1983.

Vegas Vacation. Directed by Stephen Kessler. DVD. Warner Bros. Pictures, 1997.

Chapter 6

Road Work: *Smokey and the Bandit* and the Trucker Film

Andy Johnson

This chapter will trace the development of the trucker film with a focus on the best-known example of the genre, *Smokey and the Bandit*. The film is a natural focal point for this chapter not only because of its popularity, but also because it includes most of the themes and elements that define the genre. All trucker films are, at their core, narratives of blue-collar workers trying to make a living despite challenges from others. I intend to show how pop culture's embrace of trucker films in general and *Smokey and the Bandit* in particular reflect a respect for blue-collar workers and an elevation of the trucker into working-class hero.

Film critics often point to the 1970s as a monumental decade of excellence in American cinema, and with films as powerful as *The Godfather* (1972), *Chinatown* (1974), *Nashville* (1975), *Taxi Driver* (1976), and many others, it is impossible to disagree. Many of these critically acclaimed films spoke to the uncertainty and fear felt by audiences in the 1970s by rejecting old Hollywood conventions and challenging audiences with grittier subjects and flawed antiheroes. Audiences responded by making these films hits and launching the careers of young directors Martin Scorsese, Francis Ford Coppola, Roman Polanski, and others. Other young directors, such as George Lucas and Steven Spielberg, took a different tack and sought to distract audiences from their real lives by using cutting-edge special effects to make them scream in horror (1973's *The Exorcist*, 1977's *Jaws*) or marvel at battling spaceships in far-flung galaxies (*Star Wars*, 1977). The high quality of film in the 1970s brought massive crowds to movie theaters and profoundly changed the way the film studios handled movie distribution and promotion. The blockbusters of the 1970s encouraged studios to distribute the films as widely as possible and advertise them nationally, instead of the previous method of opening films in a handful of theaters and letting word-of-mouth build the films' reputations. The blockbuster approach rejected big-city coastal favoritism and allowed for geographic parity that gave more Americans the opportunity to experience the same films at the same time. When the summer heat got too oppressive, or the winter chill too biting, Americans could escape together to the welcoming confines of the movie theater and join in a national dialogue over shared narratives and common heroes.

Working-class Americans in the 1970s needed the escapism of the blockbuster. During the decade, they faced an energy crisis, a gas shortage, recession, the messy and demoralizing end of the Vietnam War, and the scandal-laden presidency and resignation of Richard Nixon. People needed heroes, but the complicated events of the decade made them cynical toward authority and traditional heroes. The 1960s had offered counterculture icons arising from rock music and the hippie culture, but working-class Americans found little about them that reflected their respect for hard work and traditional values. As the 1970s progressed, however, the working class found itself betrayed by its authority figures, living in increasingly crime-infested areas, and struggling to meet the inflation of basic necessities. People wanted escapism, but also wanted heroes who would provide models for how to cope with such difficult times.

From the lonesome highway and in a cloud of diesel smoke, one heroic icon emerged to give the working class hope, or if not hope, at least a good time at the movies: the truck driver. Truckers combine the mystique of the cowboy with the technology of the twentieth century. Their work requires them to travel long distances transporting goods from one place to another, but instead of using a horse to herd cattle across windswept plains, truckers use a semi to haul various kinds of loads across ribbons of asphalt. The ache in the back from hours in the saddle or the seat would be familiar to both cowboys and truckers, and both would know the longing for loved ones left at home. In her book *Trucker: A Portrait of the Last American Cowboy*, Jane Stern makes explicit comparisons between cowboys of the Old West and truckers. Through interviews, photo galleries, and poems from various authors, Stern draws a distinctive picture of the lives of truckers and how they mirror the Old West icons. She notes that when truckers call each other "cowboy," they usually do so sarcastically, because it "refers to a driver who is reckless or spends all his money on fancy boots and custom chrome for his truck. A true-blue trucker is supposedly content to listen to the sound of highway being eaten up under his wheels, while a cowboy must have a stereo tape deck with country-western music to keep his gears meshing. Today's 'cowboys' are the Old West's 'dudes'" (6). A humble dedication to work defines both the original Old West cowboy and the modern-day trucker. By the 1970s, however, the cowboy of the Western film had changed from a white-hat-wearing paladin of good into a more conflicted and morally ambiguous hero. The violent antiheroes of Sam Peckinpah and Sergio Leone had replaced the noble cowboys of John Ford and Joseph Kane. The scene was set for a new icon to emerge, one who could reflect the ideals of the past while facing the challenges of the present. The decade was primed for the trucker.

Cinematic representations of truckers did not begin in the 1970s. Films featuring truck-driving protagonists existed as early as 1928 (*Crooks Can't Win*), and trucking was central to the film noir classics *They Drive by Night* (1940) and *Thieves' Highway* (1949). While truckers provided sympathetic working-class characters for the cinema, Scott Von Doviak notes, "Hollywood was in no hurry to embrace the trucker as an archetypal hero worthy of silver screen immortality" (124). It probably didn't help that the anticommunist blacklist frightened filmmakers away from making movies that championed blue-collar workers, which could have led to the issue of unionization. Indeed, the blacklist forced the director of *Thieves' Highway*, Jules Dassin, to flee the United States for France after the release of the film. Truckers would have to wait several decades to see their rise as pop culture heroes.

The cinematic focus on truckers that occurred in the 1970s seems to be the result of confluences of several pop culture and real-world events: music, CB radio, the fuel shortage, and working-class disillusionment with government. Von Doviak suggests that music in the 1960s began paving the way for the trucker's ascension to working-class hero based on the popularity of truck driving songs by Red Sovine, Del Reeves, and, particularly, the huge 1963 crossover hit by Dave Dudley, "Six Days on the Road" (124). Songs that championed truckers found an enthusiastic (and somewhat captive) audience in drivers who counted on the radio for entertainment during long stretches of the road, but others were listening as well.

Von Doviak points to 1973 as the critical year for the rise of trucking culture in the United States: "The true dawn of trucker-mania arrived in December 1973 after thousands of independent owner-operators staged a nationwide blockade. Hamstrung by rising fuel costs and the new national 55 mph speed limit, these independent truckers took out their frustration on the highways of America" (126–27). Print and television news featured stories of the plight of truckers and the difficulties they faced on the road. The general public learned about the dangers, hard work, and personal sacrifices that truckers endured to deliver their goods. They also heard about the truckers' lifestyles and the cultural community truckers developed to communicate with each other. Truckers soon found that the American people sympathized with them and were surprised (and eventually frustrated) as nontruckers latched onto CB radios and the colorful jargon they heard about in the news stories. Von Doviak notes that "the rebellious independent trucker became an overnight folk hero" and that, by 1977, approximately 30 million Americans used CD radios (127).

Hollywood soon recognized the public groundswell of interest in truck driving and began producing trucker-related films to capitalize on the boom. *White Line Fever,* directed by Jonathan Kaplan, appeared in 1975 and took full advantage of the public's elevation of the trucker driver into folk hero. The promotional poster for the movie featured star Jan-Michael Vincent (as Carrol Jo Hummer) brandishing a shotgun in his left hand with his right arm wrapped protectively around his wife Jerri Kane Hummer (Kay Lenz). A blue and white Kenworth cabover jumps a hill in the background with the tagline appearing above it: "Carrol Jo Hummer—A working man who's had enough!" Carrol Jo is a Vietnam veteran who comes home with a dream of becoming an independent trucker, but who runs into difficulties from Glass House, a corrupt trucking conglomerate that attempts to control truckers and force them into hauling illegal goods. The company is not above using violence to coerce truckers, and Carrol Jo and his wife suffer at the hands of the company's thugs. The movie became something of a cult classic, but critics found little to praise beyond Jan-Michael Vincent's performance. In his January 1, 1975, review of the film for the *Chicago Sun-Times,* Roger Ebert wrote that it is Vincent's performance that "saves the movie, to the degree that it's salvageable," but that the plot reveals that, "while I know little about trucking, the film's maker arguably knows less." Ebert points out that owner-operators like Carrol Jo would not be forced to carry contraband because they choose their cargo. Audiences seemed to care little for such inaccuracies, however, and the genre continued to grow as the decade rolled on. Despite its lackluster critical response, *White Line Fever* contains several elements that subsequent trucker films would employ in shaping the genre: conflict between the working-class trucker and others who hold more money and/or initial power, the trucker's respect for (and from) other races in his socioeconomic class, and the trucker's ability to work collectively with others to fight antagonists. Later trucker films would add their own specific touches to the genre, but most of them involved these themes in some way.

In 1976, the song "Convoy" hit the charts and fueled even more interest in trucking. The song was written by Bill Fries and Chip Davis (Davis later founded Mannheim Steamroller) and sung by Fries as fictional trucker C. W. McCall. The duo had created McCall as a character in a series of bread commercials for their employer, Omaha advertising firm Bozell & Jacobs. The commercials became so popular they began writing songs for the character (http://www.cw-mccall.com/legend/). The song became such a huge hit, it inspired a (disappointing) film adaptation in 1978 directed by Sam Peckinpah and starring Kris Kristofferson, Ali MacGraw, and Ernest Borgnine.

By the mid-1970s, trucker-mania was in high gear. CB radios filled American homes and vehicles, and trucker narratives filled the movie theaters. Prominent directors like Peckinpah (*Convoy*, 1978) and Norman Jewison (*F.I.S.T.*, 1978) and beloved actors like Henry Fonda (*The Great Smokey Roadblock*, 1976) and Kris Kristofferson (*Convoy*) had gotten on board. The year 1977 became the apex for trucker films with the release of three distinctly different offerings that reveal the diversity of the genre: *Citizens Band* (also known as *Handle with Care*), *Breaker! Breaker!*, and *Smokey and the Bandit*.

Citizens Band is Jonathan Demme's thoughtful, character-driven exploration of the CB radio craze. The Altmanesque narrative revolves around a number of CB users in a small town whose lives intersect over the CB and, eventually, in person. Truck driving is not the explicit focus of the film, but the truckers in the film not only provide motion to the plot, but also reveal the struggles of the townspeople for adventure versus their desire for stability and community. Philandering trucker Chrome Angel (Charles Napier) uses his transitory lifestyle to juggle two marriages and at least one mistress. His bigamy catches up with him, however, as he becomes stranded in the town and both wives come to take care of him. His story indulges in the stereotype that truckers have multiple lovers located along their routes, but this film posits a resolution of the issue that seems to be pure "swinging seventies": why not all just get along and live together?

The film contrasts Chrome Angel's free-wheeling lifestyle with the sedentary life of townsperson and retired trucker Papa Thermodyne (Roberts Blossom). Papa Thermodyne barely interacts with his son, but talks animatedly with truckers over the CB. Retirement has devitalized him and the CB allows him to reconnect to some memorialized shreds of history, when he was young and driving the highways. His desire to leave finally over-whelms him, however, and his ill-planned escape on a rainy night is the catalyst that brings the townspeople together to search for him. While *Citizens Band* features few scenes of truck driving and the actual working life of truckers, it does show the powerful impact that trucking can have on a person's identity and the nostalgia felt by truckers forced by age to park their rigs. The colorful characters and the respect with which Demme treats them makes the movie worth watching and raises it above many other trucker films.

Breaker! Breaker!, which also hit movie screens in 1977, is notable mainly for being Chuck Norris's first starring role. Norris plays J.D. Dawes, a trucker whose brother and fellow trucker Billy (Michael Augenstein) has been illegally detained by a drunken judge who brutally controls a corrupt town. As one would expect, the movie allows Norris to show off his martial arts skills as he fights what seems to be the entire male population of the town in an effort to rescue his brother. The town appears plucked from the Old West, with dirt streets and Western-style buildings, and the plot echoes a classic Western in which a good-hearted cowboy takes on a corrupt town, so Norris's character fits squarely into the image of trucker as modern cowboy. It is important to note, however, that J.D. Dawes does not defeat the villains on his own: alerted by CB, a convoy of fellow truckers comes to his aid and demolishes the town with their rigs. In trucker films, drivers are part of a community always ready to support its members. The truckers in *Breaker! Breaker!* take great delight in crashing through buildings, chasing the townspeople from the dusty streets, and creating general mayhem while protecting one of their own. Their actions manifest real, physical power that presents a real threat to the self-created governmental power of the judge and his corrupted town.

The third of the trucker trinity to appear in 1977, *Smokey and the Bandit*, included the themes of previous trucker films, but added established stars like Burt Reynolds and Jackie Gleason and a fast, distinctive Pontiac Trans Am for an explosive mix that became one of the top-grossing films of the year and the most famous and influential trucker film ever. With the hugely popular *Smokey and the Bandit*, the trucker film hit its high water mark in pop culture. In a year that produced films that helped define the concept of blockbuster, *Smokey and the Bandit* came in fourth in U.S. box office gross for the year, bringing in more money than competitors *The Spy Who Loved Me*, *The Deep*, and *The Rescuers*, among others (Shone 64). Only *Star Wars*, *Close Encounters of the Third Kind*, and *Saturday Night Fever* earned more money in 1977.

What was it that made *Smokey and the Bandit* so popular? It offered nothing particularly revolutionary, unlike *Star Wars*, which dazzled audiences with its ground-breaking special effects. Its plot is simple: truckers Bandit Darville (Burt Reynolds) and Cledus "Snowman" Snow (Jerry Reed) are challenged to pick up a load of Coors beer from Texarkana, Texas, and bring it back to Atlanta, Georgia, within 28 hours for $80,000. Complications include the illegality of the run—Coors was not legally available east of the Mississippi River before 1981—and the runaway bride Carrie (Sally Field), whom Bandit picks up, causing her potential father-in-law Sheriff Buford T. Justice (Jackie Gleason) and his son, Junior (Mike Henry), to chase them across several states "in hot pursuit." Director Hal Needham kept the actors loose and the action level high and gave audiences a fun time at the movies. Although *Smokey and the Bandit* has much in common with car chase and road films, it is at heart a trucker film and its status as the most popular trucker film ever makes it worthy of examination and discussion.

The film establishes itself immediately as a trucker film with its first scene: the sound of a semi starting and a shot of a Kenworth's twin smokestacks bellowing smoke. The opening credits then begin with a montage of various close-ups of parts of the truck and shots of the truck driving down the highway and around country roads past fields of horses. A painting on the side of the semi's trailer of a bandit robbing a stagecoach gives audiences an early suggestion that the truck's owner is something of a rebel and a colorful character, while simultaneously linking the trucker with the iconic history of the cowboy. The song played during the opening credit sequence goes even further by establishing the trucker as an equal to other American icons, both real and mythical, including Jesse James and John Henry. The song tells a story bearing similar elements to classic tall tales: Bandit, faced with his brakeless rig rushing backward downhill in a blinding rain toward innocent bystanders, slows the rig by jumping out and running beside it while dragging his feet.

In humorous contrast to the action of the song, we first see Bandit at a truck "roadeo" as he lies in a hammock, a cowboy hat covering his face. Nearby signs proclaim him a "legend" and the "king" of the truckers and offer a free autograph with the purchase of a photo of Bandit (which has been reduced to 75 cents). The comic juxtaposition is further emphasized when wealthy locals Big Enos and Little Enos Burdette approach Bandit to challenge him to the beer run. Big Enos says, "Son, you're looking at a legend." Little Enos, unimpressed, replies, "I guess a legend and an out-of-work bum look a lot alike, daddy." Bandit responds by mocking the sartorial choice of the father and son, who are outfitted in identical bright blue Western suits and white cowboy hats, despite extreme height and weight differences between the two men.

The discounted photo and lack of any fans around him makes us question Bandit's status as a legend. Once the run is underway, however, Bandit receives aid—both solicited and unsolicited—and encouragement from admirers in every state he passes through. Perhaps the film intentionally draws a distinction between fame and finance. Being a daring and legendary trucker might win someone fame, the film suggests, but Bandit is like any other trucker—a blue-collar worker dependent on the next load to pay his bills. If he stays and participates in the "roadeo," he stands to win $5,000. The Burdettes offer him $80,000 for the illegal beer run (plus bankrolling a new car), though, enough to buy a new semi. This, too, underlines his working-class status: instead of squandering the money, he wants to use it to support his work. When Snowman asks Bandit why they should risk the journey, Bandit replies: "For the good old American lifestyle. For the money, for the glory, and for the fun—mostly for the money." As the film goes on, however, it seems that money isn't necessarily the main reason for his acceptance of the challenge.

Big Enos wisely knows that while Bandit needs the money, Bandit also thrives on adventure and that making the run plays into Bandit's identity as folk hero. The Burdettes have made the challenge before, which is shown in an early scene in which another trucker is arrested with a trailer filled with Coors, and Bandit knows the risks associated with it. Once the trip begins, Snowman again asks Bandit why they're attempting the run, pointing out that it's never been done. "Well, that's the reason, son," Bandit replies. In a later scene, Carrie presses Bandit on what he does professionally. "I just go from place to place and do what I do best. . . . Show off." Clearly, Bandit is as appreciative of his legend as his fans, and he is eager to keep that legendary status alive. This showmanship echoes the folk hero aspects of other famous outlaws, such as Jesse James and Bonnie and Clyde, who delighted in public relations stunts designed to appeal to the masses while tweaking authorities. In his book *Hillbillyland*, J. W. Williamson identifies the cowboy painted on Bandit's trailer as Jesse James and suggests that Bandit is a kind of "social bandit" as defined by Eric Hobshawm: "The bandit is always bred in a rural culture. He is typically young, frequently unmarried, and totally unremarkable until circumstances—specifically some injustice—forces [sic] him into acts that the state or other dominating power regards as criminal but that the bandit's local community, vaguely defined, does not" (102). The film's Bandit is a southerner, young and unmarried, and his fame exists because of his deeds. We get little of Bandit's back-story, though there is mention of some jail time served involving Snowman and Bandit's admission to Carrie that he "used to do some crazy things. Used to." But, he is not physically imposing, or blessed with superhuman powers (despite what the song suggests). He is a blue-collar worker with an outsized charm and the confidence and good luck to grasp opportunities when presented.

Despite his legendary status, Bandit relies on the assistance of his community, as is common in trucker films. Initially, truckers might seem like rugged individuals, but it is critical that the films show that truckers form a working-class community. This keeps the trucker films grounded as stories of blue-collar workers whose collective action results in the defeat of their oppressor. Bandit's community is "vaguely defined," as with that of Hobshawm's social rebel. Snowman and other truckers are his most immediate community through their shared work. It is important to note that the truckers Bandit and Snowman count among their comrades are of various races and include young and old men and women. Similarly diverse is the larger CB radio community that assists and encourages Bandit and Snowman. From a young African American hearse driver ("The Graverobber") to an elderly white woman ("The Good Witch of the North"), it seems that Bandit's popularity crosses almost all racial, age, and gender boundaries, though the community never includes the upper class. Williamson notes that the social rebel's community is vitally important for his survival and his success:

> Some element of that community always protects the bandit, helps him escape, and spreads outrageous rumors to encourage the impression that he is superhuman or magical, that he can be everywhere and simultaneously nowhere. . . . His supporters' desire is to make the bandit immortal and thereby render the oppressor impotent, whether that oppressor be landlord, law, government, or whatever. (102)

When Sheriff Justice comes upon a chaotic scene of destroyed police cruisers in Mississippi, a bystander tells him proudly, "The Bandit caused all this. Ain't he somethin'?" and when Justice cuffs a client of a roadside RV brothel thinking he's finally captured Bandit, the irritated and embarrassed client is revealed to be a police captain instead of the outlaw. Bandit is everywhere, yet nowhere, and his community eagerly protects him and spreads tales of his exploits.

It is important that Bandit's crimes do not impact his fellow blue-collar workers (beyond what must be horrendous traffic closures due to wrecked police vehicles). Presumably, he and Snowman are unarmed and never seek to harm the police. Bandit even shows some respect to Justice on a couple of occasions, once by paying for his meal and the other by revealing his location and new destination to him. They are not vigilantes seeking to fight the system through any means necessary; they are good old boys trying to make a living and have some fun along the way. Justice seems more of a vigilante than the two truckers as he berates and threatens any other law enforcement officer who points out to him that he is out of his jurisdiction. His observation when Snowman runs him off the road is one of the most famous lines in the film: "What we're dealing with here is a complete lack of respect for the law." But, Justice shows an equal lack of respect for legal matters by failing to realize the limits of his jurisdiction and endangering other drivers and officers during his extended high-speed pursuit.

It could be argued that Justice, as with any other officer, is a blue-collar worker just doing his job. His obsessive vendetta, though, has little to do with his job of enforcing the law and more to do with personal insult. "She insulted my town; she insulted my son; she insulted my authority. And that's nothing but pure, old-fashioned communism," Justice says about Carrie, but it is clear that it is the insult to his authority that rankles him the most. This embrace of authority divides Justice from the other blue-collar workers in the film. The other law enforcement personnel seem to be doing their jobs and respecting their boundaries; Justice sees authority as greater than law. The police per se are not always the antagonists in pop culture, even in the 1970s, but Justice's uncritical embrace of his authority as a sheriff marks him as part of the corrupt establishment that seeks power no matter the consequence. One can almost imagine him paraphrasing Nixon: "When Sheriff Buford T. Justice does it, it is not illegal." He is no longer a working-class enforcer of the law, he has become the law.

Bandit and Snowman skirt the law when necessary to make a living. They are blue-collar workers facing difficult financial times who find an unusual opportunity to support their work without hurting anyone else. There are two scenes in the film, though, that introduce criminals that contrast starkly with the misdeeds of the truckers. The first involves three teen boys (one of whom wears a Coors T-shirt) who attempt to strip Carrie's car after she abandons it. They almost pull their van into the path of Snowman's truck, then their van slinks to the wrong side of the road to allow them easier access to her car. They become so entranced with stealing, they fail to hear Justice until he is upon them. His treatment of them reinforces their stupidity, especially when one views the incident in hindsight. They must be complete buffoons if this ridiculous, unprofessional sheriff can surprise and frighten them. The film gives no context for the teens, so the audience knows them only as criminals. By attempting to prey on someone innocent, the would-be car thieves suffer not only the threat of arrest, but also the indignity of the audience's derision.

The other outlaws in the film are the motorcyclists at Lamar's Sportsman's Club who threaten to kill Snowman's dog (Fred) and beat up Snowman. As with the teen thieves, the audience has no context within the film to know about the background of the bikers. Their rowdy behavior and rough appearance should be a tip to audiences that the bikers are not blue-collar allies to the trucker, however. The drug-using bikers from 1969's *Easy Rider* would have been fresh in the audience's mind in 1977, along with other biker films of the 1960s and 1970s. In most of those, the bikers are not portrayed as blue-collar workers, but as rebels who refuse working-class values in favor of outlaw communities filled with drugs, violence, and crime. Audiences in the 1970s, then, would have noticed the motorcycles lined up outside the bar as a potential threat to Snowman. The threat turns out to be real, as Snowman takes on the group of bikers to rescue Fred. While punching Snowman, the bikers can be heard mocking his profession by calling him a "gearjammer" and "kings of the road, huh?" He rebounds with good humor, though, as he heartily laughs while running his semi over the line of motorcycles when he leaves. His truck—a vehicle designed for work—has triumphed over the bikers' leisure vehicles (some motorcycles are designed for work, but not the choppers and sportsters belonging to the gang of bikers). The film delineates between those whose work might skirt the law and those whose behavior threatens everyone. Snowman and Bandit are truckers, blue-collar workers, not professional criminals or actual threats to innocent people (or dogs). Crime was an increasing problem in the 1970s—hence the popularity of the *Dirty Harry* and *Death Wish* movies—and *Smokey and the Bandit* encouraged audiences to laugh at the criminals. It was one more way the film gave audiences a good time during the uncertainty of the decade.

Presidential politics in the 1970s also favored *Smokey and the Bandit* and probably helped increase the likelihood that all Americans—not just southerners—would go to the theaters and drive-ins to watch good old boys outrun the police on a bootleg run. Bandit and Snowman are Georgians, like Jimmy Carter, who had just been elected president. Americans outside the South were curious about the new president and his southern culture, and movies like *Smokey and the Bandit* gave them an exciting (if exaggerated) tutorial. *Smokey and the Bandit* also offered a positive image of southerners, in contrast to the violent rednecks found in *Easy Rider* (1969),

Deliverance (1972), *Macon County Line* (1974), and other films. Von Doviak notes, "With the advent of Smokeymania, the hick flick reached the apogee of its pop culture influence. Good ol' boys were hot, and none hotter than Burt Reynolds" (134). It is worth noting, however, that while *Smokey and the Bandit* honored some elements of historical southern culture—such as bootlegging—it was very much a film about the New South. Bandit and Snowman interact equally and easily with the African Americans in the film, unlike Sheriff Justice who mutters to his son after seeing an African American sheriff, "What's the world comin' to?" Justice is a throwback to the fat, racist sheriffs seen in so many of the photos and newsreels of the segregated South, attacking African Americans and civil rights advocates with dogs and fire hoses. The New Southern community that Bandit and Snowman are a part of welcomes all races and signals the New South progressivity of desegregation and cooperation, which echoed the spirit of the Carter campaign. *Smokey and the Bandit* not only gave audiences relief from the negative events and fears of the 1970s, it also helped usher in a more optimistic outlook, albeit one that wouldn't last as world events created new challenges.

Although trucker films reached their peak of popularity in the 1970s, they still remained on the pop culture radar after that decade. Television shows like *BJ and the Bear* (1978–1981) and movies such as 1998's *Black Dog* featured truckers as blue-collar protagonists whose adventurous stories followed the patterns set by previous trucker narratives. These depictions avoided some of the realities of truck driving, however. Of course, who would want to see a movie about the fatigue, isolation, health problems, and paperwork inherent in the demanding profession? Nevertheless, more recent offerings have come closer to taking a more serious look at the lives of truckers. Indeed, one of the more compelling and honest trucker films appeared in 2008. *Trucker* stars Michelle Monaghan as female trucker Diane Ford, who is forced to take in her estranged 11-year-old son. The film shows the demands that trucking places on drivers as she must find a balance between her time on the road and her time at home with her son. The thoughtful film doesn't present truckers as folk heroes, but it gives them a great deal of respect for the work they do and how their careers impact their lives.

It is important to emphasize that whether the trucker is played by Humphrey Bogart, Burt Reynolds, or Michelle Monaghan, they all are blue-collar workers sharing the same goal as any other blue-collar worker: getting the job done. *Smokey and the Bandit* is the most popular of the trucker films, but its working-class themes can be found throughout the genre.

The popularity of the film and the genre are evidence that the truck driver has attained iconic status within American pop culture. Just as a cowboy riding a horse over a windswept prairie has its resonance in pop culture, so too has the image of an 18-wheeler speeding its way down a lonesome highway found its way into American mythology. Pop culture's elevation of the truck driver into a folk hero recognizes the crucial importance of the working class in the life of the United States and places the trucker within a national narrative of rugged individuals willing to set aside differences to work together to get the job done.

Works Cited

C.W. McCall. "The Legend." http://www.cw-mccall.com/legend/ (accessed January 8, 2011).

Ebert, Roger. 1975. Review of *White Line Fever* (Columbia Movie). *Chicago Sun-Times,* January 1, 1975. http://rogerebert.suntimes.com/apps/pbcs.dll/article?AID=/19750101/REVIEWS/501010372 (accessed January 16, 2011).

Shone, Tom. *Blockbuster: How Hollywood Learned to Stop Worrying and Love the Summer.* New York: Free Press, 2004.

Smokey and the Bandit. DVD, directed by Hal Needham (1977; Los Angeles: Universal Studios, 2004).

Stern, Jane. *Trucker: A Portrait of the Last American Cowboy.* New York: McGraw-Hill, 1975.

Von Doviak, Scott. *Hick Flicks: The Rise and Fall of Redneck Cinema.* Jefferson, NC: McFarland, 2005.

Williamson, J.W. *Hillbillyland.* Chapel Hill: University of North Carolina Press, 1995.

Chapter 7

City Workers, Country Workers: The Urban and Rural Working Class in Southern Film

Daniel Cross Turner

Several iconic films about the U.S. South—Elia Kazan's *A Streetcar Named Desire* (1951), John Boorman's *Deliverance* (1972), the Coen brothers' *O Brother, Where Art Thou?* (2000), and John Hillcoat's *The Road* (2009)—are steeped in matters of class. Critics often define these films as primarily about "Southernness" or a spectrum of other thematic emphases, such as gender, sexuality, violence, or artful self-reflexivity. However, the nature of work, and by extension of the working class, is equally at the crux of their meanings. What the characters do for a living largely defines how they live; their occupations typically occupy the characters' lives. How they work is at the core of how class works in these films, even as the laboring itself is usually invisible onscreen. We know most of these characters' class affiliations primarily by type: mostly we see the effects of their labor (their living environment, their physical appearance and condition, their interactions with others), rarely the productive work in and of itself.

Cross-sectioned with the ways class is defined and the ways it defines the main characters in these films is the divide between the city and the country in the American South. Some of these movies focus on the notion of an exceptional rural past for the region, something challenged in much recent scholarship, such as Martyn Bone's *The Postsouthern Sense of Place in Contemporary Fiction* (2005). By contrast, other films explore the city as the main physical and conceptual space in which to work. The country's economic clout has diminished in these cinematic versions of the modern and contemporary Souths. There's little financial future in the hills, fields, and backwoods. Instead, these films stereotypically portray rural southerners as amberized in a past fraught with economic strain, limning the line of blunt subsistence. The southern city offers some possibilities for upward mobility, although the urban environment often strips raw the psyches of those who brave the pressures of capitalist modernity. Caught between the Scylla of an economically destitute rural culture and the Charybdis of an overcrowded, grasping life in the city, the working class, both rural and urban, has too many mouths to feed. An undercurrent of Darwinian struggle taints both sectors. Even if the city tends to offer more of a structure for containing, at least for the time being, these riotous primal energies, both urban and rural working classes are tangled in survivalist dynamics that expose an underlying economic will to power. These cinematic representations unveil the South as a heightened repository for fleshing out the ideological violence of abstract market capitalism, as southern workers often find themselves forced to root, hog, *and* die (or kill). These famous films, whose characters labor under hard times, project the working class as a source of cultural-economic fear and loathing. The blue-collar South is typically depicted as a disconcerting, unruly presence that needs to be contained. Indeed, members of the working class in these movies are less likely to be romanticized than primitivized.

Kazan's film is a cinematic adaptation of Tennessee Williams's Pulitzer Prize–winning play. Like many of Williams's dramas, *A Streetcar Named Desire* focuses on issues of southernness played in tension with undercurrents of homosexuality and madness, but this work also underscores class frictions. The film is set in the French Quarter in New Orleans just after the close of World War II. In 1951, New Orleans was one of the South's—and, for that matter, the nation's—most multicultural cities, and we see and hear much of its mixed/"creole" heritage in the background of Kazan's film. Although conflicts over gender and sexuality often take center stage in scholarship on *Streetcar,* class divisions are foundational to the violent rift between Stanley Kowalski (Marlon Brando) and his sister-in-law, Blanche DuBois (Vivien Leigh). Because of severe financial straits, Blanche must leave what's left of the family plantation in rural Mississippi to live with her sister Stella (Kim Hunter) in a crowded apartment in the blue-collar district of New Orleans.

Economic divisions are emphasized early in the film by the contrast between *Belle Rêve,* the DuBois family's former plantation, and the cramped, dirty atmosphere of the Kowalskis' apartment in Elysian Fields. We discover as Stanley tears through the stack of attorneys' letters and bank notices in Blanche's traveling trunk that the plantation has been lost on a mortgage. There is a reason it is named *Belle Rêve* (French for "Beautiful Dream"): the economic impetus of the city has uprooted the presumably centuries-deep connection of the DuBois family with the country. The name also symbolizes how the white southern elite has fabricated the illusion of a placidly paternalistic plantation system, constructing the "beautiful dream" of landed gentry that masks the very real nightmare of racial subjugation; the white-columned façade of the Old South conceals the bleak economics of the slave labor that built those columns. Although the New South is less racially corrupt, it still carries elements of class imbalance. The remnants of the plantation have been lost to the banks, symbols of the impersonal, amorphous grid of urban bureaucratic capitalism. The land and what it represents—an agrarian system based on racially categorized slave labor ("Blanche," of course, means "white" in French)—are now paper thin. The old way of the South is incapable of surviving when set against the flux and productivity of urban life, with its Fordist mass manufacturing (Mitch works in "Spare Parts" for an unnamed factory in New Orleans), spreading networks of distribution (Stanley is a delivery man for the same factory) and diversified economy in all senses, including ethnically (Stanley is Polish, Pablo is Mexican, and a black woman speaks on equal terms with Eunice at the film's start). The plantation economy—as well as the accompanying illusionary mythos of the country as an idyllic respite for those at the top of the socioeconomic scale—seems a thing of the past.

Perceived differences in class status between Stanley and Blanche color each character's responses to the other. Stanley's hypermasculinity and sexually predatory nature are inseparable from his working-class affiliations. Economics are the crux of the divisions in the film: Stanley is Polish, boorish, and a working man, whereas Blanche is southern, all too refined, and a woman not accustomed to labor, even the middle-class intellectual work of a high school English teacher, a job she must vacate after she is embroiled in an affair with one of her students. Class lines are so pervasive in the film that each character's class identification is written on his or her body. Blanche is a blanched-out form of Scarlett O'Hara from *Gone with the Wind* (1939), a character also played by Leigh. Blanche is a hollow parody of the southern belle. While Scarlett, as her name suggests, is indeed fiery, full-blooded, and costumed in vivid dress against dynamic panoramas of the Technicolor Georgia countryside, Blanche's physical paleness and frailty are heightened by Kazan's mastery of black-and-white lighting techniques. Blanche repeatedly takes warm baths and sprays herself with perfume to cover any hint of the sweat of her brow. Stanley, on the other hand, is often covered in sweat and/or grime, physical emblems of his working-class bearings. In the famous scene when Stanley first meets Blanche, his undershirt is sopping with sweat since he has just returned from a highly competitive bowling match. Bowling is a typically working-class sport, and Stanley's league is particularly fierce: it is not uncommon for the competition to erupt into fistfights between rival bowlers. Stanley removes his shirt to make himself "comfortable" and avoid catching a cold, a coarse act that repulses Blanche socially but intrigues her sexually. The audience too has mixed emotions; the working class is marked as primitive, allowing space for both condescension toward Stanley as an unrefined inferior and for the projection of fantasy onto the bared body of the well-built Brando, an icon of primal sexuality.

Moreover, *Streetcar* is an actor-driven production, and the actorial styles further stress matters of class differentiation and conflict. Brando is notorious as one of the leading exemplars of "Method" acting, created by acting coach Constantin Stanislavski and developed in the 1940s and 1950s by Lee Strasberg at the Actors Studio in New York City. Method actors no longer take an objective, detached view of their characters, as in classical theater, but try to become personally invested in their roles to make them more emotionally charged and therefore more psychologically lifelike. Leigh, by contrast, was a classically trained actress. Both Brando and Leigh's performances are studies in extreme emotionalism; however, the Method provides Brando with a raw and violent emotiveness, while Leigh is awash in flighty abstractions and false conjectures of reality. Where Leigh is psychologically overwhelmed, unreal, Brando is psychologically overwhelming, too real. The power struggle between the once classy, now déclassé Blanche DuBois and the emergent force of the tough-minded, tough-bodied worker Stanley Kowalski plays out in the actors' very performance styles. Though his labor is assumed into the workings of a modern, urban-industrial environment, Stanley's performance unveils the underlying Darwinian struggle that continues to animate the economic impulses of postwar capitalism in the city. This animalistic drive is embodied darkly in Stanley's rape of Blanche, which devastates her brittle consciousness. The rape crushes Blanche's last-ditch fantasy of a financial deus ex machina in the form of "Shep Huntleigh," a millionaire southern gentleman whom Blanch "believes" is going to take her away from Elysian Fields and restore her to her proper station.

Even her exit to the state mental institution is couched in class terms. Now suffering a near-total break from reality, Blanche imagines the psychiatrist sent to subdue her is merely a kind stranger, another Shep Huntleigh-esque southern gentleman, whose gentle demeanor bespeaks gentility.

In *Deliverance*, John Boorman's filmic adaptation of James Dickey's bestselling 1970 novel, we are at once greeted with iconography that delineates the city from the country and, at the same time, the moneyed and comfortably middle class from the "dirt poor" working class. Although these strict boundaries ostensibly will be reasserted by the movie's end, the film also includes some potentially radical upheaval in terms of these accepted power lines, exposing the primal dynamics firing such stock divisions of labor. Between *Streetcar* and *Deliverance* there is a significant reversal in the spatial construction of class: where Kazan's film equates urban with working class and rural with privileged class, these divisions are inverted in Boorman's work—an inversion that reflects the changing economic history of the region as it (sub)urbanizes increasingly in the post–World War II era. The primitivist vision of class struggle is reinforced by the film's cinematic technique. Before taking on the project, Boorman had produced documentaries for the BBC and he uses a similar documentary style in bringing Dickey's narrative to the screen. The cinematography is plain, calling little attention to itself. The understated camera work heightens the experience of nature as a compelling, autonomous force, one that is never fully subservient to human artifice. The camera becomes essentially invisible, as the framework of modern technology recedes in order to stress more fully the unadulterated obduracy of the wild. Boorman used underwater cameras during the river scenes to showcase the visceral power of the rushing whitewater, presenting a memorable sense of what critic Casey Clabough has defined as the practice of "merging" in Dickey's work:

> Whereas the purely romantic artist must eventually back away from union with the other in order to preserve the self, Dickey has no qualms about giving his artistic self over entirely to the spirit or essence of the thing he beholds. Like Hegel, he believes that the individual who truly contemplates a subject/object is "absorbed" entirely by it, sacrificing all consciousness of the 'I,' and, through his artistic method, Dickey hopes to arrive at what Heidegger calls the phenomenological world view: a position in which the observer shuns traditional interpretation in favor of having the world reveal itself to him as it truly is ("things themselves!"). Intellect, preconceived sensibility, and the self—or as much of it as possible—must be forgotten or repressed to the extent that reality becomes perceptible in its rawest form. (9)

Just as the four main characters in *Deliverance* hope to merge with the overwhelming force of the natural world in this way, Boorman's bare-bones cinematography aids the viewer in recognizing this effort at transcendent merging.

The film's opening sequence intersperses images of untamed nature in the figure of a river with dialogue between four middle-aged men who are using a topographic map to plan a canoe trip on this waterway before it is dammed up to build a lake. We see immediately that the map, in its placid abstraction, will not adequately represent the primal flux of the river. The men—Ed Gentry (Jon Voight), Lewis Medlock (Burt Reynolds), Bobby Trippe (Ned Beatty), and Drew Ballinger (Ronnie Cox)—are city slickers, bourgeois types from Atlanta, that gleaming model of the tidily urbanized "New South" in the 1970s. They are itching for a weekend getaway in order to get in touch with their inner Tarzans. So they make the trek to rural Georgia, a land that seems to be not merely another place, but another time, far from modernity temporally as well as spatially, struck through with an irredeemable belatedness. As they travel into the Georgia wilderness, the men equate backwoods with backwards. They encounter what they view as a primitive culture, in large part because of its economic deprivation and lack of urbanity. Lewis sneeringly terms this segment of the Appalachian South "the country of nine-fingered people," referring to the genetic deficiencies and accident-prone lives/poor medical care stereotypically associated with southern backwoods dwellers or "hillbillies"—known today by the more politically correct term, *hillsmen.*

On the one side, the four city men wish to connect with primal, pristine nature by making this wilderness voyage to the river before it is ruined by modernity; on the other side, they are repulsed by the inhabitants and socioeconomic conditions of the southern backcountry. In the world of *Deliverance,* the desiccation of agriculture in the rural South has left little productive economic activity. As in Kazan's film, the actual labor of the working class goes largely unseen. We do meet a gas station operator who fills the tanks of the city-dwellers' station wagons, but business is obviously slow: it takes a long time to summon the operator and the pumps are rusted. The on-site house is in severe disrepair, its dissolution reinforced notably by the idiot savant "banjo boy" who plucks out a rendition of "Dueling Banjos" along with Drew, the most sensitive of the four urbanites. With the air of superiority of a modern anthropologist observing the "unusual" custom or dress of a primitive native, Bobby smugly tells the attendant, "Say, Mister, I love the way you wear that hat." The gulf of difference between them, the palpable division of class lines, cannot be crossed with such a facile and condescending effort at contact; the local flatly rejects this thinly veiled attempt to delineate and limit his social existence, responding bluntly, "You don't know nothing." Talked down to in this way, the territory talks back, but the hope of any productive communication across urban/ rural and monied/unmonied boundaries here ends in nothing.

Once the urban professionals set off in their canoes, the country— figured both as the wilderness itself in the force of the river and as the indigenous working class—strikes back with a vengeance. In the most (in) famous scene from the film, the four men encounter two armed hillsmen in the woods. Bobby is sodomized at gunpoint by one of the men, and Ed narrowly escapes a similar fate only because Lewis skillfully fires an arrow through the chest of one of the hillsmen with his compound bow. This scene has much to say about gender definitions (why is the image of male rape so culturally shattering, when cinematic representations of women being raped are pervasive?), but speaks importantly to class dynamics as well. In "The Great American Hunter, or, Ideological Content in the Novel" (1972), Fredric Jameson explores the ideological implications of this clash between the hillsmen and these four "typical professional men of the post-industrial world, men sophisticated enough to choose the good life of small business and a relatively rural environment, and to make the money they need at the same time that they appreciate folk music and camping" (184). Jameson argues that these hillsmen are leftovers from the 1930s, mere antiquated bogeymen that have been safely quarantined from the middle class, professional consciousness of the early 1970s:

> The hillbilly figures are of course a disguise and a displacement: for if the 1930's still call to mind that older indigenous heritage of American resistance and insubordination from Roger Williams to Eugene V. Debs, the threat to the middle-class way of life today has taken another form: that of the peoples of the Third World, of the Blacks, of the intransigent and disaffected young. . . . For the Thirties are dead, both figuratively and literally, and the triumph of the heroes over their class enemies can thus be draped in the mantle of historical necessity, the fantasy seeming to be confirmed by the very outcome of history itself. (185)

Per Jameson, the hillsmen offer a kind of ideological camouflage, for "since the beginning of the civil rights movement, the redneck as a political symbol has changed his meaning, and tends rather to set in motion associations of knownothingism and reaction, than of the agrarian populism of an older era" (185). Ultimately, he interprets *Deliverance*'s sleight-of-hand in giving us these outworn villains as a typical strategy of reactionary bourgeois art:

"the propertied classes have always understood the revolutionary process as a lawless outbreak of mob violence, wanton looting, vendettas motivated by ignorance, senseless hatred and *ressentiment*, terms which are here translated into degeneracy and general disrespect for life" (186). The four urban professionals are thereby "justified" in their reactionary violence against the backcountry men, and *Deliverance* offers us "a fantasy about class struggle in which the middle-class American property owner wins through to a happy ending" (186). However, the film version adds sinister strains to this supposed victory, darkening the supposed "happy" ending. On a purely structural level, Ed Gentry does win out—if winning is defined as surviving—but the rest of the middle-class American property owners are not merely marked, but marred irrevocably by their experience in the backcountry: Bobby is raped, Drew loses his life on the river, and Lewis, the physically most adept member of the foursome, is in the hospital with a crushed leg—he literally will not be able to simply walk away from this.

Furthermore, the hillsmen have cultural gravitas precisely as unexorcised specters of the rural working class. The return of the socioeconomically repressed is signaled in the film's ending. The sheer hostility expressed by the hillsmen outlasts the thin bourgeois victory, which amounts to mere survivalism. Because of Boorman's terse cinematographic style and emphasis on spare realism, we find the film's closing image all the more jolting. Now safely returned to the Atlanta suburbs, Ed suffers a post-traumatic nightmare, startled awake by an image we initially view as real: the hand of the dead hillsman bursting through the placid surface of the newly constructed lake. As Ed regains his senses and collects his consciousness, we too realize that this is "only a dream," and yet we are left with the unsettling memory of this haunting figure. Not much of a happy ending, the closing image offers no closure, but the threat of further reiterations of the post-traumatic nightmare. It leaves bleak implications hovering in the darkness of Ed's suburban bedroom: the divisions we create between the real and the imagined are thinning considerably, just as the starkly demarcated cultural spaces between the city/affluent, progressive middle class and the country/abject, degenerate working class are also destabilized. No longer invisible labor, out of time and out of mind, the hillsman's image echoes fiercely in Ed Gentry's gentrified consciousness, violently suturing the city to the country and the middle to the working class. Psychologically, he also will not be able to simply walk away from his confrontation with his socioeconomic other; from this, there will be no psychic deliverance.

In the Coen brothers' *O Brother, Where Art Thou?*, we again see cinematic holdovers from the 1930s proletariat, visualized remnants of the Depression-era South. Yet in opposition to the uncanny, traumatic presence of the hillsmen in Boorman's film, the Coen brothers convert socioeconomic conflicts into comedy, turning fears over class divisions to laughter. *O Brother, Where Art Thou?* is a comedy in both its root meanings: (1) it contains plenty of humor (it is "ha-ha" funny) and (2) it also comes to a harmonious conclusion where earlier tensions and conflicts—particularly those over economic disparity and grasping to upgrade one's class position—are resolved happily. The film's title is taken from director Preston Sturges's *Sullivan's Travels* (1941), in which a big-time director named John Lloyd Sullivan plans to make a sad and gloomy picture entitled *O Brother, Where Art Thou?* Sullivan's film will be full of gritty social realism and depict accurately the harsh struggles of the working class. The director is told by his producers that, because of his life of privilege, he knows nothing about suffering and poverty, so he decides to go undercover as a hobo. Although this experiment in class "passing" does not go as planned, Sullivan eventually reemerges from obscurity to make a triumphal return to the movie industry. Yet he finds that he no longer wishes to make tragic motion pictures, despite the fact that news reports of his adventures as a hobo have created a massive public relations buzz for his upcoming film. Instead, Sullivan now wants to produce only comedies in order to make people laugh and therefore lighten their emotional burdens in the Great Depression. Ethan and Joel Coen's version of *O Brother, Where Art Thou?* follows the pattern of Sturges's film on at least these two levels: it is indeed a comic work, though it nevertheless speaks to serious matters of class division and conflict, even if it does so with tongue firmly in cheek.

Several of the episodes in *O Brother, Where Art Thou?* are based (at times rather loosely) on Odysseus's 10 years of wandering as he attempted to return home to Ithaca after the end of the Trojan War. But these events are reset in 1930s Mississippi, which becomes something of a microcosm for the far end of economic hard times under modern capitalism. The movie describes the escape of three convicts from a chain gang—Ulysses Everett McGill (George Clooney), Pete Hogwallop (John Turturro), and Delmar O'Donnell (Tim Blake Nelson)—and their adventures as Everett attempts to make his way home to wife Penny (Holly Hunter) and gaggle of young daughters. The men, especially Pete and Delmar, are walking types of southern "white trash." Everett claims leadership of the three convicts by declaring that he is "the one with the capacity for abstract thought," diminishing the intelligence of his partners in crime: he has been convicted of a white-collar crime—practicing law without a license—while Pete and Delmar are strictly blue collar. Indeed, Delmar's neck is marked with a bright shade of red: he is a farmer by trade who lost the family land to the banks.

While we do have some shots of actual hard labor being performed by members of a chain gang, the working class down South is depicted with sarcasm in *O Brother*. Unlike the hillsmen in Boorman's film, these rednecks have been sapped of any sense of threat, more buffoons than beasts. The Coen brothers are known for storyboarding each scene before they shoot it—that is, drawing or sketching the particular camera angles and mise-en-scène for each sequence on placards beforehand to create a series of illustrations or "cartoons" that serve as models to help them visualize each scene they will shoot. Many of the scenes seem purposefully *over*drawn, the characters' over-the-top actions and expressions appear themselves cartoonish (e.g., the three convicts, still chained together in leg irons, popping up and down among the fields or falling off a moving boxcar together). The Coens' technique offers a further twist between the cartoonish scenarios and the grandiose visual scale of the film. The movie was shot in widescreen, a format usually reserved for epic films such as *Ben Hur* (1959), *Spartacus* (1960), and *Braveheart* (1995), thereby making *O Brother, Where Art Thou?,* to borrow Ethan Coen's terms, "the *Lawrence of Arabia* of hayseed movies" ("Director's Commentary"). This disjunction between form and content creates a level of ironic deflation between larger-than-life cinematography and diminished subject matter. Hayseeds aren't the stuff of epics, the movie quips, offering a bitingly parodic view of the country working class down South.

O Brother, Where Art Thou? provides a *tableau vivant* of the South at the presumed end of its history, as what has been construed the nation's most distinctive region has become increasingly "Americanized" and even globalized. The movie invokes southern history as a virtual reality, producing a computer-generated image of the region. As Roger Deakins, the film's director of photography, succinctly put it, the motion picture aims to create a vision of the "Dust-Bowl" South where "the color is a character" ("Director's Commentary"), creating digital effects that move South by Midwest, grafting Steinbeck's (or John Ford's) Dust Bowl onto Yoknapatawpha County. By computer-enhancing the film's color, *O Brother* creates a Depression-era South digitally airbrushed with an old timey feel, a product of simulation. Playing against the mythic background of Homer's *Odyssey,* the film records the transformation of the region from a site of classical to Faulknerian to mock epic. Despite—or because of—the movie's touting of a marketable brand of folksiness (witness the massive commercial sensation of its southern folk-laden soundtrack), *O Brother* trots out the ruins of the traditional South (at least as commonly portrayed in literary texts and cultural artifacts) as mere set furniture, the gravitas of its white-columned past wrecked and buried in the underbrush—visualized literally as our main characters sit around a campfire with broken white columns, overgrown with briars, in the woods behind them.

The film reflects several motifs associated with the white southern working class. The escaped convicts display an abiding dedication to the homeplace, demonstrated by Everett's voyage home to Penny and his return to the old homestead about to be flooded into oblivion by the Tennessee Valley Authority, as well as the repeated shots that feature the landscape, as if it were itself a primary character. The agrarian focus of the southern working-class economy is seen in Delmar's claim that "You ain't no kind of man if you ain't got land." With the (purely invented) hidden stash of money to which Everett is supposedly leading his fellow escapees, Delmar will buy his family farm back from the banks and resume working the fields. The emphasis on family and kinship ties is seen in Pete's devotion to his Hogwallop cousin, Wash, even after being betrayed to the police at his hands, as he hotly defends his kin against Everett's act of stealing Wash's gold watch. The working-class "essence" of the main characters is further stressed through dialect in the exaggerated southern accents of the characters as well as the setting—1930s Mississippi, what H. L. Mencken notably named "The Worst American State." In the background of the main action, political demagogue Homer Stokes shills loudly for the support of "the little man." This political platitude is comically manifested in the figure of a little person standing next to Homer wielding a broom to symbolize the working man's desire to sweep the incumbent gubernatorial rival, Pappy O'Daniel, right out of office. Moreover, the Coen brothers' film also includes references to working-class characters from specific southern literary texts. Wash Hogwallop seems born of the "white trash" tenant farmer Wash Jones in *Absalom, Absalom!* (1936), while the one-eyed Bible salesman "Big Dan" Teague (John Goodman) is a merging of Homer's Polyphemus and Flannery O'Connor's Manley Pointer from "Good Country People" (1955). In ironic fashion, *O Brother* places the above clichés in an added set of quotation marks, paralleling Michael Kreyling's argument that the South's "familiar way of making and maintaining meaning, its orthodoxy or consensus, had ceased functioning, as it were, on involuntary muscles and had become a kind of willed habit" (1).

This persistent sense of parody is apparent as the three men travel, still chained to one another, to the farm of Pete's cousin, Wash Hogwallop.

The homeplace looks like it has materialized from one of Walker Evans's Depression-era photographs, digitally retouched. The American South is pictured here as if it is a "primitive" Third World territory within the geopolitical confines of the "modern" First World nation. A boy meets the men on the dirt road in front of a falling-down shack, shotgun gripped tightly in his hands and he fires off a series of warning shots at the approaching strangers.

Child:	You men from the bank?
Pete:	You Wash's boy?
Child:	Yassir! And Daddy tolt me I'm to shoot whosoever from the bank!
Delmar:	Well, we ain't from no bank, young feller.
Child:	Yassir! I'm also suppose to shoot folks servin' papers!
Delmar:	Well we ain't got no papers.
Child:	Yassir! I nicked the census man!
Delmar:	There's a good boy. Is your daddy about?

The boy offers some resistance, though couched in comedy, to the political economy of market capitalism, making a stand, though one that we know is only momentary, against the federalist incursions of bureaucratic representatives from the bank, the law ("folks servin' papers"), and the government (the census as a means of interpolating citizens as taxpayers). In the figure of the Hogwallop boy, the working class is seen as covered in dust and bluster, no real threat to the federalist powers that be. When we meet Wash over dinner, he delivers a litany of bad news, comic in its very excessiveness as it crams together a host of apocryphal Depression-era woes that concretizes the Hogwallops as pure types, total crackers:

Wash:	They foreclosed on Cousin Vester. He hanged himself a year come May.
Pete:	And Uncle Ratliff?
Wash:	The anthrax took most of his cows. The rest don't milk, and he lost a boy to mumps.
Pete:	Where's Cora, Cousin Wash?
Wash:	Couldn't say. Mrs. Hogwallop up and R-U-N-N-O-F-T.
Everett:	Mm. Must've been lookin' for answers.
Wash:	Possibly. Good riddance, far as I'm concerned. . . . I do miss her cookin' though.
Delmar:	This stew's awful good.
Wash:	Think so? I slaughtered this horse last Tuesday; I'm afraid she's startin' to turn.

The sting is taken out of these hard times through the film's overriding parody. The events are as sad as they are true; given the comic overtones of the scene, they don't ring very true and therefore aren't very sad. The connection between economic depression and personal despair is treated light-heartedly here. Perhaps the comic tone helps to lighten the burdensome history of poverty among the rural working class, but one might also argue that making light of severe deprivation allows us to laugh off the memory of the Depression as well as the threat of a possible recurrence of such economic collapse.

The TVA flood at the end of the film is notably ambiguous. Does it offer some slight salvation for the severe financial hardships of the Depression down South? Or is it just another form of damnation? The artificial deluge suggests that the New Deal South is going to usher in a New South that, while more racially integrated, is in danger of becoming culturally disintegrated, stretched too thin over the grid of federal economic expansion. In the words of our mock hero, Everett, the federal government's plans to "hydroelectric up the whole durned state" will sweep away the South's longstanding—and sometimes backward-facing—social and cultural values, its regional identity lost to the technological matrix of flexible capitalist expansion. This concept is celebrated by Everett in the wake of the flood that rescues him and his fellow ex-cons from a lynching at the hands of the sheriff and his deputies. Holding fast to a rolltop desk while bobbing on the currents of the just-made lake, he spouts the clichés of a federalist paradigm of regional redemption through the progress of the nation-state:

Yessir, the South is gonna change. Everything's gonna be put on electricity and run on a payin' basis. Out with the old spiritual mumbo-jumbo, the superstitions and the backward ways. We're gonna see a brave new world where they run everyone a wire and hook us all up to a grid. Yessir, a veritable age of reason—like the one they had in France—and not a moment too soon. (106)

Yielding to the onrush of such transregional economic networks may lead to disconnectedness through overconnectedness. That is, hooking the South up to the federal grid may overwrite local values, dissolving the sense of a distinct southern culture. Indeed, the TVA's deliberate flooding of farmland physically as well as psychologically displaced inhabitants from long-held family lands. The film provides the unsettling recognition that, in the aftermath of such federalist reterritorialization of the South, capital may be left as the primary authenticating force. The "little man" whose vote the political figures court in their campaigns for governor may well get further washed away in the flood, a comic version of what happens to the hillsmen in *Deliverance*. Nationalism of the economy, hooking up the South to a federal web, may be little more than a shell game of shifting around class imbalances, keeping the region and especially its laboring class in a subalternate position.

John Hillcoat's 2009 film version of Cormac McCarthy's Pulitzer Prize–winning novel *The Road* imagines the aftermath of the failure of the global political economy. In essence, it realizes Lewis Medlock's apocalyptic vision in *Deliverance*. Lewis lifts weights and learns to bowhunt, he tells Ed on their trip into the backwoods, because he believes "that the whole thing is going to be reduced to the human body, once and for all," for "the machines are going to fail, the political systems are going to fail, and a few men are going to take to the hills and start over." What Ed Gentry considers a delusional fantasy in Boorman's film indeed comes to pass in the world of *The Road*. In its creation of a postapocalyptic earth filled with environmental catastrophe, abject poverty, and cannibalistic savagery, Hillcoat's film envisions the U.S. South at the nonredemptive extremity of hard times. The movie extends the region's stereotypical backwardness outward and everywhere, imagining a world of collapsing infrastructures—political, economic, social, physical—and a reversion to primitive conditions on a global scale. As the father and his young son journey through the desolate relics of east Tennessee down to the coastline of what used to be the southeastern United States, we see the splintering of what remains of regional and national economic systems; in place of the abstractions of the late capitalism matrix, we have a regression to a blunt Darwinian grab for survival. In this starkly postnational, postregional world of ecological ruin, "south" designates little more than the direction taken by father and son on a threadbare roadmap. The former class structure has evaporated: all survivors are now constant laborers, part of an endless working class. This is a vision of truly classless society, and it is as terrifying as it is bleak.

One of the movie's tacit, but most powerful effects is to demonstrate how economics are bound inextricably to ecology. Even though the mountains and the coastline are still there in Hillcoat's film, most geopolitical markers of the South and the nation have disintegrated amid the chaos of massive climate change and phenological devastation. Indeed, George Monbiot calls McCarthy's novel "the most important environmental book ever written," asserting that this "thought experiment exposes the one terrible fact to which our technological hubris blinds us: our dependence on biological production remains absolute" (1). Assigning the ecological cataclysm of the narrative to the consequences of "nuclear winter," Monbiot aptly describes the fall from civilization to primitivism, as "all pre-existing codes soon collapse and are replaced with organised butchery, then chaotic, blundering horror" (1). When "the only remaining resource is human," civilization is "just a russeting on the skin of the biosphere, never immune from being rubbed against the sleeve of environmental change" (1).

In Hillcoat's setting, the South is a land now truly beyond time, a region outstripped of the temporal flows of modernity and nationhood, leaving primitive survivalism as the zero sum game of the current economic system, if "system" is even the right word for it. The film follows father and son through a charred wasteland dimmed by the constant sift of gray ash down from sunless skies. The film shows how the catastrophic lobotomizing of environmental memory leads to the eradication of "the land" as an anchor of traditional regional identity. The postapocalyptic South has been denuded of regionalist and nationalist formations. In the center of this radically decentered postrural, posturban culture is work, now stripped of its traditional class associations: in this classless "society," hard labor becomes meaningful again, not simply in the fight for physical subsistence, but as a means for rebooting the moral underpinnings of our life's work. The father and son endure fierce hardship as they make a living merely living. The abstractions of excess accumulation have buckled violently into ruin, and in their place is the hard work of empathy, as father and son work not for self-interest but for one another. The film stresses the value of other-directed reciprocity under the extreme stresses of such conditions. It takes an almost total unraveling of market values in order to redeem the value of good works.

Save for a few brighter flashbacks to the time before the catastrophe hit, Javier Aguirresarobe's spare, at times almost monochrome, cinematography is appropriate to the dark matter of the film's content, projecting a pastiche of washed-out landscapes in dull hues. Dialogue is sparse, primarily coming piecemeal in terse conversations between father and son. The musical score, composed by Nick Cave and Warren Ellis, is equally bare, as the film stresses the overwhelming silence of this postapocalyptic world. The repetitiveness of the film mirrors the redundancy of the main characters' existence, a motif given visual form in the movie's recurrent images of father and son pushing a shopping cart through a variety of decimated scenes. The cart is a perfect symbol for what has become of late capitalism, a last remnant of the supermarket, that nexus of product placement and processed food. The cart, now loaded only with the things the two require for survival, shows the stripping away of abstract codes of value derived from the market. As an extension of the supermarket, the cart once represented the confluence of mass production and networks of distribution that greased the wheels of consumption en masse. Now, by contrast, the shopping cart has replaced ease of consumerism with its polar opposite: its wobbly wheels mark the sheer duration of endurance enacted daily, hourly by father and son in a world bereft of large-scale manufacturing and processing plants and national, even global grids for distribution. They've lost their identities as consumers and are now purely scavengers, constantly laboring for mere survival.

The film's depiction of father and son's endless grind to scavenge enough necessities to live to work another day is kept interesting by the unremitting fear that savagery will erupt at the next moment. The continuous difficulty they confront in hunting-and-gathering for food, shelter, and clothing is thus compounded by the proximity of intense suffering and death. The deeper sense of absence wrought by both plotline and technique is occasionally broken by chaotic action, as the film's gray tedium is punctuated violently with sharp episodes of trauma: the father has to fire a gunshot through the head of a man holding a knife to his son's throat, the two narrowly escape capture at a "farm"/slaughterhouse run by cannibals whose livestock is humans, the father is wounded by an arrow from a primitive bow, and so on. The pervasive threat of cannibalism converts the symbolic cannibalism of the "dog-eat-dog" impulse of modern capitalism into a "man-eat-man" world of pure survival. Hillcoat's film envisions a region where old boundaries between rural and urban no longer exist, thereby taking to its outer edge the idea of class strivings as a manifestation of a primal penchant for dominance.

And yet, despite all its postapocalyptic sound and fury and grim clashes, the movie also strikes a more hopeful tone by framing the question: in the absence of market values, where do our moral values derive from? Once the economics of class-driven capitalism have failed, does this offer the possibility of creating a system of ethics beyond the taint of abstract economics? Although the elimination of class hierarchies seems to end in sheer nightmare in the film, perhaps it gives us this desperate vision as a kind of cultural *memento mori,* warning us that we need to find a better middle ground between the extremes of modernity and total degeneracy into primitivism. The ethics of reciprocity between father and son takes us beyond sheer self-interest as the primal reason for being and constructs an alternative model of other-directed actions, what the father calls "goodness."

All four of these iconic films use region, and more particularly the partitions of city and country, as testing grounds for cathected issues of class definition and division. The "Americanization" of the South—the region's shift from an agrarian economy to more industrial and postindustrial structures in combination with the spread of urban and suburban zones— enables a diverse continuum of class dynamics, which are reflected and at times critiqued onscreen. The equation of the country with the economically elite via the Old South's plantation economy is roughly overturned in the bustling, brutal cacophony of the urban environment in Kazan's film, which is in turn reversed in Boorman's film, with the opposition of the citified bourgeois set against the bad country people. The backwards inhabitants of the rural South are laughed to scorn in *O Brother,* as parody saps away some of the historical threat of the rural underclass. However, the repressed figure of class violence returns in *The Road,* where the decimation of the physical and conceptual structures of late capitalism equally razes socioeconomic hierarchy, placing everyone in a subsistence-level class. In their images of crudeness and savagery beget by the "lower orders," these films share a penchant for primitivizing the working class. *The Road* is arguably the most obvious version of this recurrent theme coursing through these prominent films about the American South in which class conflict is defined in Darwinian terms as a primitive struggle for advantage, if not survival. However, with respect to its concern for empathetic sentiment and action expressed between the father and the son, it may, paradoxically, be the most hopeful of these works.

Works Cited

Bone, Martyn. *The Postsouthern Sense of Place in Contemporary Fiction.* Baton Rouge: Louisiana State University Press, 2005.

Clabough, Casey Howard. *Elements: The Novels of James Dickey.* Macon, GA: Mercer University Press, 2002.

Deliverance. Dir. John Boorman. Perf. Jon Voight, Burt Reynolds, Ned Beatty, and Ronny Cox. Warner Brothers, 1972.

"Director's Commentary." *O Brother, Where Art Thou?* Dir. Ethan Coen and Joel Coen. Perf. George Clooney, John Turturro, Tim Blake Nelson, and Holly Hunter. Touchstone, 2002.

Jameson, Fredric. "The Great American Hunter, or, Ideological Content in the Novel." *College English* 34:2 (1972): 180–97.

Kreyling, Michael. "Fee, Fie, Faux Faulkner: Parody and Postmodernism in Southern Literature." *Southern Review* 29:1 (1993): 1–15.

Monbiot, George. "Civilisation Ends with a Shutdown of Human Concern. Are We There Already?" *The Guardian* (October 30, 2007): 1–3. http://www.guardian.co.uk/commentisfree/2007/oct/30/comments.books.

O Brother, Where Art Thou? Dir. Ethan Coen and Joel Coen. Perf. George Clooney, John Turturro, Tim Blake Nelson, and Holly Hunter. Touchstone, 2000.

The Road. Dir. John Hillcoat. Perf. Viggo Mortensen, Kodi Smti-McPhee, Charlize Theron, Robert Duvall, and Guy Pearce. Dimension Films, 2009.

A Streetcar Named Desire. Dir. Elia Kazan. Perf. Vivien Leigh, Marlon Brando, Kim Hunter, and Karl Malden. Warner Brothers, 1951.

Chapter 8

Working-Class Children: Disappearing from Contemporary American Children's Films

Iris G. Shepard

Children's films are sites of ideological transmission between adults and children. Elizabeth Freeman in "Monster's Inc: Notes on the Neoliberal Arts Education" sees children's films as "portable professors" that enculturate children while, simultaneously, allowing adults a deeper look into our society's ideologies (85). Jillian Hinkins in "'Biting the Hand That Feeds': Consumerism, Ideology, and Recent Animated Film for Children" states, "Filmic text is embedded with ideologies and often has specific didactic intentions" (49). Henry Giroux in *The Mouse That Roared* writes: "Media culture is a substantial educational force in regulating meanings, values, and tastes" (2–3). Children's films instruct children on how to both perform childhood and find their place in an adult world by dramatizing imaginary relationships between children and all facets of their lived experience. Althusser describes the imagined relationship established by ideology between individuals and their lives: "What is represented in ideology is therefore not the system of real relations which govern the existence of individuals but the imaginary relationships of individuals to their real condition of existence" (162). Notably, the imaginary relationships that children's films have been building between children and the issue of class over the past three decades seem to be more ideologically conservative and reactionary than in previous decades. Contemporary children's films are examples of what Roland Barthes describes as the "bourgeois myth." These films appeal to a generalized humanity by obscuring social ills such as gender inequalities, racial discrimination, and the very existence of the lower social classes. While the issues of racial discrimination and gender inequality seem, at least ostensibly, to be having some limited treatment in recent children's films (think Tiana, the first African American princess, in Disney's 2010 "princess film" *The Princess and the Frog*), the issue of social class has gone primarily ignored in recent, mainstream live action and animated children's films. Many recent children's films, most notably the films produced by Disney and its subsidiary Pixar, continue to focus their films on middle- and upper-class protagonists.

For representations of the working class in children's films, 2010 was an especially bad year. Most children's films such as *Tron: Legacy, Harry Potter and the Deathly Hallows,* and *The Tooth Fairy* ignored the issue of social class entirely while others such as *Shrek: Forever After, How to Train a Dragon,* and *Toy Story 3* alluded briefly to a specific character's working-class roots dismissively as something the protagonists were destined to transcend. Disney's 2010 animated/live action film *Tron: Legacy* completely ignores the working class with its focus on Sam Flynn, the son of legendary Kevin Flynn, owner of ENCOM Corporation and creator of a virtual world known as the Grid. In *Tron: Legacy* Kevin is abducted by his own virtual world, and his son Sam attempts a rescue. The film has little plot beyond this, and so it relies on stunning, lavish computer-generated technological effects. In fact, this film could easily not be seen as a children's film except for the fact that it was marketed to children viewers in advertisement of its release in children's television shows and previews for other children's films and in the extensive comarketing that targeted children consumers. In both *Tron: Legacy*'s real world and the virtual world of the Grid, Sam is in a place of privilege because of his father's extensive estate and computer genius. This computer genius that Kevin and Sam possess, viewers are left to surmise, results from a genetic proclivity and unlimited access to cutting-edge technology. *Tron: Legacy* provides an example of one reason that the working class is increasingly being pushed from children's films. Over the past three decades ever-increasing technological inventions have been a major subject of children's films, and access to technology depends, to a certain extent, on wealth and opportunities often afforded by wealth. Sam Flynn has access to the virtual world created by his father and the technological access and leisure time afforded him because of his wealth.

Several 2010 children's films include characters with working-class roots, but the issue of social class is only treated marginally. For example, Shrek has "working-class" roots, and in *Shrek Forever After,* his one wish is to return to his working-class bachelor, prefatherhood days before becoming a king. This wish is granted, and the results for Shrek are disastrous. He spends the rest of the film trying to win Fiona's heart again, storm the castle, and regain his place of privilege. Hiccup, the protagonist of Dreamworks' *How to Train a Dragon,* is the Viking chief's son, but a series of misadventures and his puny size resulted in a lowly apprenticeship to a blacksmith. His thankless job echoes the position of working-class children; however, because of his ability to fearlessly communicate with dragons, he regains a position of honor in his village. In these major theatrical releases, the narratives focus on protagonists privileged by either wealth or parentage or characters who overcome their working-class roots. The real issues facing the working class are obscured.

There was one major theatrical release listed in the top 10 children's movies of 2010 that briefly treats the issue of social privilege, if not the issue of social class. Dreamworks' *Megamind,* directed by Tom McGrath and featuring the voices of Will Ferrel, Brad Pitt, and Tina Fey, tells the story of the supervillain Megamind who was sent to Earth by his parents to escape the black hole that was causing his home planet to collapse. Megamind was heading to a wealthy home with nurturing, attentive parents in Metrocity until his space pod was forced off course by the escape pod of another infant who would become Megamind's archrival: the superhero Metro Man. Megamind's space pod lands in a prison yard, and he is raised by Metrocity's criminals. At school he is ridiculed because of his strange home life, his clothes, and his appearance. Every attempt he makes to fit in with his peers and win the approval of his teacher fails miserably, so Megamind decides that the only thing he is good at is being bad. He becomes a supervillain and terrifies the citizens of Metrocity. The rest of the movie focuses on his gradual realization that he doesn't want to continue always being the bad guy. In the end, he and his sidekick Minion, a piranhalike fish in a robot suit, are able to save Metrocity from a supervillian. Megamind is hailed as the new hero of the city.

The first 10 minutes of *Megamind* offer a pretty direct critique of the role of wealth, privilege, and social class in shaping the character of an individual. Megamind, the film seems to say, would have turned out differently if he had had the same social advantages as his archrival Metro Man. The film directly contradicts one of the main messages of Disney's children's films. Keith Booker in *Disney, Pixar, and the Hidden Messages in Children's*

Films states that Disney films focus on characters that are predetermined or somehow destined to assume a certain position in life. In the nurture versus nature argument, Disney comes down on the side of nature. This emphasis of nature over nurture is seen in Disney's very first feature-length film *Snow White* up through *Tron: Legacy.* In *Snow White,* despite the attempt on her life and the backwoods refuge with the dwarves and animals in the middle of the forest, Snow White still gets the prince because, the film insists, she was destined to become a queen; it was in her nature. Dreamworks, the distributor of *Megamind,* Booker observes, has repeatedly challenged some of the dominant ideologies of Disney. In *Megamind* Dreamworks weighs in about the importance of nurture in shaping a character's life. If Megamind had received the same privileged conditions as Metro Man, he wouldn't have devoted himself to a life of crime. Disney's repeated focus on nature over nurture in children's films can lead to an irresponsible approach to social problems. Since, for example, working-class children have limited access to certain privileged aspects of society such as education, travel, certain careers and other opportunities, the ideology supported by Disney seems to imply that working-class children's inability to succeed as dramatically as privileged children is not the fault of their society but, instead, a personal flaw. Disney's consistent emphasis on nature over nurture may be a reason why working-class children haven't gotten much screen time.

Children's films have not always relied on upper- and middle-class protagonists and depictions of worlds that required substantial wealth to join. In fact, in the early days, film was used as a form of social criticism, especially of classism. Robert Sklar in *Movie-Made America,* states: "They [movies] were the first of the modern mass media, and they rose to the surface of cultural consciousness from the bottom up, receiving their principal support from the lowest and most invisible classes in America. . . . The urban workers, the immigrants and the poor had discovered a new medium of entertainment without the aid, and indeed beneath the notice of the custodians and arbiters of middle-class culture" (3–4). The first 40 to 50 years of children's films, from the silent films of the 1890s through the post–World War II era, include several films that focus on working-class kids including *Oliver Twist* (1912), Chaplin's *The Tramp* (1915) and *The Kid* (1921), and the *Our Gang* series of films (1922–1944, also known as *The Little Rascals*). Several films from the silent era actually depict social problems experienced by working-class children such as child labor, child abuse, and overly large families because of inadequate birth control methods. These films include *Children Who Labor* (1912), *The Blood of the Children* (1915), *Where Are My Children?* (1916), *Broken Blossoms* (1919), and *The Hand That Rocks the*

Cradle (1917). After World War II, children's films became more conservative. Ian Wojcik-Andrews describes the ideological shift that occurred in children's films after World War II:

> Unsurprisingly, in the post–World War II era, we see children's cinema and film emerge as a site of phenomenal commercial success and deep ideological commitment to conservative family values. Corporate Hollywood's use of film to highlight social injustice, so prevalent in the silent era and the early 1930s, fades entirely from the post-World War II era. Film as a tool for promoting social equality is assigned to Italian Neorealism (1940s), Third Worldism and Black Cinema (1980s and 1990s), Independents and women directors (1980s and 1990s). In the post–World War II era, Hollywood got in it for the money alone. (73)

After World War II children's films began moving away from depictions of working-class children to focus primarily on the imagined children of the middle and upper classes. While the 1960s did produce some films that reflected First World countercultural changes, creating what Wojcik-Andrews terms a "schizoid" image of the child (meaning that both conservative and progressive politics were present in children's films simultaneously), the past three decades have witnessed a regressive and conservative backlash to those limited changes.

Since its inception in the early 1930s, Disney has been at the forefront in producing and distributing animated films. Throughout its 80 years in children's film production, Disney has become an icon of American culture and a disseminator of middle-class family values. Disney's conceptualization of childhood has helped shape America's definition of childhood since the 1930s. Giroux states, "Disney defines the US as a white/ideological construct, suburban, middle-class and heterosexual" (127). This definition of childhood is evidenced in the imagined viewing audience. "Walt Disney and his successors recognized the importance of catering to families, but they were not interested in catering to all families but to conventional, white, middle-class, heterosexual families" (Giroux 40–41). Giroux continues, "These films produce representations and codes through which children are taught that characters which do not bear the imprint of white, middle-class ethnicity are culturally deviant, inferior, unintelligent and a threat" (103). Children who fit into Disney's definition of childhood were further indoctrinated into their role as children by these films. Children who did not fit into this definition were further marginalized.

Not only do children learn how they should perform childhood through watching children's films, but viewers and critics of children's films can see shifts in how our culture envisions children and childhood. Kathy Jackson states: "By looking at the image of children on the screen, one can gain insight into the changing beliefs about the child" (8). One main shift that seems to be occurring is a shift away from the importance of gaining adultlike qualities, say, for example, the appreciation of hard work as advanced in Disney's *Snow White*, toward a more complete devaluation of childhood. Children are encouraged to become miniature adults. Wojcik-Andrews states that the children's films of the 1990s ignore the pressing social problems facing children. He asserts that there is a growing gulf between the cinematic depictions of children and children's lived experiences (108, 111). This tendency of ignoring pressing social problems facing children has grown in the twenty-first century. For example, Pixar films have taken children out of children's films. How can there be a meaningful treatment of problems children are facing without children protagonists? The tremendous financial success of the Pixar films undoubtedly indicates that depictions of children—whether human or anthropomorphized animals or objects— are not a necessary component of successful children's films. In Pixar films, child protagonists are replaced with primarily adult anthropomorphized characters including toys, ants, fish, cars, rats, and robots. As Pixar excludes child characters repeatedly from its blockbuster films, a pattern seems to be emerging. Childhood is not valued as much as adulthood; children are encouraged to identify fully with adult characters' struggle with adult feelings and adult emotions instead of identifying with children characters who have adultlike qualities. Children are encouraged to grow into adulthood more quickly. Several of Disney's live action/computer-generated films also reveal this tendency. Disney's *Tron: Legacy* (discussed earlier) features a 27-year-old protagonist, Sam Flynn. Sam is nine when his father disappears. But after the opening five minutes back story, the focus is on the adult Sam. Children are disappearing from children's films, and as the overall number of children in both animated and live action children films diminishes, most working-class children have been cut from children's films.

Another pattern is observable in contemporary children's film. As children are being steered toward adulthood earlier and earlier through the portrayal of older protagonists in children's films, children are also being increasingly valued for their role as consumers in our society. Children have been the target of marketers since the 1930s, but marketing that directly targets child consumers grows each year. Jack Zipes in *Happily Ever After* writes: "Most importantly for Disney and other producers of fairy-tale films was the manner in which they could 'hook' children as consumers not because they believed their films had artistic merit and could contribute to children's cultural development, but because they wanted to control children's aesthetic interests and consumer tastes" (91). The main goal of the producers and distributors of children's films, even more than the transmission of ideology, is to secure a greater and greater profit. Several factors in the history of children's films have contributed to the increasing focus on the profitability of children's films. Wojick-Andrews states, "The 1960s are an important decade in the history of children's cinema and film. The ownership of the studios passes from individuals to individual corporations" (95). In the late 1970s and 1980s, children's films were doing poorly in the box office, but since the reinvention of Disney and the advent of "New Disney" in 1989 with *The Little Mermaid* and *Beauty and the Beast* in 1991, children's films have become a hugely profitable market. The increasing desire to secure a profit limits the portrayal of working-class children in two important ways. First, films attempt to reach the largest possible viewing audience. Jacqueline Rose in *The Case of Peter Pan, or The Impossibility of Children's Fiction* states that the desire to appeal to all children "serves to close off a set of cultural divisions, divisions in which not only children, but we ourselves are necessarily caught" (7). The desire to create a text with a blanket audience appeal results in films that obscure all differences and divisions of race, class, and gender. Second, because children are being increasingly desired as consumers they are depicted in children's film as consumers. The act of consumption is one of the main ways that the protagonists of children's films, whether they are anthropomorphized characters or played by actors (frequently adults), are shown to be powerful. In Pixar's *Cars,* for example, the plot revolves around consumption. The cars are shown buying organic fuel, going out to the diner, and purchasing new tires. These filmic acts of consumption encourage children viewers to associate the acts of consumption with being a powerful individual, a.k.a. an adult. Simultaneously, by viewing the film and purchasing the accompanying merchandise, children are consumers in their lived experience. Making a profit by depicting children as consumers and then providing opportunities and comarketing merchandise for them to actually become consumers in their lived experiences is the main goal of children's films. Working-class protagonists can't believably participate in conspicuous consumption; therefore, they can't model the type of avid consumption that filmmakers seek to cultivate in their viewers. Thus, the children who are privileged in children's films are those with more economic resources at their disposal: the children of the middle and upper classes.

Most children's films today choose to depict protagonists who are fairly well off. Wojcik-Andrews states: "Under late capitalism children's films do not make class disappear: They simply narrow it down and conceal it whenever possible behind all those traditional humanist themes of friendship, romance, innocence, and so forth" (141). The seeming invisibility of class in most children's films simply parallels the invisibility of the working class in our cultural imagination; we seem to think that if we ignore the issue of class and the accompanying problem of poverty that these social ills will disappear. Unfortunately, this is far from the case. According to a recent report in the *New York Times* by Erik Eckholm, poverty in the United States has hit a 15-year high with more than 43.6 million Americans living at or below the poverty level. Ignoring the working class will not make it go away.

A few children's films in the past 35 years, however, have taken on the issue of class, often with an accompanying nod toward racial diversity as well. Interestingly, Disney and Pixar's animated films typically steer clear of class issues, while a few of Disney's live action films and companies such as Warner Brothers and Columbia Pictures included more working-class children in their films. Though typically invisible, working-class children characters are more often found in live action children films and in computer-generated films designed to look and feel like live action films than in animated films. *Stand by Me* (1986) and *Newsies* (1992) are two landmark films depicting working-class children. Also, several Christmas films including the recent computer-generated motion capture films *The Polar Express* (2004) and *A Christmas Carol* (2009) contain working-class characters. The working-class children in these films are treated in one of two possible ways. They are either seen as noble savages who rise above social class (for a brief period of time) because of their inherent goodness (Chris from *Stand by Me* and Jack Kelly from *Newsies,* for example), or they are pitied and/or ridiculed (e.g., Billy from *The Polar Express*) by the other characters in the film with whom the audience is encouraged to identify.

Stand by Me, the 1986 adaptation of Stephen King's novella "The Body" directed by Rob Reiner and nominated for an Oscar in 1987, ostensibly approaches the working class sympathetically through the character of Chris Chambers (River Phoenix). The protagonist Gordy Lachance (Wil Wheaton) is shown at the opening of the film as an adult remembering a childhood journey he took with three of his buddies. His memory of the events, which shapes our understanding of the film, is colored by his knowledge that Chris Chambers, his best boyhood friend and only member of the working class, was murdered as an adult when trying to break up a fight.

From the start of the movie, viewers are conscious that the working-class protagonist will die an untimely, violent death.

The film centers on four 12-year-old boys who are setting out on a two-day trek to look for the body of Ray Bower, a boy about their age who has been missing from home for three days. Chris is the natural leader of the gang and Gordy's best friend. Accompanying them on the journey to look for the body are Vern Tessio (Jerry O'Connell) and Teddy Duchamp (Corey Feldman). The primary antagonists of the film seem to be the gang of older boys led by Ace Merrill (Kiefer Sutherland) and including Vern and Chris's older brothers; however, the boys' conversations as they are walking, and later talking around the campfire at night, focus on other, more unsettling occurrences and people in their lives than the gang of older boys.

Gordy's older brother died four months earlier, and Gordy feels that his father wishes that he had died in his brother's place. Teddy's dad is in a mental hospital after burning Teddy's ear by pressing it against the stove. Vern is overweight, and he is ridiculed by his older brother. Chris is the only character struggling with a set of typical working-class problems. Chris comes from "a bad family." When Chris and Gordy are talking by the campfire after the other boys are asleep, Chris says that the whole town just thinks of him as "one of those low-life Chambers kids." He describes an incident where he stole the milk money from his classroom, but then he felt guilty and returned it. His teacher, however, who saw him return the money, stole the money after Chris had returned it, used it to buy new clothes, and then accused Chris of never returning the money. The principal was already convinced that Chris, with his working-class roots, was prone to criminality, so he was suspended from school. The principal sided with the teacher against Chris because of Chris's lower social class. Chris feels that his life is predetermined for him. Because of his working-class background, he says that while Gordy goes on to college prep classes, he'll be stuck in shop class. He says that people assume that because of his family "he has shit for brains."

Stand by Me's treatment of class is interesting since it is set in the world of childhood during extraordinary circumstances in which normal day-to-day class markers are rendered mostly irrelevant. What the characters own is less important than personal virtues of courage and perseverance. Chris is a natural leader. He is self-sacrificing and compassionate. In the woods with his buddies, away from the judgmental opinions of the town, he can excel and succeed, but he has no illusions about how his social class affects his life in town. Wojcik-Andrews writes, "Gordie believes that friendship can transcend class. Chris is fully conscious of his own class and how it will affect his friendship with Gordie when they enter Junior High in the fall" (142). It seems, initially, that Gordie was right. With Gordie's encouragement, Chris goes on and enrolls in college prep classes. He makes it out of the stifling economic situation of Castle Rock, Oregon. He finishes college and becomes an attorney. Even though Chris is able to get out of town and become a lawyer, and apparently transcend his working-class background, his fate, as he seemed to recognize all along, is predetermined for him. In spite of his achievements, he cannot escape a violent death. He dies trying to break up a fight in a restaurant. His ability to escape from his working-class roots could only extend so far. The film's treatment of Chris's death seems to present a stark message about how inflexible class boundaries really are in America, but this message is hidden under the guise of how friendship can transcend class boundaries.

Newsies (1992), a live-action Disney film directed by Kenny Ortega, is based on the historical account of a newsboy strike in 1899 in New York City. The first few lines of the film describe the group of teenage boys as a "ragged army of orphans and runaways." These boys make a meager living by hawking papers in the streets of New York City. When *The World* newspaper owner Joseph Pulitzer (Robert Duval) raises the price that the newspaper boys pay for the papers they sell 1/10th of a cent per paper, the newsies who already can barely afford the papers they're selling, go on strike led by charismatic Jack Kelly (Christian Bale) and level-headed David Jacobs (David Moscow). Kelly's group of newspaper boys persuades the newspaper boys across the city to unify and strike. But the cruel newspaper distributers use brute force against the boys, including gangs of rough men and mounted police battalions. At a rally of all the newspaper boys, the police storm in, trampling boys with their horses, beating them, and arresting many of the boys and taking them to "The Refuge," a juvenile detention hall. When all appears lost for the striking newspaper boys, a newspaper reporter for the rival *New York Sun*, Bryan Denton (Bill Pullman), begins covering the strike, but his story is suppressed by all of the New York City papers because people in New York City are scared that news of the strike might spread to other child workers in the city. That's exactly what happens. Using an abandoned printing press, the newsies publish Denton's story and distribute it widely throughout New York City. Hundreds of additional child workers join the strike, and news of the strike and the poor working conditions of child laborers reaches the office of Governor Teddy Roosevelt. He rallies in support of the striking children, and the price increase of the papers is reversed. At the end of the film, the newsies are depicted happily celebrating their victory. A closer reading of the film, however, shows that the working-class children, like Chris from *Stand by Me,* are raised above their social class only for a short period of time. There are no real changes in the child labor system in New York City.

Newsies' portrayal of working-class children, instead of encouraging real social change, reinforces common stereotypes held about the working class. Since the film is set in 1899, *Newsies* makes the issue of social class a thing of the past. The problems faced by the teenage newspaper boys are problems that the audience can comfortably place in America's distant past. The protagonists' struggles are not issues that we usually associate with the working class of the twenty-first century. If anything, the film reinforces the idea that social class isn't a problem anymore. The audience can feel relieved that the problems of child labor and runaways and street urchins are no longer troubling the United States.

Additionally, the portrayal of the newsies themselves is so fantastical that the issue of social class seems obscured. The film is full of choreographed dance routines and songs. All of the newsies are amazing dancers. Even though the boys are dressed in ragged clothes, their physical fitness, dance training, and vocal abilities erase the discomfort that the audience might feel about their situation. It's hard to believe these boys are hungry and homeless when they seem so happy and energetic throughout the film. They seem to enjoy their work; they are just dissatisfied by the price hike. Portraying child laborers as lighthearted and carefree is a recurring problem in Disney films. Booker describes the similar treatment of working-class children, the chimney sweeps, in *Mary Poppins* who are shown singing and dancing on the London rooftops, much happier than Mr. Banks, suggesting that poor people are happier under capitalism than the rich. Booker states:

> Such suggestions are not just silly and they are not just lies. They are potentially harmful lies that give children a version of the world in which they live that is not only false but false in ways that will make it easier for the powers that be in this world to manipulate and exploit them as they grow up under the illusion that poor workers are happy workers. (33–34)

Newsies' falsified portrayal of working-class children, when seen in conjunction with the widespread dismissal of social class problems, creates a difficult situation for viewing children to navigate.

Another way that *Newsies* actually downplays the harsh realities facing children of the working class is that the victory of the strikers is so small. The newsies successfully defeated the 1/10th of a cent raise per paper, and they celebrate wildly at the end of the film. It's easy to forget that even at the beginning of the film, before the price of papers was raised, the newsies barely had enough to eat. The strike didn't result in any real change in the lives of these characters. Even a film supposedly about the working class obscures and ignores the realities of the working class. Like Chris Chambers from *Stand by Me,* Jack Kelly, David Jacobs, and the other newsies are elevated for a brief time above their working-class roots, only to be even more firmly situated at the end of the film in the inescapable social situation they were born into, but at the end of the film they seem happy with their situation.

Despite the relatively few portrayals of working-class children in films, Christmas films explore issues of class with higher frequency than do other films. The two most recent children's Christmas films that treat the issue of class are *The Polar Express* and the 2009 computer-animated *A Christmas Carol.* Sue Saltmarsh writes, "Stories, books, and films that focus on the celebration of Christmas provide a surprisingly rich source of cultural information about the ways in which children and childhood is constructed in reference to the broader social world." Saltmarsh continues: "In contemporary Christmas texts . . . children are reconfigured as integral to and a driving force within the spaces of capitalist production" (5). Christmas is depicted as a magical time when class barriers are lowered and people are more kind. Since the class divisions are imagined as being lowered, class issues are addressed with greater frequency in Christmas films. Christmas is also a time of rampant consumerism. Children are the focus of this consumerism through ritual gift giving. In children's Christmas films, there is always the presence of a character with enough excess capital to erase any disparities between children of different classes. In *The Polar Express* the benevolent gift giver is Santa Claus; in *A Christmas Carol* the gift-giver who elevates the working-class children is Mr. Scrooge. In *The Polar Express,* every child who rides the train of the title receives a gift, so in this imagined space, class positions are less important than the individual child's capacity for believing in Santa and magic. Only the children who believe in Santa Claus can ride the train to the North Pole. In *A Christmas Carol* Scrooge's generosity brings Christmas to the working-class family of Scrooge's clerk, Bob Cratchet.

The Polar Express, a computer-generated film that "feels" real, directed by Robert Zemeckis with voices done by Tom Hanks, is a Christmas narrative based on the book of the same title by Chris Van Allsburg. *The Polar Express* tells the story of a magical train that on Christmas Eve picks up children who are still longing to believe in Santa Claus and takes them to the North Pole where Santa lives with his industrious elves. The narrative focuses on a 10-year-old, middle-class boy who is struggling with his growing disbelief in Santa. He gets on the Polar Express bound for the North Pole and is immediately welcomed by singing waiters who elaborately serve rich hot chocolate. He settles into a train car full of warmth and laughter and other excited children. He belongs.

The Polar Express' last stop before continuing to the North Pole is Billy's house, located, states one child already riding on the train, "on the other side of the tracks." A sharp distinction is made between the narrator of the story and the underprivileged, working-class Billy. Billy's house is located on the edge of town, and in comparison to this small, unpainted home, viewers realize the material wealth and economic security of the narrator. When Billy is introduced, the narrator's comfortable social status is suddenly highlighted. Billy is only wearing an oversized shirt and rain boots when he comes out to meet the train, clothes of noticeably poorer quality than the matching pajama set, blue robe, and slippers worn by the narrator. Besides the one comment about the house's location, the children don't make any other observations about Billy, but as they watch him stare in confusion at the huge steam engine idling in his front yard, we viewers become complicit in making assumptions about Billy's life. We look at his pinched expression, his uncertainty, and his bashfulness and read these as the signs of poverty and a lack of experience. Billy's hesitation almost causes him to miss his train, but at the last minute, he jumps aboard. Once Billy is on the train, he doesn't come into the well-lit car with the other children where waiters are singing and dancing and pouring hot chocolate for the children. He sits alone at the back of the train, in the last car, which is dark and unheated, further acknowledging his separateness from the other children.

After riding for several hours, Billy is shown singing "When Christmas Comes to Town" at the back of the train. The narrator and his friend, an African American girl, join Billy at the back of the train. The girl begins singing with him, but Billy only sings the poignant lines of the song that mention poverty and lack. For example, about Christmas presents he sings, "All the things I've heard about but never really seen." After the song, he says to the other two children, "Christmas doesn't work out for me—never has." It's left up to the audience to assume why. Billy's family hasn't had the money to celebrate Christmas. They don't have the excess wealth to participate in rampant consumerism.

Later in the film when the children reach the North Pole, Billy finds a big white-and-green Christmas present with his name on it. He risks life and limb to keep hold of his present. At one point, when faced with what seems like a life-or-death situation, Billy chooses keeping the present even though it could have resulted in a fatal fall. His determination to hang on to his present can easily be understood as a result of his poverty. The other children watch him in disbelief. Like the viewers, they realize that the present is so special to Billy because it is one of the only ones he has ever received. I watched this film with my children, ages five and nine, and when it looked like Billy was facing certain death because he wouldn't let go of his present, my children made fun of him. The film encourages us to either pity or ridicule Billy because of his social class.

Billy is not the only member of the working class in the film. The train's engineer and fireman are members of the working class, and their role in the film is simply to add humor. The fireman and engineer joke with and scold each other in stereotypical working-class accents. They are shown as incompetent, and their lack of skill is portrayed as slap-stick comedy. For example, when the pin that controls the brake rattles loose at one point on the journey, the engineer and fireman are shown scrambling for it, bumping into each other, tripping, falling down. Then, the engineer accidentally swallows it. Meanwhile, the train is skidding toward a dangerous patch of ice. When the fireman jumps on the engineer, the pins flies out of the engineer's mouth and then out the window. The comedic scene ends with the fireman calmly pulling out another pin from his hair; the second pin had been there the whole time, making the whole breathtaking scramble to prevent a train wreck completely unnecessary. Repeatedly in the film, these two characters are set up to be ridiculed. As seen through the characters of Billy and the train drivers, in *The Polar Express* the members of the working class are both pitied and ridiculed.

The 2009 computer-generated *A Christmas Carol,* also directed by Zemeckis and featuring the voices of Jim Carrey, Steve Valentine, and Daryl Saraba, is a familiar Christmas story based on Charles Dickens's novel. The primary appeal of the film is its technological inventiveness and 3-D presentation. Scrooge, the miserly owner of a counting house, is confronted by three ghosts, and as a result of these encounters he becomes more generous. He is especially supportive to his employee Bob Cratchet and Cratchet's young son Tiny Tim who is depicted in the film as undernourished, weak, and sickly. Tim's illness and sweetness win him the sympathy of the audience. Scrooge provides financial support to the Cratchet family, and Tim gets well. Like *Newsies, A Christmas Carol* situates the issue of the working class in the distant past. While the audience is encouraged to feel sympathy for the Cratchet family, the film reifies the popular idea that the problems associated with social classes have been overcome. Also, the film ends happily for the Cratchet family, and the audience can easily forget the other members of the working class who briefly appeared throughout the film. Disney is comfortable asserting that individual greedy people are bad for society (e.g., Pulitzer from *Newsies* and Scrooge before his change of heart), but Disney does not criticize the capitalistic system that it relies on for securing an enormous profit.

Over the past 30 years, shifts in the ideologies promoted in children's films and the ever-increasing goal of producers and distributors of children's films to secure a profit have reduced the overall number of children, especially working-class children, in children films. Children's films, once seen as an avenue for critiquing the oppressive treatment of children, are used primarily to secure a profit and shape children earlier and earlier into successful consumers. Since working-class children have less access to expendable resources, they are seen as a less profitable market, and they are usually ignored by filmmakers and producers. When working-class children are included in mainstream films, the reasons usually are to give the more privileged viewing audience something to laugh at or to reinforce the dominant cultural beliefs about the working class.

Works Cited

Althusser, Louis. *Lenin and Philosophy and Other Essays.* Trans. Ben Brewster. New York: Monthly Review P, 1971.

Booker, Keith. *Disney, Pixar, and the Hidden Messages in Children's Films.* Santa Barbara, CA: Praeger, 2010.

A Christmas Carol. Dir. Robert Zemeckis. Disney, 2009.

Eckholm, Erik. "Recession Raises Poverty Rate to a 15-Year High." *New York Times,* Sept. 16, 2010. http://www.nytimes.com/2010/09/17/us/17poverty.html.

Freeman, Elizabeth. "Monster's Inc: Notes on the Neoliberal Arts Education." *New Literary History* 36.1 (Winter 2005): 83–95.

Giroux, Henry. *The Mouse That Roared.* New York: Rowman and Littlefield, 1999.

Hinkins, Jillian. "'Biting the Hand That Feeds': Consumerism, Ideology, and Recent Animated Film for Children." *Explorations in Children's Literature* 17 (2007): 43–50.

Jackson, Kathy Merlock. *Images of Children in American Film.* Lanham, MD: Scarecrow Press, 1986.

Newsies. Dir. Kenny Ortega. Disney, 1992.

The Polar Express. Dir. Robert Zemeckis. Warner Bros., 2004.

Rose, Jacqueline. *The Case of Peter Pan, or The Impossibility of Children's Fiction.* Philadelphia: U of Pennsylvania P, 1984.

Saltmarsh, Sue. "Spirits, Miracles, and Clauses: Economy, Patriarchy, and Childhood in Popular Christmas Texts." *Explorations in Children's Literature* 17 (2007): 5–17.

Sklar, Robert. *Movie-Made America.* New York: Random House, 1975.

Stand by Me. Dir. Rob Reiner. Columbia Pictures, 1986.

Tron: Legacy. Dir. Joseph Kosinski. Disney, 2010.

Wojcik-Andrews, Ian. *Children's Films.* New York: Garland, 2000.

Zipes, Jack. *Happily Ever After: Fairy Tales, Children, and the Culture Industry.* New York: Routledge, 1997.

Chapter 9

Reach for the Stars: Imagining the American Dream for Working-Class Teens in Science Fiction Film

Jennifer R. Dutch

Even before President John F. Kennedy's speech in May 1961 challenged the United States of America to place a man on the moon before the end of the decade, the limitless possibilities of space meshed with the limitless possibilities of the American Dream. By the mid-1980s, at the height of the Cold War, popular culture invited working-class teens to participate in the American Dream by imagining themselves pushing the boundaries of possibility. Both aimed at a working-class audience and depicting characters from a working-class background, three films from that period best illustrate the ways in which Hollywood attempted to recruit working-class teenagers as warriors for the American Dream. In *The Last Starfighter* (1984), Alex Rogan (Lance Guest) rose above his modest beginnings in a trailer park to become the space hero that saved the galaxy from an intergalactic war. In *Explorers* (1985), three friends used parts from a junkyard to build a spacecraft that took them into outer space to make friends with aliens. In *Space Camp* (1986), a group of "typical" American teens found their NASA camp experience took an unexpected turn when their chance to experience a test launch of the space shuttle suddenly became real. Each of these films invited American teenagers to dream about what it would be like to surpass their humble origins and reach for the stars. And yet, even while the characters experienced fantastic journeys into outer space, the plots of all three films emphasized a return to Earth, and a rethinking of the characters' humble origins. In so doing, all three films offer a contradictory message for the audience: it is possible to dream big dreams of leaving behind the limitations and frustrations of working-class life, but, at the same time, they should also be satisfied with the status quo. The films *The Last Starfighter, Explorers,* and *Space Camp* first engage the imaginations of working-class American teenagers with tantalizing images of outer space adventure and then redirect their thoughts to traditional American values by underscoring the importance of the return to Earth and the significance that home plays in assuring happiness. The message is that it is acceptable to reach for the stars, but dreamers should keep their feet firmly planted on Earth.

By the mid-1980s, there was an audience for light, escapist fantasies like *The Last Starfighter, Explorers,* and *Space Camp.* Events of the 1960s and 1970s called into question the basic tenets of the American Dream, which Jim Cullen identifies in his book *The American Dream* as "upward mobility . . . the quest for equality . . . home ownership . . . and the dream of the good life" (Cullen 8–10). After decades of social upheaval and economic uncertainty—with the Vietnam War, the civil rights and women's rights movements, stagflation, and the recession of the early 1980s—the American Dream seemed tenuous at best. Working-class Americans were in a particularly shaky position by mid-decade as pressures from Reagan-era economic policies and the transformation of the manufacturing economy into a service economy increasingly threatened their jobs, undermined their standing in society, and threatened their individual identities. As Chris Jordan argues, rhetoric related to "individual economic and cultural mobility . . . proved powerful amid a culture of widespread middle-class downward mobility in which multinational corporations' enfeeblement of labor unions marginalized working-class white males alongside women and minorities in minimum wage, often part-time service jobs" (Jordan 17). At the same time working-class Americans saw their opportunities for upward mobility vanishing alongside the manufacturing jobs that undergirded their economic stability, President Ronald Reagan preached what Chris Jordan calls "the success ethic" that was planted on a foundation of "fantasies of America as a land of second chances and fluid economic and cultural mobility" (Jordan 15). The rhetoric of the day informed working-class Americans that they had unlimited possibilities to live the American Dream and their inability to do so was their own fault. The reality was much different. While being told that economic success was based on hard work and individual merit, the middle class experienced the wrenching loss of jobs and homes. Films depicting a fantasy world where working-class characters became heroes while experiencing exciting adventures offered working-class Americans a momentary pause from the stresses of everyday concerns and worries; here were characters who offered a model for overcoming the limitations of working-class American life by reaching for their dreams.

Perhaps there was no better setting for these fantasies than the unlimited reaches of outer space. Unmarred by the upheavals that wracked the country during the 1960s and 1970s, the American space program held onto its aura of power and possibility. From the earliest days of space exploration, astronauts were cast in the role of American heroes. As Howard E. McCurdy notes, early astronauts "were presented by the press as the personification of clean-cut, all-American boys . . . they were portrayed as brave, God-fearing, patriotic individuals with loving wives and children" (McCurdy 90). Most of all, however, they were portrayed as exceptional. They were the best of the best. As Howard S. Schwartz declares, "they, our bravest and best test pilots, would ride the rockets into space and symbolically do battle with the Russians" (Schwartz 9). For a country embroiled in the Cold War, the astronauts "seemed to embody the personal qualities in which Americans of that era wanted to believe: bravery, youth, honesty, love of God and country, and family devotion" (McCurdy 91–92). These early astronauts were seen as the elite heroes who alone possessed the skills and bravery to assure that America won the space race.

At the same time, the dream of reaching the stars became incorporated in the American Dream; the limitless possibilities of space merged with America's belief in its own limitless possibilities. The idea of heroic, American astronauts pushing beyond Earth's boundaries into the uncharted reaches of space fit within America's vision of its pioneer origins. As Janice Hocker Rushing asserts, "from birth to maturity, America has drawn upon the frontier for its mythic identity. Whether fixed upon Columbus sailing the ocean blue or Buffalo Bill conquering the Wild, Wild West, the American imagination remains fascinated by new and unknown places. . . . Since the beginning, the pioneer spirit has shaped the American dream and infused its character" (Rushing 265). The dream of spaceflight became the perfect carrier for America's vision of itself and its future. As Schwartz notes, "the US manned space program was a way for Americans to talk to themselves about themselves" and "the symbol of manned space flight had become a symbol of limitless, effortless perfection in which constraint appeared only as an illusion" (Schwartz 6). America's success as a nation was symbolized by its successful space program.

By the 1980s, the dream of spaceflight had expanded to include *all* Americans, not just the best and brightest. As McCurdy notes, the American Dream of space flight was expanded so that "ordinary people could imagine themselves flying into space" (McCurdy 186). In the 1980s, this vision was in the process of becoming reality with the Teacher-in-Space program. Christa McAuliffe, a high school teacher from Concord, New Hampshire, was selected to become the first civilian in space. McAuliffe was "the girl next door" who represented the average American (Hohler 10). In McAuliffe's excitement at being chosen to go into space, Americans recognized their own dreams and embraced her as a hero. When McAuliffe's adventure ended in the *Challenger*'s tragic explosion, it left a deep scar in America's faith in the country's space program. As Grace George Corrigan, McAuliffe's mother, notes in her book *A Journal for Christa,* "from July 19, 1985 to January 28 1986, Christa was in the national eye. In that short time, she became teacher, daughter, sister, and friend to people all over the world, and, as such, her death affected each and every one" (Corrigan x). It would take decades for the nation and the space program to fully recover, if they ever did.

Released before the *Challenger* disaster tinged the American Dream of civilian spaceflight with tragedy, *The Last Starfighter, Explorers,* and *Space Camp* captured the unbridled optimism of the limitless possibilities of space and the American Dream. These films took characters with humble, working-class backgrounds and launched them into grand adventures among the stars. Ultimately, however, these films demonstrated that it was not the adventure in space that was important, but the return to Earth that carried meaning. By traveling to the stars and then returning home, these characters were able to recognize the innate strength that came from their humble origins. Though the dream of returning to space remained, it was no longer a mysterious fantasy, but a concrete reality made possible by the characters' own abilities. They no longer needed to rise above their origins, but instead came to embrace them.

The Last Starfighter opens with a shot of a single, unrecognizable planet. The music swells and the camera begins an escalating retreat away from the planet. Stars and planets rush by until the motion ceases with a shot of a single planet that is recognizably Earth. The field of view narrows until it dips beneath the cloud cover and focuses on a small trailer park somewhere in an American desert. The trailer park bustles with activity as the residents begin their morning rituals. Every detail reinforces the dreariness of the working-class roots of the residents of the trailer park. Each tiny trailer looks rundown with tiny front yards packed with kitschy lawn ornaments and banged up furniture. The small, dirt lane between the closely packed trailers is overrun with too many people crammed into such a tiny space. The noise level rises to a din as residents call to one another from across the park, dogs bark, and children play. Despite bearing the hopeful name "Starlite Starbrite," this trailer park seems more like a place to escape *from* than a place that offers the possibility of granting its residents wishes.

And escape from this small, unsophisticated trailer park is exactly lead character Alex Rogan's fondest wish. The son of a single mother, Jane Rogan (Barbara Bosson), who works a double-shift as a waitress at a local restaurant, Alex rejects the limitations of his working-class background and hopes for something more. Unlike his friends, Alex dreams of something bigger and something better than staying in the town where he grew up. Alex declares, "you guys think I'm gonna hang out here, watch you shine your pickup, go to the drive-in, get drunk and throw up every Saturday night go to City College like everybody else? Forget it, man. I'm doing somethin' with my life." Alex's ticket to doing "something" with his life is a loan that will allow him to attend a university far away from the dingy trailer park he now calls home. Alex's temporary escape from the pressures of his life is to play the *Starfighter* arcade video game. The opening welcome of the game: "Greetings, Starfighter! You have been recruited by the Star League to defend the frontier against Xur and the Kodan armada" transports Alex away from the demands of his mother and neighbors, the stress of waiting for news about his loan, and the daily realities of being an American teenager.

Matching the ambiguities of working-class life in America in the mid-1980s, the moment of Alex's most exciting triumph comes at almost the same moment as his most crushing defeat. With his girlfriend Maggie Gordon (Catherine Mary Stewart) and Otis (Vernon Washington), an older African American resident of the trailer park looking on, Alex breaks the *Starfighter* high score record—a triumph that the entire trailer park community celebrates. But when Alex finally gets the chance to tell his mother of his success, she carries much more disappointing news. Alex's triumph at setting the new high score for the game is shattered when he reads the letter denying his school loan. Instead of offering the comfort intended, Alex's mother's consoling declaration that Alex could "still go to City College with your friends" is the exact opposite. At that moment, Alex is crushed by the overwhelming knowledge that his dream of leaving the trailer park and having a different life is over. Fleeing the confines of his family's trailer, Alex runs to the outskirts of the trailer park where he crushes the letter and tosses it away. The light of the "Starlite Starbrite" trailer park sign bathes Alex in an ironic glow as he stands at the border of the trailer park; his wish is over and he can go no further.

What Alex does not realize, but the audience will soon discover is that the now seemingly insignificant fact that Alex broke the *Starfighter* record will become his ticket out of the trailer park and to adventure among the stars. As Alex stands beneath the flickering trailer park sign, a strange man named Centauri (Robert Preston) arrives in a futuristic-looking car asking for the name of the person who broke the record. When Alex identifies himself as the record-holder, he soon finds himself in this man's vehicle, driving at speeds over 300 miles per hour, and then into space. It seems Alex's dream is coming true, if in the most unexpected way. For Centauri invented the *Starfighter* game as a way to recruit warriors to join the Star League, fight for Rylos, and defeat the Kodan armada and the evil Xur. The game turns out to be more than a story—it is true. Now, with his talent affirmed, Alex is a *real* Starfighter.

But Alex is a reluctant Starfighter. Despite the wonders of traveling through space and the excitement of going through Starfighter orientation at the headquarters of the Star League, Alex immediately demands to return to Earth. Only the threat of alien assassins makes Alex join the Star League. When he is told that all the other Starfighters were killed in an attack, making him the *last* Starfighter, Alex is alarmed that in place of a fleet of warriors, there is now only one navigator, one Starfighter, and one prototype Gunstar on its "maiden voyage"—and only reluctantly takes on the mantle of Starfighter. After their first battle, Alex confronts his navigator, Grig (Dan O'Herlihy), a lizardlike alien, with the accusation, "You almost got me killed." Grig expresses his disappointment saying, "I had hoped that by putting you in the thick of battle, a great Starfighter would emerge. But alas, perhaps there was never one in you to begin with." He offers to take Alex home, promising that he could "live a long and fruitful life back there" at least "until the Kodan reach Earth."

Why is Alex so reluctant to take hold of the opportunity and become a real Starfighter? In light of his earlier yearning to leave the trailer park, the rejection of this ultimate adventure seems to ring hollow. The true source of Alex's reluctance to embrace his chance to leave the trailer park and become a Starfighter is revealed in the scene in which Centauri returns Alex to Earth. Centauri tosses Alex "communa-crystals" and informs him that they represent his "second chance" to call Centauri back and become a

Starfighter. As Alex attempts to return the gift, Centauri declares "You're walking away from history. History! Did Chris Columbus say he wanted to stay home? No! What if the Wright brothers thought only birds should fly?" But, Alex rejects Centauri's comparison exclaiming, "Look Centauri, I'm not any of those guys. I'm a kid from a trailer park." Alex's reluctance to grasp hold of adventure stems from the idea that he does not see himself as a hero—he is just "a kid from a trailer park." Centauri's next words capture not only his own disdain for Alex's choice, but also the overall message of the film. Centauri declares, "If that's what you think, then that's all you'll ever be!" The rest of the film unfolds as a way to prove to Alex, and the audience, that not only can a kid from a trailer park become a hero, but it is his roots in the trailer park that give him the strength and know-how to defeat the enemy.

The turning point in Alex's journey to embrace his new destiny as a Starfighter comes when Alex merges his experience of growing up in the trailer park with his skills as a video game player. With only one ship against the entire Kodan armada, Alex is understandably pessimistic about their chances of success. After the first run-in with the enemy, Alex and Grig take refuge in an asteroid's caves. While in the caves, Alex and Grig exchange stories about their families back home. Grig reveals that his family lives in caves below ground. Alex notes that his family lives in a house that is a "cave above ground," but that he played "hide and seek" with his brother in below-ground caves. This memory gives Alex the inspiration to hide the Gunstar in the asteroid's caves and take the Kodan command ship by surprise. As Grig begins to enter the coordinates for Earth into the navigation system, Alex declares "maybe there is a Starfighter left." Drawing strength from his memory of playing hide and seek back home, Alex manages to take the command ship by surprise and damages it.

Alex's success over the command ship marks the first time that Alex has used his family life as inspiration for his fighting life. No longer living with one foot in each world—Alex is finally able to embrace both the influence of his origins and the power of his destiny to give him the strength to outwit the enemy and win the day. His success gives Alex the confidence to take on the rest of the Kodan armada, even when it means engaging the untested, experimental weapon, the Death Blossom. Activating the Death Blossom might mean the destruction for the entire armada or it might mean death for both Alex and Grig. But, Alex has changed. He is no longer afraid. "What are you worried about Grig?" Alex jokes, "Theoretically, we should already be dead!" In the course of the mission, Alex has been transformed from the reluctant teenager who dreamed of a life beyond the trailer park, but balked at the chance at adventure, into a true Star-fighter who scoffs at danger and risks his life to assure the safety of the Star League. Without a hint of reluctance, Alex engages the Death Blossom and destroys the enemy fleet. The Gunstar drifts in space, defenseless after the Death Blossom's enormous output of energy. That is when the crippled command ship arrives for one last attempt to ram the Gunstar. At that moment, Alex and Grig work as a team and defeat the command carrier: Grig redirects power from life support and Alex takes his one shot. The command ship explodes. The war is over. When Alex and Grig return to the Star League they receive a hero's welcome and Alex is invited to "stay on and rebuild the Starfighter legion." The scene ends as Alex whispers a single word, "stay?"

The audience is left to ponder whether Alex plans to remain a Star-fighter or return to his life on Earth. The answer to the riddle is seemingly answered as the scene shifts to the trailer park as an alien spacecraft lands. As Alex emerges he is almost unrecognizable in his Starfighter uniform and, once he removes his helmet and reveals his identity, he is inundated with questions from the entire trailer park community that had gathered to view the spectacle. Alex's simple answer, "I've been to another planet," masks his heroic intervention on behalf of the Star League, an oversight that Grig quickly corrects. Grig reveals Alex's heroic status by declaring, "You should be proud of Alex, Mrs. Rogan. You should all be proud of him. He saved the Star League and hundreds of worlds, including Earth." Grig also reveals that Alex will not be staying at the trailer park, but has chosen instead to embrace his new destiny as a Starfighter. In awe, Alex's mother declares, "Oh Alex, I always knew you'd leave someday, but I never ex-pected this." Alex's reason for returning to the trailer park is to invite Mag-gie to join his space adventure. At first, Maggie is reluctant and reveals that she is "scared of leaving." Confirming his transformation from reluctant teenager to brave Starfighter, Alex declares, "This is it. This is our big chance . . . when it comes you gotta grab on with both hands and hold tight." Wavering for just a few more moments, Maggie makes her decision and rushes to Alex's side. She has decided to grasp hold of their chance.

As Alex and Maggie begin their journey to the stars, the trailer park community bids them farewell. At this moment it is not only Alex who has been redeemed in the eyes of the community, but the community that is redeemed for the audience. Where the opening shots of the trailer park made it appear to be a place to escape from, the ending of the film reveals the trailer park to be a loving community, supportive of each other's dreams, and willing to stand behind Alex and Maggie as they journey to the stars.

The trailer park is no longer a place where dreams die, but a home where dreams began. Otis sums up the change when he announces, "The whole world—the whole universe—is gonna know about us! Starlite, Starbrite— the place where Alex and Maggie left for the stars!" The film ends with a shot of Alex's spaceship blasting off into the stars while the trailer park's star sign flickers in the corner of the shot. This final image reinforces the idea that the trailer park should no longer be seen as a place where dreams go to die. Instead, it is the place where dreams are born and nourished by the loving community of trailer park residents that call the Starlite, Starbrite trailer park their home.

In this way, *The Last Starfighter* seems to end on a triumphant note. Alex is a hero. The trailer park has been revealed as a loving community to which Alex and Maggie will someday return. Beneath the festive façade, however, there is the less than celebratory message—nothing has really changed. While Alex finds success as a Starfighter, he has become embroiled in a fight in which Earth plays no major part and in which he might still lose his life. In fact, the war in which Alex now finds himself playing a major role is never really fully defined aside from the idea that the Star League is "good" and Xur is "evil." The origins of the war and the values that Alex now fights for are never clearly stated. In fighting for a cause not entirely his own in a war not of his own making, Alex replicates an all-too-familiar pattern for working-class Americans who have traditionally borne the brunt of America's wars since they are often too poor to buy their way out of uniform. Moreover, with Alex's absence the trailer park loses one of its most important residents since he often completed minor repairs and helped the residents with their chores. There is no indication of who will replace him in completing these tasks. Perhaps Alex's younger brother, Louis (Chris Hebert), or another resident will be called upon to be the new handyman. But if no one in the trailer park has the talent, the residents will be forced to call a professional, which will strain their already limited resources. And, when Alex and Maggie finally do return to Earth, they will still face the same problems that were there when they left. Unless Alex manages to become rich in space or famous on Earth, he will not have the money to attend the college he wanted and his skills as a Starfighter will have little applicability on the American job market. And so, while *The Last Starfighter* ends with the excitement of a space adventure, the earthly reality remains a struggle against the economic and social forces that had placed Alex and his neighbors at a disadvantage from the beginning.

The film *Explorers* also begins with a sweeping shot of the sky as the camera hovers above the clouds before dipping beneath them to fly above a city. The shot finally narrows in on the sleeping form of a young boy.

The audience joins the boy's dream of flying above the clouds and then over a mysterious landscape made up of geometric designs. The boy, Ben Crandall (Ethan Hawke), is startled awake. He jumps out of bed and begins to draw the landscape from his dream. What Ben does not realize, but will soon find out, is that his dream and the drawing that he made will be the ticket to the grand adventure in space he always dreamed of experiencing. He will need help along the way from his best friend, Wolfgang Müller (River Phoenix), and a new friend, Darren Woods (Jason Presson). Together, the three friends will go on an adventure to the stars.

But first, the film establishes the fact that the boys' *real* lives are far from perfect. Ben is a dreamer. He immerses himself in science fiction and spends his time daydreaming about space travel and aliens. Ben's obsession with science fiction makes him a target for bullies at school and a mystery to his father who does not understand Ben's interest in aliens. Darren lives in a small, rundown house with peeling paint and a junk car in the driveway sitting with its hood propped open and weeds growing out of its engine. More disturbing is the fact that Darren indicates that his father, whose usual job is to "haul junk," but who is currently unemployed, is sometimes abusive. While Darren does not explicitly say that his father is abusive he does mention that his dad "taught me how to run. He can't catch me anymore." Obviously, Darren's home life is very unhappy. Wolfgang also suffers from misunderstandings and a difficult home life. A brilliant scientist, Wolfgang is the eldest son of immigrant parents with thick German accents. Wolfgang's only refuge from his many siblings and parent's eccentric habits is his basement laboratory where he conducts his experiments. For these three characters, their working-class origins are a source of frustration, anger, and even pain; escape to the stars becomes a dream that all three can embrace.

And it will take all three to make the dream come true. Ben the dreamer, Darren the realist, and Wolfgang the scientist—without the individual talents of each of these characters the trio would not be able to grasp hold of the chance to become space explorers. For Ben's dream is more than just a dream; it is a blueprint for space travel sent by aliens. From Ben's drawing, Wolfgang is able to construct a computer chip that creates a force field. Darren provides access to the junkyard where they find an old Tilt-O-Whirl amusement park ride that they transform into a spaceship they name the *Thunder Road*. When the maiden voyage of the *Thunder Road* goes awry due to lack of oxygen, the bond between the three friends is reaffirmed when they *all* share the same dream that gives them the solution for an unlimited supply of oxygen. The three friends have truly embraced the same goal to escape Earth and meet aliens in space.

And that is exactly what Ben, Darren, and Wolfgang are now able to do. With an unlimited supply of oxygen, they are able to allow the aliens to guide them to an enormous spaceship. But once the three friends board the ship, the experience is not at all what Ben was expecting. His grand hope of meeting all-powerful aliens does not fit in a somewhat smelly spaceship. "I hate to say this," Ben admits, "but this isn't the way I thought it would be at all." The aliens themselves, although green with buglike bodies and antennae, also fall short of Ben's imaginings. The first words Wak (Robert Picardo), the male alien, speaks to Ben is "What's up, Doc?" Wak's entire vocabulary seems to be from cartoons, commercials, and stand-up comedians. In fact, everything that Wak and his sister Neek (Leslie Rickert) know about humans came from watching television transmissions from Earth. Even more alarming is that the violent way in which encounters with aliens are presented in the very movies that inspired Ben's dreams of one day meeting aliens, plus the presence of deadly germs, have kept the aliens at a distance. As Ben declares, "But this is just the movies. This isn't the way we really are. . . . This isn't real." While Ben expected the aliens to share the secrets of the universe, it is Wak and Neek who hope that Ben can explain humans to them.

Ben's disillusionment with meeting *real* aliens serves to demystify the experience. Far from the wise creatures of his imagination, Wak and Neek are often silly and strange. In fact, they are in many ways very much like Ben and his friends—excited to have an adventure and meet strange, human aliens. The idea that the aliens are just like Ben and his friends is reinforced when a larger ship pulls alongside their vessel cutting the meeting short. As Wak and Neek hurry Ben, Darren, and Wolfgang back to the *Thunder Road,* an enormous green alien enters the hangar where the boys are about to board the *Thunder Road,* he is shouting and waving his arms. "It's their father. I'm telling you, it's their father," Darren observes, perhaps recognizing the body language of an enraged father yelling at his children from his own experience. Suddenly Ben realizes that Wak and Neek are "just a couple of kids," just like Ben and his friends. As the camera pans upward from the father alien's feet to his face the shot lingers for a moment on his tool belt. This marker indicates that Wak and Neek are also from a working-class background—their father has a job that involves using tools. What Ben and his friends have discovered is that there is no refuge in space, just new friends who may share their dreams, but also share their problems.

When Ben, Wolfgang, and Darren make it back to Earth, the *Thunder Road* crashes into the water, disappearing beneath the surface. They will not be able to return to space unless Wak and Neek once again send them dreams to construct a new space vessel. For Ben, Wolfgang, and Darren, however, space travel is no longer a realm of mysterious wonder, but an expected reality. And so, when the three boys once again enter the strange dream world sent by the aliens, they are once again ready to take up the challenge to return to space and reunite with their new friends.

For the audience, the film *Explorers* provides two contradictory messages. On the one hand, Ben, Darren, and Wolfgang are able to draw upon their talents as a dreamer, a realist, and a scientist to make their dream of exploring space and making friends with aliens come true. On the other hand, when the boys return to Earth, they are still outsiders with the same problems that they had before their adventures. Moreover, the mystery of space travel has been replaced with the idea that the aliens' lives are similar to Ben, Darren, and Wolfgang's experiences. Wak and Neek are working-class kids, just like the three friends, and may share the same dreams, but also live with the same difficulties and challenges. As such, there is no real escape from the realities and difficulties of working-class life—even in space. The audience, therefore, receives both the promise that they too can fulfill their dreams, but that the result may not be as freeing as they might hope.

The film *Space Camp* also opens with the sweeping vista of outer space before shifting to focus on a little girl sitting in the middle of a field of wheat gazing up at the night sky. The little girl, Andie (Hollye Rebecca Suggs), is watching anxiously for an American spacecraft to pass overhead. In the background, her mother calls her from the door of the farmhouse to come inside and watch the event on television. But, Andie prefers to witness the astronauts' flyover firsthand. Every time there is motion in the sky she sits up, but falls back when she realizes it's a "shootin' star" or "just another wisher." Finally, when she sees what she believes is the spacecraft, this small girl growing up in heartland America with the humble working-class roots of a farm family expresses her dream of one day becoming an astronaut and going to the stars herself. "I'm going up," Andie declares, "I am. I'm going up."

Fast forward and Andie (Kate Capshaw) is now grown up. She has fulfilled her dream of becoming an astronaut, but has been notified that she is "not going up" on the next mission. Her husband, fellow astronaut Zach Bergstrom (Tom Skerritt), consoles her, saying "you'll get your chance next time." For Andie, the dream remains alive and she replies, "You're damn right I will." To add a deeper level to her disappointment, Zach informs Andie that, instead of going to space, she will be joining him as an instructor for the summer at Space Camp. The prospect of working with "a bunch of kids" definitely does not live up to Andie's dream of reaching the stars.

Joining Andie's "Blue Team" at Space Camp is a rag-tag group of "clean-cut, all-American" kids from a wide range of mostly working-class backgrounds. There is Kevin Donaldson (Tate Donovan), who traded his father a summer at Space Camp for a new Jeep but is far from happy about the experience. He has an instant attraction to Kathryn Fairly (Lea Thompson) who arrives at Space Camp in her father's biplane and declares that she wants to be "the first female shuttle commander." Sharing a bunk with Kathryn is Tish Ambrosei (Kelly Preston), a beautiful blonde who behaves scatterbrained, but actually is brilliant and remembers everything she reads. Then there is Rudy Tyler (Larry B. Scott), an African American teen who starts out treating Space Camp like boot camp. Finally, there is Max (Joaquin "Leaf" Phoenix), a young boy whose age would place him in Junior Space Camp, but whose experience and enthusiasm convinces Andie to accept him into the teen group. The unofficial mascot of the group is Jinx, the multimillion dollar robotic failure that becomes friends with Max.

The film's earliest scenes are devoted to demonstrating each of the characters' weaknesses. Kathryn is so focused on becoming a commander, that she undervalues the role of pilot when Andie gives her that assignment. Kevin clings to his reckless attitude and refuses to take responsibility for his new role as commander. Tish feels burdened by her ability to remember everything she reads. Rudy was teased by his friends back home for being interested in science and, while he loves the subject, expresses doubt that he can ever master the subject. Max cannot escape being younger than everyone else and seeks refuge in his friendship with Jinx. Even Jinx is burdened by his programming, so that he "literally does everything he is told."

The Blue Team's weaknesses are on full display during a simulation spaceflight in the training module. Max is terrified when he attempts a simulation of a space walk. Tish opens a door at the wrong time and nearly makes Rudy drop Max's chairlift. Rudy is confused by a panel that he's trying to rewire and almost causes a fire. Kathryn abandons her post as pilot to help Rudy, meaning no one is at the controls during reentry. Kevin gives up and just watches the screen as the shuttle crashes to Earth. At the end of the simulation Andie expresses her disappointment saying, "You're all dead because you didn't work together as a team." In disbelief at the level of her anger, Kevin responds that "it's just Space Camp."

These weaknesses, however, turn into strengths when the Blue Team is given the opportunity to sit in the space shuttle during a rocket test which, with Jinx's help, becomes a *real* launch and the Blue Team finds itself unexpectedly in orbit. Since the shuttle is ill equipped for a real mission in space, the Blue Team soon loses touch with Mission Control because its short-range radio cannot pick up the signal. More important, the shuttle only has a limited supply of oxygen, one that will run out before they can land. In order to get back to Earth safely, each of the characters will need to overcome his or her greatest weakness. As Andie declares, "What's important now is how we get back home. . . . Folks, I'm gonna need all your help to get there." In order to make it home, they *must* act as a team.

In turn, each of the characters overcomes his or her limitations. Ditzy-seeming Tish figures out that the shuttle can communicate with Mission Control by flashing lights on the panel controls in Morse Code, a skill she picked up by reading a book once. Andie proves her skill as a pilot by navigating the shuttle to the space station, Daedalus, where they can attain a supply of oxygen. Only Max, the youngest and smallest member of the crew, can fit in between the space station's supports to retrieve the bottles of oxygen. Rudy, who once doubted his own ability to learn scientific facts, is the only one who can correctly guide Andie's attempt to attach the oxygen bottle to the ship without causing an explosion that would destroy the shuttle.

When Andie attempts to attach the second canister of oxygen, the valve explodes and she is rocketed against a wall and then floats helplessly unconscious into space, held to the shuttle by a tether. Unaware of the danger, Mission Control chooses that moment to assert their control over the shuttle in order to ready it for landing. In so doing, they close the shuttle bay doors, trapping Andie in space. Kathryn confirms that they can press the manual override button and rescue Andie. However, that would mean they would miss the window of opportunity to make a safe landing at Edwards Air Force Base. As the seconds tick by and Mission Control prepares to ignite the engines, Kathryn's finger hovers over the manual override button. At the last second, Kevin pushes the button as Kathryn remains frozen. This is Kevin's moment of redemption. The carefree boy who refused to take responsibility for his team in the simulator takes control of the situation and makes a life or death choice—saving Andie's life while knowingly putting the lives of the rest of the crew in danger. It is a choice that Kathryn realizes she was not able to make. "You did the right thing," Kathryn reassures Kevin, "Andie's part of the crew. You took responsibility for her. Somebody had to. That's what makes a good flight commander. I'm a good pilot, but I'm no commander." For Kevin and Kathryn, their adventure in space has changed the way they see themselves.

With Andie hurt, it is up to the members of Blue Team to save themselves—they will truly need to act as a team. Saving Andie's life meant they missed the chance to land at Edwards Air Force Base and, with one canister of oxygen, they do not have enough air to last to the next opportunity. First, Rudy comes up with the idea of trying to land somewhere different. Then, Kathryn remembers that a shuttle had once landed at White Sands, New Mexico. With only a short time until the window of opportunity opens, Tish redoubles her efforts to attract Mission Control's attention with her message. Finally, in an effort to help save Max's life, Jinx arrives at Mission Control and recognizes the Morse Code that the rest of the officials had missed. Finally, the shuttle has the chance to get back to Earth safely.

Now it is Kathryn's turn to prove herself. With Andie hurt, there is no one else to fly the shuttle during reentry. As Kathryn maneuvers the shuttle for reentry, she loses control and it enters a "flat spin." This is the same problem that she had difficulty mastering in the multiaxis trainer. With intense focus, Kathryn manages to stabilize the shuttle and keep it at the correct angle to avoid burning up during reentry. Congratulating her on the safe reentry, Rudy declares, "You did it, Kathryn." "No." Kathryn replies, "We all did it." With contributions from every member of the group, the Blue Team makes it back to Earth safely.

The film ends with the shuttle's triumphant landing. In their journey into space and ultimate return to Earth, the Blue Team members overcame their self-doubt and became a real team. For members of the audience, the triumphant conclusion to the film provides the reassurance that their own dreams could come true. While most members of the audience may not have dreamed of going into space, the film provides a hopeful message that, in America, hard work and dedication can bring about a happy ending. For if these "typical, all-American teens" can fly among the stars and return safely to Earth then anything is possible.

And yet, while the film makes clear that the Blue Team members managed to overcome their weaknesses to survive their unexpected mission in space, it never addresses the underlying causes for those weaknesses—the social, economic, and cultural factors that were the root of these characters' difficulties. Why is Kathryn so focused on becoming the first female shuttle commander? Why is Tish afraid to show off her inherent intelligence and focuses her energy on clothes and makeup instead? The film raises these issues as flaws in Kathryn's and Tish's characters, but does not touch the underlying issues related to society's definitions of proper gender roles that inform Kathryn's and Tish's choices. The same is true for Kevin and Max, who both struggle with the pressures of society's expectations as they grow closer to adulthood. The film underscores Kevin's initial irresponsibility and Max's immaturity, but never addresses the underlying ideals of masculinity and manhood that they are pitted against. For Rudy, the only African American character in the film, race is not even raised as an issue. And yet, there are clear indicators that Rudy feels out-of-place. Why does he begin the Space Camp experience by treating it like boot camp? Why do his friends make fun of him for an interest in science? Is it because the expectation is that an African American male is more likely to join the military than to become an astronaut? Finally, there is Andie—the little girl who dreamed of flying in space and who grew up to become an astronaut. At the beginning of the film, her dream was still unfulfilled—NASA did not choose to send her into space, she only got there by accident. And so, while *Space Camp* provides a seeming glimpse of dreams fulfilled and characters who overcome their limitations, the film does not provide answers to the problems that caused the limitations in the first place. The expectations based on gender, race, economic status, and age that were in place when the shuttle blasted into space are still in place when the characters return to Earth. The film ends when the shuttle touches the ground. In so doing, the film avoids grappling with the difficult issues and repercussions of the adventure.

All three films, *The Last Starfighter, Explorers,* and *Space Camp,* offer their audiences contradictory messages. On the one hand, the films celebrate their main characters' abilities to overcome the weaknesses and limitations that originate in their working-class backgrounds. Alex, Ben, Darren, Wolfgang, Kathryn, Kevin, Tish, Rudy, Max, and even Andie all transform into space-traveling heroes who fulfill their dreams and fly among the stars. On the other hand, however, these films seem to celebrate the status quo by equally emphasizing the return to Earth where the inherent problems of gender role differences, racial inequalities, and economic disparities go unaddressed. In fact, the films seem to celebrate these characters homes by transforming a downtrodden trailer park into a loving community, eliminating the difference between aliens and earthlings by making them just like us, and by simply ignoring the underlying causes of the characters' limitations. In so doing, the audience receives the second message that they should be happy with their lives as they stand. Matching the contradictory messages of Reagan-era politics that simultaneously celebrated working-class abilities to live the American Dream while blaming them when they fell short, these films offer their audiences the promise that they too can reach for the stars, but no reassurance that, when they do, they will come away with anything but stardust on their fingertips.

Works Cited

Castle, Nick. *The Last Starfighter.* Universal Studios, 1999. DVD.

Corrigan, Grace George. *A Journal for Christa: Christa McAuliffe, Teacher in Space.* Lincoln: U of Nebraska P, 1993.

Cullen, Jim. *The American Dream: A Short History of an Idea That Shaped a Nation.* Oxford: Oxford UP, 2003.

Dante, Joe. *Explorers.* Paramount, 2004. DVD.

Hohler, Robert T. "*I Touch the Future . . .*": *The Story of Christa McAuliffe.* New York: Random House, 1986.

Jordan, Chris. *Movies and the Reagan Presidency: Success and Ethics.* Westport: Praeger, 2003.

McCurdy, Howard E. *Space and the American Imagination.* Illustrated Edition. Washington: Smithsonian, 1997.

Rushing, Janice Hocker. "Mythic Evolution of the 'New Frontier' in Mass Mediated Rhetoric." *Critical Studies in Mass Communication* 3 (1986): 265–96.

Schwartz, Howard S. "The Symbol of the Space Shuttle and the Degeneration of the American Dream." *Journal of Management* 1 (1988): 5–20.

Winer, Harry. *Space Camp.* MGM, 2004. DVD.

Chapter 10

"No Free Rides, No Excuses": Film Stereotypes of Urban Working-Class Students

Richard Mora and Mary Christianakis

While scholars have examined the charismatic, prophetic adult (teacher, coach, or principal) character in the urban high school film genre (Bulman 2005; Bulman 2004; Bulman 2002; Grant 2002), the depiction of urban working-class students in these films has received much less attention. In this chapter, we seek to address this gap in the literature by analyzing a sample of some of the most popular films within the urban high school genre—*Blackboard Jungle* (1955), *Cooley High* (1975), *Class of 1984* (1982), *Teachers* (1984), *The Principal* (1987), *Stand and Deliver* (1988), *Lean on Me* (1989), *Dangerous Minds* (1995), *High School High* (1996), *The Substitute* (1996), *One Eight Seven (187)* (1997), *Light It Up* (1999), *Coach Carter* (2005), *Take the Lead* (2006), and *Freedom Writers* (2007). Based on our content analysis, we argue that these films serve to perpetuate both the myth of meritocracy and the culture of poverty narrative by depicting urban working-class students as either unsalvageable or of having the potential to become law-abiding, contributing members of society only if they set aside their lifestyles and cultural ways.[1]

Visual cues at the beginning of most of these films make clear that the students come from communities that, unlike the suburban ideal with manicured lawns and white picket fences, are plagued with social disorganization and the ills that come with it—vandalism, drug dealing, and gang violence. The motif of urban decay can be seen in *Blackboard Jungle,* which opens with images of dirty streets, and dilapidated buildings in the depressed New York City neighborhood surrounding North Manual High School. Likewise, the film *Dangerous Minds* opens with scenes of an urban neighborhood—East Palo Alto—where the students featured in the film reside. The scenes include shots of vandalized walls, derelict buildings, and drug dealing that stand in contrast to the suburban Palo Alto community where the school they are bused to is located. The film *Freedom Writers* opens with visual and audio references to the rioting that took place following the 1992 acquittal of the Los Angeles Police Department officers who beat and detained Rodney King. The sound of sirens and images of burning buildings are underscored by the words: "the city resembles a war zone." Then, more text appears on the screen indicating that Long Beach, where *Freedom Writers* is set, experienced high rates of racial and gang violence following the riots. Thus, even before the main protagonists are introduced, the urban students featured in many of the films are framed as urban "others."

High School High, which spoofs the urban high school film genre, underscores how the genre depicts the inner city as a world apart from the rest of society. As Richard Clark (Jon Lovitz), a white man who up to this point has taught at a prep school, drives to Marion Barry High School for the first time, there is a street sign that reads "INNER CITY." When Clark drives past the sign, every station of his car radio plays nothing but hip hop music and there are only black people on the streets. Taken together, the visuals and the hip hop music serve as signifiers foretelling that the students at Barry High will not be white suburbanites.

A recurring trope used early on in the urban high school films—a new teacher having his or her vehicle stolen or vandalized—communicates that urban school campuses are crime-ridden. In *Take the Lead,* for example, Pierre Dulaine (Antonio Banderas), a dance teacher who volunteers to work with the students in detention, has the wheels stolen off his bicycle, which he had locked to a rail a few feet from the school's front entrance. Andrew Norris (Perry King), the main protagonist in *Class of 1984,* has his car spray painted with the message "teachers suck." In *High School High,* Mr. Clark has his car stolen a few seconds after walking away from it. While the teachers respond with disbelief at the theft or vandalizing of their vehicles, there were clear signs that the vehicles would not be safe when they arrived for the day, signs that the suburbanite teachers are too naïve to decode. Mr. Norris has his car vandalized after innocently driving his car into the faculty parking lot as a group of white punk rockers smoke at the gate and an adolescent young man defaces a sign so that it reads, "Abraham Lincoln Fukulty Parking Lot." Mr. Clark, in his case, parks in a dirt parking lot with barbed-wired fences and reserved parking spaces for the local police's Special Weapons And Tactics (SWAT) team and for the National Guard. The juxtaposition of the teachers' naïveté with the criminality in and around the schools in effect serves to differentiate the teachers' suburban lifestyle and their virtuous ways from the depiction of working-class students' lifestyle as deviant and corrupt.

In most of these films, the school's main entrance signals that it is in fact the students who make the school environment dangerous and consequently, require heavy surveillance. Students must pass through metal detectors and have their bags checked by security guards before entering. In the various films, numerous teachers, including some who themselves take guns to school, state that the layers of security are necessary for both the students' and teachers' safety. *High School High* aptly parodies the security and surveillance practices depicted in the urban school film genre, highlighting how the films frame the schools not as sites of learning but as sites of social disorder. At Barry High's main entrance, guards confiscate guns, assault rifles, cleavers, and knives while other guards roam around the school with Dobermans and assault rifles, much like the cinematic portrayal of prison facilities.

Once inside the urban schools, there are further cues of disarray and of students' anti-authoritative behavior. In *187,* which the DVD box describes as "a gritty urban-school thriller," Latino adolescent boys with the "home-boy aesthetic" (Rodríguez 2006)—baggy clothes and short hair combed back or a shaved head—deface the outside walls of classroom bungalows with graffiti during the school day, showing little respect for private property. *Freedom Writers,* which is based on a true story, depicts Woodrow Wilson High School as plagued with racial tension between gang members who are quick to fight one another. According to Yosso and García (2008), many students of color at Wilson High are portrayed as gang members because Richard LaGravense, the writer and director of *Freedom Writers,* erroneously associated the Latino, African American, and Asian students at the actual Wilson High with street gangs. What is more, some of the films underscore the disorder at the schools with music whose lyrics suggest that the working-class students pose a violent threat. In an early scene of *Lean on Me,* the hallways of Eastside High School morph over a period of 20 years as the student population goes from all white to mostly black. The hallways go from having pristine walls and clean floors to walls covered in graffiti and floors littered with rubbish, while the audio goes from Eastside's school song to the sound of sirens. Then, we see the dirty hallways filled with raucous black students and when some boys begin to fight, we hear the Guns N' Roses song "Welcome to the Jungle," which includes the lyrics: "Welcome to the jungle / . . . / I wanna watch you bleed." Hence, in the span of a few minutes, the film sets up Eastside High as a space that has gone from being white and civilized to black and wildly dangerous, like a jungle filled with untamed animals.

In *Class of 1984,* Abraham Lincoln High School, whose student population is mostly working-class white students, including a gang of adolescent Nazi punks, is no less threatening. While Mr. Norris arrives for his first day of teaching, Alice Cooper can be heard singing the rock song, "I Am the Future," which includes ominous lyrics—"take a look at my face. I am the future . . . and you belong to me"—that foreshadow the violence to come in the film. The *Class of 1984* DVD box plays up the violence at Lincoln High, an "academic abyss," by linking it to the overly sensationalized media representation of present-day public schools: "While [the film's] vision of a decaying, violence-plagued inner city school seemed over-the-top in 1982, it sadly prophesized the future of American education."

Many of the films imply that in order for troubled urban schools to adequately teach urban working-class students, students with corrupting behaviors and norms must first be removed, by force if need be. The removal of deviant students serves to warn other students that the teacher will not tolerate poor behavior and establishes teacher authority. For example, consider the advice a gun-carrying teacher at Quincy Adams High School provides Trevor Garfield (Samuel L. Jackson), the main protagonist in *187,* who is serving as a substitute science teacher: "The first one of these *homeboys* that gives you the slightest bit of shit, you march his ass down to Larry Highland. He's their counselor. Right off the bat you have to sacrifice one of them. Show them some balls. Show them who's boss." Likewise, at his first school assembly, Principal Clark (Jackson again) of *Lean on Me* puts the "miscreants" up on stage and announces to the rest of the student population that the students on stage will not be part of his school because:

These people have been here roughly five years, and done absolutely nothing. These people are drug dealers and drug users. They have taken up space. They have disrupted this school. They have harassed your teachers. . . . These people are incorrigible.

Then, Principal Clark turns to the students on stage and says the following before they are all forcefully removed from the school by security guards: "You are all expurgated. You are dismissed! You are out of here, forever.

I wish you well!" Later, when Principal Clark is questioned by a parent for having kicked out the students, he indicates that in order to save the bunch it was necessary to sacrifice those students that his staff and he considered spoiled apples: "They say one bad apple spoils the bunch. But what about 300? Rotten to the core! . . . This is a war. It's a war to save 2700 other students, most of whom don't have the basic skills to pass the state exam." Clearing out undesirable students sends a message of zero tolerance for delinquency to the community.

Some of the urban school films (*187, The Substitute, The Principal, Class of 1984*) are so overly dramatized that they come off as violent battles between heroic, vigilante teachers, principals, and school security guards on the one side, and villainous male gang members attending the schools on the other. As with other films of the good-guy bad-guy genre, the gang members are beaten up, if not killed, and thus vanquished. Jonathan Shale (Tom Berenger), the military-trained mercenary turned substitute teacher in *The Substitute*, for example, relies on a team of mercenaries to fight the gang members at his school, some of whom he had warned earlier: "I'm in charge of this classroom. I'm the warrior chief, the merciless god who stirs anything in its path. You fuck with me, and you will suffer my wrath." Similarly, in *The Principal*, Rick Latimer (James Belushi), the new motorcycle-riding school principal, and Jake Phillips (Louis Gossett Jr.), the head of school security, team up and resort to violence, rather than rely on law enforcement, to rid their school of a drug-dealing gang.

In *187*, Mr. Garfield, who had been attacked by a student at his previous school and is trying to make his classroom "a sanctuary" for his students, goes after members of Kappin Out Suckas (KOS), a tag-banging crew (i.e., a crew of graffiti taggers that engages in violence against other taggers) with a vengeance—drugging Cesar Sanchez (Clifton Collins Jr.) and cutting off his finger, and possibly murdering Benny Chacon (Lobo Sebastian), the Latino leader of KOS. Early in the film, a teacher quotes the president of Singapore, framing the violence that Mr. Garfield comes to engage in as the necessary acts of a dedicated teacher in the face of lawlessness: "When a continued state of defiance and disorder cannot be checked by the rules, then new and sometimes drastic rules must be forged to maintain order. The alternative is anarchy." Later in the film, after hearing accusations that Mr. Garfield committed violent crimes against students, a teacher union representative excuses the violence by stating that "the [school] system failed [Mr. Garfield]." Finally, consider how the summary on the DVD box of *187* describes Mr. Garfield and goes on to suggest that he turns to violence because he could no longer take the disorder at Quincy High School: "Garfield is skilled, smart, committed, the total package as a teacher. But he's also human. And what he confronts in a school turned increasingly into a battlefield may be more than he can bear." The heroes' use of violence against urban working-class adolescents is seemingly justified in these films as the acts of caring humans who are left with no choice but to assail adolescent students with brutal and inhumane natures.

Unlike the teachers, the working-class students that are gang members are depicted as disturbed individuals who merit no sympathy from the viewer because they represent the urban ills that plague the schools. For example, Peter Stegman (Timothy Van Patten), the white Nazi gang leader in *Class of 1984,* takes pleasure from tormenting Mr. Norris and his wife, Diane Norris (Merrie Lynn Ross), whom he and his fellow gang members rape, and in telling Mr. Norris, "I'm the future." In *187,* Benny, the Latino leader of the tag-banging crew Kappin Out Suckas (KOS), threatens various teachers, including one who is pregnant; further, living up to his crew's name, he "kaps" (i.e., shoots and murders) a graffiti writer in cold blood. Juan Lacas (Marc Anthony), the Latino leader of the Kings of Destruction ("KOD") street gang in *The Substitute,* deals drugs in the school and organizes attacks on teachers. Victor Duncan (Michael Wright), the African American gang leader in *The Principal,* sells drugs, punishes a gang member who begins focusing on school, and warns Principal Latimer that the school is his, that he makes the rules, and that if Principal Latimer is "trying to reach [him], [he'll] cut his hand off."

These violent, predatory characters, particularly the youth of color, are also representative of how the film industry constructs and presents one-dimensional stereotypes of those considered "others." The stereotypical depictions of some urban students as deviant and beyond redemption converge with the sociopolitical and media discourses that criminalize urban black and Latino youth. In an analysis of the cholo (i.e., the Latino gang member) stereotype on film, Mora (Abjection) points out that the depiction of cholo as an abject being who threatens the social order with his ill intentions and hyperaggressive masculinity aligns with how actual Latino youth are constructed and policed in the U.S. justice system—as both marginalized young men and migrants unworthy of membership in our society.

While the stereotype of the urban drug dealer and gang member is used to represent the deviancy of urban male youth, the stereotype of the promiscuous and/or pregnant girl is used to depict the deviant behavior of urban female youth. In the film *187,* Rita, a Chicana with gang ties who does not want to be known as "a school girl," has sexual trysts at school with multiple tag-bangers at the same time, has sexual intercourse with a male teacher, and offers herself sans clothes to Mr. Garfield at his house to repay him for helping her with her schoolwork. In *Class of 1984*, the Nazi gang at the high school pimps adolescent girls. In one scene, an adolescent girl looking to work as a prostitute agrees to have sex with male gang members as part of her evaluation. Before going off to have intercourse with the gang members, she is fawned over and caressed by the gang leader's girlfriend. Then, toward the end of *Class of 1984*, the Nazi gang members break into Mr. Norris's house and sexually assault Mr. Norris's wife, Diane, while the gang leader's girlfriend excitedly takes pictures.

Additionally, in *Stand and Deliver*, Jaime Escalante (Edward James Olmos) suggests to the class that Claudia Camejo (Adelaida Alvarez), one of his students, has many boyfriends and implies that she may be focusing more time on carnal interests than on studying, that is, the "work from the neck up," to Claudia's displeasure:

Escalante: [Claudia's] gotta do some work from the neck up. We're going to have to stay late again. Of course you know we have pizza because they deliver. We can get fried chicken, hamburgers with cheese. We'll need donations. No, really, you owe me money anyway. You don't deserve the grades you're getting. [*Claudia gets up and heads for the door*]

Escalante: Where are you going? Late for another date? She's got more boyfriends than Elizabeth Taylor.

Claudia: I don't appreciate you using my personal life to entertain this class.

The emphasis on the working-class young women's sexuality, sexual desires, and sexual escapades serves to suggest that they are not innocent "good girls." Such a depiction of working-class girls in the films is indicative of the negative manner in which their sexuality is viewed by those higher in the socioeconomic strata. Egan and Hawkes (2008), who analyzed both the media coverage of, and the scholarly and activist writings on, the sexualization of girls in Australia, the United Kingdom, and the United States, inform us that: "The disquiet over sexualization is, in part, catalyzed by the fear of class contamination. The discourse on sexualization paints a picture of overly sexual displays of 'low culture' rupturing the innocence of middle and upper middle class girls" (306).

The teen mothers in *Lean on Me*, *Teachers*, *Coach Carter*, *Light It Up*, and *High School High* serve as an archetype that signifies the loss of childhood innocence and morals among urban working-class young women. The two pregnant black girls in *Lean on Me* and *Coach Carter* contend with the possibility that the young men that impregnated them will not take "responsibility" of their unborn children and they will end up as unwed, teenage mothers, as is the case for a disproportionately high percentage of black adolescent girls. Additionally, *High School High* conveys the message that white teenage girls are susceptible to the deviant sexuality of urban girls of color (and the hypersexual nature of Latino young men). One of the students in the film, Julie, is a white adolescent girl who has two children fathered by her Latino boyfriend and is once again pregnant. When Mr. Clark asks her whether she's "learned a valuable lesson" from her third pregnancy, she makes it clear with her response that she had regular (unprotected) sex with her boyfriend and planned to continue to do so: "Oh, yes. Basically as far as vasectomies go, never use the home kit."

The depiction of the pregnant working-class student on film is indicative of the broader discourses that frame teenage motherhood as a social problem. For decades now, public discourses across the political spectrum in the United States have continued to depict teen mothers as emblematic of ongoing social ills (Irvine 2002; Rhode 1995). As Ruddick (1995) states: "In national debates [about teenage pregnancy] the adolescent mother is a symbol of sexual and social disorder; her pregnancy and even more her decision to give birth are represented as causes as well as symptoms of intergenerational cycles of poverty and despair" (126). Consequently, like the gang members in the films, the pregnant girls can be read as abject beings against which suburbanites define their children and their morality.

The central message in most of these films is that working-class urban students, including pregnant adolescent girls and those drug dealers and gang members not lost to the streets, must be willing to change their deviant behaviors and values in order for them to succeed in life and become contributing members of society. For example, at Cooley Vocational High School (*Cooley High* 1975), every school day begins with the recitation of the school code, which emphasizes appropriate moral behavior and presentation of self: "We are honest . . . responsible . . . We do not enter public transportation illegally. . . . We wear clean, neat clothes. . . . We keep our bodies clean. We avoid excessive ornamentation." The code is telling because it suggests that without the corrective intervention of school officials the black students at Cooley would embody the stereotypical and degrading characteristics the media often ascribes to working-class and poor African Americans—criminal, untrustworthy, dirty, and gaudy.

Similarly, in *Coach Carter,* which was inspired by a true story, Coach Carter (Samuel L. Jackson once again) contends that the players on his varsity basketball team, including some with ties to drug dealers, need to learn to be responsible in order to avoid living criminal lifestyles. Before the school board votes on whether or not to end the gym lockout he implemented because some of the boys on the team were not maintaining a 2.3 grade point average as they agreed they would, he tells the board members:

> You really need to consider the message you're sending these boys by ending the lockout. It's the same message that we as a culture send to our professional athletes; and that is that they are above the law. If these boys cannot honor the simple rules of a basketball contract, how long do you think it will be before they're out there breaking the law? I played ball here at Richmond High 30 years ago. It was the same thing then; some of my teammates went to prison, some of them even ended up dead.

Interestingly enough, this speech never took place in actuality; it is Hollywood taking a creative liberty for dramatic effect. As Bulman (2005) explains: "*Coach Carter* the movie is a fairy tale that resolves for the audience the thorniest problems in urban public schools with the purest and least complicated solution—a heroic outsider cuts through the obstruction of the inept school authorities, enforces law and order among the students, and makes the school safe for learning again" (75). The "fairy tale" is made all the more striking by depicting Coach Carter's players, who were mostly black, as deviant, when in fact, they were not. Bulman quotes Joe Wolfcale, a sports reporter who reported on the lockout, as stating the following about the film: "The thing that disturbs me the most is the sensationalized characterization of the kids as drug dealers and trouble-makers. They were not like that. They were pretty good kids, good citizens" (75).

As Bulman (2004; 2002) correctly argues, many of the urban school films feature a middle-class teacher or principal who with his or her effort changes the attitudes and behaviors of low-income, underperforming students. The transformation serves to promulgate the suburban middle class fantasy that the urban "other" can succeed only if he or she adopts the morals, values, and behaviors of the middle class (Bulman 2002). Speaking to his math class, Mr. Escalante acknowledges that his students face the challenge of discrimination and other "problems," but also makes clear that that will not afford them any "free rides." Rather than embracing victimization, he calls upon his students to embrace a willingness to work hard and the desire to succeed:

> There will be no free rides, no excuses. You already have two strikes against you: your name and your complexion. Because of those two strikes, there are some people in this world who will assume that you know less than you do. *Math* is the great equalizer. . . . When you go for a job, the person giving you that job will not want to hear your problems; ergo, neither do I. You're going

to work harder here than you've ever worked anywhere else. And the only thing I ask from you is *ganas. Desire.*

Like Escalante, Erin Gruwell (Hilary Swank), the main protagonist in *Freedom Writers,* tells one of her struggling students that he can succeed regardless of the challenges he faces in life—racism, gang violence, and poverty: "I know what you're up against. We're all of us up against something. So you better make up your mind, because until you have the balls to look me straight in the eye and tell me this is all you deserve, I am not letting you fail." By stating that everyone is "up against something," Ms. Gruwell dismissively minimizes the structural impediments that decrease the life chances of urban working-class students.

Additionally, in *Lean on Me,* Joe Clark (Morgan Freeman), the principal of Eastside High School, emphasizes the individualistic triumphalism that comes with the credo of the American Dream. He tells students at a school-wide assembly that each of them is responsible for his or her personal success or failure: "My motto is simple: If you do not succeed in life, I don't want you to blame your parents. I don't want you to blame the White Man. I want you to blame yourselves. The responsibility is yours!" By absolving "the White Man" of any responsibility, Clark in effect absolves governmental policies and the capitalist economic system of any responsibility for the longstanding social inequities undergirding the social hierarchies in the United States. Clark continues, telling his students that if they focus on their studies, learn, and avoid the urban perils that surround them, the American Dream is within their reach:

If you do not have these basic skills, you will find yourselves locked out. Locked out of that American Dream that you see advertised on TV, and that they tell you is so easy to get. You are here for one reason. One reason only: To learn. To work for what you believe in. The alternative is to waste your time, to fall into the trap of crime and drugs and death.

Principal Clark's lecture, like the statements by Coach Carter and Ms. Gruwell, reiterate the message in many of the urban high school films—that urban working-class students need to stop making excuses about the challenges in their lives, and need to be both self-motivated and disciplined so that they can gain social and economic status within a meritocratic society.

The "pull yourself up by your own bootstraps" Horatio Alger narrative ignores the fact that social inequalities in our capitalist society make meritocracy more of a myth than a reality (Bowles and Gintis 1977). High aspirations and hard work are not always enough for urban poor and working-class students to overcome numerous impediments to their success, including decades of stagnating wages, the loss of manufacturing jobs that in previous generations allowed many working-class students to get a foothold in the labor market and become property owners, the loss of social institutions in urban communities, and the underfunding of urban public schools, among other factors (McLeod 1995). By making little to no mention of the life-altering socioeconomic and sociopolitical issues beyond the students' control, the films place the failure of not reaching the American Dream squarely on the students' shoulders for not making the most of their education, which many in our society view as a great social equalizer. Such is the power of the myth of the American Dream that many poor students who fail to move up the social ladder despite their efforts in high school come to view themselves as solely responsible for their inability to succeed in the labor market (McLeod 1995).

Films that present middle-class educators as heroes also reinforce the "culture of poverty" argument, which maintains that poverty results not from economic hardship or lack of opportunities but rather from the poor's lack of work ethic and self-sufficiency (Bulman 2002). What is more, the culture-of-poverty argument, in effect, holds that poor black families are pathological and highly dependent on welfare (Moynihan 1965; Kaplan 1997). In numerous scenes, the urban students' parents demonstrate irresponsible behavior and drug abuse, with some of them coming across as pathologically damaged, consequently giving the impression the students' cultural deviancy is intergenerational and that poverty is passed on in a cycle of poverty. Such depictions of individuals in financial need demonize the poor by disregarding the fact that poverty is a common experience in the United States. As Rank (2003) points out, "Rather than an isolated event that occurs only among the so-called 'underclass,' poverty is a reality that a clear majority of Americans will experience during their lifetimes" (43).

In a tense scene in *Lean on Me,* Principal Clark lets it be known publicly that he believes his black students' parents are ensconced in the culture of poverty. To the displeasure of Ms. Barrett, a parent and his most vocal critic, he says black parents on welfare can get off if they tried, thus implying that their dependency on welfare is evidence of their preference to live off and cheat the state rather than of actual necessity:

Principal Clark: Sit down with your kids and make them study at night. Go get your families off welfare.

| Leonna Barrett: | How dare you talk to these people about welfare! |
| Principal Clark: | Give our children some pride! Tell them to get their priorities straight! |

By suggesting that the mothers in the room are on welfare, Principal Clark alludes to the fictitious "welfare queen" invoked by President Reagan. Feminist scholar Patricia Hill Collins identifies "the welfare mother" as one of four "controlling images" used in dominant discourse and media to subordinate African American women and girls. She explains that "welfare mother" is conceptualized as an undereducated, underemployed, breeder who is a "threat to political and economic stability" (76). Principal Clark's accusations that his students and their parents do not possess the requisite self-drive to live out the American Dream echoes the reasoning of many conservatives during the Reagan era, when funding for social services was slashed and *Lean on Me* was filmed.

The film *Light It Up* is the rare urban school film in which the main protagonists are all students and the social concerns of working-class students and their families are central to the narrative. The six (archetypal) students—a star basketball player, an artist, a punk-rocker, a member of the student council, a gang member, and a hustler—find themselves the hostage takers in a standoff situation at their high school. They respond to the subsequent media attention by making it clear that not all urban students are gang members and demanding that decrepit schools, including their high school, be renovated and provided with more funding. While the students' demands do highlight both their agency and concern for how underserved working-class students are by underfunded public schools, it must be noted that their demands are not part of an organized, proactive, and sustained movement, but rather their opportunistic reaction to finding themselves as incidental hostage takers with access to the press. In the end, the film's narrative does differ from that of other urban school films, but it nonetheless does little more than highlight working-class students' concerns and like the other films within the urban school film genre trades in the archetypes of black male youths—basketball player, hustler, and gang member.

As we have shown in this chapter, the urban high school film genre communicates variants of the Horatio Alger stories emphasizing the importance of individualism and hard work; personal traits juxtaposed against the students' working-class lifestyles and values, which are depicted as being rooted in the culture of poverty. To achieve individual school success, those students deemed worthy of receiving an education are told by middle-class adults that they must comply with authorities and overcome numerous pathologies that the films present as endemic to poor, working-class neighborhoods—anti-authoritarian youth stances, family poverty, low motivation, lack of hope, truancy, gang membership, drug dealing, and teenage pregnancy. In order to accomplish narrative cohesion of the Horatio Alger storyline, the films sacrifice those archetypal students deemed unsalvageable—drug dealers and gang bangers—by punishing them, excluding them from school, or turning them over to authorities. Missing from the films' narratives is an accurate depiction of either how U.S. schools serve to perpetuate class status or how structural and sociopolitical forces contribute to urban poverty. Consequently, these films perpetuate the myth of meritocracy and the notion that what needs to be fixed so that urban working-class students can succeed are the students themselves.

Note

1. The term *working class* is being used to refer to urban students that come from communities and households that have employed, underemployed, and unemployed adults. We avoid using the term *underclass* to refer to students coming from impoverished households and communities with high unemployment rates and, thus, are in line with Wilson (1990; 1996), who coined the term and then stopped using it because it has been misconstrued and become a disparaging epithet rather than a social class within the socioeconomic hierarchy in the United States.

Works Cited

Bowles, Samuel, and Herbert Gintis. *Schooling in Capitalist America.* New York: Basic Books, 1977.

Bulman, Robert C. *Hollywood Goes to High School: Cinema, Schools, and American Culture.* London: Worth Press, 2004.

Bulman, Robert C. "Teachers in the 'Hood: Hollywood's Middle-Class Fantasy." *The Urban Review* 34.3 (2002): 251–76.

Bulman, Robert C. "The Urban Cowboy Rides Again." *Contexts* 4.3 (2005): 73–75.

Collins, Patricia H. *Black Feminist Thought: Knowledge, Consciousness, and the Politics of Empowerment.* New York: Routledge, 1990.

Egan, R.D., and Gail L. Hawkes. "Endangered Girls and Incendiary Objects: Unpacking the Discourse on Sexualization." *Sexuality & Culture* 12.4 (2008): 291–311.

Grant, Peggy A. "Using Popular Films to Challenge Preservice Teachers' Beliefs about Teaching in Urban Schools." *Urban Education* 37 (2002): 77–95.

Irvine, Janice M. *Talk about Sex: The Battles over Sex Education in the United States.* Berkeley: University of California Press, 2002.

Kaplan, Elaine B. *Not Our Kind of Girl: Unraveling the Myths of Black Teenage Motherhood.* Berkeley: University of California Press, 1997.

McLeod, Jay. *Ain't No Makin' It: Aspirations and Attainment in a Low-Income Neighborhood.* Boulder: Westview Press, 1995.

Mora, Richard. "Abjection and the Cinematic Cholo: The Chicano Gang Stereotype in Sociohistoric Context." *THYMOS: Journal of Boyhood Studies* 5.2 (2011): 124–37.

Moynihan, Daniel. *The Negro Family: The Case for National Action.* Washington: GPO, 1965.

Rank, Mark R. "As American as Apple Pie: Poverty and Welfare." *Contexts* 2.3 (2003): 41–49.

Rhode, Deborah L. "Adolescent Pregnancy and Public Policy." In *The Politics of Pregnancy,* edited by Annette Lawson and Deborah L. Rhode, 301–35. New Haven: Yale University Press, 1995.

Rodríguez, Richard T. "Queering the Homeboy Aesthetic." *Aztlán: A Journal of Chicano Studies* 31.2 (2006): 127–37.

Ruddick, Sara. "Procreative Choice for Adolescent Women." In *The Politics of Pregnancy,* edited by Annette Lawson and Deborah L. Rhode, 126–43. New Haven: Yale University Press, 1995.

Wilson, Julius William. *The Truly Disadvantaged: The Inner City, The Underclass, and Public Policy.* Chicago: University of Chicago Press, 1990.

Wilson, Julius William. *When Work Disappears: The World of the New Urban Poor.* New York: Alfred A. Knopf, 1996.

Yosso, Tara J., and David G. García. "'Cause It's Not Just Me': Walkout's History Lessons Challenge Hollywood's Urban School Formula." *Radical History Review* 102 (2008): 171–84.

Chapter 11

Blue-Collar Heroes: War Movies and the Working Class

Marcus Schulzke

Relations between the American civil and military spheres have always been strained. For more than a century after its founding, the United States maintained a small standing army because of widespread fears of concentrated power leading to despotism (Huntington 1959). Even now, after decades of experience with a large professional armed service, there is skepticism regarding the power of the military industrial complex and the use of force in foreign interventions. Despite this deep suspicion of the military as an institution, American popular culture often celebrates military heroes. The hero is typically a hardworking, blue-collar soldier who leaves civilian life not because he wishes to fight but because he feels compelled to serve his country. He is an amateur soldier who never becomes a professional, thus preserving his link with the common man. This chapter will explore this working-class soldier in movies and show how the same character has taken various shapes depending on the war being depicted. The blue-collar soldier is alternately depicted as a heroic defender of freedom and as an exploited conscript who is used by officers and politicians, but who remains a figure of tragic nobility.

Nearly every war movie pauses at some point in the narrative to reflect on the prewar lives of the soldiers, marines, aviators, or sailors that are fighting the war. This look at prewar life can be used to open the story and introduce the characters. It can be a moment of reflection on what it would be like to be back home. It can also be something that arises casually as soldiers from diverse backgrounds relate to their new friends. However the narrative introduces this subject, this moment of reflection invariably focuses on the premilitary jobs of the soldiers, as if to establish that the characters are normal people who once worked normal jobs. These scenes make the class character of wars explicit and are the clearest source of information about the depiction of working-class soldiers. This moment of reflection is particularly common in heroic war movies. These movies also tend to show class relations as complementary; the variations are rarely enough to cause a rift in the tight-knit group of soldiers who act as a group throughout the film. There are also less obvious ways of representing class, such as by showing the relations between soldiers and their commanders. Films that show exploited soldiers often focus on the relationship between the working-class soldiers who perform the most dangerous tasks and the professionals that command them. Social class conflict is transported into the military, as the respective classes reproduce the hierarchies of civilian life and between the amateur and the professional. There is a strong tension between these roles and usually the working-class soldiers appear to have the moral high ground, even though they may lose the struggle.

The type of blue-collar soldier that appears in war movies tends to correspond more to the war being represented than to the time in which the film is produced. One rarely finds a story about World War II in Europe, the American Revolution, or the Civil War that does not show heroic, unified working-class heroes, even in the post-Vietnam era. At the same time, movies about World War II in the Pacific, the Korean War, Vietnam War, and post-Vietnam conflicts tend to be far more skeptical. The soldiers in these movies are more prone to class conflict and tend to be more critical of how they are treated by elites. This chapter focuses on some of the most popular war films to characterize these styles of representing blue-collar soldiers. Many of the countless war films produced over the last century are necessarily excluded, but those discussed indicate patterns in the representation of blue-collar soldiers. This chapter will focus on movies about the Army and Marine infantry, as these are the services that are most closely linked to the working class. Traditionally, it is the members of the working class who make up the bulk of the infantry and who must do most of the fighting.

The Heroic Citizen Soldiers

The heroic working-class soldier in film is not the product of any particular era; rather, this figure is the result of a certain kind of war. Movies about World War I and World War II in Europe consistently represent working-class soldiers in the heroic form, regardless of when the movies are produced.

This character is equally part of classics like *Sergeant York* (1941) and *The Longest Day* (1962), and more recent releases like *Saving Private Ryan* (1998). The working-class connection is often overt, as this is what distinguishes the hero as an outsider in the military establishment. In many cases, film narratives focus on the soldier's background to emphasize his common character and simple virtue. The lead character is usually an everyman—someone who represents the average American, or who at least seems to represent American values. This soldier usually works in an agricultural or manufacturing capacity until called upon to fight. Farming is a particularly common background for these characters, as this is a deeply valued profession in America. Although their occupation is associated with poverty and poor education, it is valorized because of the proximity to nature and the hard work it requires.

Sergeant York is one of the best examples of the heroic narrative. The movie follows the exploits of a real World War I veteran, Alvin York (Gary Cooper), as he grows up on a farm in Tennessee, becomes a hardworking, devout Christian, and then leaves to fight in Europe. Although York tries to avoid fighting because he is a conscientious objector, he is forced into the infantry. This helps to make him a perfect hero. He is not a professional soldier, nor does he wish to harm others. He is portrayed as a benevolent figure who wants nothing more than a small plot of land and a family. He goes to war reluctantly, but once there he outperforms the professional soldiers on both sides. York's farming background and his reluctance to fight make him appear as a modern Cincinnatus, who, once he has become a hero, will scorn fame and return to his former life. York proves himself in the Meuse-Argonne Offensive, in which he kills several German soldiers and single-handedly forces 132 to surrender. Even as a hero, he reminds the audience of his humble origins by explaining that his tactical insight is drawn from his experiences hunting on the farm. He surprises a group of German soldiers by shooting at the last soldier in the line and working his way forward. This way, none of the soldiers sees his comrades being killed and does not suspect the attack.

Other World War I movies, like *The Big Parade* (1925), *Corporal Kate* (1926), and *Marianne* (1928), show the war erasing class divisions by bringing the rich into contact with the working-class soldiers (Westwell 2006; 19). *The Big Parade* follows the exploits of a lazy rich boy who volunteers to go to France. He becomes friends with two working-class men and falls in love with a French woman who works on her mother's farm. The experience of war gives him new purpose in life and an appreciation for the members of other classes. The exploration of class in *Corporal Kate* and *Marianne* follows a similar path, though with more attention to the way class relations affected noncombatants. In each case, the privileged character learns from the working-class characters and becomes a better person because of the experience.

Many of the early heroic depictions of working-class soldiers come in movies about World War I because that was the first American war that could be transformed into the subject of film immediately following the conflict. However, the same kind of figure appears repeatedly in movies about wars fought earlier in American history. *Glory* (1989), *Gettysburg* (1993), and *Gods and Generals* (2003), which are set in the Civil War, are highly reflective movies that emphasize the value of the war and the noble sacrifices of the ordinary soldiers. Characters routinely describe their choices in the language of abstract concepts like liberty and equality. This gives even the most humble characters a superhuman aura. There are several moments in *Gettysburg* in which one soldier questions another about their motives. Union and Confederate soldiers say that they fight for states' rights or to liberate others and they do so with both elite and working-class accents. They are eloquent and idealistic, but their lofty ideals are expressed through characters who represent average Americans. This helps to characterize the war as a popular struggle fought by blue-collar soldiers who fully support the goals of the politicians and officers who lead them. These movies show the war merging classes into a common struggle. Yet even they fall short of the glorification of blue-collar soldiers one finds in movies about World War II in Europe.

Although movies about American wars before World War II usually show a heroic working-class soldier, World War II movies deserve much of the credit for establishing this film archetype. The myriad films produced in the decades following World War II present American soldiers who fought in the war as heroic citizen soldiers liberating Europe. Many follow the same narrative structure as that used in *Sergeant York*. *To Hell and Back* (1955), a biographical film about Audie Murphy, the most decorated soldier of World War II, closely resembles *Sergeant York*. *To Hell and Back* shows Murphy, who plays himself, growing up on a farm in Texas. As the oldest boy in a family with nine children, he must work at a young age after his father abandons the family. Murphy continues to support his family during the war by sending them his pay. Like York, Murphy is an unlikely hero. At 5 feet, 5 inches tall, he was rejected by the Marines and the paratroopers for being too short. Even once he convinces the Army to accept him as an infantryman, Murphy is teased about his size and appearance. However, he proves himself as soon as his unit enters battle and displays such courage and skill in subsequent fights that he is ultimately promoted to the rank of First Lieutenant and given numerous medals, including the Congressional Medal of Honor.

The epic World War II movies that follow the exploits of thousands of soldiers also explore class, but from a different perspective. *The Longest Day,* one of the foremost examples of this style, shows the first day of the Battle of Normandy from multiple perspectives in the Axis and Allied armies. The emphasis is on the scale of the battle and the coordination of Allied units, as the narrative flashes between soldiers engaged across Normandy. Although the movie does not dwell on the soldiers' backgrounds, the theme of the heroic working-class soldier is evident in the nearly flawless interactions between soldiers. The entire Allied army is shown as one unified group, which, despite some small internal disagreements, is composed of men enthusiastically and courageously fighting as a collective. As the Allies prepare for the invasion, the Americans are characterized as amateur soldiers who have little desire for war. The officers, who are largely drawn from a higher socioeconomic class than the enlisted soldiers, appear as paternalistic figures, who care for their subordinates and are willing to share their burden. The film creates the impression that Americans can forget peacetime differences and act as members of a team.

This epic style is also used in *A Bridge Too Far* (1977), which shows Operation Market Garden, a concerted Allied attempt to break through the German lines to secure control of several key bridges. This movie makes somber references to the operation's unrealistic ambitions, but parallels *The Longest Day* in many ways. The American and British soldiers are at times contemptuous of their commanders' misjudgments, yet they are unfailingly dutiful and many of the problems that lead to the campaign's failure seem to be matters of chance or accident. Once the attack is set in motion the differences of opinion are forgotten. Therefore, even when the commanders make mistakes, they and the ordinary soldiers are shown collaborating in pursuit of a shared objective. The soldiers' sacrifices are presented as noble efforts to complete a flawed plan. Even though *A Bridge Too Far* shows some conflict in the ranks, it never shatters the impression of group solidarity that transcends class lines, which is characteristic of World War II movies.

More recent World War II movies have been somewhat more critical of war and far more graphic in their representations of violence, but have largely maintained the idyllic image of World War II in Europe. In *Saving Private Ryan,* the soldiers charged with rescuing Ryan come to resent risking their lives on a dangerous mission for someone who is just like themselves. In the scenes before they find Ryan, some members of the squad come dangerously close to shattering the group solidarity by refusing to continue the mission, but Captain Miller (Tom Hanks) avoids disaster by solving one of his company's longstanding mysteries. Miller is a veteran of campaigns across North Africa and Europe. His men trust him completely, yet he refuses to tell them anything about his past. Instead, he maintains the illusion that he was born into his position and that there is nothing more to him than military life. Only when unit integrity threatens to completely collapse does he reveal that he was a teacher. The shock of the admission helps him to restore order and later he explains that the secrecy was a deliberate attempt to keep the spheres of his life separate. The civilian life must be sanctified and kept apart from the war's terrible violence.

The film shows dismembered soldiers, civilians caught in the war zone, and war crimes. This serves as an implicit indictment of war, as the horrors speak for themselves. Nevertheless, the patriotic overtones and support of this particular war are clear (Doherty 1993). The story is a veteran's reflection on the events that led to his return from the war; the movie opens and closes with reverent music, American flags, and a view of Normandy American Cemetery. Moreover, the story follows the model typical of those about World War II in Europe. The audience sees a tight-knit group of soldiers, who are ready to risk their lives for each other, battling a faceless, evil enemy. The soldiers act as part of unified groups that are undivided by class antagonisms, a characteristic it shares with most other World War II movies (Appy 1993; 125). Young describes this style of film as "sentimental militarism" based on "faith in benevolent male authority" (Young 2007; 243). Although the Rangers question their mission and some even become insubordinate, they seem to have little doubt about their place in the war and no lack of enthusiasm for fighting. The soldiers die as heroes, accomplishing their mission and killing countless enemies in the process. Only the cowardly Private Upham (Jeremy Davies), who, given his foreign-language skills and writing ability appears to be the most educated of the group, shows signs of serious trauma. The fact that Ryan is himself a blue-collar hero who grew up on a farm helps to justify the sacrifices others make to bring him back to his widowed mother.

The Exploited Soldiers

The exploited working-class soldier is a fixture of films about unpopular wars. This figure is usually a draftee, and a great deal more complex than the Sergeant York or Private Ryan character. Whereas the heroic soldier is usually charismatic, white, and simple to the point of naïveté, the exploited working-class soldier comes from all races, is often cynical or disillusioned, and is not always a loveable figure. Nevertheless, he is heroic in his own way because he fights, despite obvious inequities. He is determined to survive and in some cases even cares deeply about completing a mission that he knows will never matter. This figure is an essential component of movies about the Vietnam War. As with the heroic character, movies about the exploited soldier focus on the working-class background of the character. *Platoon* (1986), *Deer Hunter* (1978), *Full Metal Jacket* (1987), *Hamburger Hill* (1987), and *Apocalypse Now* (1979) make repeated references to the soldiers being poor and coming from underprivileged neighborhoods. This figure comes from the same kind of background as the heroes of past wars and often starts the movie with the potential to accomplish great things, but this ability is squandered by the machinations of politicians and inept commanders.

The Korean War is often called a forgotten war, and this is certainly supported by the comparatively low number of movies about it. Around 2,800 films have dealt with World War II, 800 cover the Vietnam War, and only around 110 are set in the Korean War (Edwards 2006; 178–79). *Pork Chop Hill* (1959) is one of the most famous Korean War movies, and it shows a transition in the representation of soldiers, as it characterizes them in a way that mixes elements of the heroic and exploited models. The movie follows the members of the 7th Infantry Division as they struggle to retake Pork Chop Hill from the Chinese and to hold it against a determined attack. There is something courageous about the struggle against overwhelming odds, but the battle of Pork Chop Hill is tragic. It takes place during the armistice negotiations and, although the hill has little tactical value, fighting to control the hill is seen as a way of improving U.S. bargaining power. Thus, the soldiers who fight to control the hill do so when the war will soon be over and only in order to pressure the Chinese government. The officers who order the attack neglect the men who participate in it, as they decide that it is not worth the risk of sending reinforcements to hold onto a strategically valueless hill. The justice of the war is not called into question, but the injustice of a battle that will only serve as a political bargaining chip is made clear.

In heroic war movies, the audience hears proud justifications for the war and for taking up the call to arms. Yet those about Vietnam rarely discuss motives without reference to the war's class bias. Perhaps more than any other movie about the Vietnam War, *Platoon* calls attention to the class character of war and the injustice of the draft. The central character, Chris Taylor (Charlie Sheen), is a volunteer who joins the infantry and requests to go to Vietnam, despite having a promising future. Throughout the movie, he reflects on his decision and the injustice of the war in letters to his grandmother and expresses the guilt he feels overseeing the working class fighting the war by itself.

> Well here I am—anonymous all right, with guys nobody really cares about—they come from the end of the line, most of 'em, small towns you never heard of—Pulaski, Tennessee, Brandon, Mississippi, Pork Bend, Utah, Wampum, Pennsylvania. Two years' high school's it, maybe if they're lucky a job waiting for 'em back in a factory, but most of 'em got nothing, they're poor, they're the unwanted of our society, yet they're fighting for our society and our freedom and what we call America.

The other soldiers, draftees, are shocked that someone would choose to fight. He is the lone volunteer and they are victims of a country that does not care about them. Their words and actions reflect this. None seems interested in winning the war. Their concern is surviving until the end of their tour, or at most protecting their comrades. The countdown until returning home is prominent and makes even the most abject poverty in the civilian world seem preferable to military life. The movie presents a war that is almost a form of class warfare, with the poor fighting and dying for a cause they do not believe in.

Deer Hunter follows three steelworkers from a town near Pittsburgh. Early in the movie, the audience sees the friends as they deal with relationships at home. Their hunting, which foreshadows the significance of the one-shot kill, also shows that the characters are ordinary people who enjoy a blue-collar pastime. The beginning of the film parallels the early scenes of many heroic war films, as it shows the characters' background and their journey into military service. However, that format begins to break down once the friends experience battle and see that it is much different than they imagined. *Deer Hunter* explores the psychological trauma of war, as the three friends suffer through their time in a POW camp in which the guards torture inmates by forcing them to play Russian roulette. Wracked by guilt, injured, and suffering from memory loss, the friends find it impossible to return to their former lives. The triumphal return that concludes many of the heroic war films is replaced by the struggle of the working-class soldiers to reassemble their lives and cope with loss.

Full Metal Jacket is also overtly critical of the war, but the class analysis is less overt. The characters refrain from openly discussing their backgrounds or even saying much about the justice of the war. Their backgrounds seem to be irrelevant, as they have all adopted a new identity as Marines, eager to fight and kill regardless of the cause. However, as much as the characters attempt to shed their individuality and become part of a collective, the marks of their old lives are still clear in their speech and behavior. It becomes clear that most of the characters are poor and uneducated. They are eager to identify as Marines; this identity gives meaning to their lives and justifies the risks they take, but it also leads them to dissociate themselves from their actions. Aside from Joker (Matthew Modine), few seem to understand the weight of their actions. He offers peaceful resistance through humor and is somewhat detached from the conflict because he works as a reporter rather than a rifleman. Yet he knows that he must obey his leaders and participate in the violence. Other characters are consumed by their roles. They do not reflect on their former lives or talk about what they will do upon returning home. Instead, they celebrate their acts of destruction and constantly talk about killing.

Apocalypse Now takes greater liberties with historical fact in its representation of the Vietnam War, but in doing so, it manages to capture the psychological cost of war. Nearly every character suffers from some problem. The main character, Captain Willard (Martin Sheen), is unable to live without war. Many other characters seem equally possessed by a love of death and destruction. This is particularly true of Lieutenant Colonel Kilgore (Robert Duvall), who attacks the enemy to take control of the best surfing locations. The most normal people are the captain and crew of the patrol boat that takes Willard on his mission. They are the film's working-class soldiers, as Willard makes clear when he reflects on them and how poorly suited they are for war. They are transformed along the way. Most are killed and the only survivor is so badly scarred by the experience that he seems to be a zombie by the end of the movie. Thus the movie shows the devolution of the boat's crew from normal blue-collar Americans to casualties of war.

These Vietnam War movies are unified by several themes. First, the blue-collar soldiers are not always courageous or loyal. They fall asleep on guard duty, run away from battle, question superiors, and even attack them. Soldiers in *Platoon, Full Metal Jacket,* and *Casualties of War* are shown torturing civilians, raping women, and killing indiscriminately. Those in *Full Metal Jacket* routinely visit prostitutes and kill noncombatants out of boredom. Although some of the working-class soldiers in these movies are moral, many are corrupted by the war and irreparably transformed. Second, there are deep class tensions both between the enlisted ranks and the officers and between those who went to war and those who managed to avoid the draft. This is supported by the films' narrow focus on a small group of soldiers, which allows them to depict the "us versus them" distinction. These films usually take an individual focus, unlike the epic World War II films that show countless soldiers working together as part of a determined war machine (Aufderheide 2000; 50–51). Ryan and Kellner find that this heightened individualism is a general theme of Vietnam War movies, whatever their attitude toward the war and the working-class soldier (Ryan and Kellner 1988). Finally, the working-class soldiers are victims of powers they cannot control and these powers force them to fight. Even *First Blood* (1982) makes its hero John Rambo (Sylvester Stallone) into a victim of circumstance, adding an element of critique to the film. However, this series later joins the "return to Vietnam" genre, in which the Vietnam War is redeemed by a lone warrior who is an exaggerated version of the heroic blue-collar soldier archetype (Kellner 1995; 74).

Two of the most noteworthy exceptions to the representation of exploited working-class soldiers in Vietnam are *The Green Berets* (1968) and *We Were Soldiers* (2002). The former closely resembles propaganda, as John Wayne shows a liberal reporter why America must save Vietnam from Communism amid patriotic songs and displays of American military power. By the end of the movie, the reporter has seen so many acts of evil from the Communists that he is prepared to take up arms and fight them. *We Were Soldiers* lacks the same immediacy of a film made to justify an ongoing war, but it does attempt to redeem the war with scenes of morally unambiguous combat against a large enemy force. What makes these movies particularly interesting is that they say very little about class relations. That element of the war experience is largely overlooked, as if to create the impression that class had little to do with the soldiers' entry into the war or the relations between the soldiers.

Soldiers in the War in the Pacific

Despite the heroic image of World War II in Europe, the exploited soldier is a fixture of movies about World War II in the Pacific; *The Thin Red Line* (1998), *Windtalkers* (2002), and *Flags of Our Fathers* (2006) present soldiers as being victims of circumstance, much like the movies set in Vietnam. Young argues that this might be due to the jungle setting, which calls to mind images of the Vietnam War (Young 2007). This may partially account for the negative representation, but there seems to be more than just this, as the Pacific theater was even marginalized during World War II and has always been seen as the secondary front (Dowling 2005; 97). Whatever the reason for the critical representation of the Pacific theater in popular culture, it is evidence of the strange disconnect between the memory of World War II in Europe and the Pacific. Whereas movies about World War II in Europe may show the horrors of war, films about the Pacific tend to explore the psychological costs of war and show disagreements between the ranks. They do not criticize the legitimacy of the war, as many of the movies about Vietnam do, but they present a much different image of the working-class soldier's place in battle. They show war in a harsh environment, against an enemy that is willing to use strange tactics like suicide attacks. These problems aggravate the stress of war and make it more difficult to glamorize.

Norman Mailer's novel about a reconnaissance platoon in the Pacific, *The Naked and the Dead,* was written shortly after the war and shows some of the class antagonisms that divided soldiers of different ranks. Although the 1958 film adaptation refrains from addressing class as directly as the novel, it does show internal conflicts between officers and enlisted soldiers and between different leadership styles. The film juxtaposes the life of the officers, who live comfortably as they order other men into battle, and the enlisted soldiers who must risk their lives. The former are often callous, treating their subordinates as pawns and leading them in an authoritarian manner. The dividing line between the officers and enlisted men corresponds to the characters' civilian privileges, and those who question this division, such as Lieutenant Hearn (Cliff Robertson), are punished with dangerous assignments.

The Thin Red Line is among the most reflective films about World War II. Like *The Longest Day* and *A Bridge Too Far,* it follows the actions of many soldiers. Most are left poorly developed, as though they were part of an anonymous mass of soldiers (McGettigan 2003; 50). It does not explore the characters' working past to the same extent as some other war movies. Nevertheless, its similarity to earlier epic war films allows for some comparison in terms of how the movie represents the soldiers' role in war and the interaction between ranks. The movie was a remake of a 1964 film by the same name, in which the protagonist, Private Doll, is driven insane by the war and begins attacking friend and enemy alike (Critchley 2009; 13). The movie is hardly a remake, since it deviates significantly from the earlier film, yet it explores the same psychological stress as the original. *The Thin Red Line* says little about class, but the image of the damaged working-class soldier comes through in scenes. Conflicts also erupt between the ranks, soldiers have to be disciplined, and the image of the military operating seamlessly falls apart to be replaced by a more complex representation of soldiers and war.

Flags of Our Fathers and *Letters from Iwo Jima* (2006) further develop the World War II in the Pacific style of filmmaking. Drucilla Cornell argues that these movies have an antiwar message and contrasts them to *Saving Private Ryan* in this sense (Cornell 2009). They certainly go further in showing the psychological toll of war. *Flags of Our Fathers* tells the story of the battle for the island from the American perspective and follows the lives of the Marines who famously raised the flag on Mount Suribachi. Only three of the six men who raised the flag live to see it become one of the iconic photographs of the war; the others are killed in the weeks following the event, before they learn that they have become heroes to the American public. The survivors become victims of the war propaganda and their own guilt as they go home to sell war bonds and leave their comrades to fight on without them. Ira Hayes (Adam Beach) is particularly upset, as he sees the glorification of the event as a farce. He continually complains about the public reaction to the event and the inaccuracies of the reports about it. The anguish leads him to drink frequently and he is ultimately sent back to his unit. This turns out to be what Ira always wanted. The fame proves fleeting and two of the Marines have little success when they return to the civilian workforce. Ira continues having drinking problems and dies of exposure in 1955 and Rene Gagnon (Jesse Bradford) becomes a high school janitor. In the end, even the men who receive the most publicity and whose actions are glamorized in the media return to their old lives and are forgotten by society as memory of their achievements fade.

Soldiers in Asymmetric Wars

Movies set in American conflicts after Vietnam show a somewhat different version of the working-class soldier. These soldiers are more politically conscious and better educated than the draftees of the Vietnam movies. They also have far more faith in the military and in their war than the characters of most Vietnam movies. However, they are usually portrayed as exploited figures, despite their greater sophistication, because they are ordered to fight wars by uncaring politicians and commanding officers. *Three Kings, Jarhead,* and *Black Hawk Down* (2001), which are about the first Gulf War and the intervention in Somalia, are good examples of this form. This type of working-class soldier is never an even mix of the other archetypes. Instead, he occupies a gray area between the two extremes and reflects the country's ambivalence about these conflicts.

Three Kings (1999) uses short flashbacks to give the audience a glimpse at the characters' former lives. One was a baggage handler, who is shown lifting heavy suitcases. Another performs maintenance on a copier and has his shirt ruined by the toner. Finally, there is the uneducated, but well-intentioned Private First Class Vig (Spike Jones) who does not appear to have any job and spends his time shooting things. These flashbacks come as Major Gates (George Clooney) explains his plan to steal gold from one of Saddam Hussein's secret bunkers. The other men are reluctant to take part in a dangerous operation that requires them to drive into Iraq alone and in violation of the ceasefire, but Gates convinces them to come by reminding them of how unfulfilling their old jobs were. Although the movie usually has a light, almost comedic tone, there is a serious message about the working-class soldier's fate. Gates, as an officer and professional soldier, is the antithesis of the amateur idealized in popular culture and represented by the other leading characters. He leads the three amateurs into dangerous situations that nearly kill them by promising them money that will allow them to quit their old jobs.

Jarhead (2005) is an unusual war movie in that the Marines never actually go into combat. Instead of battles, here are a series of tense moments that are never resolved by the catharsis of violence. This leads to debilitating tension among the Marines who must suffer through boredom day after day as the rest of the world forgets about them. This shows that there is a harsh reality to war even when the violence is minimal. The Marines cannot live up to a heroic image that can only be expressed in a large, morally unambiguous conflict. Their dedication is never recognized. They make an ignominious return to anonymous working-class lives without the glory of the veterans of earlier successful wars and must confront the poverty and family troubles that result from their long absence. The absence of fighting makes the personal losses they endured seem pointless.

Movies about the wars in Afghanistan and Iraq have presented the same image of the working-class soldier. As in the other movies, *The Hurt Locker* (2008) shows American soldiers struggling to understand the conflict they are engaged in. They seem relatively certain of their cause in the early scenes, but grow skeptical as the story unfolds. The war transforms William James (Jeremy Renner) and leaves him incapable of returning to a normal life. He is addicted to war and chooses it over his own family. He chooses to return to the unending war and to live there rather than to return to his family and life as a working-class civilian.

Lions for Lambs (2007) and *Stop-Loss* (2008) take a more direct look at class and are more critical of the government's conduct of wars. The former is presented through a series of flashbacks that provide information about Arian (Derek Luke) and Ernest (Michael Peña) and their decision to go to Afghanistan. There is a loose resemblance to *Sergeant York* and *To Hell and Back* in the movie that shows the path that led two men from impoverished backgrounds to military service. They attend college, perform well in classes, and receive advice from a caring professor. However, they decide to leave college and join the Army, a decision that leads them to a mountain in Afghanistan where they are surrounded by Taliban fighters. As the other subplots unfold, it becomes clear that these soldiers are courageously risking their lives for a cause they believe in, but that they are being misled by politicians. The class critique is underscored by another subplot in which Arian and Ernest's professor tries to convince a privileged student to understand the price of apathy. In the end, the two poor men die, while privileged students and politicians lead leisurely lives. *Stop-Loss* presents the same message of political exploitation by showing the journey of one soldier, Brandon King (Ryan Phillippe), who returns from Iraq only to be forced to return by the stop-loss program that prevents soldiers from leaving service after their tour has been completed. Between tours King and his friends are shown abusing their families, driving drunk, and struggling with posttraumatic stress disorder in their small Texas town. The film portrays them as scarred soldiers who have survived the fighting for whom the return to civilian life is a constant struggle.

Conclusion

The blue-collar soldier is a central figure in American war films and the way he is depicted holds clues about the popular feelings about war and the military. The character is usually a farmer or factory worker who represents traditional American values. In heroic war movies soldiers are shown overcoming great obstacles, risking their lives, and happily returning to their humble civilian lives. The exploited working-class soldiers may start with the same dedication, but they are manipulated by elites and become disillusioned. Most withdraw from the world and attempt to survive their time at war without making much of a contribution to the war effort. A few rebel against authority figures and others are transformed into merciless killers who can never return home. Contemporary war movies tend to mix these two perspectives on working-class soldiers, but they are usually closer to the latter than the former. In these movies, there is both an element of heroism and of loss. The soldiers win their battles, few refuse to fight, and most return home alive, but they are plagued with questions about the legitimacy of war and the moral worth of their own actions.

Heroic war films invariably present war as a great crusade against evil, but the representations of controversial contemporary wars cannot take such a monolithic view of war. Instead of adopting a single model, movies about recent wars tend to show the same kind of elite manipulation as those about Vietnam while still casting the ordinary soldiers in a positive light.

Regardless of a movie's stance on the morality of war, there is a consistent rejection of military professionalism. Movies as different as *Sergeant York* and *Platoon* are equally concerned with exploring the experiences of amateur soldiers and suspicious of those who make military service a career. A few war films, like *The Longest Day* and *Patton* (1970), are generous in their portrayal of high-ranking professionals, but they redeem these characters by pitting them against aristocratic British officers who lack the Americans' desire to democratize the experience of war. The heroic and exploited styles both reflect American ambivalence about the military as an institution and mistrust of those who see their occupation as forming the basis of a world distinct from the civil sphere. However, the different styles of representing working-class soldiers show that popular attitudes about the working-class soldier's relation to elites and attitudes about the legitimacy of war have changed over time.

Which image of the working-class soldier is adopted depends heavily on a conflict's perceived legitimacy. The heroic soldier is a reflection of national pride about wars that have widespread popular support. The way heroic films show seamless cooperation between soldiers of different class backgrounds emphasizes national unity and the soldiers' ability to shed their former differences and become part of an undivided, national force. Exploited soldiers can be partially detached from the guilt surrounding unpopular wars like Vietnam because they are either depicted as unwilling participants who are forced to fight or as misinformed people who are manipulated by officers and politicians. These films place most of the blame on elites and emphasize the difference between the two groups, but they also show soldiers acting ignobly in response to their exploitation and this implicates the working-class soldiers in the immorality of war. The merger of the exploited and heroic styles in contemporary war movies is evidence that there is now far more support for individual soldiers than there was during the Vietnam War, but that there is still deep suspicion of generals and politicians. This indicates a high degree of polarization between elites and ordinary people and assigns blame for the horrors of war almost entirely to the former.

Works Cited

Appy, Christian G. *Working-Class War: American Combat Soldiers in Vietnam.* Chapel Hill: University of North Carolina Press, 1993.

Aufderheide, Patricia. *The Daily Planet: A Critic on the Capitalist Culture Beat.* Minneapolis: University of Minnesota Press, 2000.

Cornell, Drucilla. *Clint Eastwood and Issues of American Masculinity.* New York: Fordham University Press, 2009.

Critchley, Simon. "Calm-on Terrence Malick's *The Thin Red Line.*" In *The Thin Red Line,* edited by David Davies, 11–28. New York: Routledge, 2009.

Doherty, Thomas. *Projections of War: Hollywood, American Culture, and World War II.* New York: Columbia University Press, 1993.

Dowling, Timothy C. *Personal Perspectives: World War II, Volume 2.* Santa Barbara, CA: ABC-CLIO, 2005.

Edwards, Paul M. *The Korean War.* Westport, CT: Greenwood, 2006.

Huntington, S. P. *The Soldier and the State: The Theory and Politics of Civil-Military Relations.* Cambridge, MA: Harvard University Press, 1959.

Kellner, Douglas. *Media Culture: Cultural Studies, Identity, and Politics between the Modern.* New York: Psychology Press, 1995.

McGettigan, J. "*Days of Heaven* and the Myth of the West." In *The Cinema of Terrence Malick: Poetic Visions of America,* edited by H. Patterson, 52–62. London: Wallflower Press, 2003.

Ryan, Michael, and Douglas Kellner. *Camera Politica: The Politics and Ideology of Contemporary Hollywood Film.* Bloomington: Indiana University Press, 1988.

Westwell, Guy. *War Cinema: Hollywood on the Front Line.* London: Wallflower Press, 2006.

Young, Marilyn B. "In the Combat Zone." In *The Practice of War: Production, Reproduction and Communication of Armed Violence,* edited by Aparna Rao, Michael Bollig, and Monika Böck, 241–52. New York: Berghahn Books, 2007.

Chapter 12

Whistle While We Work: Working-Class Labor in Hollywood Film Musicals from *Snow White and the Seven Dwarfs* to *Newsies*

Brian Granger

Two Walt Disney musicals on near-opposite ends of the twentieth century—the animated feature film *Snow White and the Seven Dwarfs* (1937) and the live-action film *Newsies* (1992)—seem on the surface to embody all that is problematic about mythologies of the American Dream, and the tendency in these invested mythologies to patronize and devalue the laboring body. As the American nation's largest or possibly most long-standing "dream factory," the Disney Corporation is a major creator and supporter of utopian fantasy representations of America, and its preferred vision of America is a world where labor inequities and scarcity are nonexistent. Like Disney, the Hollywood film musical industry is also largely understood and accepted as a major creator and supporter of utopian fantasy storytelling, and it would not be a wild assumption to say that many people see utopian fantasy as the sole justification for the continued existence of the "musical" as a cultural form. Given the shared tendency of these two culture creators to patronize and devalue the laboring body, it is easy to assume that any joint product of theirs, like *Snow White and the Seven Dwarfs* and *Newsies*, would have nothing useful to offer in a discussion of American working-class labor.

The patronizing and devaluing of the laboring body is certainly visible right away in the beginning sections of both of the aforementioned films. In *Snow White and the Seven Dwarfs* the Princess Snow White never strays far from her class privilege, and without offering the forest creatures anything in return, she simply puts the animals to work, as the song "Whistle While You Work" begins. Earlier in the forest she has shared her problem-solving strategy with the animals, by saying that she sings a song whenever she feels things go wrong. The very idea that singing can solve one's problems seems like an uncomfortable romanticization of the forced labor and homelessness Snow White is experiencing here.

Likewise, the opening number of *Newsies*, a rousing song-and-dance number called "Carrying the Banner," shows the band of young newspaper sellers bouncing happily through their boarding house and through the streets of a turn-of-the-twentieth-century New York City, all singing about how awesome and freeing it is to be a "newsie." They sing this despite the fact that they are largely uneducated, are in many cases orphans, and remain virtual wage slaves throughout the film, fighting for a few more pennies although even that increase will not actually bring them the financial independence the creators would like us to believe they find simply by having them sing and dance that utopian fantasy before the viewer. Thus, the beginning of the "Whistle While You Work" number in *Snow White*, and the "Carrying the Banner" number that begins the film *Newsies*, together seem to suggest that all film musicals are unpleasant or at least unhelpful allegories for the lives of the working class. However, an examination of representations of working-class labor in these films reveals how audiences and critics have misunderstood and underappreciated some of these film moments, and a careful look at these uncommon films reveals much about society's views of the working class and about the very structure of meaning in the musical as a genre.

Snow White and the Seven Dwarfs as a Labor Fairy Tale

Walt Disney's ground-breaking film is a good place to begin our careful examination of labor in the Hollywood film musical for a few reasons. *Snow White and the Seven Dwarfs* marks the invention of the animated feature film in 1937 by Disney and his collaborative team, and as a cartoon depiction of a centuries-old fairy tale, it represents in many ways the furthest remove from the "real" and from issues of power and injustice through its fantasy narrative and anthropomorphized animal creatures. As the Walt Disney Corporation's first musical, it holds an important place in history as a kind of standard against which other musicals are often viewed, and contains many elements still visible in the film musicals Disney continues to produce in the twenty-first century. The film is also heavily dependent on the operetta form, which links it to early film musical history as well as to the European half of the American musical's structural and conceptual origins. In short, the film is iconic, originary, and its influence in later film musicals is significant.

The romanticized approach to working-class labor in *Snow White and the Seven Dwarfs* is not only critically overlooked by viewers when Snow White tells us to "whistle while we work," but our lack of attention to the labor struggle as we watch the film is also secured through the physical exuberance of the song and dance itself. Since we know that singing and dancing actually involves physical exertion, the act of seeing on-screen characters sing and dance lets us know that an abundance of energy is present, that the struggle of labor perhaps isn't so much a struggle, and that perhaps the lyrical pep talk in film musical numbers actually have affect, since they appear to us to be working so completely for the characters.

For example, while Snow White sweeps a broom and serves as a kind of overseer for the house cleanup during the song, the forest creatures do all other chores imaginable and exert their entire bodies and energies in doing so. The collective exertion here appears entirely voluntary and the anthropormorphized creatures all appear to be smiling as they clean. However, while the animals labor unproblematically as Snow White's cleanup crew, some interesting things do happen. At one point in the number some small mammals use their brushy tails to sweep the piles of dust they have gathered into a hole at the base of a nearby wall. This continues until a sudden burst of air expels this mess of dust from the hole and sends the sweeping animals tumbling. A mouse emerges from the hole and chatters wordlessly at the ones who had been sweeping dust into its home. Later in the song, a squirrel climbs the rafters of the house and uses its brushy tail to spin up and gather old cobwebs, creating what looks like a dusty wad of cotton candy or used cotton swab around the edge of his tail. As he begins to spin up another web, a very upset spider jumps out to scold the squirrel in the same wordless manner as the mouse.

These moments in the song number are clearly meant to be adorable and comic, but they are remarkable more for the way they disturb the narrative of work being told through the song in general. The mouse and the spider are the two smallest animals in the scene, and thus both moments are situations where the life of a littler creature is being disrespected, its home and personal space invaded. While there is a good intention behind Snow White's directives, and the air of productivity that the song number creates is presented as a refreshing change for the house, we see that others can be mistreated if we are not attentive. These moments, though brief, force the viewer to question the nature and purpose of work and its potential consequences—an impressive achievement for a film that seemed at first glance to have very little to say about the lives of the physically laboring classes.

Snow White retains her remarkable class privilege throughout the film. When nighttime approaches she agrees, with only brief hesitation, to sleep upstairs on a few of the tiny beds, while the dwarfs must fend for themselves for spaces on the crowded first floor of the house. Snow White asks the dwarfs if they will be comfortable, before she goes upstairs to the beds. The moment she leaves, the dwarfs fight over a sole pillow so vigorously that they tear it to shreds—a consequence of the lack of resources they now experience due to Snow White's presence in their house. We see various shots of the dwarfs sleeping uncomfortably, and if we consider the long day they have waiting for them in the mines, it is difficult not to bristle at the way her class presence displaces the men from their own beds entirely.

Yet Snow White also continually displays a deep affection and generous spirit during her time with the dwarfs, and another brief moment reveals the sense of equity that ultimately resonates through the film. After a fine dinner we see a scene where the dwarfs dance and frolic, entertaining Snow White in a celebration of their earthy folk essence. Rather than letting Snow White maintain her class privilege all evening, the dwarfs finish their song and turn to her, saying, "Now you do something." It is the first and only real demand the dwarfs give Snow White in the film, and the comment serves as a kind of class equalizer. She must contribute to the evening just as each of them must, a fair return for the entertainment the labor of their bodies has just provided. Though Snow White has cooked the dinner, this is part of her original deal with the dwarfs, a labor she has exchanged for her ability to board at the house. The moment also serves to identify Snow White as a member of the community, for the comment is a clear indication at that point in the film that Snow White has been fully accepted by the dwarfs.

Understanding film musicals, whether their narratives directly address issues of labor or not, requires this kind of careful, moment-by-moment analysis, a kind of analysis that for much of the history of pop cultural and theatrical scholarship has been underused by those who study the musical as a genre. The analysis in this chapter is derived primarily from the work of film theorist Rick Altman, and to a lesser degree from Carl Plantinga and Richard Dyer, scholars working in the areas of film reception theory and performance studies, respectively. This analysis is particularly necessary at this point in history because it directly addresses the two major problems in popular and academic discourse about Hollywood film musicals and their relationship to images of working-class labor. Altman's work and the work of other scholars helps shape my own theories about the complex way labor is addressed and avoided within the Hollywood film musical.

The Two Problems with Discussing Labor in Film Musical Discourse

Film musicals operate through what Richard Dyer calls "utopian sensibilities," the five types of which can be found in most entertainments: energy, abundance, intensity, transparency, and community (184). Dyer proposes that expressions of these utopian sensibilities are not restricted to the narrative of a film musical but are actually more often expressed extra-logically through such nonnarrative elements of the film as dance, music, nonnarrative lyric content, color, scenery, qualities of character. In other words, the social relevance or "point" of a musical is understood through conceptual elements.

Reading a film musical through its representations of labor requires us to accept the fact that much of the meaning in a musical, whether that content concerns labor or any other subject, will be written into the show and expressed through indirect, conceptual ways, like the ways Dyer delineates. It cannot be overstated that film musicals are high-concept works (incredibly, this holds true for all musicals even when, to the typical spectator, the film seems on the surface to be very low or simplistic in concept, such as *Mama Mia* (2008) or *High School Musical* (2006), for example). The very fact that film musicals are high-concept works therefore requires us to view them carefully and critically. Thus, while many teachers, scholars, and film reviewers understand enough about musicals to grasp that the form traffics in some way with utopian fantasies, their reflections tend to end there. They simply cannot believe, without testing their assumption, that a careful look at any musical would yield anything worth discussing (in fact, it seems that the more popular a musical is in the mainstream, the less likely it is that such a film will see extended critical consideration), and thus the lack of thorough critical attention to film musicals, especially with an eye toward representations of labor, is the first major problem.

The second major problem with discussing Hollywood film musicals is that on the rare occasion when sincere and critical attention is given to these films, scholars have a tendency to analyze film musicals the same traditional way that nonmusical films have been analyzed—by considering the narrative and plot structure as the primary source of meaning, thereby misunderstanding the function of musicals from the outset. Because most film musicals do not deal directly with the labor struggle of the working classes in their narratives, and rarely even bother to show representations of that difficult physical labor on screen, a study centered primarily on the plot of a film musical will fail to "see" the conceptual meaning and function of the film, and as a result will leave much unnoticed that is relevant to the lives of working-class people. In order to address these two major problems, and to create more nuanced and useful criticism of Hollywood film musicals and the way working-class labor is represented in them, and even before we can return to *Snow White and the Seven Dwarfs* and to *Newsies,* it is imperative that we understand the theory of the way film musicals are structured *conceptually,* in order to make sense of how depictions of working-class labor within the film musical's symbolic and visual fields are often misunderstood or underappreciated by critics of these films.

Rick Altman's Theory of Film Musical Structure

The theory of the conceptually organized, dual-focused film musical structure comes from Rick Altman, in his important book *The American Film Musical* (1987), a thorough examination of the musical and a convincing manifesto for a new and coherent way to study the musical as a genre. Briefly summarized, Altman's book-length theory of the musical goes like this: We traditionally look at film structure by considering the plot, and discern meaning in the film by paying attention to the link between scenes involving one central character. It is a linear way of looking, a method that puts an emphasis on a causal progression of events, and is perfectly familiar to us since childhood from the countless plot-centered stories we have encountered. For Altman, the advancement of a film musical's story is not primarily dependent on a linear plot (though such a plot may actually be operating in the film) but through a not necessarily linear series of paired segments or scenes that match a male and a female lead character in a romantic pairing, and this male-female pairing is layered with other paired social values, highlighting a sense of duality in the world of the film. The success of the romantic pairing, usually by the end of the film, is a gesture toward the utopian resolution of the various, secondary opposing dualities that, in the real world, exist in a paradoxical relationship. In order to discover a film's function, Altman argues that we must discover the film's "constitutive dualities," since all parts of the film will restate the film's primary and various secondary dualities throughout its structure (Altman 27–32). The notion of a basic male-female symbolic duality is the first central part of Altman's theory.

The other part of his theory concerns the most common variations in the way this basic duality is expressed and the different social concepts or values attached to the central male-female pair. The variations and their associated narrative structures are explained as different subgenres of the film musical, and so the variations that characterize each subgenre help distinguish one type of musical from another, since Altman argues that on their most basic level all film musicals operate from the same underlying romance-based duality. Altman articulates the three primary subgenres of the film musical as the fairy tale musical, the show musical, and the folk musical, and his efforts to offer a critical structure to the study of film musicals through this dual-focus theory is his great contribution to the field.

However, his overreliance on the presence of a romantic male-female pair is a real flaw in the theory. Altman's argument that the primary duality that organizes all film musicals is made up of two symbolic opposites engaged in a sexual attraction (Altman 48–49) is a theoretical approach that serves his analysis of mid-century romantic comedies well, but seems to collapse when this approach is applied to other musicals across the larger history and range of styles in the genre. I argue that delimiting his theory, to say that the important key for film musical meaning is simply an organizing, opposing duality or group of concepts—thus removing the romance requirement—would make the theory more applicable to all film musicals and helps clarify what is useful to us in *Snow White and the Seven Dwarfs* and in *Newsies* in terms of the representations of labor in those films. A brief return to the structure of *Snow White and the Seven Dwarfs* will not only help explain Altman's theory of film musical organization as it concerns the building blocks of film musical meaning (the opposing dualities within a given film), but will also show how a delimited variation of Altman's theory has more utility in examining the film.

If we take the traditional, plot-centered approach to the film, we see that *Snow White and the Seven Dwarfs* fails on a number of levels, as a plot. Primarily because fairy tales that end in marriages are thought to be romances, if we look at the plot of the film it appears to be a shockingly weak romance. At no point in the film, for example, does the Prince save Snow White from her various dangers or struggles. His saving kiss at the end has a random, deus ex machina feeling, a shoddy, last-minute feeling—if we evaluate the film according to its plot. If we look for a union of romantic opposites in the film, following Altman too strictly, we also see failure. The Prince simply does not appear as a representative of an opposing social value. Altman seems as though he is making a concession specifically for this film when he states that in fairy tale musicals where no romantic pair is present, the young girl is often paired with an older man or men who become her co-conspirators (30–31).

Yet the Prince is, in fact, present in the film in order to provide a romantic pairing, so such a theory would still require the Prince and the dwarfs to be aligned in social value. Their one shared moment, grieving together before Snow White's glass coffin, fails in my mind to secure such an important symbolic alignment, and the desire to see the romantic pairing as central to this text feels like an unnecessary imposition. But if we examine the film according to the concepts revealed through the patterning of scenes, without prioritizing the existence of a romantic pairing, we see that *Snow White and the Seven Dwarfs* is successfully and consistently organized around the opposing notions of industry and productivity of place, on the one hand, and the kindness of home and generosity on the other. All the scenes in *Snow White and the Seven Dwarfs* point to one concept or the other, or to the blending of the two concepts seen at the film's happy ending.

The concept of home is the one with which Snow White is mostly aligned, and this is seen clearly in the sense of beauty and community—whether amid animals or dwarfs—that her presence facilitates. The dwarfs represent a positive aspect of productivity and industry, but one that is not yet connected to the home. This is precisely why Snow White finds their home so remarkably untidy and dusty, while we discover them later at the mines as virtual embodiments of the idea of productive labor. The conceptual point of the film is to bring these two opposing concepts together by the end.

As mentioned earlier, this conceptual focus opens up new possibilities for considering the representations of working-class labor in film musicals. In discussing the characteristics of the folk musical, for example, Altman says "The folk musical carries along with it an impression of pioneer days when . . . the only applicable theory of value was the labor theory" (305), in essence acknowledging that the concept of working-class labor actually determines in part the way we categorize a musical as "folk." However, Altman does not go on to explain how that determination operates. I would not replace Altman's argument of the primacy of the romantic coupling with an equally faulty argument about the primacy of the labor struggle; it is enough to simply argue here that (1) each musical is, in fact, about a labor struggle on some level, though a concern over labor might not be the central conceptual concern; (2) the labor struggle is avoided or mediated in different ways depending on the specifics of the subgenre the film is operating within; and (3) viewing every musical through the lens of working-class labor issues is a productive and progressively critical task. Before concluding with an extended analysis of the opening number of *Newsies*—a scene I hold as quite underappreciated in its embodiment of labor meanings—it is useful to look briefly at the history of the film musical in light of its conceptual subgenres.

Subgenres and a Brief History of the Hollywood Film Musical

Stanley Green's catalog, *Hollywood Musicals: Year by Year,* attempts to list all major film musicals from each year, beginning with the genre's origins with *The Jazz Singer* (1927), and offers the reader a brief plot summary with each title given. Green makes many untested generalizations about the genre and is less than critically thoughtful about why older film musicals worked, but his book is a useful way to look for immediately discernible patterns in subgenre and in the way film musicals deal with labor. Considering Green, then, and using Altman as a critical compass, we can make some basic and by no means definitive observations about film musical history by saying that in the earliest years of the film musical, two forms of storytelling were most popular in it: the fairy tale musical, which drew heavily on the stage operetta form for its European style and content, and the show musical, which drew just as heavily on the minstrel, vaudeville, and burlesque stage traditions for its American style, content, and nonlinear plot elements. The first successful film musical, *The Jazz Singer* (1927), was a show musical with folk musical elements. Yet fairy tale musicals were making it to the screen in the genre's early years, in films like *Sunny Side Up* (1929), in which a working-class shop girl falls for a wealthy man, and in the Jeanette MacDonald–Maurice Chevalier series of fairy tale musicals including *The Love Parade* (1929), *The Smiling Lieutenant* (1931), and *The Merry Widow* (1934). MacDonald went on to partner with Nelson Eddy in *Naughty Marietta* (1935), which led to their pairing up in seven more operettas, some of which were fairy tales in structure.

The basic structure of the musical fairy tale centers on a working-class character who must find an attachment to a romantic other, generally a member of the wealthier class. Because economic/labor transcendence through marriage or romantic partnership is indeed a real avenue of escape, it is a romanticized notion that easily accounts for the proliferation of film musical plots featuring cross-class romantic partnerships—plots that circulated continuously from the early years of the film musical well into the 1930s.

The show musical had been a popular subgenre of the film musical from its inception with *The Jazz Singer* (1927). Yet the 1930s through the World War II years saw the predominance of the show musical, perhaps—as many have argued elsewhere—because Americans in those troubling years desired entertainments that would offer joy and escapism, and the show musical tends to indulge those desires. Simply defined, the show musical is a musical in which the main character earns his or her living as a performing artist of some kind, and the spectator is treated to various displays of their artistic work and to some glimpse into their personal life or struggles. The ideological goal of the show musical was always to celebrate art, the human spirit, and of course commerce, in the face of struggle, and this goal is exemplified in *Gold Diggers of 1933* (1933), which, as Mark Roth reminds us, was the only one of the show musicals of the era to convey the seriousness of the impact of the Depression on the lives of people (Roth).

The show musical subgenre can be broken down further into two types of show musicals that predominate in the history of the film musical: the backstage musical, in which the focus is on the making of, or putting on of, the show; and the biopic, in which the focus is on the individual genius and his or her artistic journey. Examples of the backstage musical during the height of the show musical's popularity include the Judy Garland–Mickey Rooney series *Babes in Arms* (1939), *Babes on Broadway* (1941), and *Girl Crazy* (1943), as well as numerous patriotic musicals in which the staging of a show, either for or with soldiers, is seen as a true service to the American war effort.

If audiences during the Depression era and war years were most entertained by the show musical and its variants, as a way of escaping the dire times, then we might say that the postwar years through the early 1980s—until the rise of MTV and the revolution in musical storytelling it created—was dominated by the folk musical. In search of a definition of the folk musical, Altman identifies for us the four main qualities of the subgenre. He argues that the folk musical presents a "mythicized version of the cultural past" (272); the folk musical puts an emphasis on family groupings and the home (274); because of the overt focus on community, that the folk musical is location-oriented; and that within the folk musical it is the fact of musical expression and not the aesthetic quality of that expression that takes precedence.

The folk musical has diverse origins: the pioneering musical *Showboat* (1936 version); the socially minded federal theater of the 1930s; the longer minstrel tradition that preceded the musical as America's favorite stage entertainment; religious drama and educational oratory tradition; popular social movements; as well as the realist turn in American arts and letters. Throughout the late twentieth century, these qualities of the folk musical subgenre were visible in varying degrees in nearly all of the popular film musicals of that time. Some examples from the height of the folk musical era include *Seven Brides for Seven Brothers* (1954), *Oklahoma!* (1955), *Carousel* (1956), *The Pajama Game* (1957), *West Side Story* (1961), *Mary Poppins* (1964), the Beatles film *Yellow Submarine* (1968), *Sweet Charity* (1969), and *Fiddler on the Roof* (1971), *Hair* (1979), and *Popeye* (1980). Post-MTV-arrival films like *The Best Little Whorehouse in Texas* (1982), *Beat Street* (1984), *South Park: Bigger, Longer & Uncut* (1999), *Team America: World Police* (2004), *Rent* (2005), and *Sita Sings the Blues* (2008) may seem initially like odd late additions to this list, but mythic history or a sense of myth-making, a sense of location, a sense of community or family, and the expression of the common person are present in all the folk musicals mentioned here.

There is a dark side, however. While many folk musicals express a desire for social change on the narrative level, the only clear change its working-class characters experience is in the realm of their self-defined identities. Like the fairy tale musical and the show musical, the hiding or devaluing of labor happens here, too, in the form of romanticizing the reality of the labor struggle and physical effort of those characters. The power structures that give rise to the various inequities of the world in the folk musical remain uncontested in the end by displacing a potentially radical individual character's struggle with power into a struggle over belonging to community, not advocating for real change.

This, then, is the real trouble I have with most Hollywood film musicals throughout the genre's history: working-class labor is positioned as problematic, as something to be avoided or escaped, and if escape is not possible, then it is to be masked or hidden altogether. In almost all cases, the physical effort and difficulties of working-class labor are positioned either in opposition to the imagined life that the romantic relationship would provide (the fairy tale), in opposition to the imagined or engaged moment of the artistic performance (the show musical), or are repositioned as the kinds of unproblematic labor that offers the transcendence the film's characters search for (the folk musical).

Newsies as a Labor Folk Tale

The folk musical *Newsies* is refreshing in its direct engagement with issues of labor, concerning, as it does, a historic labor strike of newspaper sales boys in New York City in 1899. By attempting to be concerned with issues of labor on the narrative level (already a rarity in the history of the film musical), the film reveals in surprising ways how it moves against the standard approach the Hollywood film musical takes to the issue of working-class labor. The film was not a popular, critical, or financial success for the Disney Corporation, and this is partly explained by the general absence of laborers as plot story material in mainstream Hollywood musicals, and partly by the lack of understanding of film musical structure explained earlier. I do not claim that *Newsies* is entirely progressive. Like *Snow White and the Seven Dwarfs*, the contrary movement in the film is momentary, but it reveals the film as worthy of much more critical attention. *Newsies*— as a major media representation of the working class—is relevant to labor studies, to film and performance studies, and to a more critically engaged and wider-reaching musical theater scholarship.

The film begins in darkness, then presents a layered montage of sepia-colored photos and a voice-over summarizing the historical achievements of the newsies. The first real action sequence of the film begins when the camera focuses on the close-up of a memorial plaque of some kind, commemorating "Horace Greeley, Journalist & Publisher, 'Go West Young Man,' 1811–1872." The camera rises slowly, revealing that the plaque fronts the base of a public statue of Greeley. A young boy is sleeping along the top of this base, and as the camera continues its move up the form of the statue, we see the image of a second young boy sleeping in the lap of the Greeley statue—an image of homelessness and child neglect that would be horrible if the boys' faces did not look so angelic and wiped-clean of dirt (though their limbs and clothes are clearly dusty). The boys appear to be having a perfectly comfortable sleep despite the uncomfortable setting, and this is highlighted by the image of the boy sleeping in the lap of the Greeley statue, as though this Greeley, metal and nonliving as he may be, were the father of these two boys or of all the newsies. This iron father clearly does not change or improve the boys' material or economic condition, but the brief choreography of the moving shot suggests that the boys gain some sort of comfort in the cold metal of his presence.

Other readings of the statue-as-bed are operating here as well. To choose the public statue as a bed—instead of the base of a bush, tree, or alley corner, and so forth—suggests a certain social impropriety and boldness, a kind of wild freedom and intrepid spirit. There is risk for the characters in this particular choice: the young boys could be seen as vandalizing the statue through their unorthodox use of it, and their choice could be seen as brazen and socially inappropriate since the commemorative statue is a resting place for the public gaze. In sleeping on and around the statue, the youth are daring the public in the film to "see" them and their need.

The choice to sleep on the statue can also be viewed as an act of aggression toward the city fathers and mothers and the class elite who have most likely provided the funds that sponsored the creation of the Greeley monument. The newsies' actions can be seen as a way of rejecting the authority of this upper class, as well as rejecting the authority and honor accorded to Greeley, and the values he is understood in this world to represent. Finally, their choice to perch there for the night aligns them in boldness with the spirit of Greeley himself, and in this way the children become his spiritual children through the visual choreography of the scene.

The notion of the noble homeless is certainly problematic, but the scene manages to evade the weight of that suggestion by emphasizing the peacefulness of their sleep (assuring us that the nights they spend are somehow safe ones) and the symbolic presence of a powerful father figure in the metallic Greeley. The newsies are, according to this sequence, not only healthy and strapping enough to endure nights spent outside, but in their potentially ironic embrace of Greeley and his values they, too, become heroic and worthy of their own commemoration. There will be no deep exploration of the obvious lack and neglect in the lives of the newsies, and this is emphasized symbolically through director Kenny Ortega's carefully choreographed camera movement.

The next action sequence is a close-up of the various rolls and belts of a large newspaper press, spinning white and black-inked paper at blinding speed, while a young male worker reaches up into the works, as if to check to see if the papers are feeding through properly. Another shot shows another worker looking up as the reams of printed paper shoot past, with a look of slight anxiety. This is dangerous work, high-stakes work, but the personal danger to the print shop workers themselves is minimized by the brevity of their appearance here and by the energy of the full orchestra, which comes in simultaneously with the press worker images as if suggesting a larger, more positive purpose for this clearly dangerous labor. The spelling out of the film title in newsprint-like letters is superimposed over the images of papers streaming through the press, and this image gives way to a street-front view of a building whose sign reads, "Newsboy Lodging House." This brief title sequence, from the first appearance of the press to the final shot of the lodging house, articulates for us the operating duality of the film, a rubric under which all other elements must be organized if the semiotics of the film and its use of images of labor are to be understood and fully appreciated.

On the one hand, we have the realm of the relentless energy, vitality, financial promise, solidity, reliability, and inescapability of industry, though to be in that world means great risk, even death, to one's individual body. Then as a contrast to an image of industry, we have the realm of physical rest (perhaps even lethargy), peacefulness, community, family, and emotional support represented by the lodging house and the very idea of the Home; although to be in that world means to live in the continuous material uncertainty of class and ethnic discrimination. The juxtaposition in this title sequence of *industry* and *home*, of individual versus communal interest, is also a preoccupation for immigrants living in America and is the central struggle of the film. The film is announcing itself not as a musical comedy with a romantic couple and the possibilities of their relationship at its center, but as a folk musical with an argument about American urban labor and its promises at its center. The fact that the film's function and symbolic message have been set up so tightly in this opening sequence is something that continues to be overlooked, and is one of the many reasons that *Newsies* deserves to be better known.

The opening scene continues as we go inside the lodging house and follow the newsies as they rise, dress, and wash up for the day, in the song-and-dance number "Carrying the Banner." The boys' singing clearly emphasizes how routine their petty fights and work-related anxieties are, as well as how their youthful energy will arm them for the day's struggle. While we might see them steal from each other, disregard each other's privacy, and monopolize resources that could be shared, the newsies all appear religiously devoted to helping each other move forward in their business.

One newsie is framed consistently as the mature one, the newsie all the others seem to already hold in high esteem. We see him greeted as "Jack" (played with wonderful vitality by a young, pre-Batman Christian Bale), and his leadership is visible in the way the others defer to him or seek his advice during the number. Dressed and ready, the newsies bolt through doors and into the corridors, with a camera shot of Jack fixing on his cap, and the whole gang proceeds down into the street and the awakening city with exclamations about how "fine" it is to be a newsie. And together they celebrate their lives when they sing: "We's as free as fishes . . . sure beats washing dishes!"

The filmmakers intend this moment, like the ones that surround it, to build to the number's anthemic release into fuller song and an all-out group dance sequence. In proclaiming the freedom that newspaper selling offers them, and in drawing a distinct line between what they do and other forms of labor known to them (the washing of dishes), the newsies articulate a class-oriented desire to be one's own boss and control one's own movements during the course of a work day. However, like the beginning of Snow White's "Whistle While You Work," the act of smiling and singing a catchy tune seems, at first, to be more of the same problematic romanticization of hardship and neglect that bothered critics about the singing chimneysweeps in 1964's *Mary Poppins* (Szumsky 100) and the singing homeless in *Rent*.

The newsies sing and dance their way through more verses to a street uncluttered by wagons or pedestrians, and their last line in this section, "Carrying the banner through the slums," begins with the newsies pausing together before the camera cuts to a shot of a nun. The camera angle is from below looking upward, and as the camera quickly moves upward and outward we hear a handful of female voices in a slow, beautiful harmony. The camera lifts and widens to show three nuns, singing from atop a large wagon, where they smile and hover over a large bin of rolls and a barrel filled with water. They sing "Blessed / children / Though you wander / lost and depraved," and the camera cuts briefly to a shot of the newsies, who cease their cavorting and shuffle over to the nuns. The moment marks the first sound in the film of female voices—spoken or sung—so the fact that it is a trio of sacred women who introduce female sound to this world is significant. The presence of the nuns at first might suggest a greater benevolence in the harsh world of the newsies, and the initial camera angle from beneath the nuns, who we then see in the next shot are sitting atop the wagon, replicates the actual viewing position of the boys as they approach the nuns and listen to their angelic appeals.

Yet the nuns end on the word "depraved"—a clear judgment of the boys—before they continue the stanza, singing, "Jesus / loves you / You shall be saved." They smile and ladle out tin cups of water and pass out rolls to the boys, some of whom we see receiving this good will with great satisfaction, and the moment runs the risk of romanticizing the struggle of poor, working children by suggesting that despite their hardship there will be food and drink provided for them. But this romance of Christian charity is undercut by a near-Brechtian moment of visual alienation as the camera holds Christian Bale as Jack, leader of the newsies, in its frame. As the nuns sing he does not approach, but instead looks on with an expression that appears initially to be scorn, which then softens slightly to a smirk of ridicule or skepticism. As James K. Lyon reminds us, "Brecht rejects the basic Christian motivation of doing good to salve a bad conscience. He has no use for conscience, much less for a Christian God who frightens men into following him" (Lyon 806). Like Brecht, Jack seems to be unmoved by the nuns' plea, and decides at the last minute to take some of the bread before moving on with his companions.

While the newsies briefly partake in the free water and bread, and various boys sing in tandem about their anxieties for the work day, a woman enters and begins to make her way through the crowd, moving past the boys and staring into their faces. She touches a few of them gently on their shoulders to see them better, clearly searching for someone. Because the newsies are already singing, the woman's slower, higher melody becomes a kind of descant. Melodically, it is the nun's melody the mother has entered with, and she begins it in the same light, choral vocal tone, singing, "Patrick / Darling / Since you left me / I am undone . . ." The woman is clearly looking for her child, yet the newsies ignore her, giving her only the briefest look of pity if they do acknowledge her. As she finishes the stanza, she switches to a more emotional vocal register—her chest voice—and belts out the remaining lines in a kind of cry, singing, "Mother / loves you / God save my son!" There is no help for the mother. Yet this very fact, which intensifies what the spectator sees as her palpable fear, works in tandem with Jack's disinterest and the Greeley statue pan shot to visually and lyrically darken what would otherwise be an extension of the uncomfortable romanticism of this entire number.

The pulsing chorus singing continues past the end of the mother's plea as the newsies gather as a group around the plaza, where we again see the Horace Greeley statue from the initial shots of this number. Two bullies appear, and as the opening number surges to a close, we see Jack skillfully evade the bullies in a physical chase that is part cowboy and part swashbuckling pirate. Strong, shrewd, and seemingly infinitely resourceful, Jack embodies in this moment the essence of the newsies' spirit and their willingness to fight anyone bold enough to cause them trouble.

Critics of the film seem to either dislike the film because its romantic plot feels tacked on (a view that a misguided, plot-centered approach to the film will support), or, as Tom Zaniello argues, because the Disney Corporation scrubs this image of the newsies beyond realistic recognition, preferring instead for a depiction of youth workers who are somehow too wholesome, too well-fed, and too clean to be believable (Zaniello). Disney, and other

Hollywood film musical creators, may be guilty in general of what Brian E. Szumsky calls "disrepresentation," in which, for the sake of a dollar, serious ideological or historical content is trumped by entertainment value (98). Yet in the case of *Newsies,* these kinds of criticisms collapse under careful examination.

In a recent and important study of the film, entitled "Carrying the Banner: The Portrayal of the American Newsboy Myth in the Disney Musical *Newsies,*" journalist Stephen Siff makes a comparative study between the film's representations of the newsies and the accuracy of those images when compared to the evidence surviving in the historical and literary records from that era. Working from Robert A. Rosestone's theory of the five areas of "truth" that all historical films deal with—factual truth, narrative truth, emotional truth, psychological truth, and symbolic truth—Siff evaluates the accuracy of *Newsies*' dramatic representations of labor (17). He comes to the surprising conclusion that, "Ironically, the Disney musical took the strike more seriously than period journalists did, even when it showed signs of becoming a children's general strike. Although *Newsies* distorted journalistic history, it also successfully dramatized it in a way that preserves the strike in popular memory" (31). In other words, an unprecedented historical moment in which children stood up for themselves as laborers was given little respect by the journalists of the day, and would have arguably fallen out of public memory by now if it weren't for the work of the musical. *Newsies* and *Snow White and the Seven Dwarfs* are not perfect, but they are films that convey, in their limited but interesting ways, arguments in support of the working class. It is hoped that new work will emerge that investigates the way labor is represented in Hollywood film musicals, which will in turn generate more critical understanding of the representations of the working class in these films.

Works Cited

Altman, Rick. *The American Film Musical.* Bloomington: Indiana University Press, 1987.

Dyer, Richard. "Entertainment and Utopia." In *Genre: The Musical: A Reader,* edited by Rick Altman, 175–89. London: Routledge & Kegan Paul, 1981.

Green, Stanley. *Hollywood Musicals: Year by Year.* Milwaukee: Hal Leonard, 1990.

Lyon, James K. "The Source of Brecht's Poem 'Vorbildliche Bekehrung eines Branntweinhändlers.'" *MLN* 84, no. 5 (German issue) (October 1969): 802–6.

Newsies. Dir. Kenny Ortega. Perf. Christian Bale, Bill Pullman, Ann-Margret, Robert Duvall. Walt Disney Home Video/Buena Vista Home Entertainment, 1992. VHS.

Roth, Mark. "Some Warners Musicals and the Spirit of the New Deal." In *Genre: The Musical, a Reader*, edited by Rick Altman, 41–56. London: British Film Institute Readers in Film Studies/Routledge, 1981.

Siff, Stephen. "Carrying the Banner: The Portrayal of the American Newsboy Myth in the Disney Musical *Newsies*." *IJPC Journal* 1 (Fall 2009): 12–36.

Snow White and the Seven Dwarfs. Dir. David Hand. Perf. Adriana Caselotti, Lucile La Verne, Harry Stockwell, Roy Atwell, Stuart Buchanan. Walt Disney Video, 2001. DVD.

Szumsky, Brian E. "'All That Is Solid Melts into the Air': The Winds of Change and Other Analogues of Colonialism in Disney's *Mary Poppins*." *The Lion and the Unicorn* 24, no. 1 (January 2000): 97–109.

Zaniello, Tom. *Working Stiffs, Union Maids, Reds, and Riffraff: An Expanded Guide to Films about Labor*. Ithaca: ILR Press/Cornell University Press, 2003.

PART II

Blue-Collar Music

Chapter 13

Workingman's Song: The Blues as Working-Class Music

Terrence T. Tucker

The blues maintains an unusual place in the tradition of African American music and American mainstream identity. While jazz, rock and roll, and hip-hop all have clearly defined histories that move from distinct black spaces and sources to be appropriated by white cultural ideas, perspectives, and desires, the blues has curiously remained less affected, as figures like Eric Clapton do not seem to carry the cultural weight of a Frank Sinatra or an Elvis Presley or Eminem. This, in large part, has been because country or bluegrass music has been most associated with the mix of joy and pain, of celebration and mourning that characterizes blues music. Yet our understanding of the power and persistence of blues music in America and in the formation of American national identity rests on two points. The first is the interdependent relationship between the expressive culture of African Americans and white cultural formation and perception. The mutual influence has been well documented by both historians and cultural critics, whether in the evolution of collective identity formation, in the production of sources of entertainment, or in sociopolitical, economic, or legal philosophies. The second has been the reality that the blues has permeated the emergence of *every* black musical artform since slavery. Despite our attention to the more celebrated genres, the blues animates the musical forms even as the styles and circumstances that produce different genres change. The blues has continued to act, as Houston Baker famously pointed out, "a forceful matrix in cultural understanding" that transforms "experiences of a durative (unceasingly oppressive) landscape into the energies of rhythmic song" (7). That matrix allows for a multitude of directions and interpretations that has made the presence of the blues a continuing and vital force in African American expression.

Like Baker, I believe the "blues should be privileged in the study of American culture to precisely the extent that inventive understanding successfully converges with blues force to yield accounts that persuasively and playfully refigure expressive geographies in the United States" (11). In particular, the presence of the blues among the American working and underclass, although taking other musical or expressive forms, remains necessary in the twenty-first century. While race remains the great American subject we dare not discuss, class hierarchy and exploitation continues to act as a presence we dare not see. Virtually any reference to class division is labeled as class warfare and, indeed, disrupts our viewing of the static racial dichotomy (i.e., whites as privileged, blacks as impoverished). More important, there is virtually no discussion of how the working and underclasses resist collectively the crushing impact of wage stagnation, food/gas increases, and an exclusive job market. This chapter argues that blues culture must be recognized for its ties to black expressive culture as part of American national expression and embraced to produce a response to the crisis we face. The events of the first decade of the twenty-first century—9/11, Hurricane Katrina, the Great Recession, anxiety over anti-Americanism—have been most acutely felt by the working class. The response has been uncritical fear, anxiety, and rage. By serving as an important influence on country music and bluegrass, the blues remains a distinct black tradition that indirectly serves as the primary source of entertainment and ideology for the white working class. I contend, therefore, that the blues sits at the center of an American tradition of hope and if embraced in its uncensored form can act as an important source in the production of an American ability to confront the multiple internal tensions and national crisis.

In "Goin' up the Country: Blues in Texas and the Deep South," David Evans points out that blues artists were initially linked "with the class of displaced migratory workers seeking cash work in the levee camps and lumber camps, building roads and railroads, picking cotton during the harvest season, hauling wood or coal, working on the riverboats, or seeking work in the towns and cities. He avoided being tied to land, either as an owner or through a long-term sharecropping arrangement, as this meant the loss of mobility and acceptance of the social status quo" (36). The figure of the bluesman has sustained its appeal in large part by sticking to the subjects and spaces that these workers frequently experienced. Those spaces were recognized by the working and underclasses of both races. According to Evans, the bluesman, "preferred to sing and play for tips on street corners and in parks, on passenger trains and riverboats, and at railroad stations, pool halls, bars, cafes, brothels, house parties, dances, and traveling shows" (36–37). The blues seizes on themes of rootlessness, of disenfranchisement, and of a temporal existence dramatized by the dramatic, the romantic, and the absurd. The ability to depict the daily struggles of these larger themes results in a confrontation not only with the larger forces of economic exploitation and racial discrimination, but with byproducts of those larger forces; in taking on, and ultimately transcending disillusionment, rage, loneliness, and nihilism, the blues becomes a significant American form grounded in working and underclass experiences and voices. Although there is certainly a tradition in America of creating forms of entertainment that act as escapism, including those that stereotype African Americans, Ralph Ellison's belief that American is "part Negro American" would suggest that blues culture must also be part of American expressive culture. This chapter seeks to reveal the connections and complexities that blues music has to both the African American community and culture and the white working-class and expressive culture.

Charles Wolfe points out, "As the 1930s drew to a close, the blues was assimilated into more and more forms of commercial country music. The 'blue yodel' was gone, a victim of overexposure, and there were no longer many country artists who thought of themselves as blue specialists" (262). Not surprisingly, country and blues music take on topics, the politically volatile or incorrect, the sexually explicit, or the dramatically mundane, that leave them outside of popular and critical discussions of definitive and mainstream American artforms. More important, they are more difficult to discuss because of their often racy topicality and because they are more solely based on an intimate, visceral connection between artists, audience, and subject. Instead of the focus on composition and form, technological advances or individual celebrities, country and blues traditionally evoke core emotional responses from the dramatically compromising or the surprisingly and touchingly commonplace. As a result, both have been relegated, in the eyes of many, to rural, localized artforms, with country associated with white "hillbillies and trash," and blues music—when not completely ignored—is seen through portraits of old black men and Mississippi juke joints. Perhaps they, more than any other musical forms, reinforce racialized boundaries that are traced to staunch cultural differences. Country remains distinctly white while the blues are thought to be distinctly black. However, even Bill Monroe, thought of as the father of bluegrass, by 1940 was "giving notice that 'the taste of the blues,' as [Monroe] put it, would be a major part of the new music he was inventing. The notion of white blues was no longer novel, and producers no longer thought of it as an automatic ticket to big sales, but it was on its way to becoming a part of the deep fabric of country music" (Wolfe 263). The relationship between blues and country and bluegrass music has mirrored the dichotomy of race that has characterized the relationship between blacks and whites and whose material examples appear in the institutions of slavery and Jim Crow segregation. For Wolfe, "Just as jazz bands eagerly tacked the label 'blues' on almost any dance tune, early country artists were quick to add the 'blues' suffix to a variety of songs of all type. Yet, although the major record companies maintained, the field sessions that recorded the music were themselves quite integrated" (236). What those sessions revealed is the "give and take between white and black music 'in the field' was always greater than the segregated record series implied" (237). Like the institutions of Jim Crow or voting rights, the seemingly fixed status of the color line adopted by members of both races often masks a cultural interdependency.

More important, what we see is not a separation of genres that might occasionally intersect, but an active consistent relationship between two artforms that resembles the more complicated relationship between African Americans and whites that was cloaked behind the staunch presence and violent maintenance of Jim Crow segregation. What emerges is the realization of the blues that moves beyond traditionally "black" forms of music. Such an entangled relationship plays a significant role in constructions of both blackness and whiteness as well as the perceptions and ideology that members of both groups adopt. Thus, while these forms of music all emerge from distinctly rural cultures in the South and Midwest, our conception of music remains segregated. Yet the white artists themselves, as Wolfe points out, "found in the blues rich inspiration. As they adapted and reworked both material from the city blues and the more indigenous country blues, they soon forged their own version of the music: a genre called white blues," which became a popular type "of early country music" (237). Both have been instrumental in the formation of working-class culture and ideology, and therefore the influence of blues on country music and on the conception of the white working class makes blues music a central presence in working-class perspective as a whole. What becomes significant, however, is the specificity with which the blues depicts a distinct, collective African American experience, even though, as a segregated musical form, the blues reveals a significance that reaches beyond the boundaries of African American culture.

Commenting on the eventual appearance of Amiri Baraka's 1963 study *Blues People,* Allan Moore sees the previous absence of such a work as a "clear comment on its 'low' status as music, on the minimal values placed on understanding the culture, and indeed on the lack of interest in understanding how music functions socially in general. Baraka saw the emergence of the blues as marking the transition from the African as transient to the African as American" (9). Although frequently ignored for its collective sociopolitical importance, the blues has become increasingly well studied because of the irresistible charm of its individual performers and the continuing devotion of its (white) fan base. This chapter, however, situates itself away from viewing the blues as an artform that exists solely for pleasure and entertainment; instead it looks at the cultural significance of blues and its ability to push back against racist oppression and class exploitation. Perhaps more important, as Jeff Todd Titon points out, "most blues researchers understood that roughly until the 1950s and the era of the Civil Rights Movement, blues was a music of the African American underclass: they had invented it, nurtured it, and popularized it primarily in their own communities" (16). While generally well-known and well-established, Titon's recognition of the blues as generally the domain of the underclass assumes that there was little impact on the white working class. Aside from its influence on country music and eventually rock and roll, the blues-toned perspective that permeated the African American community would become a part of American mainstream ideology.

So, then, it is not the artists who fail to recognize the ways in which the blues comes to represent multiple racial and working-class interests, but the larger culture's investment in the maintenance of a segregated and specifically white-dominated America. For instance, Paul Oliver has said, "Traditionally the white man in the South has had an avuncular relationship with the Negro and if, in growing from youth to manhood, he has had to shake off the rule of the mother, he has been unable to reject the father-figure of the white boss. If Negro songs display an adolescent absorption with pornography they afford some outlet for repressed aggression canalizing, at least, the frustrations of stunted growth. Recently the blues singer has been lionized in some small sections of the white community, and not every singer can adjust himself to the situation" (256). Oliver points out the practice of younger whites turning toward African American musical expression as part of their defiance of the social/religious strictures of the older generation. It is the adoption not only of African American expressive art that challenged the society's desire to make racial segregation pervasive, but the frank subject matter and language that reject (white) middle-class bourgeois values and rhetoric. While Oliver may be correct in suggesting that the "frustrations of stunted growth" expressed in the blues appeal to white youth, their eventual invocation of white privilege leads to the appropriation, exploitation, and adoption of those forms and renders that defiance hollow because the form becomes disconnected from the source and subjects that initially caught the attention of whites. Blues music has been more resiliently connected to African Americans because it acts as the source of expressive culture instead of a mere byproduct. The blues continues to emerge from the second-class status with which African Americans find themselves, beginning with slavery. Instead of viewing the blues as a (brief) answer to the angst of white adolescence and rebellion, this chapter is interested in the impact the blues has on the working class and how it influences our understanding of the relationship between the white working class and the sizeable African American community. Part of the larger culture's investment in a segregated America cloaks the ability of the blues to build connections across racial lines and to speak directly to the anxieties, fears, and joys of the working and underclass. That other artforms emerge from, or are shaped by, blues culture speaks to the pervasiveness of African American culture in American life. However, it also reveals a shared site of despair, longing, and resistance that is part of the working-class's relationship to mainstream, hegemonic forces, ones that transcend artificial racial boundaries we frequently erect. The importance of the blues is that it rejects a "small section of the white community" that uses its influence to produce an economic industry and cultural elite that requires their critical reviews and praise to filter which works are "deserving" and which works are not. The system assumes that the working class is unable to appreciate or recognize avant garde work and that the cultural elite must protect and inform what artforms should be acclaimed. However, the blues reveals the presence of the white working class and the adoption of blues themes and styles that frequently resist the elite and actively seeks to generate a portrait of the everyday struggles of the working and underclass in rural towns and midsize cities.

Blues Music and the Threat of Blackface Minstrelsy

Paul Oliver points out, "Most writing on the blues appears in books on jazz apart from the few specialized studies of blues that have appeared. Works on Negro life and culture and on the popular Negro art seldom give more than the most superficial attention to blues" (166). Many have assumed that jazz is synonymous with blues and have used the significant influence of blues on the formation of jazz as a means to consider the two interchangeable; yet the popularity of jazz and the appropriation and narrowing of a definition of jazz excludes the blunter, guttural, and confrontational style that often appears with the blues. The blues is certainly less politically correct, and its artists are as likely to take on sexually explicit subjects as they are politically conscious topics. Allan Moore has revealed, "It was only after 1950 that middle-class black aspirations began to be achieved, and as the Civil Rights movement gained momentum through the 1950s, and as accommodation to the status quo became more widely replaced by a discourse of struggle, the blues faded from black awareness, as embodying a message which was out of tune with the times" (4). While the entrance of African Americans into the democratic tradition and American mainstream are and should, to some extent, be lauded, the result of integration has been the marginalization of expressive forms and critical perspectives that were catalysts in African American resistance struggles. The willingness of, say, urban blues to confront the issues of overcrowding, migration, and police brutality makes it a key form in the conveying of black frustration at white racist oppression. With integration, the popularity of the blues centered instead on the desire for white pleasure and entertainment, a process that simultaneously minimized the ability of blues music to produce the unease that Eric Lott often assigned to minstrelsy in his seminal work *Love and Theft: Blackface Minstrelsy and the American Working Class.*

In the book, Lott rightly points out that the significance of the blackface minstrel show is that it acts as a site that fulfills "the particular desire to try on the accents of 'blackness' and demonstrates the permeability of the color line" (6). Minstrelsy, of course, is the first example of white appropriation and exploitation of black expressive culture and while it may be its most grotesque distortion, it may be its most telling. This chapter draws a number of parallels between blues music and the black cultural practices from which minstrelsy draws. This is not, of course, to suggest that blues music possesses the racist underpinnings and stereotypical constructions that minstrelsy did. But both reveal what Lott has described as "less a sign of absolute white power and control than of panic, anxiety, terror, and pleasure" and for Lott the minstrel show helped "facilitate safely an exchange of energies between two otherwise rigidly bounded and policed cultures, a shape-shifting middle term in racial conflict which began to disappear (in the 1920s) once its historical function had been performed" (6). Minstrelsy established an interracial tradition that seeks and maintains a "cultural marker or visible sign of cultural interaction" that solved the problems of conflict and attraction that are part of our national racial history. While minstrelsy may have fallen out of favor as a cultural marker, it did not eradicate the desire for a marker of some sort, whether for white escape, pleasure, rebellion, or profit. Even though ensuing markers like jazz or the blues provided an opportunity for African American control over what types of performances were produced, the ability of whites to marginalize, erase, or ignore the presence of African American culture in popular entertainment and culture often stunted a transformative integration of black expressive tradition into American national identity. What we saw instead was an assimilation that demanded the maintenance of white privilege and of a cultural conformity that eventually made jazz much easier to absorb than blues' often racy, taboo, and plainspoken style. Additionally, this assimilation has cloaked Ellison's idea of America as "half Negro" and has allowed for the maintenance of the belief that the two "bounded and policed cultures" exist virtually absent of cultural sharing, especially with regard to the working classes.

Like minstrelsy, uncensored—and by uncensored I mean a tradition flexible enough to both engage and critique commercial culture—blues tradition reveals what Lott refers to as "contradictory racial impulses at work, impulses based in the everyday lives and racial negotiations of the minstrel show's working-class partisans" (4). I am particularly interested in rejecting the idea of "working-class racial feeling as uncomplicated and monolithic, and historians of working-class culture have usually concurred—or made apologies" (4). If we begin to recognize that the black and white working classes are more dynamic than is typically acknowledged, the common interaction materially and culturally that the white and black working and underclasses have with each other makes the influence of blues tradition in both bluegrass and country exceedingly apparent. Instead of seeing the blues and black music generally as if the white working class becomes the last group to embrace, if ever, black expressive forms, we should recognize that the blues first enters the fabric of American national identity and popular culture from its exposure to and interaction with working-class white cultural perspectives and responses. This reality rejects the idea that the development of the artform occurred within an historical and racial vacuum. James Cone believes that "Taking form sometime after the Emancipation and Reconstruction, [the blues] invited black people to embrace the reality and truth of black experience" (110). By situating the emergence of the blues in a post–Civil War context, we can see the blues as an answer to the realignment of white supremacy after Reconstruction whether through the sharecropping system, the prison industrial complex, and violent enforcement of segregation. Even when the blues is not interrogating explicitly the social, political, and economic exploitation of post–Civil War

America, it speaks to the byproducts of those systems of oppression. For these reasons, the blues has been sustained by distinct African American experiences and spaces and avoided the historical treatment of African American expressive culture. Lott points out that a "heedless (and ridiculing) appropriation of 'black' culture by whites in the minstrel show" resulted in "guilty whites all the more because they were so attracted to the culture they plundered" (8). Interestingly, it has often been the presence of African Americans and the appropriation of black expressive forms that have acted as the space where the frustrations and anxieties of the white working class were placed. Instead of a critique of the political and economic elite, blame for the plight of the white working class has traditionally been placed with the African American community, either as a proof of their privilege or a threat to their advancement. African American expressive culture, then, has not only become a source of entertainment but, when appropriated and exploited by whites, has reified perceptions of white superiority by seizing black stereotypes. The fear of incurring the mark of blackness fed into the working-class whites' attempts to distinguish themselves from blacks in the eyes of the white elite. Thus, the need to not only prioritize and maintain white privilege, but to marginalize distinctly "black" cultures as "different," "taboo," and separate, resulted in making culture and race synonymous. However, the continual fascination with and engagement of the color line reveal the inability of maintaining such strict racial and cultural boundaries. The blues, then, underwrites the cultural relationship between African Americans and whites by disrupting the strict boundaries that working-class whites enforced by taking on subjects and forms that often spoke to the working and underclass while avoiding the sophisticated filtering appropriation process of the cultural and class elite that we see with other musical forms. It is, then, a return to the blues that stands to have a constructive impact on national identity, race relations, and class crises.

The Blues as Working-Class Music

The working-class roots of the blues are, of course, not separate from its significant role in African American life. Although we continue to cite Africa as one of the primary sources of the blues, it is out of the realities, and in particular the labors, of the slave, the sharecropper, and the working man that the blues has been most acutely defined. Often seen as both a rejection of the imposition of white Christian theology and a salve against the crushing weight of racial and economic exploitation, the blues often manifested itself in the form of work songs that took on topics considered taboo by the church and a tone considered dangerous in front of whites. James H. Cone points out, "The blues are about black life and the sheer earth and gut capacity to survive in an extreme situation of oppression" (108). And yet, David Evans has pointed out that the blues historically "had less appeal" for "the religious segment of the black population who viewed the blues as sinful, or for the upwardly mobile and educated class" (21). Evans, of course, argues that the need for musicians to make a living inherently makes the blues a commercial venture and, thus, susceptible to the capitalist forces that often sacrifice more complex or experimental forms and controversial subject matters in order to increase popularity and profits. As a result, our conception of blues becomes one dominated by themes of romance and tragedy, whether they are tales of wild nights or heartbreak. Similarly, images of the working and underclass frequently assume an absence of any critical consciousness among individuals who seek entertainment as a reprieve or an anesthetic that evades the socioeconomic forces that surround them. However, Samuel Charters reveals that "It is out of all these elements—the singing of the West African griots, the holler, the work song, the song traditions of the southern countryside, and even slack-key guitar—that the blues was formed" (27). Thus, the blues emerges as a working-class soundtrack that foregrounds ritualized pleasure as opposed to critical examination of the byproducts of hegemonic oppression. The need for a cultural, political, economic elite to make decisions and solve problems for the whole is justified by establishing a hierarchy based on images of what behaviors, objects, or practices are considered normal or desirable. So, for example, the cultural elite might decide to privilege the preservation and celebration of the form in order to increase its value and associate the form with the cultural sophistication and superiority that frequently excludes the working and underclass. While Cone points out that the "work songs" from which the blues emerges, "were a means of heightening energy, converting labor into dances and games, and providing emotional excitement in an otherwise unbearable situation. The emphasis was on free, continuous, creative energy as produced in song" (109), discussion of the blues decontextualizes the music in favor of the aspects of the form that more easily fit into an idealized American narrative, one influenced by the bourgeois ideology that we see in the attitudes of the elite.

A key example is in the treatment of Shakespeare whose works were wildly popular in the United States throughout the nineteenth century, particularly in the burlesques found throughout the frontier. However, at the beginning of the twentieth century, working and in-depth knowledge of Shakespeare became a rite of passage that signaled membership in the educated class. The process maintains and enforces a cultural hierarchy that is often made interchangeable with a class hierarchy; it also ignores forms the elite deem "low art" and relies on stereotypical portraits as a means of exclusion. The hierarchy separates the form not only through the development of a language that the elite shape and deploy, but also through the maintenance of a static, idealized portrait that discourages the dynamism of the working class. In contrast to an approach that removes any type of historical context, the blues, according to Cone, "While not denying that the world was strange, described its strangeness in more concrete and vivid terms. Freedom took on historical specificity when contrasted with legal servitude. It meant that simple alternatives, which whites took for granted, became momentous options for newly 'free' black slaves. It meant getting married, drinking gin, praising God—and expressing these historical possibilities in song" (113). In August Wilson's 10-play cycle, the blues plays a central role and mines the tension between the attempts at American individualism and African American collective voice. His blues artists, in his plays *Ma Rainey's Black Bottom* (1984) and *Seven Guitars* (1996), alternate between seeking fame and using the blues as part of resisting the forces of white supremacy. The former comes by succumbing to labels and market expectations of blues at the expense of their cultural traditions and even their band mates. The latter embraces Wilson's infusion of the blues as part of the daily experience of all the African American characters in his plays. When his characters, like Levee in *Ma Rainey* and Floyd in *Guitars,* become more enamored with profit than they do with the ability of African American expressive culture to resist white supremacist capitalism, they commit a type of cultural suicide that leads to their death, often at the hands of the more nationalist figure of the play. Evans believes, "With its social institutions under siege, a sense of individualism grew in the black community, and this is reflected in blues and the other new musical forms that arose at this time. . . . Individualism, of course, was a growing factor in white society at this time, related to industrial competition, but for whites it often became a vehicle for opportunity and success. For blacks it was a matter of survival" (21). Wilson's plays, of course, openly refuse to separate the oral performance of blues music and culture from the collective spirit and subjectivity of African Americans. His plays mirror the attempt by the blues and its artists to navigate the competing forces of the market versus cultural tradition, individualist versus collective spirit.

Here we see how the combination of African and European influences shapes the context from which blues emerges, African American identity and culture. As Evans notes, "Songs of social commentary, praise and derision, boasting and self-pity are also common in many African traditions, and aspects of the lifestyle of blues singer and the social position of the outsider can be observed in African minstrel and griot traditions" (24). However, we also see how the contradictory cultural impulses produce the "double consciousness" that W.E.B. DuBois made famous in *The Souls of Black Folk* (1903). So, the rugged individualism that has been a hallmark of American national identity had a significant impact on African American culture as a means of escaping the violent stereotype of a monolithic black community used to sustain slavery and eventually used to erect Jim Crow segregation. However, the move toward individualism is met with extreme resistance and conflict within a community that often uses its collective perspective and cultural responses to reject the alienation and depression that eventually emerges not only in an industrial, modernist post–World War I America, but because of the crushing forces of white supremacy that often overwhelmed African Americans and whose only and most constructive recourse was to pull from the collective strength and voices of the African American community. Despite the benefit of individualism at certain moments, the push toward a narrow individualism also threatens the most important intersection of African American and mainstream American ideas; specifically, the realization of democratic ideals that allow dynamic individualism within an inclusive collective. It is that mix of dynamism and inclusion that fuels the blues and more easily works as an important element in contemporary American identity and perspective.

Conclusion

James Cone rightly contends, "The blues are not art for art's sake, music for music's sake. They are a way of life, a life-style of the black community; and they came into being to give expression to black identity and the will for survival" (124). Because I contend that African American music underwrites much of the American national and cultural narrative, the presence of the blues can resonate with working-class whites who are facing similar threats of disillusionment, disenfranchisement, and rage. Additionally, the embrace of an unfiltered blues culture has the potential to refashion the traditional and problematic relationship between the white working class and African American expressive culture. Our need to racialize musical forms, as a byproduct of our need to sustain racial difference, even in a "postracial" America, ignores the potential class solidarity that can emerge between races by looking at the similarities with which they engage questions about the environment that surrounds and influences them. Whether those environmental forces are poverty, rage, anguish, or passion, the blues transforms those feelings into a grasp for hope, an articulation of tragedy, and a celebration of life regardless of how flawed it might be. Evans informs us, "blues introduced to popular song a new frankness, breadth of subject matter, and assertiveness. The songs demanded to be taken seriously, thus causing their singers and the subculture they represented to be taken seriously as well. Blues were distinctly secular and worldly, unsentimental, sexually explicit, and ironic, with an undertone of deep dissatisfaction" (22). Narrower definitions have sought to localize the traits displayed in blues music into a paradigm that not only includes a full range of individual relationships and emotions but which remains disconnected from an exploration of the larger forces of white supremacy, material-driven capitalism, and religious fundamentalism that will drive the frank treatment of subjects of blues songs. Not surprisingly, a similar frankness, unsentimentalism, and secularism exists within working-class culture as well as other "low" arts from hard-boiled detective fiction to anti-Prohibition bootlegging. Although a strong religious strain has been a hallmark of African Americans and the white working class, we frequently see malleability between the sacred and the profane similar to the line between whites and African Americans. The blues rejects the strict fundamentalism that has been associated with Protestantism even though many blues artists, like B. B. King, began in the church and incorporate any number of elements in the gospel tradition into their music. Steve Tracy sees the presence of what he refers to as "optimism" acting as "implicitly or explicitly a defiance of defeat through the acts of creating and performing themselves; optimistic in its assertion of voice and humanity in a world that restricted or denied them both" (90). Part of maintaining an uncensored blues tradition is in viewing it as a separate, autonomous space that exists outside the commercialism that often dictates how the mainstream sees musical forms and the cultures with which it is associated. Tracy suggests that the result of the popularization of the form "has seen the blues leave juke joint and back porch for tours such as the American Folk Blues Festival in the 1960s and early 1970s, and events sponsored by large tobacco and alcohol companies anxious to cash in on the blues' appeal. Nevertheless, one can encounter blues and gospel in small, informal venues where it continues to serve its intimate, personal functions unconnected to the commercialism that sometimes threatens to engulf it" (100–101). Tracy recognizes the significance of the form but also its fundamental desire to resist middle-class bourgeois ideals and rigid, formal social interactions that placed a premium on clearly defined, separating lines. Blues' engagement of call and response and of the exploration of unrestrained emotions, for example, pursues the collapse of boundaries between artist and audience and between the audience members themselves. Tracy sees the blues as flexible enough to participate in the larger mainstream culture without sacrificing the elements that often critique or reject that culture. So while cultural integration, or postracialism in terms of the twenty-first century, are widely celebrated as the realization of racial reconciliation, the need remains for a blues that operates without the tendencies of appropriation and exploitation that characterize the intersection of race, expressive culture, and mainstream entertainment. In the case of the blues, not only does a separate space allow for an unrestrained deployment of African American oral and cultural tradition but it also openly embraces a working-class sentiment that challenges the materialism and restrictive codes that are often applied by the cultural and moral elite.

The blues rejects the penchant of the elite to act as the warden or the steward of important, quality artforms and expressions. Instead, artists frequently prioritize their work based on an emotional investment with the audience in which the audience is not passively entertained by the artist, but participates as part of a critical examination of themselves and the world in which they live. Both artist and audience mine their emotional, political, and economic realities as a way to confront and transcend the forces that are shaping those realities. However, while other expressions fall into despair and nihilism, the blues pulls from a tradition of hope. It is the tradition of hope that will be most useful for the working and underclass in the twenty-first century, if a willingness to embrace the impact of African American cultural tradition emerges.

Houston Baker has claimed that the blues "is a point of ceaseless input and output, a web of intersecting, crisscrossing impulses always in productive transit" (3). The blues becomes important because it neither anesthetizes nor succumbs to the forces that impinge on its subjects; instead it confronts those forces and its responses in the hopes of, as Ellison might say, "squeezing from it a near-tragic, near-comic lyricism." As a result, we must realize that the presence of the blues both as artform and as critical matrix can have a significant impact on the formation and execution of a twenty-first-century American national identity and culture. Understanding the dynamic becomes important because the characteristics and possibilities of uncensored blues music may be more important than ever in a twenty-first century in which a variety of national tragedies and traumas have had a lasting impact on the working class. The blues—and its blues people—can provide an important perspective and a transcendence that helps its subjects and audience confront—instead of avoiding or silencing—the forces and emotions impinging on them.

Works Cited

Baker, Houston. *Blues, Ideology, and Afro-American Literature: A Vernacular Theory.* Chicago: U of Chicago P, 1984.

Charters, Samuel. "Workin' on the Building: Roots and Influences." *Nothing but the Blues: The Music and the Musicians.* Ed. Lawrence Cohn. New York: Abbeville, 1993.

Cone, James H. *The Spirituals and the Blues: An Interpretation.* New York: Seabury Press, 1972.

Evans, David. "Goin' Up the Country: Blues in Texas and the Deep South." *Nothing but the Blues: The Music and the Musicians.* Ed. Lawrence Cohn. New York: Abbeville, 1993.

Lott, Eric. *Love and Theft: Blackface Minstrelsy and the American Working Class.* New York: Oxford UP, 1995.

Moore, Allan. "Surveying the Field: Our Knowledge of Blues and Gospel Music." *The Cambridge Companion to Blues and Gospel Music.* Ed. Allan Moore. Cambridge: Cambridge UP, 2003. 1–12.

Oliver, Paul. *The Story of the Blues.* Philadelphia: Chilton Books, 1969.

Titon, Jeff Todd. "Labels: Identifying Categories of Blues and Gospel. *The Cambridge Companion to Blues and Gospel Music.* Ed. Allan Moore. Cambridge: Cambridge UP, 2003. 13–19.

Tracy, Steve. "'Black Twice': Performance Conditions for Blues and Gospel Artists. *The Cambridge Companion to Blues and Gospel Music.* Ed. Allan Moore. Cambridge: Cambridge UP, 2003. 89–101.

Wolfe, Charles K. *Classic Country: Legends of Country Music.* New York: Routledge, 2001.

Chapter 14

Going "Stateside": The Beatles, America, and the Meanings of Class

Sandra Trudgen Dawson

On September 21, 1964, the *New York Times* reported what was clearly seen as an acutely awkward social moment. A British "beat" band was touring the United States and had agreed to play for a charitable cause supported by the privileged elite of New York. As the band played, the reporter noted the striking contrast within the make-up of the audience. "Coolly elegant women in mink coats and pearls, together with men in black tie and in no need of a haircut, found themselves in the Paramount Theater last night sitting amid 1,800 hysterical teenagers." New York's social elite felt ill at ease but, as the journalist explained, the discomfort of the moment was mediated by the fact that "the Beatles were at the Paramount, the show was for charity and all was tolerated" (Talese). The Beatles represented the newly popular British "beat" music scene, the hysterical teenagers their fans, and the chic and elegant men and women the wealth of postwar America. Philanthropy tied the three groups together yet, as the journalist suggested, the unity of the event was momentary, socially uncomfortable, and largely illusionary. Although Americans had earlier declared the Beatles "harmless," their music and their celebrity created social unease, exacerbated generational divisions in the United States, and threatened to internationalize American popular music ("Americans Decide").

Many scholars argue that the popularity of British "beat" music in the United States and the subsequent "British invasion" of America began with the Beatles tour in early 1964 (Miles 8). The charity event at the Paramount was a clear indication of the marked triumph of the Beatles tour. This was an unexpected achievement and constituted the first successful inroad of any British band into the postwar American market, paving the way for other British bands like the Dave Clark Five, the Rolling Stones, and single artists like Petula Clark. The Beatle phenomenon, dubbed "Beatlemania" in the press on both sides of the Atlantic, received considerable attention at the time and has continued to intrigue scholars of musicology and popular culture, as well as music enthusiasts.[1] Most focus on one question: how did they do it? How were the Beatles able to capture the imagination of a generation, enter the top 100 hits repeatedly from 1964, and subsequently open up the U.S. market to more British bands and performers? Some scholars explain their success by arguing that the Beatles offered a dramatic change from the songwriting styles of Tin Pan Alley and the Brill Building. They wrote and performed their own songs, unlike the popular American artists who relied on professional songwriters to create not only their music but also their performance style for them (Scheurer; Fitzgerald). Others maintain that the Beatles were greatly influenced by American popular music, especially African American blues and jazz and so, they insist, the Beatles music was not original but simply an imitation of American sounds, and that accounts for their popularity. Contemporaries surmised that the success of the "fabulous four" was due to their "cheeky" Liverpudlian accent and humor. When the Beatles performed on *The Ed Sullivan Show* on February 9, 1964, they were seen by 73 million Americans, more than 60 percent of the total population. Indeed, the Beatles appeared on *The Ed Sullivan Show* for three consecutive weeks beginning with this first performance (see Inglis, "Beatles"). This drew crowds of hysterical fans to Beatles concerts and, more important, fuelled the demand for Beatles records and memorabilia. Journalists at the time recognized that the band and the "attendant frenzy, Beatlemania, did not just happen" but was the result of "artful contrivance" and the work of "promotional wizards" (Philips 1). Some of the Beatles' success, then, was the result of the business acumen of their manager, Brian Epstein, and mass marketing by Capitol Records (Braun 90–92). Another contemporary explanation for the success of the Beatles and those that followed centered on the cultural milieu. Commentators assessing Beatlemania argued that the band and British "beat" music offered a distraction for the nation mourning the untimely death of President John F. Kennedy (Inglis, "Beatles" 93–108). The Beatles entered the U.S. market at the right time with the right array of talents.

None of these arguments alone seem sufficient to account for the phenomenal popularity of the Beatles and the subsequent British bands. Instead, I'd like to suggest that the success of the Beatles, the Rolling Stones, the Dave Clark Five, and the other invading Brits of the 1960s was a result of their challenge to the meaning of gender, class, and race in both postwar Britain and postwar America. These groups interrupted boundaries of social class and created discomfort, as the opening story suggests. The British invasion took place at the moment when the reality of American society as a "melting pot" was challenged by the emergent civil rights movement, women's liberation, and the anti-Vietnam protests and when Britain's middle class was eclipsed by the celebration of working-class culture and the memory of a "People's War" against social injustice, the latter a term coined during the Cold War as part of an attempt to construct a viable postwar British national identity (Jones 35). The shifting social attitudes in the two postwar societies created a cultural space for a band like the Beatles, altering the nature of the relationship between Britain and the United States and complicating the meaning of class.

In such a milieu, I would like to suggest that the Beatles operated as cultural mediators, able to translate certain forms of music rendered incomprehensible by advertising and accepted constructions of gender, race, and class to a generation of Americans who had already begun challenging the status quo. This was only possible, however, because of the celebration of regional difference and working-class cultures in postwar Britain. It was during this short-lived moment that regionally based groups like the Beatles became empowered and saw themselves as mediators of working-class music from both sides of the Atlantic, to young consumers ready for change. In this sense, their music was greatly influenced by African American artists whose music was marginalized in the United States. The Beatles were then able to mediate and repackage elements of African American music and translate it into a form more easily understood by an audience more willing to listen to a foreign, white band. In other words, the Beatles "sanitized soul," mediating an unknown subculture—American black music—to American teenagers, and providing many Americans with their "first exposure to rhythm 'n' blues" (Cooper and Cooper 67).

Before the Beatles monopolized the U.S. popular music market, however, they first conquered the British market. As one scholar argues, the long years of war and austerity were over, and the Beatles were indicative of a new optimism and a new sense of entitlement (Miles 50). The Beatles became celebrities practically overnight in late 1962 with their first British hit single "Love Me Do." Journalists clamored with fans to take pictures and interview the "fab four." The first biography of the Beatles, by Michael Braun, was published in 1964. Michael Braun, an American, lived and toured with the Beatles for three months and wrote journalistic entries that provided readers with intimate details of the Beatles' personalities and attitudes to fans, their manager, food, and the press. John Lennon's response to the biography suggests the image Braun gave of the Beatles was one that the "fabulous four" endorsed. According to the blurb on the cover of Braun's book, Lennon quipped, "A true book. He wrote how we were, which was bastards." To the twenty-first-century reader, Braun's account is far from sensational. The Beatles appeared to enjoy each other's company and reveled in a common and exclusionary humor that only they appeared to understand. While their backgrounds varied slightly, the Beatles were understood to represent genuine Liverpool working-class culture, and, for some members of the press, this seemed to be part of the attraction. Lawrence Malkin of the *Chicago Tribune* wrote that all the band members were "'blitz babies' from the backstreets of Liverpool," and this common working-class background appeared to be the "key to their success" in Britain and the United States (A3). This statement suggests that it was something about the commonality of the Beatles' class background that made the right mix for success in the 1960s.

Ringo Starr was the most authentically working class of the four band members. Starr (born Richard Starkey) grew up in poverty and experienced an interrupted education because of childhood disease. The other three Beatles came from lower middle- and securely middle-class homes. John Lennon, George Harrison, and Paul McCartney were intelligent and as such were given the opportunity of a good education and even college careers as part of Britain's social reform that stemmed from the Butler Act (1944). The legislation extended universal primary and secondary education to all Britons until the age of 15 and further education at colleges and universities for those who wished to continue their education (Middleton). Gone were the qualifications of social class and economic status. Education was free and available to all Britons on the same basis. Passed while Britain was still at war, the Butler Act represented a sea change in attitudes toward entitlement and social class in Britain. Lennon and McCartney were both offered grammar school educations previously reserved for wealthy middle-class students. Paul, however, was the only one who took full advantage of this postwar settlement.

Educational reform was just one aspect of what scholars term the "postwar settlement" that established an extensive welfare state in Britain. When the 1945 elections returned Labour overwhelmingly to power, the

Party presented the country with a slew of social reforms that were continued by subsequent Conservative governments until the 1970s (Ellison, Francis). Historians refer to the decades following World War II as the "postwar consensus" as both major parties enacted housing, health care, education, and even cultural reforms. Postwar working Britons were rehoused in uniform brick council houses on enormous housing estates; they attended newly built grammar and secondary modern schools; and they received free health care through the National Health Service. Outside of school, children played in neighborhood parks and listened to music on radios or jukeboxes in the local cafés. For those interested in further studies after school, local art colleges offered a liberal arts education and the Arts Council provided low-priced theater and music performances in most of the major cities.[2]

The Arts Council was a continuation of a wartime government project to offer a distraction from the hardships of war. Live music concerts entertained Britons at lunchtimes in war factories, in hostels, and on military bases. The radio provided continuous entertainment and comedy programs at work and at home and became an integral part of daily life for all social classes during the war. Before World War II, the British Broadcasting Corporation (BBC) transmitted radio shows intended to "uplift" and educate the listening public with classical music and highbrow programming. During World War II, the BBC continued these but also selected more popular variety shows. These included community singing and songs by British artists like Vera Lynn, Flannagan and Allen, Gracie Fields, and George Formby who sang songs like "White Cliffs of Dover," "Underneath the Arches," "Sally," and "When I'm Cleaning Windows." Many of the most popular artists embraced their working-class roots and sang with prominent regional accents. Indeed, the same artists made dozens of films that celebrated working-class life, culture, regional accents, and dialects. For example, Gracie Fields and George Formby starred in a number of films including *Shipyard Sally, Sally in Our Alley, Sing as We Go, George in Civvy Street,* and *Zip Goes a Million* (see Jeffrey Richards). The songs, films, and comedy of these artists contributed to a popular wartime culture that came to be seen as an important facet of a national identity forged through the common experience of war.

As I have noted elsewhere, the comedy and variety shows featuring regional accents, working-class humor, and music continued after 1945, embracing working-class culture in a way that had been frowned upon in prewar Britain (*Holiday Camps*). Postwar politicians and members of the royal family took pains to celebrate the working class and the culture that enabled workers to survive six years of war and the decade of austerity that followed.[3] Television aided in this respect. By 1965, more than 90 percent of Britons owned a television and viewers had the choice of three channels, BBC One, BBC Two, and Independent commercial television (Inglis, "Men" 7). It was the BBC, however, that broadcast the hugely popular Royal Command Variety Performance that by 1963 included an act by the Beatles, who were asked to perform at the Royal Command Variety Performance in London in November 1963. These annual command performances were attended by members of the royal family. An invitation was an honor. When the Beatles were invited to perform, it was a formal recognition of their popularity and the value ascribed to the culture they represented in postwar Britain (Conekin).

The overt celebration of the working class was, in part, due to the continued need for their support during the Cold War. National Service meant that even after the war in 1945, young men between the ages of 17 and 21 were conscripted into military service for 18 months. Historian Adrian Horn writes about this generation of teenagers who waited for two years between leaving school and joining the military. Horn maintains this two-year period was a time when young men and women expressed themselves through their music choices and their clothing and developed cultural resistance (85). Postwar teens rejected the austerity that governed their parents' lives and chose to spend their discretionary income on records and specific clothing items that demonstrated their individual association with a particular subgroup (Hebdige). The "Teddy Boys" of the 1950s emerged as one such significant subgroup and the "Mods" of the late 1950s appeared as another. Within the subgroups, music surfaced as a critical signifier. American music had dominated Britain during the war and continued after 1945 to offer a hegemonic popular culture. Nevertheless, exports from the United States also included minority music, namely rhythm and blues and rock 'n' roll. These musical offerings, however, met resistance from the BBC, which controlled radio programming and refused to play rock 'n' roll or rhythm and blues. Some scholars have suggested that there was an entrenched resistance to playing black music on white-owned radios that the BBC's regulations enforced. Horn contends, however, that once jukebox distributors and owners saw the potential profits from the burgeoning postwar teenage market, they began putting rock 'n' roll records in the machines and the popularity spread unhindered by the BBC. Jukeboxes in Britain then delivered American popular music in an "undiluted form" to the growing number of teenage Britons waiting for National Service with discretionary income (Horn 85).

National Service finally ended in 1960. The Beatles and their generation of "blitz babies" were the recipients of the postwar social programs and celebration of working-class culture. At the same time, they were also the first generation of postwar teenagers not to have their education or employment opportunities interrupted by compulsory National Service. These social benefits were substantial and afforded the individual members of the British invasion bands the opportunity to mediate an identity that was distinct and separate from that of their parents' generation. For the individual members of the Beatles and numerous others in Merseyside, the path to that identity lay through popular music.

Music proliferated in certain urban areas and Liverpool was no exception. As American tourists and service personnel traveled to Europe through Liverpool, they brought with them popular rock 'n' roll and rhythm and blues records that were difficult to obtain in Britain. A decade before affordable air travel, transatlantic liners provided the link between Britain and the United States. According to one biographer, the large number of travelers meant that "Liverpool stood closer to America than any other place in Britain" (Norman 43). As some scholars point out, this is how the members of the Beatles were introduced to American popular music. Indeed, some of the first musical numbers the Beatles played in Hamburg and at the Cavern in Liverpool were covers of American artists like Chuck Berry, Little Richard, and the Shirelles (Gould 107). This has led many commentators to speculate on the authenticity of the Beatles' music. Yet, as one scholar points out, all popular music has a genealogy. What the Beatles were able to do was to successfully offer something that appeared to be simultaneously fresh and familiar, "masterfully working through white and black pop traditions, they offered a novel, synthetic focus: an altered perspective, not a foreign landscape" (qtd. in Inglis, "Beatles" 96). In other words, the success of the Beatles and the subsequent invading British bands lay in the fact that they were not creating a completely new genre but that they were presenting an older form from a new angle.

The members of the bands openly acknowledged their debt to other musical genres. In his autobiography, Keith Richards claims that British bands like the Beatles and the Rolling Stones "translated black music" for the white American audience. Richards acknowledges that the British bands were not necessarily creating something new but that they acted as "cultural mediators." At a time when African Americans faced overt racism and lived in de facto segregated communities, bands like the Beatles and the Stones articulated African American rhythms that, from the lips of young white English men, gained greater commercial appeal (Cooper and Cooper 61–78). Richards's comment also suggests that he believed British working-class artists and African Americans understood each other in a way that white Americans could not. African Americans were automatically constructed as working class in the minds of many Americans. White America, on the other hand, believed itself to be middle class. This racializing of class meant that white Americans failed to appreciate the value or even understand black music when presented by African American artists because they placed the music in a box, segregated by race and class, before hearing it. Richards, on the other hand, claimed he and others like him heard the music without prejudice. Richards claims that he had no idea that Chuck Berry was black when he heard the music. His appreciation of black music was color blind, unlike in America where class was racialized and music was segregated (Richards).

When the Beatles arrived in the United States, the civil rights movement was gaining strength and visibility. African Americans challenged segregated education, public transport, and housing districts. America had fought for the ideals of democracy in World War II with the aid of African American servicemen and women war workers and they demanded that the United States practice what it preached. Unlike Britain and the rest of Europe, American wealth grew throughout the war years and postwar American society reflected this. The United States marketed itself self-consciously as a classless society where all citizens were members of the middle class. The civil rights protestors demanded that African Americans be included in the new middle-class nation. They defied exclusion in all areas of American life, including popular music. African American girl bands like the Shirelles dominated the charts, challenging the notion that black artists could not become part of the mainstream. At the same time, these girl bands were carefully groomed and styled to appeal to a white middle-class audience (Douglas 660–63). Some scholars have argued that the Beatles and the subsequent British invasion bands displaced the girl bands that had challenged both the race and gender boundaries of popular culture. The Beatles presented the United States with alternative popular music that was white and male and that did not challenge gender roles and racial distinctions. In other words, the Beatles arrived at the moment that the social order was confronted by the demands of the civil rights and the women's movements.

Against the background of social unrest, the United States emerged as one of the two world superpowers after 1945 and expressed this power by offering citizens an enormous array of consumer goods. The middle class grew larger in the 1940s and 1950s and the urban landscape replicated the growth. Suburban living, unlike the council estates in Britain, included single-family homes on a third to half an acre or more. Like Britain, television was popular. By 1955, the majority of American homes had at least one television and enjoyed a variety of shows on a multitude of channels (Spiegel). American middle-class youth enjoyed a rapidly expanding commercial culture as entrepreneurs recognized the growing market of teenagers as the baby boomers grew to adolescents. Like Britain, educational opportunities for Americans grew as the United States competed with the USSR. White, male, middle-class Americans expected to attend college and expected to enter careers as corporate executives, and they expected to receive wages comparable to their position within the middle class.

When the Beatles appeared in the United States as overtly working-class individuals who worked few hours and received huge wages, this challenged the entire economic basis of social class. After their appearance on *The Ed Sullivan Show* in February 1964, the immediate reaction was one of relief as well as muted criticism of their appearance. The Beatles had already become something of a sensation in Britain and in command of significant amounts of money for each performance, but American commentators saw the Beatles as harmless young men who represented a small British cultural expedition to the United States. Indeed, after their appearance on *The Ed Sullivan Show,* correspondents from coast to coast agreed that the "overwhelming reaction, apart from those who were provoked into the private mental orgies that teenagers reserve for their latest heroes, was one of relief." Televised Beatlemania appeared to be an anticlimax that spoke well "for continuing British-American understanding." In fact, "apart from the outrageous bathmat coiffure, the four young men seemed downright conservative . . . asexual and homely," argued one correspondent, and they "behaved in a more civilized manner than most of our own rock-and-roll heroes" ("Americans Decide" 8).

Within days, however, criticism increased. Students at Purdue University were particularly withering of the Beatles. The American students criticized the Beatles for their lack of college educations, lack of talent, and lack of work ethic. Beatles supporters, however, argued that the students' criticism of the band was unfair. One Beatles supporter wrote, a college education did not mean entitlement to higher wages than those without a college education. Further, the supporter claimed the entire system of free enterprise upon which America was built meant that "anyone who can think of something ingenious, new, and in the public demand . . . [is] . . . free to reap as much money and success" as is possible (Reep 18). "Just because they [the Beatles] make a large amount of money for a small amount of work is no reason to criticize them as having no talent," claimed Sally Silverstein of Chicago. Indeed, Silverstein continued, teenagers enjoy the music the Beatles produced and so critics should listen to the music rather than simply criticize it as "'jack-hammer beat' or 'calliope-like shrieks'" (Silverstein 18).

The criticism of the English beat band did not only center on the amount of money they earned per performance and their music. The reaction of the fans elicited discomfort and divided generations. As reports of "Beatlemania" spread, reports of frenzied teenagers and screaming adolescents filled the newspapers as the Beatles toured the United States. Robert Alden reported that in Manhattan, "at least a dozen teen-age girls were injured in a nearly hysterical pursuit of their idols—the Beatles" (Alden 26). In a letter to the editor, Joseph John of Milwaukee wrote scathingly of the Beatles' "apparent lack of talent," which was surpassed only by their followers' "lack of taste." Nevertheless, the Beatles had performed an important function in the United States. According to John, "they shamefully show the immaturity of our teenagers. Youth's seemingly irrational outbursts of emotion and their unswerving loyalty do nothing more than cancel any respect that adults may have had for adolescent values." In other words, the Beatles had highlighted divisions between the youth and the older generation. For this reader, as long as "America's young display total lack of intellectual, emotional and social maturity, we [the older generation] will have to put up with the agonizing sound of Beatles and their related kin" (12). For this observer, the success of the Beatles and other beat bands lay in the immaturity of American youth rather than musical talent.

The American fans, in general, were young teenage girls although, as the band toured, more young men and women became fans. One sociologist assessed the reasons for the attraction. Dr. Renee Fox wrote that the most important answers to the "Beatlemania question runs much deeper than sex, status, and adolescent revolt." It stemmed, Fox contended, from the fact that the Beatles were the "personification of many forms of duality that exist in our society." They were male and yet their "hair dos" were feminine. The Beatles' "fancy clothes suggest a sophistication that stands in contrast to their homespun style of performance." Further, Fox claimed, while much had been made of their poor, working-class background, "they are accepted by the upper crust, having attracted the auspicious attention of the Queen Mother, Princess Margaret, Mrs. Rockefeller, and President Johnson." Overall, Fox concluded, the attraction of this working-class band lay in the Beatles' "realistic attitudes towards their own success and their eventual eclipse" (qtd. in Braun 137).

So what did the Beatles think of themselves? All the band members gave themselves five years before the phenomenon would be over and they would be rich enough not to have to work (84). This was considerably longer than Ray Bloch, the musical director of *The Ed Sullivan Show*, expected them to last. He gave the band a year (Braun 105). What neither the Beatles nor Bloch imagined, however, was the subsequent popularity of other British bands like the Rolling Stones, the Dave Clark Five, Herman's Hermits, and artists like Chad and Jeremy, Dusty Springfield, and Petula Clark. The Beatles began the British Invasion of the United States and the British bands that followed acknowledged their debt to them. Thus the Beatles were enshrined in popular culture and memory as the group that began it all.

From an historical standpoint, then, there are multiple meanings behind and explanations for the British invasion in general and Beatlemania in particular. Perhaps the most all-encompassing explanation for the Beatles' success was their ability to function as cultural mediators. As outsiders, they internationalized American popular music styles, adapted them, and then used them to break the American music monopoly in Britain. As musicians, they benefited from the social reforms of postwar Britain and the cultural legacy of a "people's war," including the accompanying change in attitudes toward class. The celebration of the British working class was short-lived but it dramatically changed the expectations of a generation. As Lennon explained, "We were all on this ship in the sixties, our generation, a ship going to discover the new world. And the Beatles were in the crow's nest" (qtd. in Miles, 298). Going "Stateside" was both metaphor and reality for the Beatles and a postwar generation looking for a new world and a new social order. In the United States, the forces of social change were from more grassroots sources. The folk revival of the 1960s challenged the institutions that determined social class as a mix of race and economics. Bob Dylan and Joan Baez perhaps most profoundly protested the social and political status quo. The civil rights movement challenged the racialized class system that excluded African Americans from the middle class. In addition, women were placing new pressures on American society, claiming rights and demanding a voice. The success of the Beatles lay in their ability to present Americans with a distraction from racial and gender issues. By maintaining a working-class heritage and Liverpudlian accent and humor, the Beatles were able to blur race and class in their musical and personal styles, and offer a culturally mediated form of music that was both foreign and familiar.

Notes

1. For example, see Miles, Gould, Turner, O'Donnell, MacDonald, Norman, Martin, and Braun.

2. The Arts Council of Britain replaced the wartime Council for the Encouragement of Music and the Arts. The Arts Council offered low-priced tickets for the National Theater, the National Portrait Gallery, and the British Museum in London.

3. Rationing and a policy of austerity continued in Britain until 1954. See Zweiniger-Bargielowska.

Works Cited

Alden, Robert. "Wild-Eyed Mobs Pursue Beatles." *New York Times* 13 February 1964: 26.

"Americans Decide the Beatles Are Harmless." *The Times* 11 February 1964: 8.

Braun, Michael. *Love Me Do.* 1964. London: Penguin, 1995.

Conekin, Becky. *Autobiography of a Nation: The 1951 Festival of Britain.* Manchester: Manchester UP, 2003.

Cooper, Laura E., and B. Lee Cooper. "The Pendulum of Cultural Imperialism: Popular Music Interchanges between the United States and Britain, 1943–1967." *Journal of Popular Culture* 27.3 (1993): 61–78.

Dawson, Sandra Trudgen. *Holiday Camps in Twentieth Century Britain: Packaging Pleasure.* Manchester: Manchester UP, 2011.

Douglas, Susan J. "Why the Shirelles Mattered: Girl Groups on the Cusp of a Feminist Awakening." *Women's America: Refocusing the Past.* Ed. Linda Kerber et al. 7th ed. New York: Oxford UP, 2011. 660–63.

Ellison, Nick. "Consensus Here, Consensus There . . . but not Consensus Everywhere: The Labour Party, Equality and Social Policy in the 1950s." *The Myth of Consensus.* Ed. Peter Catterall and Harriet Jones. Basingstoke: Macmillan, 1996. 17–39.

Fitzgerald, Jon. "Lennon-McCartney and the 'Middle Eight.'" *Popular Music and Society* 20.4 (1996): 41–52.

Francis, Martin. "Not Reformed Capitalism, but . . . Democratic Socialism: The Ideology of the Labour Leadership, 1945–51." *The Myth of Consensus.* Ed. Peter Catterall and Harriet Jones. Basingstoke: Macmillan, 1996. 40–57.

Gould, Jonathan. *Can't Buy Me Love: The Beatles, Britain and America.* New York: Three Rivers P, 2007.

Hebdige, Dick. *Subculture: The Meaning of Style.* London: Routledge, 1978.

Horn, Adrian. *Juke Box Britain: Americanisation and Youth Culture, 1945–1960.* Manchester: Manchester UP, 2009.

Inglis, Ian. "The Beatles Are Coming! Conjecture and Conviction in the Myth of Kennedy, America, and the Beatles." *Popular Music and Society* 24.2 (2000): 93–108.

Inglis, Ian. "Men of Ideas? Popular Music, Anti-Intellectualism and the Beatles." *The Beatles, Popular Music and Society: A Thousand Voices.* Ed. Ian Inglis. Houndsmill, Basingstoke: Macmillan, 2000. 1–22.

John, Joseph. "Agonizing Beatles." Letter. *Chicago Tribune* 14 February 1964: 12.

Jones, Harriet. "The Impact of the Cold War." *A Companion to Contemporary Britain, 1939–2000.* Ed. Paul Addison and Harriet Jones. Oxford: Blackwell, 2005. 23–41.

MacDonald, Ian. *Revolution in the Head: The Beatles' Records and the Sixties.* 3rd ed. Chicago: Chicago Review P, 2005.

Malkin, Lawrence. "Beatles Bring Screams from Teenagers." *Chicago Tribune* 29 December 1963: A3.

Martin, George, with Jeremy Hornsly. *All You Need Is Ears.* New York: St. Martin's, 1979.

Middleton, Nigel. "Lord Butler and the Education Act of 1944." *British Journal of Educational Studies* 20.2 (1972): 178–91.

Miles, Barry. *The British Invasion.* New York: Sterling, 2009.

Norman, Philip. *Shout! The Beatles in Their Generation.* 3rd ed. New York: Fireside, 2003.

O'Donnell, Jim. *The Day John Met Paul: An Hour by Hour Account of How the Beatles Began.* London: Routledge, 2006.

Philips, McCandlish. "Publicitywise." *New York Times* 17 February 1964: 1.

Reep, Diana C. Letter. *Chicago Tribune* 18 February 1964: 18.

Richards, Jeffrey. *Film and British National Identity: From Dickens to Dad's Army.* Manchester: Manchester UP, 1997.

Richards, Keith, with James Fox. *Life.* New York: Hachette Digital, 2010.

Scheurer, Timothy E. "The Beatles, the Brill Building, and the Persistence of Tin Pan Alley in the Age of Rock." *Popular Music and Society* 20.4 (1996): 89–102.

Silverstein, Sally. Letter. *Chicago Tribune* 18 February 1964: 18.

Spiegel, Lynn. *Make Room for TV: Television and the Family Ideal in Postwar America.* Chicago: U of Chicago P, 1992.

Talese, Gay. "Beatles and Fans Meet Social Set: Chic and Shriek Mingle at Paramount Benefit Show." *New York Times* 21 September 1964: 44.

Turner, Steve. *The Gospel According to the Beatles.* London: John Knox P, 2006.

Zweiniger-Bargielowska, Ina. *Austerity in Britain: Rationing, Controls, and Consumption 1939–1955.* Oxford: Oxford UP, 2000.

Chapter 15

The Boss and the Workers: Bruce Springsteen as Blue-Collar Icon

Ryan Poll

From his blue-collar image to his exhausting, epic concerts, Springsteen explicitly situates himself as a working-class rocker. But beyond the iconic images, legendary concerts, and fist-pumping anthems, Springsteen's songs offer complex narratives of working-class experiences in a changing U.S. economy. The characters in Springsteen's songs stare at the American Dream from the dirty side of the display window. His songs feature characters who sludge through the working day longing for brief respites of leisure time ("Night," "Out in the Streets"); characters who have been laid off ("The River," "Johnny 99"); characters who watch their local economies collapse ("My Hometown," "Youngstown"); and myriad characters who are physically, psychologically, and spiritually ruined by the dehumanizing conditions of capitalist labor. Springsteen's music makes visible the multiple violences germane to capitalism, and his music documents how working-class culture is inextricable from imagining a more humane, empathetic, and socially just world.

Working-Class Alienation and Violence

During his induction to the Rock and Roll Hall of Fame, Springsteen explained that he wore working-class clothes on stage to honor his parents. "My parents' experiences," Springsteen said, "forged my own" (Sawyers 2). Springsteen grew up experiencing the shame, humiliation, and instability experienced by many working-class families. Born in 1949, he was raised in Freehold, New Jersey, a segregated, blue-collar town located 15 miles from the Jersey shore and 50 miles from New York City. Springsteen's father, Douglas, held various jobs attempting to make ends meet, including stints as a rug mill worker, taxi driver, bus driver, prison guard, and as a worker in a plastics factory. His mother, Adele, worked as a legal secretary. Their financial situation was so dire that Adele frequently needed to borrow money from a nearby financial institution in order to produce the appearance of a stable "normal" home (Alterman 11–13; Marsh 325–27).

As a child, Springsteen watched his father's increasing despair, alienation, silence, and anger. Only later in life did he understand that his father's condition was related to capitalism: "I grew up in a house where there was a lot of struggle to find work, where the results of not being able to find your place in society manifested themselves with the resulting lack of self-worth, with anger, with violence" (Masur 22). From a young age, Springsteen was able to see through the American myth that hard work, discipline, and dedication could lead to economic mobility and material comfort. Instead, while a teenager, Springsteen recognized that the working people around him—his grandparents, his parents, his friends—were caught in a cycle of constant struggle. Nobody, Springsteen recalls, seemed to have a chance of escaping their position as exploited, underpaid laborers. As the narrator of "Born to Run" observes, his hometown was a "death trap."

Springsteen's salvation was rock and roll. On multiple occasions, Springsteen acknowledged that music gave him a reason to live. The music of Elvis, the Crystals, the Ronetts, Chuck Berry, the Animals, the Beatles, and Bob Dylan offered an escape from working-class life, and it offered a community of meaning and fulfillment (Marsh 28; Masciotra 2; Masur 27). For Christmas 1964, Adele Springsteen took out a loan for $60 and purchased for her 15-year-old son his first electric guitar (Masciotra 3). (Springsteen fondly retells this beautiful story in the song "The Wish.") Eleven years later, with the release of *Born to Run* (1975), Bruce Springsteen became a rock star. The album became a critical and commercial success, and the media hype surrounding Springsteen ballooned to stratospheric heights. In the same week in October 1975, he graced the cover of both *Newsweek* and *Time*, and newspapers and reviews across the nation hailed Springsteen as the Next Big Thing. Springsteen achieved his childhood dream to become a rocker, but he did not leave his working-class origins; rather, he became a working-class rocker.

Springsteen's first three albums—*Greetings from Asbury Park, N.J.* (1973), *The Wild, the Innocent & The E-Street Shuffle* (1973), and *Born to Run*

(1975)—are all rooted in his experience growing up in working-class communities. However, these albums display a romantic desire to transcend the conditions of class, as is evident in songs such as "Thunder Road" and "Born to Run." With the release of his fourth album, *Darkness on the Edge of Town* (1977), Springsteen found his focus. In this dark, stripped-down album—a stark contrast to the Wall of Sound that propels *Born to Run*—Springsteen wrote more explicitly and consciously about working-class conditions and experiences.

Darkness on the Edge of Town is a brooding album about working-class alienation. More than a hundred years earlier, Karl Marx identified alienation as one of the dominant symptoms of working-class labor (Tucker 133). Capitalism, Marx elaborates, alienates workers from meaningful, respected, and creative labor, and instead, it positions workers as quantifiable, replaceable figures stripped of their humanity and from their potential as human beings. This exclusion from valued labor multiples into other forms of alienation: from family, from friends, from community, and from one's self.

Darkness begins with the hope of escaping the "Badlands" of capitalist exploitation and alienation. The opening song erupts and races forward with heavy percussions and a simmering smoldering guitar rhythm. But the hope of transcendence dissolves over the course of the album. *Darkness* paints a bleak picture in which no matter how hard someone works, those who are not born into a privileged capitalist life have little chance of escaping the conditions of exploitation, humiliation, and alienation inextricable from capitalist labor. The album's final song, the harrowing title track, "Darkness on the Edge of Town," unfolds on the shadowy, despairing margins of capitalist culture. In this seemingly permanent darkness, the promise of escape articulated on the album's opening seems impossibly distant.

Throughout *Darkness,* Springsteen illustrates the contradictions of working-class life. On the one hand, the album's characters fully submit to the capitalist system. They work long and grueling hours without complaining about their situation, nor critiquing a system that privileges profit over people. However, while these working-class subjects externally comply with a capitalist system, internally, a complex, violent battle rages. On "The Promised Land," for example, the narrator explains how he follows the script authored by the dominant, capitalist culture. He goes to work every day, works hard, and remains submissive. However, rather than labor leading to any sense of upward mobility, dignity, and pride, it proves to be a dead-end job that is dehumanizing and unrewarding. Although the characters on the album appear as subservient workers who respectfully call their boss "mister," internally, a mounting rage simmers.

Springsteen's music recognizes that the condition of working-class alienation is intimately linked to violence.[1] The narrator in "The Promised Land" is figured as a fuse who, at any moment, may "explode and tear this whole town apart." Similarly, the song "Factory," also from the *Darkness* album, foregrounds how working-class alienation leads to violence. "Factory" sounds like a dirge, and Springsteen's vocals are intentionally flat and defeated. The word *work* repeats 12 times in the song, symbolizing the repetitive, soul-killing labor of factory life. "Factory," based on Springsteen's father, follows the unchanging daily pattern of working life under a Fordist regime from the whistle blow that demarcates the beginning of the workday to the whistle blow that announces the end of the workday. Nowhere in the song is there any indication of pride in the work being done, nor any dignity in being a worker, nor any sense of community. In perhaps his most poignant line documenting the violent paradoxes of working life in capitalism, Springsteen sings in the second verse: "Factory takes his hearing, factory gives him life." This contradiction is based on biography. Douglas Springsteen's work at a local plastic factory led to permanent hearing loss. On the one hand, the labor conditions in the factory are dangerous and damaging. However, on the other hand, these exploitative conditions provided the salary Douglas Springsteen needed to help house, feed, and clothe his family. The conditions of capitalist labor provide life and death at the same time.

In the final verse, the factory whistle blows, announcing that the men are "free." In a haunting image, the men leave the factory gates with "death in their eyes." This image signifies multiple forms of death: the death of the worker's body under taxing and unsafe labor conditions; the death of the worker's soul under capitalism; and a more imminent death. The narrator promises, in the final lines of the song, that somebody, anybody, is going to "get hurt tonight." Springsteen highlights that the consequences of alienated labor is a culture of violence and death.

The characters in *Darkness on the Edge of Town* recognize the myth of the American Dream, and they are angry. But rather than transform this anger into collective action against the market system, these characters internalize their anger and enact their anger on random targets. What these characters lack, in short, is a developed class consciousness.

From an Industrial to a De-Industrializing U.S. Economy

After *Darkness on the Edge of Town*, Springsteen's lyrics become even darker. This is because what is worse than the experience of alienation due to factory labor is the experience of alienation caused by not being able to find any work at all. Since the 1970s, manufacturing and industry jobs have fled the United States at a rapid pace. Consequently, multitudes of working-class individuals have lost their jobs, and unlike previous eras of recessions and depressions, there is no chance of being rehired because these jobs, workers have been told, are not returning. This is the defining pattern of the post-Fordist capitalist regime in the United States.

A post-Fordist regime is an era of intensified dislocation and destabilization for the working class, especially for white men in the United States who enjoyed relative prosperity in the previous era of Fordism.[2] In that era, the one in which Douglas and Adele Springsteen were born into, capitalists invested heavily in constructing factories and manufacturing centers in specific spaces (such as Freehold, New Jersey). This spatially fixed model of capitalist production enabled relative stability for working-class communities. If Company Y, for example, builds a factory in Town A, then the company and the town have, theoretically, a symbiotic relationship. Company Y provides jobs that benefit the surrounding community, and in return, workers generate the value and profit to keep Company Y satisfied (if capitalism could ever be satisfied). However, in a post-Fordist regime, this model of spatially fixed capital dissipates. Industrial spaces become de-industrialized as capital becomes more mobile and flexible in its singular search for greater profits. Throughout the United States, industrial spaces are de-industrializing as capital moves with greater ease and efficiency across the globe in search of the most exploitable labor and the most favorable conditions to maximize profits (tax breaks, State kickbacks, corrupt or corruptible governments, etc.; Harvey). In this new regime of capitalist development, if workers in Town A demand health care, Company Y no longer needs to negotiate with labor. Rather, Company Y simply leaves Town A.

Springsteen's music documents the United States' transition from a Fordist, industrial economy to a post-Fordist, de-industrializing economy. From the 1980s onward, Springsteen gives voice to working-class subjects who lost their jobs and who are informed that their jobs will *never* come back. Springsteen sings, in short, of the continuing trauma of labor within a globalizing market. "The River," the title track from the 1980 album, focuses upon a young worker who grew up in a town where "They bring you up to do like your daddy done." The fate of this character is ostensibly determined at birth. From a young age, the narrator is resigned to a life of construction because this is what his father did, and presumably, this is what his grandfather did as well. However, what is worse than the limited (and limiting) opportunities for working-class subjects is the absence of available work altogether. When the narrator of "The River" begins his job as a construction worker, he receives his "union card." But by the third verse, the narrator informs him that there's no work to be found "on account of the economy." While Reagan would soon be celebrating a new "Morning in America," Springsteen gave voice to the intensifying darkness and hopelessness for working people across the nation. The dire situations described in *Darkness* intensify in subsequent songs as Springsteen's social vision transforms with the economy's transformations. In a de-industrializing U.S. economy, the notion of doing what your parents have done becomes an untenable goal. In "The River," this absence of hope is symbolized by the title image. Initially, the river represents a space of promise. At the river, the narrator fell in love with his current wife, discussed his dreams, and imagined their future together. However, by the song's end, the river is dry, and the narrator asks, in one of Springsteen's most poetic lines: "Is a dream a lie if it don't come true / Or is it something worse?" In a postindustrial economy, the dream of economic stability, of a comfortable working-class life, of a future with promising possibilities, dissolves.

Beginning in the 1980s, Springsteen penned song after song about workers unable to find work. In "My Hometown," the concluding song on *Born in the U.S.A.* (1984), the narrator witnesses the death of his small industrial city. In the opening verse, an eight-year-old listens as his father tells him to take pride in his hometown. However, by the song's end, this place called home is destroyed by a changing economy. Main Street's once-vibrant commercial center has become a long stretch of abandoned stores. Moreover, the textile mill, the community's economic center, has permanently closed its doors. The foreman not only fires the workers but informs them that these jobs are never coming back. All the concessions that the town made and sacrificed for the factory to flourish and to be profitable—presumably for decades—comes to naught. The workers in the narrator's "hometown" have become disposable figures. At the song's end, the narrator of "My Hometown" faces the daunting task of uprooting his family in a desperate search for work in the nebulous south. The family's pending move to a new region is not a hopeful journey toward a potential promised land, as California is frequently figured in the popular U.S. imagination. Rather, this migration is rendered as a desperate attempt to find any work anywhere.

This pattern of working-class trauma continues throughout Springsteen's canon. In "Seeds," an outtake from *Born in the U.S.A.*, Springsteen sings of a family who travels to Houston in hope of finding work in the oil town. However, when the family arrives, there are no opportunities and the family becomes hopeless and homeless. The hard-hitting, angry song kicks into overdrive when the narrator sees a limousine and desires to spit on this symbol of conspicuous consumption. A decade later, on the song "Youngstown" (1995), Springsteen focuses on a factory in Youngstown, Ohio. The song is based on a real factory that built weapons to help the United States wage its multiple wars from the Civil War through Vietnam. In the song, Springsteen looks at class relations in a particular place over a long historical period. Built in 1803, the factory has employed and exploited generation after generation of blue-collar workers. A laborer describes his job, working with taconite, coke, and limestone, as suited for the "devil." Nevertheless, as the song makes clear, workers are willing to endure the unhealthy, hellish conditions of millwork as long as there is a guarantee of work.

The 1995 song documents a major transformation in Youngstown. Similar to the fate of the factory in "My Hometown," the factory in "Youngstown" permanently shuts down. The excuse that capitalists provide workers is that "the world's changed." After years of enduring work suitable only for the devil, the whole community of Youngstown is abandoned by capital's singular quest for profit. The factory that flees Youngstown, of course, is not unique. At the song's end, Springsteen links this local story to a national story (and an implied global story). Throughout this new world order, the same narrative, Springsteen emphasizes, repeats again and again, from the Appalachian coal mines to the Iron Range of Minnesota. The globalization of capitalism results in the displacement and dispossession of working-class communities throughout the Untied States.

This process of de-industrialization is the final act of betrayal that enables the narrator of "Youngstown" to recognize capitalism as a system that systemically exploits the working class. Moreover, the narrator is now able to recognize that the United States is not a democracy that serves the interests of all people. The narrator reflects how the workers in Youngstown built the machinery of death to support the United States' multiple wars, and how these workers sent their sons and daughters to fight in these same wars, most recently in Korea and Vietnam. However, it is only when the Youngstown factory abandons the community that the narrator asks: "Now we're wondering what they were dyin' for." The narrator intuits that capitalists and the United States have abandoned the working class.

The song expresses an explicit class consciousness that recognizes that the government works on behalf of capital, and not on behalf of labor. Moreover, this song, and many others in Springsteen's canon, recognizes that those who fight the United States' wars are composed predominately of the working class—the class that capitalists and this nation-state mercilessly left behind. This recognition exists at the heart of many of Springsteen's songs from "Born in the U.S.A." (1984), about a soldier returning from the

Vietnam War only to find no available work, to "Gypsy Biker" (2007), about a soldier returning home from the Middle East in a body bag. In the opening lines of "Gypsy Biker," Springsteen spews in anger: "The speculators made their money / On the blood you shed."

Hey, Boss: What's Your Politics?

In 1984, President Reagan—with his neoliberal vision of busting unions, dismantling welfare programs, and preaching "trickle-down economics"— ran for re-election against the Democratic candidate Walter Mondale. In the midst of the campaign, George Will, a popular conservative columnist and unofficial advisor to Reagan, penned an infamous article that positioned Springsteen as a national icon. "I have not got a clue about Springsteen's politics, if any, but flags get waved at his concerts while he sings songs about hard times. He is no whiner, and the recitation of closed factories and other problems always seem punctured by a grand, cheerful affirmation: 'Born in the U.S.A.!'" (107). A few days later, President Reagan aligned his social and political vision with Bruce Springsteen. At a campaign stop in New Jersey, Reagan proclaimed: "America's future rests in the message of hope in songs of a man so many young Americans admire, New Jersey's Bruce Springsteen" (Garman 213).

Although his music is often in dialogue with the ideals (and betrayals) of nationalism, Springsteen disassociated himself from the president. In a concert in Pittsburg, he remarked: "The President mentioned my name the other day, and that got me wondering what his favorite album might be. I don't think it's the *Nebraska* album. I don't think he's been listening to this one" (Masciotra 11). On *Nebraska* (1982), Springsteen sings of the multitudes excluded from Reagan's ideological vision of a bright, prosperous new "morning" in America. *Nebraska* gives voice to those who darken Reagan's ideological image—to those who have been taught the American Dream, yet for whom this dream remains forever out of reach.

Springsteen begins his critique of Reagan's America by turning to his own biography. *Nebraska* is his most personal and intimate album to date, consisting mostly of Springsteen's lone voice, acoustic guitar, and harmonica. Despite earning worldwide fame and fortune, Springsteen recorded *Nebraska* in his home with cheap, easily accessible equipment. In songs such as "Used Cars" and "Mansion on the Hill," Springsteen sings from the perspective of his younger self, growing up in a struggling working-class family. In "Used Cars," the young narrator expresses the shame and humiliation he feels when his neighbors see him in a used car—the only type his family can afford.

Similarly, in "Mansion on the Hill," Springsteen recalls how as a child, his family would drive to look longingly at the gated mansions located high in the hills. These homes symbolize the widening abyss separating the working class from the capitalist class. Moreover, they symbolize the inherent injustice of capitalism. While those who work in the factories can barely make ends meet, those who own the means of production live in extravagant luxury signifying a new aristocracy. *Nebraska* is filled with songs about working-class characters whose dream is not to live on a mansion on a hill; rather, these alienated characters live without *any* dreams and without *any* hope.

Similar to *Darkness, Nebraska* suggests that an alienated working-class culture leads to senseless, random violence against the self and against the outside world. *Nebraska* is about the intertwining of alienation and violence, and song after song features characters erupting into violence. From the opening title song told from the perspective of a serial killer—loosely based on Charles Starkweather and Caril Ann Fugate's killing spree in 1958 and Terrence Malick's cinematic adaptation, *Badlands* (1973)—to "State Trooper," to "Highway Patrolman," to "Atlantic City," the album is rife with violence. However, this is not an album of nihilism. Rather, Springsteen explains that this violence is preventable because it is underwritten by capitalism's system of exploitation and abandonment. "Johnny 99," for example, begins by announcing that an auto plant in Mahwah, New Jersey, shut down. This form of capitalist violence is inspired by a real event. In 1980, the Ford Motor Company closed its Mahwah plant, and subsequently more than 3,300 people lost their jobs. For 25 years, the plant had become central to the town's economy. When Ford closed the auto plant, practically overnight, the town crumbled. The story of Mahwah is symptomatic of American working-class conditions in late capitalism. Throughout the United States, more than 250,000 autoworkers lost their jobs in the early 1980s. The president of the United Auto Workers described the traumatic experience as follows: the "kind of permanent layoff at Mahwah [was] much more shattering than anything during the Depression. At least in the 1930s workers had hopes of being called back to work. In Mahwah they don't" (Garman 2004, 226).[3]

"Johnny 99" is about the America that Reagan both ignored and helped decimate. Not only did capital not "trickle down" as Reagan promised, but moreover, Reagan helped create the social conditions to intensify the process of de-industrialization. Springsteen personalizes this social and political process and intimates the distressed psychology of someone who loses his or her job in this globalizing economy. In "Johnny 99," the titular character loses his job without being able to find any other form of employment.

Consequently, the narrator cannot keep up with his mortgage and the bank threatens to foreclose on his home. In response, the narrator gets drunk, takes a gun, and randomly shoots a night clerk. At the song's end, the judge asks the narrator to explain his crime. While the narrator accepts responsibility, he also explains the material conditions that led to this act of violence. As "Johnny 99" and other songs within Springsteen's canon suggest, what underwrites the violence plaguing many contemporary working-class communities—from small rural towns to inner cities—is capitalism's perpetually violent conditions that pay low wages, offer little job security, and no safety nets to ensure the basic conditions of living from homes to health care.

However, the album *Nebraska* ends with a note of promise. The closing song, entitled "Reason to Believe," focuses on people in situations that seem beyond hope. And yet, Springsteen suggests, what makes us human is our extraordinary ability to believe and to have hope even against the most incredible odds. This is a salient motto of Springsteen's mature music. A willingness to believe in a better future is not just for our own welfare, but for the welfare of all.

Working-Class Culture and Social Justice

One way out of working-class alienation and despair is to find a community that is meaningful, life affirming, and of course, class conscious. After *Born to Run*, Springsteen explicitly placed himself within a working-class tradition and community that simultaneously critiqued capitalism and offered hope for a more socially just world. As Springsteen matured, he became a more serious student of working-class culture in its multiple forms. He studied Harry Smith's *Anthology of American Folk Music* (1952); the music of Johnny Cash, Bob Dylan, Hank Williams, Robert Johnson, Jimmie Rodgers, and Pete Seeger; John Ford's *The Grapes of Wrath* (1940); Ron Kovic's memoir on the Vietnam War, *Born on the Fourth of July* (1981); James Agee and Walker Evans's *Let Us Now Praise Famous Men* (1941); Dale Maharidge and Michael Williamson's *Journey to Nowhere: The Saga of the New Underclass* (1996) . . . and the list continues (Cullen 234; Garman 2004, 223; Sawyers 10).

Perhaps the greatest influence on Springsteen's developing class consciousness was Woody Guthrie.[4] In 1980, Springsteen read a copy of Joe Klein's biography *Woody Guthrie: A Life* (1980). For the River tour (1980–1981) and the Born in the U.S.A. tour (1984–1985), Springsteen incorporated Guthrie's "This Land Is Your Land" into his concerts. From

Klein's biography, Springsteen learned that Guthrie's song was written as an indignant response to Irving Berlin's "God Bless America" (Garman 2004, 223; Marsh 278–79). In contrast to Berlin's erasure of class relations, Guthrie expresses solidarity with the oppressed and downtrodden, and offers a radical nationalism that includes all people. "This Land" recognizes the injustices within the United States and articulates a vision where all people must work together to redress any form of social and economic violence.

Twenty-three years later, for President Obama's inauguration, Springsteen repeated this song. Only this time, he stood beside folk legend Pete Seeger, Seeger's grandson Tao Rodriguez-Seeger, and a racially and ethnically diverse chorus. With the Lincoln Memorial in the background, Springsteen and company asked the 400,000 people who congregated on the National Mall to join in and participate. In this rendition of the song, the group included Guthrie's most radical verse—a verse that Springsteen opted not to sing in the 1980s. It begins with the image of a barrier and a sign. The "sign was painted, it said private property; / But on the back side it didn't say nothing," which leads back into the chorus, and the idea of a shared land and a common good.

Springsteen's efforts to situate himself in a progressive, working-class context became explicit two years earlier with the 2006 release of *We Shall Overcome: The Seeger Sessions.* On this album, Springsteen revisits and re-imagines the diverse canon of working-class folk music in its many guises including gospel, New Orleans jazz, and Appalachian folk. Folk music focuses upon class relations in a historically specific, space-specific context *and* within a larger context of the long history of class struggle. In the first decade of the twenty-first century, Springsteen sings of the workers who built the Erie Canal ("Erie Canal") and of working-class subjects who lost their homes in the Dust Bowl ("My Oklahoma Home"). And he sings "We Shall Overcome" like a prayer heard for the first time. Folk music connects the past to the present while gesturing toward a more socially just future. Moreover, folk music offers a tradition of innovation in which singers alter canonical and familiar songs in order to address and account for modern times. Consider, for example, how Springsteen altered "How Can a Poor Man Stand Such Times and Live" (released on the *American Land Edition*). The song was originally penned in 1929 by Blind Alfred Reed in response to the Great Depression; in 2006, Springsteen added several verses in response to Hurricane Katrina. Springsteen links the tragedy catalyzed by Katrina to the Great Depression, mandating that we understand what happened in New Orleans within the paradigm of class relations, and not exclusively as a natural disaster.

In the second verse, Springsteen sings from the perspective of President George W. Bush. The president infamously took days to respond to the tragedy unfolding in New Orleans, and even when he did respond, he never supplied the goods and services necessary to address the worst "natural" disaster in the United States' history (Dyson). In the song, Bush arrives in New Orleans, tours the damage in New Orleans, and promises the "poor black folks" that he will stand with them and assist them in their time of need. But then, the president just leaves. Springsteen asks in anger: "Tell me how can a poor man stand such times and live?"

In the following verse, Springsteen offers glimpses of the horrors in New Orleans. Springsteen sings of bodies floating down Canal Street, and he sings with indignation that those who could not leave the city were simply "left to drown." However, the song ends with the promise of social justice. After accusing the State for failing to care for its citizens, Springsteen responds with anger and with faith that a judgment day will soon arrive, a concept crystallized in the image of "a righteous train rollin' down this track."

This image of the train appears in the uplifting song, "Land of Hope and Dreams" (2001), a song that articulates Springsteen's vision of radical democracy, community, and inclusivity. In contrast to a car, the preferred symbol and mode of transportation in Springsteen's earlier songs, the train becomes a symbol of collectivity upon which all people are invited to board. On this train, everyone has a right to dream and to hope, and equally important, a fair chance to realize these dreams and hopes. This image crystallizes Springsteen's motto, repeated throughout his concerts in the early 1980s: "Remember, nobody wins unless everybody wins" (Marsh 499). This motto of collectivity and community challenges capitalism's ideology of individualism and its winner-take-all approach.

Springsteen remains an important working-class cultural producer because his music makes explicit that working-class culture is always tethered to social justice. Whereas capitalist culture curtails empathy and collectivity, Springsteen's music opens to all people who suffer injustices. In "Streets of Philadelphia" (1993), for example, Springsteen—often celebrated as an icon of hypermasculinity and heterosexuality—sings from the perspective of a gay man living with AIDS who is ostracized by his surrounding community. The song "American Skin (41 Shots)" (2000) tells the tragic true story of Amadou Diallo, a Guinean immigrant who was murdered by four police officers. The officers, who claimed that Diallo resembled a suspect, fired 41 shots at the unarmed 23-year-old as he reached into his pocket to retrieve his identification. The police officers were subsequently tried and acquitted. Rather than allow this story to slip into the recesses of history,

Springsteen crafted a powerful, enduring song for which he won an NAACP Image Award (Pardini).

Springsteen's music gives voice and humanity to individuals oppressed, vulnerable, and dehumanized by our current world (dis)order. In *The Ghost of Tom Joad* (1995), an album which re-animates the folk vision of Steinbeck, Ford, and Guthrie, Springsteen confronts an issue that these artists avoided in their iterations of Tom Joad: race and racism. Rather than focus exclusively on white, working-class characters, Springsteen relocates the Joad struggles to the Southwest. Five of the songs on the album focus on Mexican immigration ("Across the Border," "Balboa Park," "The Ghost of Tom Joad," "The Line," and "Sinaloa Cowboys"). In contrast to the racist rhetoric that symbolically strips immigrants of their humanity and dignity, Springsteen's music personalizes and humanizes migrant stories. Whereas earlier in his career Springsteen avoided wrestling with the intersections of class and race, as Springsteen's political vision has expanded, his music has become more sensitive and explicit that capitalist exploitation and racist practices frequently go together.

In a 2005 concert in Detroit, Springsteen introduced "Matamoros Banks," a song from *Devils & Dust* (2005), in which he continues to sing from the perspective of Mexican immigrants who dream of a better life in the United States. In the song, tragedy strikes when an immigrant drowns trying to cross the treacherous waterway separating Mexico and the United States. Before performing the song, Springsteen referenced a book he read recently on the subject, Jorge Ramos's *Dying to Cross: The Worst Immigrant Tragedy in American History* (2005), and Springsteen discussed with his audience the need for Americans to recognize that countless people die every year trying to get into the United States to do some of the most demanding and dangerous jobs. "We need," Springsteen emphasized, a "humane immigration policy."[5] Springsteen then launched into his song "Matamoros Banks," with the implicit understanding that a true working class respects the rights of all working people. The working class, Springsteen insinuates, has no single country, no single gender, no single ethnicity, no single religion, and no single color.

In the middle of the nineteenth century, Marx claimed that the working class must be an international movement to combat the globalizing development of capitalism. Today, we live in an age of global capitalism, and Springsteen's music offers politically committed music that recognizes and wrestles with these global entanglements. Springsteen's origins are in a working-class community, and he sings of the alienation experienced by workers everywhere. But his music seeks to transcend this feeling of working-class alienation in order to forge a coalition of working-class collectivity built on an expanding sense of empathy, community, and empowerment that overcomes any restrictive boundaries.

Notes

1. For an alternative reading of alienation in Springsteen's music, see Michels.
2. Cowie and Boehm offer an astute analysis of "Born in the U.S.A." that focuses on the changing working conditions and changing identity formations for working-class Americans in late capitalism.
3. The above paragraph is indebted to Garman 2004, 226.
4. For an analysis of Guthrie's influence on Springsteen, see Garman 2000 and 2004.
5. This performance can be viewed online at http://www.youtube.com/watch?v=lsOSG6FXW3M (accessed 22 February 2011).

Works Cited

Alterman, Eric. *It Ain't No Sin to Be Glad You're Alive: The Promise of Bruce Springsteen.* Boston: Back Bay Books, 2001.

Cowie, Jefferson R., and Lauren Boehm. "Dead Man's Town: 'Born in the U.S.A.,' Social History, and Working-Class Identity." *American Quarterly* 58.2 (June 2006): 353–78.

Cullen, Jim. "Tom Joad's Children." Excerpt from *Born in the U.S.A.: Brice Springsteen and the American Tradition.* In *Racing in the Street: The Bruce Springsteen Reader.* Ed. June Skinner Sawyers. New York: Penguin Books, 2004. 231–40.

Dyson, Michael Eric. *Come Hell or High Water: Hurricane Katrina and the Color of Disaster.* New York: Basic Civitas Books, 2005.

Garman, Bryan K. "The Ghost of History: Bruce Springsteen, Woody Guthrie, and the Hurt Song." *Racing in the Street: The Bruce Springsteen Reader.* Ed. June Skinner Sawyers. New York: Penguin Books, 2004. 221–30.

Garman, Bryan K. *A Race of Singers: Whitman's Working-Class Hero from Guthrie to Springsteen.* Chapel Hill: U of North Carolina P, 2000.

Harvey, David. *The Condition of Postmodernity: An Enquiry into the Origins of Cultural Change.* Cambridge, MA: Blackwell, 2004.

Marsh, David. *Bruce Springsteen: Two Hearts: The Definitive Biography: 1972–2003.* New York: Routledge, 2003.

Masciotra, David. *Working on a Dream: The Progressive Political Vision of Bruce Springsteen.* New York: Continuum, 2010.

Masur, Louis P. *Runaway Dream: Born to Run and Bruce Springsteen's American Vision.* New York: Bloomsbury Press, 2009.

Michels, Steven. "Who's The Boss? Springsteen on the Alienation and Salvation of Work and Labor." *Bruce Springsteen and Philosophy: Darkness on the Edge of Truth.* Ed. Randall A. Auxier and Doug Anderson. Chicago: Open Court, 2008. 17–28.

Pardini, Samuele F. S. "Bruce Springsteen's 'American Skin.'" *Racing in the Street: The Bruce Springsteen Reader*. Ed. June Skinner Sawyers. New York: Penguin Books, 2004. 329–36.

Sawyers, June Skinner. "Introduction." *Racing in the Street: The Bruce Springsteen Reader*. Ed. June Skinner Sawyers. New York: Penguin Books, 2004. 1–25.

Springsteen, Bruce. *Born in the U.S.A*. Columbia Records, 1984. Compact disc.

Springsteen, Bruce. *Darkness on the Edge of Town*. Columbia Records, 1978. Compact disc.

Springsteen, Bruce. *The Ghost of Tom Joad*. Columbia Records, 1995. Compact disc.

Springsteen, Bruce. *Magic*. Columbia Records, 2007. Compact disc.

Springsteen, Bruce. *Nebraska*. Columbia Records, 1982. Compact disc.

Springsteen, Bruce. *The River*. Columbia Records, 1980. Compact disc.

Springsteen, Bruce. *We Shall Overcome: The Seeger Sessions: American Land Edition*. Sony, 2006. Compact disc.

Tucker, Robert C., ed. *The Marx-Engels Reader*. 2nd ed. New York: W. W. Norton, 1978.

Will, George F. "Bruuuuuce." *Racing in the Street: The Bruce Springsteen Reader*. Ed. June Skinner Sawyers. New York: Penguin Books, 2004. 107–9.

Chapter 16

Performing Working-Class Patriotism: Musical Responses to 9/11

William DeGenaro

Setting the Stage

It has become commonplace to claim that the terrorist attacks of September 11, 2001, changed virtually every facet of life in the United States. From art to commerce, popular culture to the political landscape, few areas remained untouched by the events of 9/11. Almost immediately, for instance, the mass media inundated audiences with working-class iconography and heroic images of working-class individuals. Stories and photographs of New York City firefighters and police officers risking their lives and even perishing by entering the burning towers and, later, sifting through rubble and breathing the toxic air at Ground Zero, were ubiquitous. These images of working-class heroism, though disturbing, paradoxically provided solace for a grieving and frightened nation and prompted patriotic rhetoric about "the American spirit," "work ethic," and "grit." In the years leading up to 9/11, working-class labor tended to be somewhat invisible in the popular media—and at times even demonized (especially the work of civil servants in urban centers) by a nation critical of trade unionism. NYPD and New York firefighters T-shirts and ball caps became fashionable. Groups of civil servants dressed in blue-collar uniforms became de riguer on 9/11 telethons and fundraisers, magazine covers, and even the 2001–2002 season premiere of *Saturday Night Live,* that venerable New York City institution, which aired weeks after the attacks. In a moment, even those prone to believe the mythology of "lazy union members" began to celebrate blue-collar laborers as heroes. Whereas the professional and managerial classes appeared ineffectual on 9/11—witness the reports about intelligence failures among the hierarchies of the CIA and FBI, not to mention images of George W. Bush reading a children's book as he's told of the attacks—the working classes were canonized as selfless, larger-than-life, and patriotic.

The world of popular music responded to this cultural climate in fascinating ways. To be sure, musical genres like rock and roll and country and western were exploiting working-class iconography for nearly five decades before the attacks of 9/11. Entertainers and artists, as well as fans and members of the respective subcultures, made working-class uniforms fashionable: boots, blue jeans, leather jackets, flannel shirts, and so forth. At various historic and pop culture moments, these uniforms have been worn critically (the rock and roll counterculture of the 1960s), ironically (the grunge movement's affinity for flannel), and/or commercially (the pop country community's embrace of rodeo gear in the 1990s), but during each era, the pose has by and large been a deliberate embrace of working-class chic. But 9/11 represented a particular challenge, an imperative even. The groundswell of patriotism—a patriotism entangled in issues of class due to the intense reverence for heroic blue-collar workers—presented an overwhelming imperative for the privileged classes to appear self-effacing and genuine. So even an indie rock band like the Strokes, critical darlings in 2001 and much-buzzed about online and within hipster circles, decided to pull a song called "New York City Cops" ("they ain't too bright," the lyrics proclaim) from their debut album. The press widely reported the elite backgrounds of band members while showing images of the band in the aforementioned jeans and leather jackets.

Coming from an elite background has long been perceived as a threat to credibility; in the weeks after 9/11, it was a threat to legitimacy. To be working class somehow aligned individuals with patriotism and suggested an identification with civil servants, not to mention—given the socioeconomic make-up of the voluntary armed forces—to the military. But of course popular music stars are rarely working class, regardless of the uniforms they wear. Perhaps if you are a pop star who grew up in a working-class family and/or posses a particular ideology or sensibility and/or attract a particular audience, you partly maintain that "working-class" status (think of Bruce Springsteen), but having great amounts of wealth, cultural capital, and discretionary time probably make the connection to working-class identity tenuous at best. But the imperative to appear patriotic after 9/11 was embodied by expressions of common cause and the adoption and even exploitation of blue-collar chic. For example, at one popular telethon, the Rolling Stones—the epitome of the popular music artist as corporation—opted to perform "Salt of the Earth," a relatively obscure selection from their catalogue. The song's lyrics include a toast to blue-collar laborers; Mick Jagger referencing both "hard working people" and "the lowly of birth" seemed appropriate and sensitive—an odd ethos for a band long known for being full of bad boys. Of course the Rolling Stones have numerous iconic hits including "Satisfaction," "Brown Sugar," "Honky Tonk Women," "Gimme Shelter," "Paint It Black," and "Start Me Up," to name only a few. Their catalogue boasts some of the most recognizable rock and roll songs ever written. So performing a relatively obscure number is noteworthy in and of itself. In part, Mick Jagger strutting as the band launches into the crowd-pleasing opening riff of "Satisfaction" might have appeared more than gauche, given the nature of the proceedings. The song selection nonetheless speaks to the cultural moment, a moment whose cultural logic of unity ("today we are all one") included a class dimension (perhaps something like "today we are all working class"?)—a dimension that was newly intensified in the wake of 9/11 yet also drew on the rhetoric of the classless society that already had wide circulation before the attacks.

This cultural moment when being patriotic and being working class became entangled and popular music reflected that dual imperative needs parsing. This chapter explores and attempts to taxonomize some of the responses to 9/11 in the world of popular music, paying special attention to several key types of representations of class consciousness and patriotism. After surveying some examples of 9/11 songs from the worlds of country music and rock and roll, I offer extended case studies of two longer and more sustained musical projects that offer more complex and nuanced representations of the post-9/11 landscape. Scores of diverse artists from various popular genres of music responded to 9/11 explicitly in their art; just a few examples include indie rockers Ryan Adams and Juliana Hatfield, metal bands Ministry and Iced Earth, classic rock icons Paul McCartney and Bo Diddley, and even the bubblegum pop-rap group Black Eyed Peas. Christine Lee Gengaro argues that the wide variety of musical response to 9/11 is indicative of "the diversity of ideas about what America means" (25). This is not an exhaustive analysis of all of those musical responses, but rather an examination of some of those representations that explicitly and/ or implicitly invoke something akin to working-class identity.

The Jingoistic Response

Certainly one of the prominent themes in musical responses to 9/11 was flag-waving. Even after the initial period of telethons and radio bans on "anti-American" music (for instance, removing John Lennon's apparently offensive ballad "Imagine"), the rhetoric of American exceptionalism continued to circulate in song. Critics have pointed out that this jingoism was not wholly original and compared these patriotic songs to the wave of popular jingoistic hits after the bombing of Pearl Harbor (Gengaro 28). Indeed, the theme became arguably more prominent as the United States prepared to invade Iraq in 2003. Many of the popular jingoistic lyrics told working-class narratives and included references to blue-collar lives, real or mythic. Aging classic rockers Lynyrd Skynyrd linked working-class identity and patriotism in their single "Red, White, and Blue," which managed to inject humor and wordplay into an explicitly jingoistic anthem. The song uses the colors of the flag to reference, respectively, the narrator's neck, hair, and collar. The clever (albeit commonplace) and funny lyrics suggest that members of the working class uniquely constitute the fabric, so to speak, of the nation, a common refrain in post-9/11 discourse. The colors of patriotism literally become the colors of working-class identity, in the lyrics, and the first-person plural narrative attempts to establish common cause, as when Lynyrd Skynyrd sing "We don't have no plastic L.A. friends." The band divorces itself from the ineffectual professional/managerial class and makes the requisite claim of being of the people.

Like the Rolling Stones performing "Salt of the Earth," Lynyrd Skynyrd backgrounds their own privileges and foregrounds humility in order to forge a tasteful, and also effective, identification with their audience. Not only do these examples speak to the cultural moment, they also suggest a broader insight about class in America: many working people expect self-effacement from the rich celebrities who provide entertainment and escape. As much as Americans like to fantasize about being Mick Jagger or Keith Richards, we also like hearing them reject or mock elitist values.

While Lynyrd Skynyrd represent the rock community in the jingoistic camp, even more representatives from the country and western community juxtapose working-class iconography and patriotism in their responses to 9/11. Perhaps the most notable, and extreme, example is Toby Keith's "Courtesy of the Red, White, and Blue (The Angry American)," an unapologetic apologia for both revenge and military aggression. In addition to violent and bellicose clichés, the metaphor-mixing lyrics include the direct, nearly apoetic, "we'll put a boot in your ass / it's the American way." Significantly, the line references a boot, a collective boot. Not a shoe, but rather the foot-wear that invokes working-class attire. In Keith's narrative, America as a collective asserts a uniquely working-class prerogative to enact revenge on the enemy. That mythic collective establishes legitimacy for the artist and constructs a unified "we" comprising artist and audience, who are all American, all good guys, and all working class.

That rhetorical move on the part of the popular artist requires a certain amount of self-effacement. Like Keith, Alan Jackson and Darryl Worley, both members of the pop country community, appeal to the mythic and cliché "common man" to establish a post-9/11 ethos. Jackson's "Where Were You (When the World Stopped Turning)" stands out as one of the most popular 9/11 anthems and has a similar, everyman theme ("I'm just a singer of simple songs," Jackson sings). The song references the narrator's relationship with Jesus and also his lack of familiarity with Middle Eastern geography, creating an interesting and somewhat problematic juxtaposition that suggests the righteous are working class, Christian, apolitical (a somewhat disingenuous claim given that the song advocates a particular position vis-à-vis military action), and nonexperts. The ballad places patriotism among other legitimate, affective responses to the events of 9/11. The song's narrator rhetorically asks the audience whether anger, fear, and/or patriotism were part of the reaction to the attacks and also juxtaposes the self-effacement and near anti-intellectualism (*I'm a good fellow who doesn't need to know about global politics because I'm Christian*) with praise for the working-class heroes of New York City, referenced in the song as "The heroes who died just doing what they do." Pop culture analyst Martha Bayles has pointed out that one hopes "not many Americans share Jackson's complacent ignorance" (B16).

Worley, meanwhile, in "Have You Forgotten?," also makes use of a regular-guy persona in a song even more explicitly framed as a prowar screed. Worley refers to the much-debated question of whether or not broadcast media ought to show graphic images of 9/11 deaths. The song's broader thesis is the need for anger and the productive value of anger, which keeps Americans from "forgetting," as the song's title suggests. Worley constructs a strawman argument against those who would question the value of war in the Middle East with lines like "you say we shouldn't worry about bin Laden." Of course no reasonable pundits during the early years of the wars in Afghanistan and Iraq were suggesting that America shouldn't *worry* about Osama bin Laden, but even the problematic link helps Worley create an affective appeal about both public policy as well as the (national and class-based) identity of the good guys. Like other battles of the so-called culture wars, the rhetoric of "everyday people" enjoys wide circulation. Of course, this rhetoric was not wholly new in the post-9/11 era; country music in particular had thrived on the tropes of everyday people for decades. But jingoism and "common man" tropes after September 11 circulated *at the exclusion* of alternative points of view (witness the shunning of the Dixie Chicks after critical comments about the Bush administration).

The Critical Response

Another group of working-class–themed country and rock songs came out in the wake of 9/11—a group of songs that took a more critical tack in their response to the attacks, either focusing on human character or explicitly problematizing the jingoism present in mass and popular culture. Whether implicit or explicit in their critique, this grouping of songs can be said to have a critical outlook, in the sense that their lyrics are reflective about their representation of the people, places, events, and implications of 9/11. Further, the examples I point to offer a working-class perspective either by virtue of the artist's persona or the subject matter of the song itself.

Consider Neil Young, a rock and roll artist with a blue-collar persona who perpetually wore old blue jeans and flannel shirts decades before grunge artists made the uniform fashionable. Young oozes working-class credibility, attracts a diverse fan base including numerous members of the working class, and exudes class consciousness. Young commented on 9/11 with his poignant but somehow unsentimental ballad "Let's Roll." Its title borrows the words spoken by a heroic passenger on United Flight 93 who with his fellow passengers stormed the plane's cockpit, brought the craft down over rural Pennsylvania, and likely prevented a further attack, perhaps on Washington, DC. As a work of art, the Neil Young song knows its subject is a hero and doesn't condescend to declare him as such. In this sense, the song offers what I am calling a "critical" response to 9/11, a response that opts to reflect on humanity instead of stating a partisan commonplace. "Let's Roll" offers a character study and puts listeners inside the head of the passenger where he considers his situation and expresses his own conflicted emotions. Wistful, the narrator seems to know his mission is a suicide mission, but also expresses paradoxical hope. In a further expression of conflict and even paradox, the narrator appears confident of his mission's righteousness. The lyrics declare, "You've got to turn on evil," which could be a line from one of the jingoistic songs if not for the critical balance that comes from a line like "I hope that we're forgiven," which allows for ambivalence.

266   Blue-Collar Pop Culture

Alternative country artist Steve Earle also focuses on humanity and offers a critical character study—albeit one far more controversial than Neil
Young's subject. In "John Walker's Blues," Earle goes so far as to humanize
the "American Taliban" John Walker Lindh, the young American man who
joined the terrorist organization made infamous by Osama bin Laden and
of course became a pariah in the American media. Like Young, Earle has a
blue-collar sensibility; although a long-time outsider (a rebel among rebels)
in the world of country music, he made his way in popular music by singing songs about small-town and working-class Americans. "John Walker's
Blues" uses the acoustic stylings of another such ballad and early on gives
listeners the impression the song is about a typical outcast, later turning
in quite a different direction. The song paints a picture of a young outcast
who converts to Islam, adopts an extremist ideology, and truly believes he's
doing what is right. Not only does the song invoke Earle's (and country
music's) other ballads of working-class young men, the song also contains
lyrics that invoke post-9/11 themes of heroism, albeit with the ironic twist
of coming from one of the "enemy." Earle sings, "Sometimes a man's got
to fight for what he believes" and "our hearts were pure and strong" and
you almost forget who is speaking these words. Certainly humanizing John
Walker Lind in the wake of 9/11 caused controversy, but Earle manages to
focus critically and reflectively on a nuanced human being. Although their
subjects are worlds apart, both Young and Earle avoid explicit political
sloganeering in favor of keeping a human being in the foreground.

But the critical camp also showed itself to be capable of some sloganeering of its own. Earle also released a song in the years following 9/11 called
"The Revolution Starts Now" that never explicitly mentions the attacks of
9/11 or the subsequent military actions in Iraq and Afghanistan but exists
in the popular consciousness as a critique of the post-9/11 mindset and
post-9/11 foreign policy, likely due to both Earle's political ideology, not
to mention the song's inclusion in Michael Moore's piece of leftist political
theater *Fahrenheit 9/11*. Like "John Walker's Blues," the song begins with the
trappings of a working-class ballad: "I was walkin' down the street in the
town where I was born." However, the song maintains a more abstract and
didactic structure, repeating the titular phrase as a kind of call to action. A
less subtle example of the politically explicit critical school is Ani Difranco's
"Self-Evident," a diatribe against George W. Bush that takes the form of
a spoken word performance piece. Difranco, long associated with various
leftist causes, has perhaps the most explicitly class-conscious ideology and
public persona of any artist mentioned in this analysis. Further, her do-it-
yourself ethos (she manages her own record label, her own merchandising,

and virtually every other artistic and commercial facet of her work as a singer-songwriter and performer) and work ethic is blue collar.

In "Self-Evident," Difranco plays the role of provocateur much more brazenly than Steve Earle does in "John Walker's Blues." She situates 9/11 within American foreign policy and indicts then-President Bush (who she declares is not really the president) for his illegitimacy and his ineffectualism. Frankly, the song is shocking, albeit epideictic, ceremonial, and unlikely to engage anyone but those already in agreement with Difranco's radical politics. Although on the opposite end of the political spectrum, Difranco reduces complex politics to sound bites as reductively as does Toby Keith. And just as the prowar jingoism glorified working-class life and the heroism of the everyday individual, Difranco's song vilifies Bush not only for his actions and policies but also for his privilege. She refers to "some prep school punk's plan to perpetuate retribution" and, later suggests that America is "under the thumb of some blue blood royal son." On various points along the political spectrum, there was credibility to be had by aligning with the workers against the elite. Such was the political climate after 9/11 and such was the state of popular music that chose to take up the events of 9/11.

The Elder Statesman Responds: Springsteen's *The Rising*

Perhaps no popular music star has a stronger identity as a working-class rocker than Bruce Springsteen. From his own familial origins to his fan base to the subject matter of his critiques of the American Dream ("Atlantic City," "Youngstown," "The River," and many, many others) to his legendary work ethic during sweaty, marathon concerts, Springsteen has a blue-collar ethos. His post-9/11 concept album *The Rising* eschews politics and partisan slogans—of the political right or political left—in favor of a nuanced set of meditations on the state of the nation in the months following the attacks. In a thorough scholarly analysis, Gengaro calls the record "finely wrought portraits of the stages of grief, and descriptions of the experiences of the heroes, the saved, and the lost" (26).

Indeed, the entire album is full of just that—meditations. A pair of songs late on the album work in tandem to posit a better place and a better time. The title track centers on a sacred celebration, "in a sky filled with light." The next song, "Paradise," promises the existence of heaven, which he characterizes as a site of reunion. Throughout the album, Springsteen's lyrics and at times maudlin melodies create poignant but not-quite-sentimental spaces in which to reflect on national identity through the lens of narrative.

Most of the album's songs take the form of stories of individual Americans who embody the national ethos in the months after 9/11. "Lonesome Day" not only offers solace to anyone suffering but also urges restraint—albeit with more than a little ambivalence—when faced with a revenge impulse: "Better ask questions before you shoot." Consider Springsteen's lyrics as a reflective counterpoint to Darryl Worley's narrator wishing that more violent images be broadcast on television so as to elicit productive rage. Springsteen's lyrics acknowledge that revenge would offer affective relief, but follows up that acknowledgment with the somewhat radical (in early 2002) suggestion that restraint might be wise. Revenge is a thematic presence elsewhere too; in "Empty Sky," Springsteen sings, "I want an eye for an eye / I woke up this morning to an empty sky." The presence of a desire for revenge is a realistic component of the album and yet time and again, Springsteen suggests that anger might not last forever. This simple but profound *this too shall pass* theme recurs throughout the album, notably on "Waitin' on a Sunny Day," which is even more of a narrative—a love story actually—than "Lonesome Day." The song's love story conceit gives the song a comforting edge; Springsteen's ballads, after all, are *familiar* to such a wide American audience. So too is Springsteen's emphasis on love stories about the working class, and "Waitin' on a Sunny Day" is no exception. Springsteen sings, "Hard times, baby well they come to us all" and gives the song a familiar context, situating the pain of 9/11 as a kind of extension of other, socioeconomic, challenges the mythic "we" have faced. Like Steve Earle's post-9/11 reflections, the song starts out sounding like any other story of working-class woe. One of the album's most familiar tracks, "My City of Ruins" (written before 9/11, as critics such as Gengaro point out) also begins with a signature Springsteen trope: a vivid, free-verse description of a collapsed town. He sings of "boarded-up windows" and "empty streets" and the song sounds like classic Springsteen tracks like "My Hometown." Here, though, blue-collar de-industrialization serves as a metaphor for understanding and coping with a different type of destruction, 9/11.

Elsewhere on the album, Springsteen's fictional lovers invoke with subtlety the stories of firefighters, and again the music advanced familiar Springsteen themes of working people. The "Into the Fire" lyrics, for instance, read like a note to a fallen 9/11 firefighter from a grieving lover. Lines like "The sky was falling and streaked with blood" sound explicitly like 9/11 allusions. Later, the song goes on to use second-person pronouns to simulate a maudlin love note. "Empty Sky" also seems to take the form of a love letter. And in the explicitly titled "You're Missing," his narrator plainly states, "Your house is waiting / for you to walk in." The lyrics certainly invoke 9/11, especially given that the song was released in 2002, and yet they also connect intimately to Springsteen's large catalogue of songs about blue-collar lovers. The album manages to be both new and familiar.

Elsewhere, Springsteen changes his narrator and sings from the point of view of the fallen hero. "Nothing Man," certainly one of the darkest songs on the album, creates a humble, working-class narrator from small-town USA whose "brave young life was forever changed." This is perhaps the moment on *The Rising* that comes the closest to sentimentality, but we see first of all that Springsteen, the mature and seasoned artist, feels confident enough to risk singing from this perspective. Further, we are reminded that 9/11's pathos certainly lent itself to affective and weighty artistic expression. Springsteen allows himself to create a strictly emotive narrative; the risk pays off, I believe. Likewise, Springsteen risks including a narrative of Arab lovers who live "'neath Allah's blessed rain" in the aptly titled "Worlds Apart." The song does not rise to the level of "John Walker's Blues" in terms of provocative appeal, but helps the album, as a holistic comment on 9/11's effects, have a round and even global approach. Bayles points out that Springsteen's sampling of Islamic prayer in "Worlds Apart" is an apt, almost transgressive, response to the Taliban's ban on popular music.

Springsteen's career has focused in large part on creating empathic narratives of working-class experience and *The Rising* is no exception. It is a work of art by an artist at the peak of his creativity, taking risks, comforting an audience, invoking the themes his music always invokes, and yet rising, so to speak, to the challenges of commenting on the post-9/11 landscape in a way that is reflective, critical, and rooted in storytelling as much as it is rooted in sociopolitical consciousness. Springsteen's voice transcends leftist critique even, as his narrators reach for wisdom and perspective. Ultimately, forgiveness (as a theme and as a critical stance) seems to win, although consistently tempered with a realistic ambivalence. The album closes with Springsteen's narrator praying for the ability to forgive: "With these hands, I pray Lord . . . I pray for your love."

The Punks Weigh In: Green Day's *American Idiot*

Punk rock—particularly the political and class-conscious variety of the brash genre—has been less inclined than anthemic, Springsteen rock to espouse an ethos of love and forgiveness. And during the post-9/11 moment, Green Day seemed less able than Springsteen to project authority and credibility beyond a very small audience. Green Day seemed like has-beens in 2001, the year of the attacks. Known primarily for their pop punk chart-toppers of the mid-1990s, the band seemed to most observers past its prime. Indeed, many critics blamed Green Day for spawning the shopping mall punks that dominated modern rock radio in the years leading up to 9/11. However, like Springsteen, Green Day chose to tackle 9/11 by way of a nuanced, poetic, album-length meditation on the state of post-9/11 United States of America and in doing so made the most critically acclaimed music of the band's career. Whereas Springsteen created multiple tone poems, Green Day created an album-length narrative (albeit an abstract one), a rock opera of sorts.

Green Day released its concept album *American Idiot* in 2004 and the record went on to win Grammys and get adapted into a musical stage show, unlikely fates for a Green Day release. *American Idiot*'s references to September 11 are oblique; in fact, the album is more explicitly about 7–11 than 9/11. Green Day narrates the story of a young man named Jesus of Suburbia (a possible allusion to Hanif Kureishi's novel *The Buddha of Suburbia*), disillusioned with life in a working-class suburb, who runs away to the city, befriends a rebellious punk rock hero named St. Jimmy, but never escapes the sensation of alienation and loneliness. Throughout the loose narrative, Jesus of Suburbia searches for space where resistance and an alternative to dominant culture exist but he continues to come up short. The record visits familiar punk rock tropes: alienation among youth culture, dominant culture's imperative to conform, the boredom of suburban life, and lack of hope among young working-class males. However, as a statement on the post-9/11 American landscape, Green Day manages to transcend these familiar tropes and create an angry missive directed at purveyors of a politically right-wing ideology during the first George W. Bush term.

Perhaps the album found commercial and critical success because the band avoided the explicit sloganeering of, say, Ani Difranco. Although *American Idiot* is an angry record, it lacks the provocative punch of "Self-Evident," or even a song like "John Walker's Blues." Green Day largely avoids specific references to the events of 9/11 (fewer even than Springsteen's 9/11 album) and largely avoids mentions of familiar leaders, although references to President Bush pop up at times. Still, it is an album that continues to resonate as one of the seminal time capsules of the post-9/11 political climate. Further, *America Idiot*—despite its poetic obliqueness—can be read as a commentary on the socioeconomic dimensions of post-9/11 frustration and alienation.

On the title track, Green Day proclaims, "I'm not part of the redneck agenda" and listeners, especially listeners in 2004 when the album saw its release, cannot help but imagine country-pop singers like Toby Keith. The song "American Idiot," with references to "propaganda," suggests that the media and the government work together to propagate lies. Green Day leader Billie Joe Armstrong creates an image of a working-class suburb where at least one member of the alienated citizenry (Jesus of Suburbia) does not believe the "redneck" party line. A critical response to the class politics and partisan politics of 9/11anthems like "Where Were You?," the song makes an affirmative and angry statement that not all members of the mythic "everyman" class think alike.

In the album's lyrics, Green Day describes the Jesus of Suburbia character with many of the familiar markers of working-class identity, including a lack of cultural capital, a lack of power and agency. Jesus of Suburbia, having been fed a "steady diet of soda pop and Ritalin," watches the changing political landscape on television, sitting on a couch in a dystopic but familiar suburban hell. "We are the kids of war and peace / from Anaheim / to the Middle East," Armstrong sings, implicitly referencing military action in Iraq and Afghanistan. Both the media and the corporate nation-state are targets of scorn on the album. Repeatedly, Green Day refers to a media that is complicit in justifying war and squelching dissent, and the lyrics blur the line between government hegemony and corporate hegemony. On the popular single "Holiday," Armstrong sings, "The company lost the war today," a vague but somehow damning critique of the military-industrial complex, circa 2004, a year that saw increasing traffic of private contractors to the front lines of the post-9/11 wars.

"Holiday" also contains imagery that is (at least obliquely) suggestive of 9/11. The image of an "armageddon flame" seems to invoke the horrors of 9/11. Likewise "Are We the Waiting" refers to dreams of "screaming" and a "dirty town . . . burning down." The lyrics are vague and somewhat esoteric but the violence and destruction potentially conjure images of 9/11, especially since much of *American Idiot* centers on the dulling but influential things that Jesus of Suburbia sees on television. It's easy to imagine the Jesus character as a blue-collar kid with few opportunities, watching the events of that September unfold on television (as most Americans did), his anxiety and disillusionment increasing. Little wonder the name of *American Idiot*'s most popular ballad is "Wake Me up When *September* Ends" (italics added).

Like Springsteen, Green Day connects post-9/11 anxiety with socioeconomic insecurity. Green Day's "Boulevard of Broken Dreams" sounds at times like a Springsteen ballad about a town where few financial (or ideological or creative) options seem to exist: "I walk this empty street / on the boulevard of broken dreams." The images are not that dissimilar to

Springsteen's "My Hometown." Later on *American Idiot,* in the song "Letter Bomb," Green Day sings "The dummy failed the crash test / Now collecting unemployment checks like a flunky along for the ride." As is the case with many songs from *The Rising,* tracks on *American Idiot* use deindustrialization, unemployment, and socioeconomic frustration as metaphors to help Americans wrestle with the challenges of 9/11. Unlike *The Rising,* the Green Day record maintains a bitter edge. It's hard to imagine Springsteen singing, "I started fucking running / Just as soon as my feet touch ground," lyrics that come from Green Day's "Homecoming." The ethos of *American Idiot*—released two years later than Springsteen's record—is bleaker, less comforting, and was more commercially successful.

Some Concluding Thoughts

As ethnomusicologist Revell Carr suggests, folksongs about disasters have a dual burden of serving as "aural monuments" to the disasters as well as prompts to help everyday people return to regular routines. Put another way, songs about trauma represent how we are both changed and unchanged by tragedy and disaster. It's not so much that we listen to remember and forget, but rather that we listen to meditate on existential realities. And 9/11 certainly shifted and redefined our collective existential realities. Social class is another reality, both existential and material, one rooted in identity, ethos, politics, lifestyle, culture, work, and economics. Popular artists seized familiar tools like class consciousness and demagoguery and audience identification to build bonds with listeners and at times challenge them during a disastrous and bleak period of U.S. history. As fans, critics, and Americans, we retain these monuments on our MP3 players and CD shelves and they take us back to the years following 9/11, reminding us of the political and emotional landscapes. We listen on our commutes or while cleaning the house and they connect us to the routines to which we have returned.

But by performing working-class identities, these songs also remind us that a mythology of social class surrounds us in the United States, a mythology that affects our attitudes, language, and even public policy. What gets Americans through "hard times"? What are the implications of pervasive feelings of alienation? What struggles define our lives? What is our relationship to national leaders and the choices they make? Do we dare resist and transgress or do those moments of dissent threaten our collective well-being? These questions provide the basis for reflection on post-9/11 life as surely as they provide the basis for thinking through our response to class division in U.S. society. The post-9/11 songs of Springsteen, Green Day, and others suggest that class in America is not only a material reality but in equal parts a performance. Paradoxically, class divides us while also uniting us in a shared engagement with dominant myths. Americans accept these myths to varying degrees but all of us are confronted with performances of the mythology—even while listening to pop music. Post-9/11 music explored these class mythologies in interesting, sometimes critical, sometimes commercial and manipulative ways. Let us return to the music, listen, and reflect on the degree to which popular art supports and/or transgresses dominant culture's sometimes problematic ideas about the working class.

Works Cited

Bayles, Martha. "Can We Find an Anthem for 9/11?" *Chronicle of Higher Education* (27 September 2002): B16.

Carr, Revell. "'We Will Never Forget': Disaster in American Folksong from the Nineteenth Century to September 11, 2001." *Voices* 30 (2004): 36–42.

Difranco, Ani. "Self-Evident." *So Much Shouting, So Much Laughter.* Compact Disc. Righteous Babe. 2002.

Earle, Steve. "John Walker's Blues." *Jerusalem.* Compact Disc. Artemis. 2002.

Earle, Steve. "The Revolution Starts Now." *The Revolution Starts Now.* Compact Disc. Artemis. 2004.

Gengaro, Christine Lee. "Requiems for a City: Popular Music's Response to 9/11." *Popular Music and Society* 32 (2009): 25–36.

Green Day. *American Idiot.* Compact Disc. Reprise. 2004.

Jackson, Alan. "Where Were You (When the World Stopped Turning)?" *Drive.* Compact Disc. Arista. 2002.

Keith, Toby. "Courtesy of the Red, White, and Blue (The Angry American)." *Unleashed.* Compact Disc. Dreamworks Nashville. 2002.

Lynyrd Skynyrd. "Red, White, and Blue." *Vicious Cycle.* Compact Disc. Sanctuary. 2003.

Rolling Stones. "Salt of the Earth." *Beggar's Banquet* (1968). Remastered Ed. Compact Disc. Abkco. 2002.

Springsteen, Bruce. *The Rising.* Compact Disc. Sony. 2002.

Worley, Darryl. "Have You Forgotten?" *Have You Forgotten?* Compact Disc. Dreamworks Nashville. 2003.

Young, Neil. "Let's Roll." *Are You Passionate?* Compact Disc. Reprise. 2002.

PART III

Blue-Collar Sports

Chapter 17

Blue-Collar Ballplayers: Sports Movies and Class in America

Derek C. Maus

With professional and some amateur sports (e.g., NCAA basketball and football) in North America being a multi-billion-dollar business at the outset of the twenty-first century, one may be tempted to view issues of class within this context from an overly reductive perspective. Frequent labor issues have beset each of the four most prominent North American professional leagues—the National Football League (NFL), Major League Baseball (MLB), the National Basketball Association (NBA), and the National Hockey League (NHL)—resulting in the cancellation of part or all of at least one season for each since 1982 due to either a players' strike or an owners' lockout. Despite substantial public relations efforts on the part of players' unions,[1] these disputes have largely been perceived as arguments between millionaire players and billionaire owners rather than as a class conflict with much relevance for the vast majority of the population (other than perhaps the interruption of a major source of entertainment). Beyond the fiscal realities of these sports lies a considerably more complex picture of class relations, partly based on a set of mythologizing impulses regarding class mobility within American popular culture and partly based on the historical economics of American professional sports.

American films about sports, and especially those about baseball and boxing, have been extremely influential in valorizing the figure of the professional athlete as a member of the working class in a Weberian sense.[2] For the most part, sports films do not stratify class beyond a fairly simple binary construction that places players (and usually their coaches) in opposition to an elite class of owners, league administrators, and other peripheral non-player types whose primary interest in sports is personal financial gain. In both fictional and journalistic accounts, players (in some cases earning salaries tens of millions of dollars per season[3]) are frequently identified with such working-class epithets as "lunch-pail," "journeyman," or "blue-collar" in an effort to separate them from the almost universally reviled ownership class and their collaborators in organized crime, especially illicit gambling. As such, sports become a metaphorical frame of reference in which the idealized class dynamics of the "American Dream" find fertile ground for symbolic reinscription. James Truslow Adams offered a succinct articulation of this philosophy in *The Epic of America* (1931):

> The American Dream is that dream of a land in which life should be better and richer and fuller for every man, with opportunity for each according to ability or achievement. . . . It is not a dream of motor cars and high wages merely, but a dream of social order in which each man and each woman shall be able to attain to the fullest stature of which they are innately capable, and be recognized by others for what they are, regardless of the fortuitous circumstances of birth or position. (214–15)

As depicted in film, sports offer the American working class not only a meritocratic opportunity for upward mobility, but also a realm in which quintessentially American values are rewarded with "the fullest stature" of success.

The class dynamics depicted in American sports films are not Marxist in as much as players almost never aspire to become or to supplant owners; rather, they generally seek to defeat the owners' plans to taint the virtue of "the game" in some way. In the process of defending the integrity of their sport, the players usually "win" something literal and/or symbolic for themselves, but this reward is almost never actual ownership. In this way, the class conflict between players and owners remains largely embedded within an economically capitalist, politically liberal-democratic, and mythologically Judeo-Christian framework, rarely (if ever) straying into the vocabulary of revolution or radicalism. Class relationships in American sports film are inherently normative to the foundational rhetorics of the United States (e.g., the declaration of the right to "life, liberty, and the pursuit of happiness") as well as to the reformist populism of Robert La Follette and Theodore Roosevelt. Much like the antitrust laws of the early twentieth century did not reject capitalist class structures but rather sought to ensure a relatively equal opportunity and fair competition within them,

American sports films attempt to reestablish the "fairness" of the playing field against any forces that would rig the game in such a way that talent and forthright effort are not the prime determinants of success.

The roots of this tendency predate the development of the motion picture industry altogether, arising out of the rapid industrialization and the concomitant aesthetic development of literary realism and naturalism in the United States during the late nineteenth and early twentieth century. The class sensibilities expressed in such novels as Theodore Dreiser's *Sister Carrie* (1900), Frank Norris's *The Octopus* (1901), and Upton Sinclair's *The Jungle* (1906) parallel the predominant tenor of subsequent American sports films, especially in regard to their depictions of an uncaring oligarchic system that cynically abuses the labor of the ordinary worker/ballplayer. Even before the minimum salary for a player in the majors rose to more than 16 times the per capita income in the United States, as was the case in 2009, professional athletes have historically been paid well above the average worker's wage. Nevertheless, strife between owners and players has been couched in the fiery rhetoric of class conflict since the earliest days of professional baseball, the first large-scale instance of professional sports in the United States. St. Louis Cardinals outfielder Curt Flood famously challenged Major League Baseball's "reserve clause" in 1969 by stating "I do not feel I am a piece of property to be bought and sold irrespective of my wishes" (qtd. in Ward and Burns 411), but his was far from the first expression of class-based outrage on the part of professional athletes. John Montgomery Ward, a member of the Baseball Hall of Fame as a player and the organizer of the Brotherhood of Professional Base Ball Players (the first formal labor union of professional athletes), published an essay in *Lippincott's Magazine* in 1885 titled "Is the Base-Ball Player a Chattel?" in which he prefigures Flood by equating the reserve clause with immoral and dehumanizing treatment of workers: "Instead of an institution for good, it has become one for evil; instead of a measure of protection, it has been used as a handle for the manipulation of a traffic in players, a sort of speculation in live stock, by which they are bought, sold, and transferred like so many sheep" (Sullivan 165). Ward adopts a similar idiom in the 1889 "Brotherhood Manifesto" that announced the formation of a player-owned league (the Players' League) to compete with the allegedly monopolistic National League. In this document, the business practices of the National League's owners are repeatedly denounced as unfair, avaricious, and even contrary to the nation's principles:

There was a time when the [National] League stood for integrity and fair dealing: to-day it stands for dollars and cents. Once it looked to the elevation of the game and an honest exhibition of the sport; to-day its eyes are upon the turnstile. Men have come into the business for no other motive than to exploit it for every dollar in sight. . . . We ask to be judged solely upon our work, and believing that the game can be played more fairly and its business conducted more intelligently under a plan which excludes everything arbitrary and un-American, we look forward with confidence to the support of the public and the future of the national game. (Sullivan 188–89)

Despite the predictably harsh reaction by the owners[4] and the rapid demise of the Players' League, this antagonism within the nation's most popular (and thus iconic) professional sport provided the fundamental ethos by which American sports films in general came to depict the conflict between the virtue of players and the duplicity of owners.

David Shields insightfully summarizes the player/owner dichotomy in sports films as a moral distinction between several pairs of opposed symbols:

If the player often becomes a Christ figure, the owner is clearly a stand-in for the Pharisees, the Roman officers, the Jewish priests, the money-changers. . . . This suits vs. jocks animus is, in a way, the narrative tension of nearly every sports movie, for these films return again and again to the opposition between the social (which is corrupt) and the body (which is miraculous). . . . The movie—any sports movie—becomes a praise song to life here on earth, to physical existence itself, beyond striving, beyond economic necessity. (Shields)

It is in this final sentence that Shields oversteps himself, for the American sports film is very much concerned with economic necessity, whether it is the minor league baseball players in *Bull Durham* (1988) dreaming of making it to "the Show" (i.e., the Major Leagues), where "[y]ou hit white balls for batting practice, the ballparks are like cathedrals, the hotels all have room service, and the women all have long legs and brains," or former boxer Terry Malloy's famous lament in *On the Waterfront* (1954): "I coulda had class. I coulda been a contender. I coulda been somebody, instead of a bum, which is what I am, let's face it." Though *On the Waterfront* is not centered on sports, the story of the criminal union running the docks unfolds through a sports metaphor via the character of Malloy, who took a dive in a fight at his brother's insistence in order to make some money from crooked gamblers. In doing so, Malloy lost his chance at sporting glory and is reduced to becoming "muscle" for the corrupt Mob, a condition he only redeems near the end of the film in Hemingwayesque fashion by taking an actual beating from Mob boss Johnny Friendly's (Lee J. Cobb) goons without being morally defeated by them. Even a relatively slapstick sports film like *Caddyshack* (1980) directly engages economic reality, with working-class teenager Danny Noonan (Michael O'Keefe) seeking to earn a scholarship to college (an option for upward class mobility seemingly not available to him by any other means) by winning a golf tournament at the exclusive country club at which he works as a caddy. Winning the tournament does not prove to be enough by itself, as Danny also finds himself having to kowtow to the elitist and corrupt worldview of the club's wealthy cofounder Judge Elihu Smails (Ted Knight). Danny eventually rejects both the judge's philosophy and his scholarship money, but wins the money to go to college anyway through his golfing skills by defeating the judge and his partner in an absurdly fraudulent match-play competition punctuated by the explosive destruction of the course. These films and many others make it clear that the players are not separated from economic necessities, but rather that the fairness of access to those necessities is the central issue. They make the argument that a ballplayer as talented as "Crash" Davis (Kevin Costner) *should* make it to "the Show" rather than languishing anonymously in the lowest level of the minor leagues; Terry Malloy *should* have been able to "be somebody" as a result of his skills in the ring instead of having to become a class-traitor abusing the other stevedores on the waterfront; and Danny Noonan *should* be able to go to college without having to cheat everyone like Judge Smails does. All of these stories reinforce the basic rhetorical premises of class mobility in American culture both by validating the "Protestant work ethic" of industriousness and rectitude and by fostering nonrevolutionary class solidarity against the broadly defined elite class that "cheats" to gain and to maintain its social power.

The theme of the virtuous worker-athlete being manipulated, corrupted, and/or taken advantage of by the insatiable greed of team owners, gamblers, promoters, and others with a monetary stake in their performance is pivotal for most American sports films. If a player resists the myriad temptations to "sell out" his gifts, he becomes a working-class hero who embodies the Horatio Alger "rags to riches" myth in sporting form. In doing so, he reinforces the meritocratic American Dream ideology that promises just rewards for hard work and self-discipline. Timothy Morris's point about this trope within baseball fiction can be extended to American sports films in general:

> The strict logic of the game provides for continuous comparison among players to ensure that a team fields its best lineup and that the best players in

a league or age group are consistently recognized for their talents. Meritocracy is therefore on every page of baseball fiction. One looks through these representations of meritocracy directly to an underlying cultural value of merit that is never challenged. The better an individual's performance, the more that individual should be recognized and rewarded. (116)

Sylvester Stallone's character of Rocky Balboa, for example, is born into poverty in the rough working-class neighborhood of Kensington in Philadelphia and all of his values—perseverance, courage, physical endurance, loyalty—are those idealized in the laborers that appear both in Alger's novels and in Weber's formulation of the "Protestant work ethic." Over the course of the six films in the series, Rocky rises from being an unknown fighter training in a club with the decidedly unglamorous name of the "Bucket of Blood" to become the heavyweight champion of the world. To emphasize his particularly American brand of heroism, in *Rocky IV* (1985) he even becomes the defender of national honor in a Cold War contest against a Soviet fighter whose "excellence" is tainted for American audiences as much by the political ideology he represents as by his use of steroids, both of which are forms of "cheating" from the class perspective of the American Dream.

A host of other films subscribes to this basic formula of glorifying the underdog who triumphs against the odds because of his or her innate merit, including *National Velvet* (1944), *Hoosiers* (1986), *Rudy* (1993), and *Miracle* (2004). *National Velvet* helped to establish this trope by depicting the journey of a horse named "The Pie" from the gates of the glue factory to victory in the Grand National, one of England's most important equestrian competitions. Despite the film's English setting, all of the primary characters in the film are strongly associated with the working-class values of the wartime United States. Velvet Brown (Elizabeth Taylor) is a 12-year-old butcher's daughter with a deep love of horses and a seemingly impossible (because of her age and sex) dream of riding the winning entry in the Grand National. Mi Taylor (Mickey Rooney) is a former jockey who now drifts and works odd jobs for Brown's father. Several times in the film Mi must resist the temptation to steal from the Browns to relieve his relative poverty, and this moral decision parallels his stewardship of Velvet and her unlikely prize gelding. Without his "proper" decision to forego theft, his skill as a horse trainer would be morally tainted. The Pie is initially shown as an unmanageable horse destined for destruction when Velvet wins him in a raffle. With Mi's help, she intends to tame him and make him into a champion because both she and Mi see his innate athleticism where others only see wildness. Velvet's ever-practical father, though, intends to turn the Pie into a workhorse, a task for which he proves wholly unsuitable and which the film suggests is an unworthy outlet for his exceptional physical talents. After Velvet and the Pie win the race, they receive multiple offers to cash in on their newfound celebrity, but Velvet refuses them and returns happily to her humble working-class life in Sussex.

In a similar vein, two films directed by David Anspaugh sentimentally exalt the simple virtues of small-town Midwestern life through a David-versus-Goliath sports metaphor that symbolically suggests that the proper dedication and attitude can overcome any physical competitive disadvantages. *Hoosiers* tells the story of a high school basketball team from a small farming town in Indiana that wins an unlikely state championship, whereas *Rudy* chronicles the efforts of Daniel "Rudy" Ruettiger (Sean Astin), the undersized son of a steelworker in the steadfastly blue-collar town of Joliet, Illinois, to play for the iconic Notre Dame Fighting Irish football team. Although it is chiefly the transcendent basketball skill of star player Jimmy Chitwood that leads the Hickory team to victory in *Hoosiers,* all of the players, including the short and seemingly untalented Ollie (Wade Schenck), contribute at various points in the season, reinforcing the working-class virtue of selfless collaboration. Simply making the team and playing a single down for Notre Dame is victory enough for the pint-sized Rudy, whose desire to do so is in large part a tribute to a childhood friend who died in an explosion at the steel mill in his hometown. When Rudy finally does get into a game at the end of the 1974 season, he makes a tackle and is carried off the field by his teammates. It hardly matters that the actual play is utterly irrelevant to the outcome of the game, as the film's rhetoric is almost entirely about individual perseverance in the face of adversity. Unlike in *Hoosiers,* the team's performance is irrelevant, since Notre Dame was a dominant college football program during the 1970s. Instead, the film's class rhetoric is one that asserts one of the most fundamental tenets of the American Dream ideology, that the opportunity for achieving success—whether symbolized by playing football for Notre Dame or by playing first base for the New York Yankees like the ever-humble would-be engineer Lou Gehrig (Gary Cooper) in *Pride of the Yankees* (1942)—is open to all who apply themselves diligently.

In recent American sporting history, few events embody the unlikely victory scenario more than the U.S. hockey team's victory over the Soviet Union during the 1980 Olympic Games in Lake Placid. This story is retold in *Miracle* and emphasizes the "ordinary American" nature of each of the players and of coach Herb Brooks. An early scene in the film even catalogues this "everyman" status as all the players in turn introduce themselves by name and by hometown. As the players list the names of large cites and small towns from the Upper Midwest and New England, the players' faces show a recognition that the chance to represent the country is ostensibly equal despite these differences in background and the team pulls together to play for the "right" reason—national, not personal, glory—and wins the gold medal as a result. As in *National Velvet, Hoosiers,* and *Rudy,* economic class is only obliquely referenced in *Miracle,* but all of these films rely on the implication that success results from adherence to the idealized values traditionally ascribed to the working class in American culture.

The converse of this equation also holds true. When a character succumbs to the lures of money and colludes with the oligarchs to betray the sanctity of the game he (or, infrequently, she) plays, it is usually depicted as a betrayal of the working-class fans who idolize him. The quintessence of this image is "Shoeless Joe" Jackson, one of eight players on the disgraced 1919 Chicago White Sox team who were accused of fixing the World Series in that year in exchange for money from gamblers. Jackson figures prominently in two films—*Eight Men Out* (1988) and *Field of Dreams* (1989)—but it is in the former that the betrayal of the American meritocratic ethic (and, by extension, the working-class fans that presumably value it) by the so-called Black Sox is most directly suggested. After the scandal breaks and the White Sox' loss in the World Series is revealed to have been a willful fraud (though the film casts doubt on Jackson's role in that fraud), one of his young fans wistfully asks Jackson to "Say it ain't so, Joe," to which the player only responds by casting his eyes downward and walking away, thereby reenacting a possibly apocryphal exchange originally reported in the *Chicago Herald and Examiner.* In *The Longest Yard* (1974, remade in 2005), Paul "Wrecking" Crewe (Burt Reynolds) is a former NFL quarterback who has been sent to prison for stealing and wrecking his girlfriend's expensive sports car during a high-speed chase. Once in prison, his *truly* reprehensible action (within the context of sports films, that is) is revealed, namely that he "shaved points" during games in which he played, for which he was expelled from the league. A fellow inmate named Caretaker (James Hampton) straightforwardly explains the nature of Crewe's betrayal: "Most of these boys have nothin', never had anything to start with. But you, you had it all. You could have robbed banks, sold dope or stole your grandma's pension checks and none of us would have minded. But shaving points off of a football game, man, that's un-American!" This theme is also present in *Blue Chips* (1994) and *He Got Game* (1998), which depict cheating—especially illegal recruitment of players—in collegiate basketball, as well as in

The Harder They Fall (1956) and *Raging Bull* (1980), whose plots revolve around corruption in boxing.

For most such characters in sports films, the betrayal of their talents in exchange for a short-term monetary reward is an unpardonable sin, since it disrupts the metaphor of "the game" as realm in which the American Dream is sacrosanct. Breaking the rules of a sport becomes not only a violation of the social contract that temporary elevates athletes to a semidivine status but also a threat to undermine the rhetoric of "fair play" (i.e., equal opportunity) that has helped mitigate the extreme class inequalities within American capitalism since the time of the "robber barons" in the late nineteenth century. Athletic talent in sports films essentially becomes a kind of temporary dispensation from the normal demands of the working class, one that comes with an implicit obligation to be used ethically and unselfishly. This theme echoes such distinctly American philosophies of privilege as Andrew Carnegie's "Gospel of Wealth" and W.E.B. Du Bois's racial notion of *noblesse oblige* among the "Talented Tenth," as well as various religious traditions that acknowledge divine favor through alms-giving (e.g., Christian tithing, Islamic *zakat,* Jewish *tzedakah*). As the title of the third film in Kevin Costner's baseball trilogy suggests, one should play *For Love of the Game* (1999) and the rewards will follow accordingly. In that film Costner plays a pitcher named Billy Chapel who is nearing the end of a distinguished career during which he has presumably made millions of dollars in salary but remains personally unfulfilled. The film chronicles the simultaneous culmination of Chapel's personal life and his career as an athlete: he pitches a perfect game (an exceedingly rare feat that will provide him with baseball immortality) in what turns out to be the last game of his career and he finally discovers the meaning of his love for Jane Aubrey (Kelly Preston), both of which the film suggests are his real compensation for playing the game the "right" way, which (like Velvet and the Pie in *National Velvet*) includes stepping back from the limelight once he has received his reward.

Because the cultural vocabulary of sports is almost entirely symbolic and because the recent explosion of player salaries problematizes the fundamental rhetoric of class solidarity between players and audiences, the actual economics of "the game"—whether it is baseball, boxing, football, and so on—are rarely directly depicted. *Jerry Maguire* (1996) stands as a notable exception in accomplishing the difficult task of asking audiences to sympathize with the plight of a sports agent and a football player mutually seeking a multi-million-dollar contract. It does so largely because it avoids any questioning of the actual economics of a system that deems an $11.2 million contract to play football to be "fair" and focuses rather on redeeming

Maguire (Tom Cruise) and wide receiver Rod Tidwell (Cuba Gooding Jr.) as virtuous figures who have learned to earn their rewards through hard work and honesty, unlike the unproven, entitled hotshot newcomer, Frank Cushman (Jerry O'Connell). As a result, the film's signature line of "Show me the money!" functions not as the crass statement of greed one might expect, but as an unlikely *cri de coeur* of class solidarity within the rhetoric of the meritocratic American Dream in its sporting form. In their pioneering 1949 work *Social Class in America* W. Lloyd Warner, Marchia Meeker, and Kenneth Eells discuss how this kind of seeming cognitive dissonance is resolved within American culture at large:

> Many Americans by their own success have learned that, for them, enough of the Dream is true to make all of it real. The examples from history, from the world around us, and from our own experience provide convincing evidence that, although full equality is absent, opportunity for advancement is present sufficiently to permit the rise of a few from the bottom and a still larger number from the middle to the higher economic and social levels. Although we know the statement that everyone is equal but that some men are higher than others is contradictory, and although some of us smile or become angry when we hear that "all of us are equal but some are more equal than others," we still accept both parts of this proposition either by understressing one part of the proposition or by letting all of it go as a paradox we feel to be true. (4)

American sports films provide such "examples from history" (albeit usually a fictionalized history) and in doing so facilitate the acceptance of the American Dream in the face of the paradoxes and contradictions that would otherwise threaten to undermine it entirely. *Jerry Maguire* reinforces the idea that this idealized system of class advancement can still work as it should, even in the grotesquely skewed economics of professional sports at the turn of the millennium.

Most other American sports films prefer to allude to the economic conditions of their respective "games" in symbolic terms as broad and vague as those of an editorial cartoon. Owners are frequently depicted as stereotypical "fat cats" whose only motive is profit and/or power, without any regard for the loyalty of fans, players, or coaches. These owners have no skill at the actual sports they oversee, a point emphasized by their typical depiction as obese, elderly, and/or female, each of which lies outside the traditional ideal of the American professional athlete. Moreover, their understanding of "the game" is wholly commodified; they lack appreciation for its subtleties and utterly reject its glorification of hard-fought victory and fair play in favor of immediate personal gain. Three baseball films released from 1984 and 1989 illustrate this characterization, which by analogy also serves as a relatively mild critique of class relations during the Reagan-Bush era. In *The Natural* (1984),[5] the Judge (Robert Prosky) is trying to wrest control of the New York Knights from his partner "Pop" Fisher (Wilford Brimley), who also manages the team. If the Knights fail to win the National League, Fisher must sell his share of the team to the Judge, who attempts to sabotage the Knights' efforts by stocking the team with what he believes to be subpar players, such as the film's protagonist Roy Hobbs (Robert Redford). Even though Fisher is also an owner of the team, he is strongly aligned with the players and with working-class values throughout the film. Fisher still wears a player's uniform rather than a suit in his role as manager and he mentions repeatedly that his father wanted him to be a farmer instead of a baseball player. His assistant coach Red Blow (Richard Farnsworth) establishes the salient contrast between the Judge and Fisher when he tells Hobbs that Fisher "gave his heart and soul to the game" and deserves a better fate than what has befallen him.

A similar plot device is used more comically in *Major League* (1989), in which the moribund Cleveland Indians franchise is inherited by a former stripper named Rachel Phelps (Margaret Whitton) who seeks to move the team to the warmth and opulence of Miami. She can only accomplish this goal if the team's attendance drops so low as to trigger an escape clause in the team's stadium lease with the city. She accordingly stocks the team with a collection of players she is assured are neither marketable nor talented and lures a career minor leaguer named Lou Brown (James Gammon) out of retirement to manage the team. The undesirability of the Indians' job is made clear when Brown weighs their job offer against continuing in his position as a tire salesman, saying that he has "got a guy on the other line asking about some white walls." Although the team is predictably bad, they are not initially bad enough to guarantee the success of Phelps's plans, so she removes the creature comforts that are the prime marker of having "made it" (cf. the quote from *Bull Durham* above), taking away the players' chartered airplane and forcing the team to travel to road games in an old bus, something associated strongly with the minor leagues (sometimes called the "bus leagues"). As such, she violates the class taboo regarding performance and reward that underpins the rhetorical logic of American professional sports (at least in film), and when the players become aware of her mercenary motives (and the threat they represent to their own continued employment), they band together and decide to win the league championship to frustrate Phelps's plans. Lou Brown's "old-school" values of discipline and honest effort ultimately win over all his players, including the highly paid but underachieving veteran Roger Dorn (Corbin Bernsen) and ex-convict relief pitcher Rick Vaughn (Charlie Sheen), crafting them into the classic underdog that achieves team glory by playing "the right way" and frustrates Phelps's overly selfish motives.

The motives of the ownership class are further denigrated in *The Natural* through the revelation of the Judge's connections to a shady gambler named Gus Sands (Darren McGavin), who has corrupted the one exceptional player on the Knights' roster prior to Hobbs's arrival. As a result, the power struggle between the Judge and Fisher becomes the moral decision that Hobbs—the titular "natural" (i.e., transcendent) talent—has to face in the film and this conflict is rhetorically couched in visual and verbal metaphors related to class throughout the film. This distinction is exemplified by Hobbs's conflicting attraction to both the saintly, hard-working Iris Gaines (Glenn Close) and the graspingly materialistic Memo Paris (Kim Basinger), who is so associated with money that Hobbs pretends to produce a coin upon their first meeting. Each time Roy succumbs to Memo's wiles, his ability to save the Knights is damaged, and it is only through his simultaneous rejection of Memo, Sands, and the Judge in favor of Iris that the film's over-the-top happy ending is effected.

A similar intertwining of owners and gamblers as class enemies takes place in *Eight Men Out* (1988), though there is no direct connection suggested between tight-fisted Chicago White Sox owner Charles Comiskey (Clifton James) and gambling kingpin Arnold Rothstein (Michael Lerner). However, when Comiskey (ironically nicknamed "Commie") uses a legal technicality to refuse to honor a contractual reward for the brilliant performance of his star pitcher Eddie Cicotte (David Strathairn), Cicotte and several other White Sox players feel justified in taking large sums of money from Rothstein and other underworld figures to "fix" the World Series by playing poorly. From the outset of the film, Comiskey's extreme miserliness—exemplified by giving the team flat champagne upon winning the pennant—is posited as the ultimate source of the corruption that destroys one of the most talented teams in baseball history. When a small-time racketeer named "Sport" Sullivan (Kevin Tighe) expresses his doubt that White Sox player Chick Gandil (Michael Rooker) can "find seven men on the best club that ever took the field willin' to throw the World Series" Gandil wryly responds that Sullivan "never played for Charlie Comiskey." Comiskey's tight-fistedness is so galling to Gandil that he blithely suggests that being "the best" has ceased to be of value, not just for him but for several of his teammates as well. Such a devaluation inverts the fundamental symbolism of the American sports movie and Cicotte drives this point home even as he confesses to his involvement in the scheme: "I always figured it was talent made a man big, you know? If I was the best at something. I mean, we're the guys they come to see. Without us there ain't a ballgame. Yeah, but look at who's holding the money and look at who's facing a jail cell. Talent don't mean nothing. And where's Comiskey and Sullivan, Attell, Rothstein? Out in the back room cutting up profits, that's where. That's the damn conspiracy." Although the film does not exonerate the "Black Sox" as a group, it does suggest that their choices were severely and unfairly limited by economic forces beyond their control.

The film emphasizes the purported innocence of "Buck" Weaver (John Cusack), one of the players implicated in the scheme, and repeatedly places him in solidarity with the working class. Not only does Weaver walk to the ballpark through the working-class Southside Chicago neighborhood in which he also lives, but while doing so he interacts with a host of ragged young boys, who in turn idolize him. Moreover, the film depicts Weaver's own living situation as considerably less luxurious than that of players like Cicotte, who justifies his own corruption through an appeal to financial necessity. Weaver's choice to refuse the gamblers' money thus affirms the integrity of both the game and the working class, making the profligacy of figures like Comiskey and Rothstein seem diabolical in contrast. Even the appointment of Kenesaw Mountain Landis as the first commissioner of baseball, an action undertaken by Comiskey and the other owners to restore confidence in the integrity—and concurrent profitability—of the game, is presented in terms of suppressing the working class (Comiskey cites Landis's fervent prosecution of "Big Bill" Haywood, Victor Berger, and other labor leaders during the late 1910s as his chief ethical qualification). Each of these films exemplifies the manner in which American sports films have come to juxtapose the virtue of honest teamwork against the vice of dishonest individualism as a trope of player/owner class conflict. No matter how wealthy a player becomes, if he "gives [his] heart and soul to the game" he is implicitly still separate from the oligarchy of the owners, since the deciding class distinction—as with the American Dream—is moral, not monetary.

Another set of films foregrounds economic necessities even more explicitly in depicting the ways in which sports relate to the American Dream. The notion that sports can be the "ticket out" of poverty, especially for nonwhites in the United States and Latin America, is central to a number of recent films, including the documentary *Hoop Dreams* (1994) and feature films such as *Hardball* (2001), *Seabiscuit* (2003), *Million Dollar Baby*

(2004), *Cinderella Man* (2005), *Sugar* (2008), *The Blind Side* (2009), and *The Fighter* (2010). Most of these films are fairly conventional in their depiction of baseball (*Hardball*), horse racing (*Seabiscuit*), boxing (*Cinderella, The Fighter*), and football (*The Blind Side*) as vehicles for personal redemption and class mobility consistent with the American Dream ideology. For example, *Hardball* is the melodramatic story of a privileged slacker named Conor O'Neill (Keanu Reeves), whose gambling debts compel him to coach a Little League baseball team from the violent and impoverished Cabrini-Green housing development in Chicago. Following a sports film formula established over the decades by such films as *The Bad News Bears* (1976) and *The Sandlot* (1993), O'Neill not only develops the fractious team into winners but also rediscovers his own virtue in the process. As is the case with *The Bad News Bears* and *The Karate Kid* (1984, remade in 2010), the team's victory in *Hardball* is also defined by class issues in that the team is initially depicted as lacking the physical resources (e.g., proper equipment, uniforms) to compete against its well-heeled rivals. The team's eventual success at baseball thus suggests that the players have learned lessons that can make them economically competitive as adults.

On the other hand, *Hoop Dreams, Million Dollar Baby,* and *Sugar* all critique the conventionally idealistic class rhetoric of professional sports and sport films, emphasizing the oft-elided racial and ethnic inequalities that figure into the equation. *Hoop Dreams* chronicles the attempts of two gifted basketball players, Arthur Agee and William Gates, to follow in the footsteps of fellow Chicago native Isiah Thomas and escape life in the projects by playing in the NBA. The film contrasts the hardships of life in Cabrini-Green with the various opportunities for class mobility that basketball offers. In addition to the ultimate goal of playing professionally, these include access to a better (and safer) high school, the chance for an otherwise unlikely college education, and the various legal and extra-legal lures of the collegiate recruiting scene. Although both Gates and Agee earn college scholarships and ultimately earn degrees, neither comes close to making the NBA and the film implicitly questions whether they will be perceived as having lived up to their "hoop dreams" or not. *Million Dollar Baby* begins with a fairly typical boxing scenario with a working-class boxer named Maggie Fitzgerald (Hillary Swank) enlisting the help of a gruff but noble trainer named Frankie Dunn (Clint Eastwood) to realize her goal of becoming a professional boxer. Dunn hones Fitzgerald's raw skills to the point that she earns a shot at a million-dollar purse in a title fight. At this point, the film departs from convention as Maggie is defeated not through her own moral failings or by superior talent, but rather by a dirty punch from her opponent that leaves her paralyzed and suicidal. The film resists all attempts to romanticize Maggie's injuries as a worthy sacrifice for the money she earned as a boxer and ultimately repudiates the ironclad cultural logic of the American Dream. Finally, *Sugar* follows the career of a pitcher named Miguel "Sugar" Santos (Algenis Perez Soto) and his efforts to rise from the poverty of San Pedro de Macorís in the Dominican Republic by making it to the Major Leagues. Sugar is signed as a teenager by a major-league team but sent to a minor-league team in Iowa to develop his skills. The film focuses not only on Sugar's culture shock in the unfamiliar world of the American Midwest, but also on his dehumanizing status as a relatively inexpensive prospect from the Dominican Republic. His nickname functions both as a marker of the "sweetness" of his athletic talents, but also a reminder of the colonial economics of the sugar plantations on Hispaniola; the metaphor of slavery, though never made explicit, looms in the background of Sugar's experiences in the minors, linking his story with the protests of Ward and Flood. As he loses his confidence, his performance suffers and the club replaces him with another prospect from San Pedro. Sugar leaves the team and moves to New York to live among the Dominican working-class émigré community there, playing baseball simply for fun again rather than as a means of making a living.

In a more middle-class context, *Field of Dreams* (1989) epitomizes the typical class dynamic of American sports films, even alluding to the American Dream ideology in its title. *Field of Dreams* monetizes the notion of baseball's sacredness through the metaphor of a magical baseball diamond that farmer Ray Kinsella (Kevin Costner) builds while faced with the foreclosure of his Iowa farm. When Kinsella responds to a mystical voice telling him "If you build it, he will come" by plowing under a sizable portion of his corn crop, his decision is met with disbelief by his wife and brother-in-law, both of whom are worried about the couple's immediate economic situation. Moreover, Kinsella's fellow farmers, who already view him as something of a romantic dilettante, perceive this act as further evidence that he fails to understand the kind of hard work required of a farmer. When Kinsella begins seeing old-time baseball players emerge from the remaining cornfield, though, he realizes that the baseball diamond represents a mystical, redemptive notion of America that transcends the economic realities of the farm crisis of the late 1980s. Over the course of the film, Kinsella follows the obscure commands of the voice and uses the field to redeem and to rehabilitate a series of characters, including a disillusioned 1960s radical named Terrence Mann (James Earl Jones), a country doctor and former ballplayer named Archibald "Moonlight" Graham (Burt Lancaster), and the disgraced members of the 1919 Chicago White Sox, among others. Like "Pop" Fisher, he gives his "heart and soul" (risking his family's home and financial well-being in the process) to "the game" in order to help others, a sacrifice that is ultimately rewarded not only through a metaphysical reconciliation (symbolized, as at the end of *The Natural,* by a game of catch) with his father but also through a commercialization of American ideals that Mann homiletically suggests will heal the societal ills of the late twentieth century:

> [P]eople will come Ray. They'll come to Iowa for reasons they can't even fathom. They'll turn up your driveway not knowing for sure why they're doing it. They'll arrive at your door as innocent as children, longing for the past. Of course, we won't mind if you look around, you'll say. It's only $20 per person. They'll pass over the money without even thinking about it: for it is money they have and peace they lack. . . . People will come Ray. The one constant through all the years, Ray, has been baseball. America has rolled by like an army of steamrollers. It has been erased like a blackboard, rebuilt and erased again. But baseball has marked the time. This field, this game: it's a part of our past, Ray. It reminds us of all that once was good and it could be again.

The film ends with an aerial shot of the field and a line of headlights extending into the distance, implying that these people are already on the way. The reclamation of a mythic American past representing "all that once was good" becomes inextricably linked with an exchange of money that will allow the struggling middle-class Kinsellas to retain their house and farm, thereby unambiguously reaffirming, as most sports films do, the class dynamics of the American Dream.

With few exceptions, this ethos prevails throughout the history of American sports films. For every moment of mildly revolutionary language—for example, a parody of Marx uttered in *Eight Men Out* by Ring Lardner (John Sayles, also the film's director) as he observes that all the sportswriters busily feeding themselves at Comiskey's buffet have "nothing to lose but [their] bar privileges" by criticizing the existing economic structure of the game— there are dozens of stories that reaffirm the Social Darwinism within the American Dream, suggesting that athletic talent is a God-given privilege that *must* be used properly. As Crash Davis tells young phenom Ebby Calvin "Nuke" LaLoosh (Tim Robbins) in *Bull Durham,* "You got a gift. When you were a baby, the Gods reached down and turned your right arm into a thunderbolt. You got a Hall-of-Fame arm, but you're pissing it away." The ideal cinematic American athlete represents virtue that remains untainted by worldly lures such as the Porsche and "quadraphonic Blau-punkt" that LaLoosh lists as evidence that he has used his "gift" properly. Success in American sports films almost invariably requires the retention and expression of an idealized set of working-class values.

Notes

1. The failure of these attempts was perhaps inevitable in the wake of infamous comments such as those by players Patrick Ewing ("People don't understand. We might make a lot of money, but we also spend a lot of money") and Kenny Anderson ("If this goes on much longer, I might have to sell one of my cars") during the owners' lockout that interrupted the 1998–99 NBA season (qtd. in Banks 153).

2. For sociologist Max Weber, class distinctions were not simply a matter of economic status, but also a matter of common social status, especially in regard to access to ownership and other forms of social and political power. Weber defined a "class situation" as "the typical chance for a supply of goods, external living conditions, and personal life experience, in so far as this chance is determined by the amount and kind of power, or lack of such, to dispose of goods or skills for the sake of income in a given economic order. The term 'class' refers to any group of people that is found in the same class situation" (Weber, "Distribution of Power" 181). Regardless of their individual salaries, all professional athletes are thus in a similar class situation vis-à-vis owners in that they have no means to "dispose of" (i.e., earn money for) their athletic skills other than in the organized leagues and teams. Within the "given economic order" of professional sports, players are excluded from ownership until after their playing careers are ended. For this reason, charges of "collusion" among owners to determine salaries or to otherwise influence the players' labor market are among the most contentious of labor-management issues in North American professional sports. Major League Baseball's ongoing exemption from antitrust laws is, for example, a major source of tension between players and owners.

3. The pursuit of Cliff Lee, a highly desired free-agent pitcher, in the wake of the 2010 baseball season is indicative of the way the mythologizing impulse regarding players' ostensible working-class identity operates within media discourses. Lee's decision to accept a contract with the Philadelphia Phillies for less money ($24 million per year for five years) than he was offered by other teams was described by ESPN's Jerry Crasnick as "[leaving] a huge pile of money on the table by Blue-Collar Joe standards," but is ultimately sensible because "Philadelphia loved him. And he loved Philadelphia back." Moreover, Crasnick echoes nearly every article dealing with Lee's decision in emphasizing that Lee is an "Arkansas country boy" (Crasnick).

4. *Spalding's Official Base Ball Guide* for 1890, a publication produced by the National League's leader, Albert Spalding, repeatedly casts Ward as a self-aggrandizing "master mind of the whole revolutionary scheme . . . to lift them[selves] into the position of professional club magnates" and uses the conventional union-busting

language of the time in branding the Brotherhood's actions as a "system of terrorism" that enslaved the "weaker class" of players who were "seduced by" the Brotherhood's promises (Sullivan 198–201).

5. The film version of *The Natural* is almost diametrically opposed to the novel by Bernard Malamud on which it was based in regard to its protagonist's ethics about taking money from corrupt owner Judge Banner to throw a pivotal game. Whereas the cinematic Roy Hobbs (Robert Redford) refuses the money and hits a dramatic game-winning home run in what is presumably his final at-bat, the Roy Hobbs of the novel strikes out like Casey in Ernest Lawrence Thayer's famous poem and weeps at his disgrace.

Works Cited

Adams, James Truslow. *The Epic of America*. Boston: Little, Brown, 1931.

Banks, Kerry. *The Unofficial Guide to Basketball's Nastiest and Most Unusual Records*. Vancouver: Greystone Books, 2005.

Crasnick, Jerry. "Cliff Lee, Phillies Get Their Wish." http://sports.espn.go.com/mlb/hotstove10/columns/story?columnist=crasnick_jerry&id=5923794 (accessed January 13, 2011).

Morris, Timothy. *Making the Team: The Cultural Work of Baseball Fiction*. Urbana: University of Illinois Press, 1997.

Shields, David. "Is This Heaven? No, It's a Sports Movie." http://espn.go.com/page2/movies/s/shields/020827.html (accessed January 13, 2011).

Sullivan, Dean A., ed. *Early Innings: A Documentary History of Baseball, 1825–1908*. Lincoln: University of Nebraska Press, 1995.

Ward, Geoffrey C., and Ken Burns. *Baseball: An Illustrated History*. New York: Knopf, 1994.

Warner, W. Lloyd, Marchia Meeker, and Kenneth Eells. *Social Class in America: A Manual of Procedure for the Measurement of Social Status*. Chicago: Science Research Associates, 1949.

Weber, Max. "The Distribution of Power within the Political Community: Class, Status, Party." In *From Max Weber: Essays in Sociology*, edited by H. J. Gerth and C. Wright Mills, 180–95. New York: Oxford University Press, 1946.

Weber, Max. *The Protestant Ethic and the Spirit of Capitalism*. Translated by Talcott Parsons. New York: Scribners, 1958.

Chapter 18

Disco, Tattoos, and Tutus: Blue-Collar Performances on Wheels

Rebecca Tolley-Stokes

Evolving from straight endurance races on roller skates that date back to the 1880s, roller derby has a long history in American culture. Roller derby became a contact sport during the Depression years of the 1930s, eventually becoming a spectacle somewhat in the mode of professional wrestling in the 1960s and 1970s. Remaining on the margins of American culture, roller derby failed to gain the widespread following of wrestling, however, and soon began to fade, until it was revived in the early twentieth century as a mostly amateur grassroots sport, dominated by female competitors who made the sport something of an expression of feminine strength and capability, while maintaining many of the earlier entertainment aspects. The fortunes of the sport, meanwhile, have been dramatized in a number of fictional films, indicating the ongoing presence of roller derby in the American consciousness.

Film depictions of roller derby mirror the sport's popularity during the decade represented while also contextualizing class, gender, and racial identities of its athletes and audiences. From 1950 to 2009 four films were devoted to roller derby, including *The Fireball* (1950), *Kansas City Bomber* (1972), *Unholy Roller* (1972), and *Whip It!* (2009). The 1975 science fiction film *Rollerball* was also tangentially related to roller derby, using an ultra-violent futuristic version of the sport as a commentary on the fascination with violence in American culture. The four films based more directly on roller derby, meanwhile, oriented potential roller derby athletes—and appreciative audiences—to the sport's organization, philosophies, strategies, culture, and practices. *The Fireball*, starring Mickey Rooney, inaugurated the genre at the sport's golden era at mid-twentieth century while *Kansas City Bomber* and *Unholy Roller* chronicled the sport's seedier days of decline until the sport's revival in Austin, Texas, in the twenty-first century, which is depicted by *Whip It!*.

Athletes enter arenas for various reasons: Because they can, because they're good, because they're rewarded—either monetarily or with recognition. Many parlay their talents into realization of the American Dream. It is no secret that blue-collar athletes strive toward this dream of middle class comfort, or more. And in fact our films teach this through their examples. Boxing may be the best-known example of this phenomenon, with the protagonist of *Rocky* (1976) and its sequels becoming one of the leading examples of a working-class athlete working to rise in wealth and status. But a variety of films (covering various sports in various modes) have been devoted to blue-collar athletes struggling for success in sports ranging from mainstream sports such as football, as in *Rudy* (1993) or *Invincible* (2006), to more marginal sports, such as bowling, in *Kingpin* (1996), or surfing, as in *Blue Crush* (2002).

Roller derby, of course, is even more marginal, but in many ways it is more suited to blue-collar athletes than any of these. Among other things, it requires relatively little equipment, other than the obvious need for roller skates. On the other hand, the mechanical nature of this equipment also makes roller derby a particularly American sport, linked to development of a specific technology. It is, in fact, worth looking at the history of roller skates as background to the history of roller derby.

Roller skates were originally developed by Belgian inventor Joseph Merlin in the mid-eighteenth century, as an alternative for ice skaters who could not maintain their athletic practice in the warmer months. Roller skating did not, however, gain widespread popularity at that time. It was introduced as an upper-class leisure activity in New York in 1838, and only the "best families" were invited to skate at rinks cropping up across the nation (Herrold 1997, 60). In fact, churches recommended the wholesome pursuit to their parishioners.

James Plimpton's improvement of the roller skate in 1863, which allowed easier turning and leaning on the foot due to the addition of a rubber pad, expanded the activity beyond the upper class, yet the first rink Plimpton opened was open to white men only and required application for membership, including proof of good character. Blue-collar women had few opportunities to skate due to lack of leisure time and money (Herrold 1997, 15). Yet, the wealthy had means to bring the rink to their homes. In 1908 Mrs. Johnston Nicholas Brown of Newport, New Jersey, invited friends to an end-of-season party at a private rink she had had constructed at her summer home ("Newport Roller Skates" 1908). After the addition of ball bearings and toe stops made roller skates more functional, individuals and rink owners readily purchased them.

Meanwhile, whereas prohibitive costs such as clubs, link fees, and country club memberships maintained the upper-crust status of golf and other sports necessitating specialized equipment or locales, roller skating transcended its original identity. By 1916, roller skating appeared as a decidedly demotic activity in *The Rink,* a short film starring Charlie Chaplin. Subsequently, it moved beyond its reputation as a leisure activity for the cultivated classes and became a democratic leisure pursuit. By this time, however, adults had begun to abandon the pursuit and it became associated more and more with children and teenagers. Still, cheap, mass-produced skates and rink tents allowed roller skating to spread across the classes, races, and the United States, though this democratization of the activity caused many to begin to regard it as a "lowbrow" pursuit (Poletti 2009, 43). Still, roller skating became more and more popular, entering a Golden Age that lasted from 1926 to 1954. During the Great Depression roller skating was affordable for everyone, though skating rinks were segregated, with black skaters allowed one evening per week at most establishments.

Leo Seltzer created roller derby in the 1930s. The decade was ripe for fads. Seltzer established the Transcontinental Roller Derby Association in Chicago in 1935. The opening event on August 13, 1935, featured 24 skaters—12 of each gender—who slept at the rink, skated on maple wheels, and skated up to 110 miles each day until someone reached 4,000 miles. Skaters could win prizes ranging from $1,000 to as little as $250 and this money beat what they could earn in their blue-collar jobs as "a butcher, a candy wrapper, a steel mill worker who holds eight roller-skating records, a commercial artist, a tattooed French sailor who had a lady's portrait scraped off his hip in a fall last fortnight, a golf-club maker and a pretty 21-year-old girl who claims to be a cousin of Herbert Hoover" ("Sport: Roller Derby"). By 1938 the marathon evolved into a game and spread to other cities such as Louisville, Kentucky, and Kansas City, Missouri.

Roller derby was popular during World War II, but struggled to maintain audiences after the war. However, noting the enthusiastic audience response to fights breaking out between players, Seltzer moved to make the sport more violent to attract crowds, and violence became linked with roller skating by association. Both roller derby and roller skating began to be increasingly regarded as crude activities, suitable perhaps for the working classes only. As the working-class association with roller skating and the roller skating rink advanced through American popular culture, roller derby became a popular televised sport in the 1950s, partly because it was relatively easy to cover with the large and immobile cameras of the time. ABC aired roller derby bouts three times each week. The banked track was a perfect stationary arena to tape and broadcast the sport to home viewing audiences. In Memphis, Elvis Presley was so enamored by roller derby that he rented the Rainbow Rollerdome for private parties in which he and his friends created their freestyle roller derby games. Presley and his guests copied moves such as whips that they learned by watching athletes on the banked track (Coffey 1997, 218). Much like the fads of the 1930s, promoters hoped to capitalize on skating's popularity by sensationalizing attractions to draw larger crowds to their venues. Oaks Amusement Park in Portland, Oregon, featured a roller-skating elephant in the 1950s.

In the early 1960s, Seltzer's son Jerry Seltzer took over roller derby and based the sport in the San Francisco Bay area. Today's adults in their 40s, 50s, and 60s recall his incarnation of the franchise that they watched on television through 1975 when the last roller derby bout was televised. During this era, roller derby came to be considered a pseudosport in the same vein as professional wrestling because the outcome (including injuries, falls, and fights) was scripted. However, as roller derby waned, the invention of plastic polyurethane wheels in 1976 caused roller skating itself to surge in popularity, and roller skating entered its second prolific era, Roller Disco, from 1977–1983. Empire Rollerdome in Brooklyn, New York, claims to be the "Birthplace of Roller Disco" and was the first rink to hire a DJ to replace organ music ("Places That Matter").

At Venice, California, the 18-mile bicycle path along Ocean Front Walk extending from Torrance to Santa Monica was a perfect spot for skating and vendors rented skates for enthusiasts to experience the revival of roller skating. Roller skating was "the biggest thing to hit Venice and attracted thousands of skaters each weekend" (Lockwood 114). Revenue generated by tourists wanting to skate or watch skaters played a large part in the city's revitalization, affluence, and inflated rents and real estate prices. Further, the influx of tourist dollars provided buskers, panhandlers, and street vendors regular income. Crowds flocked to participate; street performers joined as well, and Venice was dubbed "the roller skating capital of the world." Similarly, on the East Coast, enthusiasts could roller skate through New York's Central Park. Taking roller skating outdoors in the 1970s plus the popularization of inline skates or roller blades in the 1980s led to the decline of the indoor roller skating rink (Poletti 53).

Ironically, today's roller skating rinks are promoted as family-friendly. They offer arcade games, pool tables, and concessions, while serving as a popular birthday party destination for the range of children of various classes: blue collar, white collar, and pink collar. The rinks' continued existence, coupled with residual roller skating childhood nostalgia and skill of Generation X women, helped spread the resurgence of roller derby in the twenty-first century in an all-female flat-track manifestation.

The first true roller derby film, *The Fireball* (1950), was released at a time when the sport wasn't called roller derby and didn't follow the rules we know today. Here, Mickey Rooney, still a major Hollywood star, plays Johnny Casar, an orphan dropped off at St. Luke's Home for Boys. Stymied by his failure to be adopted by a family, his diminutive size, and his lack of natural talent in any area, Johnny copes by tossing books into the incinerator, disemboweling footballs, and ripping apart baseball gloves. He leaves St. Luke's after Father O'Hare asks him to see a counselor. Father O'Hare expects his return that night, but is surprised and delighted when Johnny finds his place in the world instead.

Johnny's identity as a foundling provides him a blue-collar context. Despite the education he received at St. Luke's, his speech is peppered by poor grammar such as repeated use of "ain't." His strategies for coping with homelessness and poverty—breaking into and sleeping inside cars and pawning property that doesn't belong to him—indicate his lack of social status, his borderline class identity, and his lack of social capital.

Casar discovers that he's a quick study at skating and learns about the International Roller Speedway from Mary, his skating instructor, who describes her real career as a speed skater. She travels across the country for eight months at a time as an athlete with the Bears, a team with the International Roller Speedway; he thinks it's no life for a girl. Her salary is $7,000–$8,000 a year winning purses and men like Mack, her teammate, make $10,000–$15,000 a year.

The movie follows Casar's success as an athlete, his entrée to higher society and sophisticated clothing, and a few bumps on the track. *The Fireball* presents roller derby as a vehicle for upward mobility and as a means to realizing the American Dream. Johnny's increasing skill on the banked track parallels his rise in social class and increase in income. While the game exhibits the violence inherent in a full-contact sport, it is represented as a relatively respectable enterprise. The audience is presented as polite and well-dressed, and audience members interact with team members and management on a formal level and observe social boundaries as well as physical boundaries such as the rail dividing them from the athletes.

In 1972, as the sport moved through its less wholesome "pro wrestling" era, two roller derby movies were released: first, *Kansas City Bomber* and then *Unholy Rollers*. The two films share similarities, but are also quite different. *Kansas City Bomber* stars Raquel Welch as K. C. Carr, the sexy star of the Kansas City Bombers, though she is traded to the Portland Loggers. The opening sequence illustrates her athleticism and rapport with the Kansas City crowd. K. C. Carr winks at fans in the audience and they cheer her on.

Police officers dot the audience, which represents an integrated blue-collar crowd. Hippies flash the peace sign. Toothless grandmas cheer and boo. Babies bounce on their mothers' laps and suckle from bottles held in front of them. Each team is co-ed. Women sprint, or jam, in heats against one another until their time runs out and then the men from opposing teams take their place on the banked track. Only jammers wear helmets and the game includes punching, fighting, tripping, and dirty tricks like the clothesline—which is a blow to an opponent's neck with an outstretched arm, or two.

The opportunity to make money and achieve fame encourages K. C.'s pursuit of roller derby. Her two children live with Mrs. Carr, whose identity is not revealed; she could be K. C.'s mother or mother-in-law. K. C. left her job as a secretary when she didn't want to follow through on her boss's sexual advances, even when they included an overture toward marriage. Even though life as a married woman promises some form of middle-class comfort, K. C.'s ambitions for social mobility preclude her from taking the easy way out via marrying up. Skating promises good money for the present, but K. C. gives little thought to the future other than becoming the top player on her team and in the nation; the sport as a means to support her children doesn't seem feasible given her demanding practice and travel schedule. In fact, later in the film after K. C. and her new boss, Henry, the Loggers' manager, become romantically involved, he promises a starring position on a new roller derby team in Chicago and tells her to bring along her children.

The Loggers' audience is not so different from the one attending the Kansas City Bombers' bouts. A woman wearing a cross on a chain around her neck shakes her fist at the banked track and yells, "Hit her!" Another woman in the audience taunts members of the Loggers and Bombers with repeated obscene chin gestures. The Loggers' audience goads skaters by throwing litter onto the banked track. Crushed tin cans, wadded up programs, and foodstuffs fly over the rail onto the players and the track causing injury to players who don't avoid the hazards quickly enough.

The action and plot points position K.C. against the team's current star, Jackie. As K.C.'s popularity soars, Jackie soothes her wounded ego with alcohol. In the concluding scenes, the rivals skate in a grudge match. The winner stays in Portland while the loser accompanies Henry to the new Chicago team. Henry tells K.C. to fix the match so that Jackie wins and stays in Portland. But he also reneges on his promise to bring K.C.'s children to Chicago. And so before the match K.C. tells Jackie they should skate for real to see who the best skater is and forget about fulfilling Henry's preordained outcome. The audience loves the kicking, hair-pulling, girl-on-girl action. In the end, K.C. prevails and crosses the finish line to win the bout and remain in Portland. Her wish to stay close to her children is realized and she extends compassion to Jackie by offering her the opportunity to start over on a new team, regain her star status and her dignity.

From the outset the script and settings of *Kansas City Bomber* inform the movie audience that roller derby is a slapdash venture, thus indicating that the audience doesn't deserve any better. The custodian at the Multnomah County Civic Center mutters about the cheap guy who won't pay for a cloth to cover the announcers' table nor will he pay for an electronic Victrola. Instead the roller derby audience endures a stuttering recording of the national anthem.

Much like *Kansas City Bomber, Unholy Rollers* features an integrated audience depicting cross-sections of American society by including black, white, and Hispanic persons in the audience. They scream "Kill the motherfuckers." The roller derby audience of the 1960s and 1970s, as seen by television audiences, featured "Aqua net hairdos, turquoise eye shadow, plaid sport coats and bushy sideburns," which may be blue-collar markers or merely, in retrospect, a sign of the unfashionable times (Joulwan 2007, 47). Karen Walker, played by Claudia Jennings, attends roller derby as a spectator. When her foreman at the cat food cannery makes another pass at her, she tells him to get his hands off and quits her job on the line.

Like Johnny Casar and K.C. Carr, Karen invests her dreams in roller derby as a means of pulling herself out of her blue-collar circumstances, helping her make money and reach the American Dream, and discovering an activity capitalizing on her natural talents. Interestingly, K.C. and Karen chose roller derby instead of withstanding sexual harassment from male bosses. Roller derby provides them with the agency to physically protect themselves and to lash out in aggression toward others. Roller derby also transports women from their ordinary lives into a setting where they can "try on identities very different from their own" (Douglas 2010, 30). Whereas Johnny and K.C. separate their personal lives from their roller derby personas, that is, the violence they inflict and accept on the banked track isn't evident in their personal lives, Karen is volatile off the banked track and brings this aspect of her personality to roller derby, an arena in which such outbursts are acceptable for women, especially.

As Karen tries out for the Avengers, the local team she watched play in the opening scene, the owner and his son discuss the potential players. One asks the other "Where'd you find them?" He answers: street corners, the unemployment office, parks, and restaurants, suggesting that they may come from society's lower echelons. The owners decide that Karen could be terrific. She and a few guys make the team. The owner says to take the black guy, too, that the Demons, a rival team, will want him. Karen's interest in roller derby lies in the fact that as a professional skater she can make big bucks. She and the other fresh meat are coached to let the audience know they're in pain. They listen to examples of different screams appropriate for particular falls or kicks. The coach indicates prime spots for accident staging so that the audience has the best view of smash-ups.

At her first game Karen is introduced to the audience as being from the "food processing industry." While she warms the bench, the owners talk to one another about people coming from all walks of life to reach for the "shining star of success" that the roller derby offers and privately commend Karen for being spunky on top of her innate sense of showmanship. Karen visits a tattoo artist and has the Avengers' insignia inked onto her forearm. The Avengers' owners admire her gusto and talk about her tattoo really working its magic with the audience at the next bout Karen skates in. Karen brandishes her forearm to the audience after each successful move she makes on the banked track. Soon Karen's life is filled with moving out of her rental housing and buying a home overlooking the interstate. She's moved up, but still can't command California's finer views on her salary. She stars in a local commercial and the money from that, along with her roller derby salary, allows her to purchase a custom hot rod car.

The variations in the movies released in 1972 offer viewers different depictions of roller derby and its performers. While both feature volatile players, women stepping outside of traditional gender norms, enraged audiences, and intrateam rivalries, the lifestyles they portray are distinct. *Kansas City Bomber* is demure in comparison to *Unholy Rollers'* seediness. Although Raquel Welch made *Playboy* magazine's list of sexiest women of the 1970s and graced its cover in 1979, at the time *Kansas City Bomber* was filmed Welch's disgust at nudity in films was clear. Yet, Claudia Jennings, star *of Unholy Rollers,* was *Playboy*'s Playmate of the Month in November 1969 and Playmate of the Year in 1970. Scenes at strip clubs, tattoos parlors, and firing ranges upped the explosive nature of *Unholy Rollers* and likewise its main character, the sociopathic Karen Walker. The spotty cinematography, poor screenwriting, and limited acting skills of the cast mark *Unholy Rollers* as one of many exploitation films made in the 1970s that Jennings starred in. Undoubtedly, its sex, violence, rebellion, and mayhem contributed to negative societal notions of roller derby and its association with blue-collar culture. On the other hand, K. C. Carr spends her downtime at home, dating Henry, or visiting her children.

Another film of the 1970s informs our notions of roller derby and the role of sports as an opiate for the masses: *Rollerball* (1975). Certainly inspired by a blend of roller derby and other sports, rollerball is a death match played by two male-only teams who manipulate motorcycles, steel balls, roller skates, and each other as a means to entertain the masses. James Caan stars as Jonathan E., an athlete sporting blue-collar origins living in a dystopic world in which allegiance is given to totalitarian corporations, attractive women are concubines, the corporate class wears grey suits in the box seats, and the masses crammed in seats closest to the fencing enclosing the arena sometimes die because of their proximity.

Jonathan E. is an invincible athlete and this presents problems for the corporation that sponsors his team, because rollerball was created to demonstrate the futility of individualism. If the rollerball players do not function as a team, they die. The corporation teaches that no player is greater than the game, but Jonathan E.'s survival, popularity, and refusal to retire from the game—which is being forced by the corporation—illustrate the opposite.

Unlike *Kansas City Bomber* and *Unholy Rollers, Rollerball* leaves viewers admiring Jonathan's resistance to the status quo. His overt challenges regarding class identity undermine corporate power and the strictly codified and enforced society that the corporations constructed. And to a greater extent, his rage against the corporate machine affirmed the perspectives of viewers who grew up in the socioeconomic unrest of the 1960s and 1970s. The death and violence of rollerball inform our expectations of bloodlust in roller derby.

In retrospect, *Rollerball* heralded an end to roller derby movies, and essentially to the sport itself, until its recent revival, which was brought to a larger audience in *Whip It!* in 2009. Here, Ellen Page stars as Bliss Cavendar, a disaffected high school student and part-time waitress living outside of Austin—in the hamlet of Bodeen—who finds her life's purpose on the banked track. Bodeen is a small company town whose main industry is the BlueBonnet ice cream factory. Bliss and her friend Pash (Alia Shawkat) yearn to escape their life in this "armpit of a town."

Bliss's mother, a postal carrier, transports Bliss and her younger sister to beauty pageants in the family's worn pickup truck. Mrs. Cavendar believes pageants are the vehicle for turning her daughters into ladies, rocketing their social mobility, and allowing them to socialize with appropriate women who will ensure their future success as Texas women in a relatively traditional, passive mold.

Roller derby, of course, provides a more active alternative. *Whip It!* departs from the roller derby movie formula set up by *The Fireball, Unholy Roller,* and *Kansas City Bomber* in many ways, and eerily models itself after the unspoken anticorporate ideal promoted by *Rollerball.* The league depicted in *Whip It!* mirrors the organizational structure of Women's Flat Track Derby Association (WFTDA) roller derby leagues. These leagues are owned and operated by the players. Though this change in organizational structure is not explicitly conveyed in *Whip It!,* its existence undergirds the film. Each woman is part owner of the league and is responsible for performing, or skating, in bouts, as well as working the back end in the league's organizational structure to coordinate bouts, order merchandise, promote the team, obtain sponsors, and often set up chairs at bouts and clean up the venue afterward.

Organized as nonprofits, contemporary roller derby leagues share their proceeds with local social service organizations like homeless shelters, battered women's shelters, animal shelters, and so on. Earlier roller derby leagues both on film—specifically *Kansas City Bomber* and *Unholy Rollers*—and in reality followed a typical sports franchise ownership model in which players are drafted, traded, and used until they are useless in the owners' eyes. Skaters had little input into the organization's direction or their schedule and were at the mercy of their owner's whims. However, in exchange for the loss of autonomy, derby skaters of the last century earned salaries and made professional careers for themselves in the sport.

In *Whip It!,* roller derby's legitimacy as a sanctioned sport is questioned by characters' remarks and events. Pash asks Bliss if she really thinks that her roller derby career is going anywhere as they make up from an estrangement and misunderstanding. In a subsequent scene Pash tells how she lost her best friend "to a gang of roller skating she-males." Mrs. Cavendar warns Bliss about her teammates: "What do you think the world thinks of those girls with all those tattoos? Do you think they have an easy time finding a job or getting a loan application or going to a decent college or finding a husband?" Mrs. Cavendar displays her wisdom and perspective about adolescence when she tells Bliss that in two or three years "This will be over. This is a moment. You don't understand. You have to support yourself."

Depictions of roller derby skaters inked with tattoos in *Whip It!* reflect the reality of roller derby as it is performed in the twenty-first century. Bliss admires the first roller derby skaters she sees in Austin. They sport visible tattoos on their arms, legs, and chests. In their knee-high socks, short skirts, layered tops, and studded belts, they display unpolished, outrageous, and confrontational attitudes, projecting what is essentially a punk rock sensibility, echoing the blue-collar origins of the punk movement itself. Their multiple piercings—lips, noses, eyebrows—and multicolored dyed hair demonstrate their alternative lifestyles and unconsciously pay homage to Ann Calvello, a tattooed, pierced, and tanned skater known for multicolored hair and her bad-ass athleticism. After all, roller derby skaters exhibit a "general preference for nonstandard body piercing" (Dundas 2010, 195).

While uniforms in *Whip It!* are standardized, they allow a small amount of embellishment per skater. Plus, the skaters' individuality is easily displayed by their choice of stockings or the visibility of their tattoos. In WFTDA league play, standardization of uniforms varies from league to league. For instance, the Texas Roller Girls traveling team's appearance is professional and consistent given their matching skates, uniforms, tights, and plain helmets. Part of the uniformity is due to the team's genealogy and ability to attract sponsors to pay for their uniforms, helmets, pads, and airfare to bouts. When it was established in 2001 the skaters used a "punk rock approach to attaching names to backs of jerseys with safety pins" (Joulwan 2007, 157). In many start-up leagues skaters dress for an audience in fishnet tights, tutus, short plaid skirts, and frilly panties or bloomers emblazoned with messages to the fans. The fire marshal evacuated the warehouse where Texas Roller Derby bouts are held because it was illegally filled past its capacity with spectators. This was never a problem in *Unholy Rollers* or *Kansas City Bombers* when bouts were held at coliseums or civic centers. In *Whip It!*'s predecessors, police officers attended the bouts as audience members. Whether they attended to manage violent outbursts or were merely enjoying the sport as spectators was unclear on film, yet bottles and knifes flew past skaters in the 1970s. "Security guards have also found fans throwing chunks of metal and shooting BB guns at the skaters. In Los Angeles, one fan was arrested for possession of a .22-claiber gun" (Levy 1975, 38).

In the end, *Whip It!* relies upon the predominant theme of roller derby movies—and sports movies in general—for much of its conflict: rivalry. As with *The Fireball, Unholy Rollers,* and *Kansas City Bomber, Whip It!* deposits a new skater in a situation where she strives to prove her worth as an athlete only to encounter rivalry from another teammate. Refreshingly, however, the rivalry between Bliss and her antagonist, Iron Maven (Juliette Lewis), is reconciled at the end of the championship bout. Though Iron Maven's team prevails in the end and wins, Bliss offers to share her knowledge with her nemesis and teach her a few new tricks. Iron Maven promises to take Bliss up on her offer.

Both Iron Maven and Bliss exhibit characteristics associated with blue-color identity. Iron Maven's toughness, heavy make-up, ratty hair, and clothing mark her as a woman with lowbrow taste. Melissa Joulwan characterizes roller derby skaters as the "girls who went to my high school—the girls with feathered hair and parents who worked nights, they smoked at the bus stop, talked during assembly, organized pencil drops in class, and regularly threatened to beat me up in the locker room" (Joulwan 7). In fact, Joulwan, who skated with the original Texas Roller Girls, describes one skater as having the "physique of a day laborer: sinewy, tanned arms and legs, with a slight hint of a beer belly. Her face looked like she's run into the business side of a cast-iron skillet. Everything about her was hard; the equivalent of the hooker no one makes a movie about—the one without the heart of gold" (Joulwan 23).

Bliss's blue-collar identity is less obvious. While her background reveals her class status, her clothing choice—dark colors, tights or leggings with skirts, band T-shirts, and combat boots—taste in music, and sense of irony demonstrate punk rock elements within her identity. Bliss is a certain type of girl, burgeoning with a "resplendent neo-punk aesthetic" that is on a journey to potentially refashion herself (Mabe 2008, 89).

Women's flat track roller derby is by nature a communal effort. Its roots lie in both the punk rock and do-it-yourself philosophies adopted by youth culture. The affluent hire professionals to provide services for them while the nonaffluent do everything themselves (Larson 34). But do-it-yourself philosophy encapsulates more than an economic divide between haves and have-nots. Its "practitioners choose to reinvent tradition as a remix, engaging with it through parody, satire and nostalgic irony, quite in the same way that Sid Vicious mocks and riffs upon high culture in the opening minute of the Sex Pistols' 1977 remake of Paul Anka's 'My Way.' It is important to acknowledge that DIY craft as a movement emerged as part of community activism, with a lineage that can be traced back to the 1980s and the punk movement, 'zine activity and into the early 1990s with the Riot Grrrl movement. In its essence, this new type of craft represents a form of expression that often flies in the face of the 1970s second-wave feminist rejection of creativity in the domestic sphere" (Stevens 2009).

While punk rock's British origins are blue collar, in the United States the movement's numbers stemmed from the disaffected middle class (Traber 38). Middle-class women are supposed to be "diplomatic, conciliatory, and nurturing" (Douglas 2010, 127). Roller derby provides a space in which middle-class women can adopt personas that reflect blue-collar attitude and philosophy. They can express anger, aggression, and the power of their athletic bodies in the contact sport of roller derby. Further, the divide between personal life and one's skating persona allows women to "kick an opponent's ass and not feel guilty about it in the morning" (Joulwan ix).

Whip It! adds layers of complex conflict and emotional sophistication to the roller derby motion picture formula. Its coverage of themes such as the mother-daughter and father-daughter relationships or desire versus duty set it apart from its predecessors. Bliss's father Earl Cavendar (Daniel Stern) is the only man in a family of three women. His next-door neighbor exhibits his masculinity and parental pride by hammering signs advertising his sons' football affiliation and jersey numbers in the yard of their blue-collar neighborhood of homogenous ranch homes. Earl wistfully watches the neighbor pass the football with his son in the front yard.

Earl's ability to express his natural interest in athletics is stymied given his daughters' girly identities. He wants to tag along with Bliss and Pash when they say they are attending a high school football game, but they discourage him from coming since they are actually driving to Austin to watch an exhibition match between the Texas Roller Derby Hurl Scouts and the Holy Rollers. Bliss nearly outs herself when she watches a televised football game with Earl in the back of his work van—he doesn't watch sports at home because he must pick his battles wisely with Mrs. Cavendar—by commenting on how well a block was executed. In one of the concluding scenes of *Whip It!*, Earl hammers a homemade sign into his front yard featuring his daughter's #22, her derby name Babe Ruthless, and TXRD. Her father's public acknowledgment of her athleticism legitimizes the pursuit and her interest in roller derby. It also remasculinizes Earl as he has fulfilled his biological and masculine imperative to spawn athletes. Planting the sign in his yard reconnects him to his masculinity. The stenciled sign references roller derby's do-it-yourself philosophy and situates Texas Roller Derby's status as an upstart sport because the teams haven't advanced to a commercialized stage where their promotional levels mirror that of high school football teams.

The demographics of the fictional Hurl Scouts mimic the reality of women's flat track roller derby; a mixture of hard-bodied athletes and women who lack training and who work in a variety of day jobs. Bliss hasn't skated since she was much younger. Bloody Holly (Zoe Bell) is a former figure skater and the Manson Sisters (Kristen Adolfi and Rachel Piplica) left the women's hockey league in Ottawa to join the league. In *Whip It!* the Texas

Roller Derby's MC announces that the women are just like their audience, waitresses, nurses, and teachers, which indicates a blend of blue-, white-, and pink-collar identities. As the sport grows and local WFTDA leagues appear, the original skaters who were short on athleticism—but demonstrated stylish panache—are being edged out of the sport by women athletes with serious backgrounds in soccer, basketball, running, and other sports.

Another departure from the established roller derby movie formula exists in *Whip It!*. Audiences watching the Texas Roller Derby mirror the demography of Austin, which boasts a bohemian culture welcoming punk rockers, hippies, trendsetters, and just plain folks in their pearl-button front Western shirts and cowboy hats. The audience reflects a diverse crowd, in background, race, and ethnicity. An individual wearing a Davy Crocket–era raccoon-skin hat—worn for its kitsch factor—sits amidst boys sporting dyed fauxhawks, girls with pink dreadlocks, and rock-a-billy/psychobilly couples accoutered in 1950s-era dress. Additionally, audience members wear Rastafarian hats and mesh trucker hats—ironically, of course. Joulwan described the Austin scene as consisting of "boys in punkabilly, Dickies, wife-beaters, tattoos, glistening pomaded hair, girls in fishnets, short tight skirts, capris, red lips, black eyeliner and vintage handbags" (Joulwan 4). Bikers and old-school derby fans flock to bouts. The derby demographic was described as "a crossroads of carnie culture and very low-end sport encompassing a broad section of hipster American, appealing to women in both recognized alterna-cities like Austin and Seattle and more blue-collar places, where perhaps the game's rough-and-tumble nature outweighed camp as an attraction" (Dundas 200).

Eva Destruction (Ari Graynor), the only black skater on the Hurl Scouts (there may be others skating in the league, but Eva is the only black with a speaking part), interacts with the audience by grabbing a can of Pabst Blue Ribbon from one, gulping it down, and spewing it back onto the crowd. The audience loves this. They love and support roller derby. They revere the skaters' athleticism and appreciate the team's performance. This audience, as opposed to the volatile, angered audiences depicted in *Kansas City Bomber* and *Unholy Rollers,* observes the boundary of the rail and provides a wave for Smashley Simpson (Drew Barrymore, who also directed the film)—a check-out girl at Whole Foods by day—when she crowd-surfs after a mishap sends her spinning off the banked track. They don't litter the track with cans, wadded paper, or other detritus because they value the safety of the skaters and understand that the injuries are real.

All roller derby films except *Whip It!* portray the sport at a time when its athletes received pay. When corporations owned teams, players drew salaries and had travel, food, and lodging paid for. While the opportunities for travel that drew women to play roller derby in the 1930s and in subsequent decades exist now, many players must arrange their personal travel and pocket the expense. Mary, the ingénue in *The Fireball* (1950), reported roller derby paid well. Women made $7,000 a year by winning purses. In 1950 that was decent money. Likewise, Karen Walker in *Unholy Rollers* (1972) earned enough money from her Avengers salary and product endorsements to buy and furnish a home and a custom-painted hotrod vehicle. K. C. Carr left her two children with their grandmother because she could not let the opportunity for earning big money playing roller derby pass her by. The discrepancy in pay between male and female skaters first seen in *The Fireball* was substantiated: "Roller derby is very sexist. Weston makes about $50,000 a year. Her male counterpart, Charlie O'Connell, gets about $75,000 for the same work—almost. The men start the game, scoring all the important points, but everyone knows that the women are the stars" (Epstein 21). The cost of playing roller derby in *Whip It!* and in the majority of WFTDA leagues is absorbed by individual players.

The lack of economic reward may seem to limit the promise of present-day roller derby. However, the formation of junior and brat leagues that are affiliated with established women's-only leagues promises something for the future of the sport. Skaters relish signing autographs for their young fans and they are keen on being role models for young girls (Joulwan 209). As these young skaters feed into the leagues play will advance to a higher level and may prevent those less athletic members of the team from playing or trying out.

Until the twenty-first century, roller derby films touted the sport as vehicles allowing skaters to surmount their blue-collar origins and achieve the American Dream. Johnny Casar escaped his orphan origins, discovered his bliss in skating, and attained his dreams of stardom by raking in the dough on the banked track. Roller derby allowed K. C. Carr to assume unfeminine behaviors of athleticism and aggression, discover her athletic talent, find a means to support herself as a single working mother, and shuck off mundane blue-collar clerical work. Once Karen Walker joined the Avengers her life improved in many ways. She left her rental and bought a cottage. She furnished the cottage in a luxurious manner. Karen ordered a custom-painted and stallion-adorned muscle car that provided her with agency and another tool with which to express her rage.

Watching roller derby films or attending bouts provides escape, entertainment, and a sense of community for people of varying income levels, but data reveal that blue-collar fans constitute the majority of fans sitting cheering on skaters. According to a 2010 survey of roller derby fans, skaters, and volunteers/affiliates conducted by the WFTDA, participants' household incomes ranged between $35,000 and $75,000 per year. At least 91 percent have some college education, but the percentages who earned college degrees are 34 percent (fans) and 37 percent (skaters). The data can be interpreted in many ways, but simply said, people with relatively low incomes and little post–high school education constituted the majority of roller derby skaters and roller derby fans.

Within roller derby films, all the athletes parlay their skating skills into the sport as a means to escape predictable, soul-deadening blue-collar jobs—or a life of crime in the case of Johnny Casar—for work that paid well, allowed them to travel, offered regular recognition of their athletic prowess, and presented opportunities for creativity and strategizing lacking in their office and factory jobs. Athletes and audiences alike turn to roller derby as a means to free themselves from the trappings of middle-class constraints. They adapt and adopt blue-collar markers of attire, beverage preferences, and other lifestyle indicators to co-opt middle-class strictures.

Works Cited

Coffey, Frank. *The Complete Idiot's Guide to Elvis.* New York: Alpha Books, 1997.

Douglas, Susan J. *Enlightened Sexism: The Seductive Message That Feminism's Work Is Done.* New York: Times Books, 2010.

Dundas, Zach. *The Renegade Sportsman: Drunken Runners, Bike Polo Superstars, Roller Derby Rebels, Killer Birds, and Other Uncommon Thrills on the Wild Frontiers of Sports.* New York: Riverhead, 2010.

Epstein, Andrew J. "Roller Derby: A Photo Essay." *The Advocate* 188 (1976): 20–21.

The Fireball. Dir. Tay Garnett. Perf. Mickey Rooney and Beverly Tyler. 1950. Fox Films. 1998. Warner Home Video. VHS. Herrold, Susan L. "Roller Skating in the 1870s and 1880s: The Cause, Effect, and Clothing of the New Athletic Women's Sport." MS Thesis, University of Wyoming, 1997.

Joulwan, Melissa. *Rollergirl: Totally True Tales from the Track.* New York: Touchstone, 2007.

Kansas City Bomber. Dir. Jerrold Freeman. Perf. Raquel Welch and Kevin McCarthy. 1972. Metro-Goldwyn-Mayer. 2005. Warner Home Video. DVD.

Larson, Jan. "Getting Professional Help." *American Demographics* 15 (July 1993): 34–38.

Levy, Maura. "Violence Is Golden." *WomenSports* 2 (1975): 36–39, 68.

Lockwood, Charles. "Wheels and Deals Keep California Venice Spinning." *Smithsonian* 10 (March 1980): 112–21.

Mabe, Catherine. *Roller Derby: The History and All-Girl Revival of the Greatest Sport on Wheels.* Golden, CO: Speck Press, 2008.

"Newport Roller Skates." *New York Times* October 25, 1908: 13+.

"Places That Matter: Empire Roller Skating Center." placeMATTERS: A Joint Project of City Lore and the Municipal Art Society. http://www.placematters.net/node/1161 (accessed May 15, 2010).

Poletti, Romy. "Residual Culture of Roller Rinks: Media, the Music and Nostalgia of Roller Skating." MS Thesis, McGill University, Montreal, 2009.

"Sport: Roller Derby." *Time* 27, no. 5 (February 3, 1936): 24.

Stevens, Dennis. "DIY: Revolution 3.0 Beta." American Craft (October/November 2009). http://www.americancraftmag.org/article.php?id=8837 (accessed May 10, 2010).

Traber, Daniel S. "L.A.'s 'White Minority': Punk and the Contradictions of Self-Marginalization." *Cultural Critique* 38 (Spring 2001): 30–64.

The Unholy Rollers. Dir. Vernon Zimmerman. Perf. Claudia Jennings and Louis Quinn. 1972. American International Pictures. (n.d.) VHS. *Whip It!* Dir. Drew Barrymore. Perf. Ellen Page and Drew Barrymore. 2009. Fox Searchlight Pictures. 2010. 20th Century Fox Home Entertainment. DVD.

Women's Flat Track Derby Association. "Roller Derby Demographics: Results from the First-Ever Comprehensive Data Collection on Skaters and Fans." http://wftda.com/files/WFTDA-Roller-Derby-Demographics-March-2010.pdf (accessed May 13, 2010).

Chapter 19

Driving to Victory: NASCAR in American Culture

Bob Batchelor

There are few certainties in the world, but one exists in NASCAR: fans universally hold an undying—almost cultlike—love and respect for Dale Earnhardt Sr., the iconic stock car driver who died after crashing on the final lap of the 2001 Daytona 500. In the days and weeks immediately after his death, commentators compared the loss to what the nation felt when Elvis Presley passed away. At the time of his death, Earnhardt's iconic stature led many fans and observers to argue that Earnhardt was not merely another racecar driver; he *was* NASCAR. The immediate question centered on whether or not the stock car association could ever overcome the loss. The season would continue, but how would the fans react to their hero's passing?

In tribute, spectators raised three fingers in the air on the third lap of every race for the remaining 2001 season. Many vehicles soon displayed a "3" decal with the words "We'll never forget," "The Legend Lives On," or "In Memory Of" in salute to Earnhardt's legacy. Although the death of "The Intimidator" shocked race fans, it became apparent that the sport would continue on, although without its favorite son. Inevitably, another question emerged as fans began processing their emotions and ties to Earnhardt: who would replace him in fans' hearts?

Perhaps not surprisingly, the new favorite son was Earnhardt's boy Dale Jr., at that time a promising young driver who manned the blazing red, number 8 Budweiser car. Although in only his second season in NASCAR, the younger driver had already won two championships in the Busch Series (stock car racing's top minor league competition) and two races in his rookie year on the senior "Winston Cup" (now "Sprint Cup") circuit, finishing second in the Rookie of the Year contest. Journalist Jeff Bartlett explains, "The loss of Dale Sr. could have a hugely negative impact on Winston Cup unless someone rises up to the mantle. It's a weighty burden, but Little E seems to be maturing to the task" (27). In the years since, however, the obligation of replacing NASCAR's king have weighed on the heir apparent, who is hugely popular, but has been unable to replicate his father's winning on the racetrack.

This chapter focuses on NASCAR's role in contemporary blue-collar culture by grappling with the significance of the Earnhardts, particularly as standard bearers for "classic" and "corporate" stock car racing. Looking back, now more than 10 years after Dale Sr.'s death, it seems inevitable that "Junior" would take his father's place as the soul of NASCAR. In that decade span, the younger Earnhardt developed not only into the sport's most popular driver, but also one of the most influential and recognizable faces across sports marketing. Just like his father, Dale Jr. has grown bigger than auto racing, becoming an iconic figure in his own right.

The death of Dale Sr. and the rise of Dale Jr., however, marks a critical turning point in NASCAR history. As a result, the Earnhardts serve as a kind of lightning rod for NASCAR fans and media. In its most basic form, one could view this as pitting "old" and "new" NASCAR against one another, the former epitomized by the career, legend, and popularity of Dale Earnhardt Sr. versus that of his son, Dale Jr., the manifestation of contemporary NASCAR. At its heart, the comparison comes to a head at the way Earnhardt Sr. rose to the top of the sport through winning, while Earnhardt Jr.'s critics charge that he received (and continues to receive) preferential treatment because of his name, not his skill as a driver. Viewed as racers, the distinction between father and son is fairly clear, but as businessmen they are more alike than fans might understand.

From a business perspective, any schism between the two men is blurry. The Earnhardt family symbolizes both the traditional, blue-collar roots of early NASCAR and today's big business appeal. Interestingly, the sport's fan base has changed simultaneously as the definition of "blue-collar" has transformed as well. For example, in the 2008 presidential election, "NASCAR dads" were considered an important voting block, lumped together based on traditional family values and a sense of striving blue-collar socioeconomic status—the kind of men who drive SUVs, shop at Home Depot and Lowe's, but yet make lots of time for their families and children.

This brand of consumerism is essentially at the heart of "corporate" NASCAR and the way the sport as a product is marketed today. And, while

Dale Jr. symbolizes the way the sport is sold on the contemporary corporate stage, Dale Sr. actually began this move by growing in stature beyond the sport itself, becoming universally iconic, rather than just a star within the parameters of his individual sport. It is as if Dale Earnhardt Sr. and NASCAR rocketed in popularity and importance concurrently, riding the wave of increasing popularity through televised races and multichannel marketing opportunities that gave them both virtually unlimited platforms.

NASCAR's obsession with marketing and advertising, however, has always been closely entwined with what happens on the track. Unlike other major sports, for example, drivers wear fire suits plastered with corporate logos. Also, the season-long championship is sponsored by a corporation—traditionally the "Winston Cup" though now replaced by the "Sprint Cup." This aspect of NASCAR is a large part of its heritage and culture, just as it is among blue-collar Americans. Perhaps that is why many corporations pay such close attention to stock car racing and pour millions of dollars into sponsorships—NASCAR fans are loyal customers. It is as if racing fans delight in not only rooting for their favorite drivers, but also for their treasured brands. Brand strategist Marty Neumeier examines why consumers commit to brands, explaining, "People base their buying decisions more on symbolic cues than features, benefits, and price. Make sure [the] symbols are compelling" (150). The tight link between NASCAR and its sponsors' logos—even the way drivers talk about one another based on car numbers or sponsor, rather than driver name—gives fans multiple ways into the sport's culture that is in large part based on consumerism, rather than team or athlete dedication like in other sports.

Dale Earnhardt and Classic NASCAR

For hardcore NASCAR fans, Dale Earnhardt Sr.'s authenticity began and ended on the racetrack. He personified winning, often dominating the opposition through sheer will to win or in the bump-and-run style that earned him the nickname "The Intimidator." For fellow competitors, seeing the Goodwrench Number 3 in the rearview mirror meant that things were about to get interesting. While other drivers would carefully work the car ahead of them to cautiously pass on the high or low side, Earnhardt would often put the nose of his car on the back bumper of the one in front and nudge it out of the way, taking off as the vehicle got loose as a result.

Earnhardt represented two traits that fans loved: first, the ability to drive through, around, or over the competition to win; and second, that one could achieve great heights while still being "normal," which meant embodying homespun traits, such as being a straight-talker and enjoying traditional blue-collar, southern hobbies, like hunting, fishing, and drinking beer. The scowl that his competitors viewed on the racetrack was quickly replaced by the broad smile fans saw off the track. His success and grit combined to make him NASCAR's star of stars. Leigh Montville explains, "He was a constant Clint Eastwood, taking care of the bad guys and picking up that fistful of dollars at the end. He was old and still good and still hip, a phenomenon right there in American culture" (8).

In many respects, Earnhardt was the prototype American success story, steeped in hard work, being raised by good country folks, and tied to the nation's agrarian past. In addition to this apple pie version of Earnhardt's journey to the top of his sport was his famed tough-guy persona and willingness to push (some would say break) the rules to win. These elements came together to create in Earnhardt a kind of modern-day John Wayne. Like the film star and icon, the racecar driver could seem gigantic, doing things in a car going 190 miles per hour that no one had ever seen before, while at the same time retaining a humility and tie to traditional values that made him "one of us" in the fans' eyes. Few modern athletes have managed this dual role well, but in Earnhardt's case, it seems as if he wrote the book.

Although today's fans look back on Earnhardt's career with love and deep nostalgia, he can also be viewed as the real bridge between old and new NASCAR from a business perspective. As Dale's legend and fame grew, his role in maintaining and marketing his personal image also became more important, though most fans certainly did not dwell on his expanding role as a celebrity or spokesperson.

Unlike most modern celebrity athletes, Earnhardt did not face complaints regarding him "selling out" or fan backlash as he became a millionaire many times over. In this regard, he joined a select group of iconic athletes and entertainers who maintained their popularity almost in spite of their success, the small group possibly including Bruce Springsteen, Michael Jordan, and Robert DeNiro. Perhaps if Earnhardt had lived longer, some fans would have inevitably turned on him—even the stars mentioned above faced some criticism as their careers wore on and age made them seem more fallible—but it is a scenario difficult to imagine.

In addition to the creation and maintenance of his legend, Earnhardt actively worked with racing officials to build the sport as a whole. The behind-the-scenes moves Earnhardt made to build the NASCAR brand included strategy sessions with former president Bill France Jr., which fans would have never conceived from his persona. NASCAR chairman and chief executive Brian France said, "Dale had an innovative business mind that changed NASCAR nearly as much as his right foot did" (30). One estimate, for example, reveals that Earnhardt accounted for as much as 40 to 50 percent of all the memorabilia sold at races prior to his death (Wilde 34).

According to Leigh Montville the Earnhardt legend was set to grow. NASCAR and Fox had big plans for showcasing Dale Sr. to the world after paying $1.6 billion to televise half the season, including the Daytona 500— NASCAR's Super Bowl and first race of the season. The television network introduced many production innovations so that fans could see and feel the excitement on the track, which had befuddled racing coverage for decades. But, they also needed a star to showcase and build the narrative around. Fox executives and broadcasters saw the senior Earnhardt as the ticket to viewer loyalty and the revenues fans would generate. "The idea," Montville says, "lying underneath all the technological bells and whistles, was to show how great these people really were. And the greatest of them all was Dale Earnhardt" (7).

Pushing through the fog of nostalgia surrounding Earnhardt and assessing his career in light of where NASCAR had been and was going at the time of his death, one sees that he really set the stage for the future. Steve Handschuh, former president of NAPA, says, "His influence was phenomenal. Dale Earnhardt did more to fuel the explosive growth of NASCAR than any other driver" (qtd. in Wilde 35). Given Dale Sr.'s fan support and the additional marketing push by Fox via its television deal, it seems inevitable that NASCAR would have fared much better had its main star lived.

Dale Junior and Corporate NASCAR

Dale Jr., despite a career that lacks the dominance of his father, is the current face of NASCAR for both serious fans and those who are casual observers. For the former, he is the personification of the Earnhardt racing clan and the embodiment of his father, the sport's most iconic figure. For the casual spectator, Junior is a familiar name and face, linked to a broad array of brands and advertising campaigns that make him a celebrity in and out of auto racing. It is in these clashing views of Junior that one finds the challenges many long-time fans have with current stock car racing. To put it bluntly: today's NASCAR is "corporate."

Here's the way this scenario breaks down: in contrast to "classic" NASCAR, the contemporary version is overly concerned with brand sponsorship at the expense of the actual racing taking place on the track. The focus on the business end of NASCAR has brought vast sums of new money into the sport, which enables drivers and teams to become well off without having to win races. The control over the sport, in many ways, tightened at the top, giving more power to NASCAR as a regulatory body and to the sponsors who fill its coffers.

As a result, sponsors exert an inordinate amount of control over drivers, essentially turning them into robotic, walking billboards. The media training and seemingly rote memorization of talking points, for example, are in stark contrast to the way drivers used to express themselves and lends to the idea that today's racers are inauthentic. Five-time NASCAR champion Jimmie Johnson, for example, gets a great deal of criticism for having a vanilla personality, even though he leads a great team and wins consistently in clutch races and has won an unprecedented five straight Sprint Cup titles.

Wearing the Earnhardt mantle places Dale Jr. in an odd position. Fellow driver and Hendrick Motorsports teammate Mark Martin pinpoints Junior's challenge, explaining that he "has the weight of [the] Nascar world on his shoulders" (qtd. in Jordan). Until he wins consistently and becomes a champion like his father, his detractors will question why he is the anointed one. However, based on his name and personality traits, he is undeniably NASCAR's most popular driver—and not by a slim margin, either.

Despite the famous name, Junior has the "like the guy next door" public persona that fans adore. He seems "normal" in a different way than his father, more like the guy one would have a beer with at a backyard barbeque than Dale Sr. who was into macho outlets, such as speedboat racing and hunting.

Dale Jr. is polarizing as well because it seems as if NASCAR is rooting for him to win as vociferously as fans. Journalist Larry Woody compares Junior to golf's Tiger Woods in that PGA Tour and television executives want to see him in contention because ratings soar (even after all of Woods's off-course shenanigans that became tabloid fodder). Woody says:

> It doesn't require a Nielson survey or a marketing study to gauge Junior's impact on the sport—just look at the grandstands at any track when he's challenging for the lead. The fans go nuts. And despite his past slump, Earnhardt continues to out-sell every other driver in Official NASCAR Merchandise. ("NASCAR")

For NASCAR, Dale Jr. might as well be a walking ATM. Fans flock to purchase a seemingly unending supply of Junior merchandise. Another journalist called him the sport's "clown prince because Nascar has a huge vested interest in Earnhardt, perhaps its greatest money-producing driver" (Jordan).

As the seasons go by without a win and Earnhardt never seems a real threat to win the Sprint Cup, commentators are wondering what's up with the driver, which opens him to additional criticism. George Diaz of the *Orlando Sentinel*, for example, called Junior "NASCAR's biggest enigma" and questioned his commitment to the sport, saying, "His father is a NASCAR icon. And depending on who you talk to, Earnhardt Jr. is either poised to make a run at relevancy soon, or is an over-hyped driver who would be working at an AutoZone store if it wasn't for his last name" ("Dale Earnhardt Jr.").

Generations Collide on and off Track

Today's NASCAR centers on two often-conflicting issues: racing and business. On one hand, drivers often talk about taking care of business on the track, in other words, going out and doing the things necessary to win. In terms of business, though, the race is only a part of the driver's world. Increasingly, as the sport has grown more corporate, sponsor obligations take up more time that in essence detracts from the preparation for racing.

The notion that racecar drivers are robotic in interviews and media opportunities has wider implications on the track too. A common criticism is that they are willing to simply ride around and pick up the big, corporate money–infused paycheck at the end of the race, rather than fight it out for victory. Junior might be the epitome of this idea, given his prolonged slump, going winless over multiple seasons, despite joining the powerhouse Hendrick Motorsports team that includes Johnson, four-time champion Jeff Gordon, and wily veteran Mark Martin. He fails to win, yet still remains the overwhelming fan favorite and grows increasingly rich through celebrity endorsements.

While the generational collide has consequences on competition, there is another challenge that the sluggish economy exposed that might have more important repercussions for NASCAR's future: if a sport's fan base is drawn primarily from the working class, then during difficult economic times, they will have to make difficult decisions about spending their money as consumers.

The recession that rocked the American economy in the late 2000s and early 2010s left few industries untouched. Even NASCAR, which seemed to have broadened its fan base dramatically in the 10 years leading up to the economic panic, could not withstand the one-two punch of high unemployment and all-encompassing belt-tightening taking place in American homes and businesses.

As a result, for the first time in recent memory, NASCAR now does not sell out mega-stadiums at many of its races. Ironically, while the technology has improved tremendously over the years, making races more enjoyable to watch on television, the increased cameras also reveal row after row of empty seats. On closer inspection, viewers also noticed that many cars in the field, particularly those from the smaller teams, held fewer sponsor decals, one of the most unique aspects of NASCAR vehicles.

When races fail to sell out, it not only hurts the sport, but local communities also suffer. For example, at the "Monster Mile" in Dover, Delaware, attendance at the twice-a-year Sprint Cup races has dropped for three straight years, from 145,000 in 2006 to 82,000 five years later. While the latter number may seem large in comparison to the kinds of crowds that show up for baseball, basketball, or hockey, NASCAR needs to continue growing to justify the large TV contracts and ad dollars it commands. Delaware officials estimated that the two race weekends drew about $94 million into the local economy, according to an economic impact study commissioned in 2001. Ten years later, the region will feel fortunate to draw half that amount, says Denis McGlynn, chief executive of Dover Motorsports, owner of the Dover International Speedway (Frank).

From the fan's perspective, there simply isn't enough money to justify the expensive tickets and concession prices dictated by NASCAR at the height of its popularity prior to the recession. Realizing that economic times have changed dramatically, executives at some tracks that no longer fill up are attempting to find ways to bring fans back to the stands.

New Jersey fan Joe Neyra, who ventures to Delaware for the race each year, brought his seven-year-old son because of reduced ticket prices. "I think it's great that tracks are coming out with affordable ticket packages," he told a local newspaper. "Many of the people who are here are living paycheck by paycheck. This is more of a blue-collar sport, so [the tracks] have to find ways to make it affordable for the average fan" (qtd. in Frank).

According to McGlynn, there are generational challenges at play as well. First, he explains, fans of Dale Earnhardt Sr. and classic NASCAR are less interested in the sport today based on their favorite drivers retiring and a series of rules changes that some fans do not like, most noticeably the way the season champion is decided by the new "Race for the Chase" system. NASCAR expects some older fans to leave, but the challenge is that young fans are not taking their places. Not only are younger fans spoiled by the ability to watch races at home on high-definition, big-screen televisions, but they are less likely to own RV campers (a racing tradition) or be willing to shell out for the huge gas bills necessary to get to races (Frank).

Corporate NASCAR and American Culture

The long-term challenge for NASCAR is directly related to its role in defining its own ethos and role within American culture, which can be characterized as stock car racing's transition from its moonshine-running outlaw past to its present and future as a sanctioned, rule-abiding sport. Pat Jordan pinpoints the change as the sport moves away from its southern roots, saying, "Today many of the best Nascar drivers, like Jimmie Johnson and Jeff Gordon, are not southerners at all (both are from California) and are clean-shaven, well-spoken men who never banged around dilapidated race cars on red clay tracks" ("In the Name"). This transformation is epitomized by the careers of the Earnhardts: the father, a ninth-grade dropout who fought his way into the sport's elite, and the son, though southern, handed his opportunity based on his name and potential star power.

Without a tinge of irony, Rick Hendrick, Earnhardt Jr.'s boss and owner of Hendrick Motorsports, says that Dale Jr. is his own man now and out from under his dad's shadow: "He has his own fans, people who love him 'cause he's blue collar" (qtd. in Jordan). The brashness of labeling someone like Dale Earnhardt Jr. "blue collar" is one of the most confounding aspects of being a NASCAR fan and reveals the depths the sports' southern culture is ingrained in its constitution, even as it undergoes this post–Dale Sr. transformation.

While NASCAR grapples with its changing culture, its fans face a different reality. The recession, powered by widespread unemployment (particularly among blue-collar workers), multiple-front wars in the Middle East, and real estate woes that more or less depleted most people's net worth, caught NASCAR off-guard and exposed the organization's weaknesses. While some observers believed the fallout provided an opportunity for auto racing to reassess its standing with both hardcore and casual fans, most people seemed willing to just weather the challenges. Track executive McGlynn explains, "It was a perfect storm of bad things that could have happened. The good news is we're still here. Are we as robust as we were 10 years ago? No. But we're not going away" (qtd. in Frank).

It seems that the problem with the hunkering-down mentality is that NASCAR may slip in relevancy, just after it was poised to enter the "big four" sports of football, baseball, hockey, and basketball in the American mindset. Several years ago, it seemed NASCAR might overtake all of them, except football, but there is a hint now that, like major league baseball, still drawing fans to the ballpark but only at the center of the American popular consciousness during the World Series and perhaps the All-Star Game, the sport might dominate the national zeitgeist only a couple of times a year, like when it runs the Daytona 500 and when its Sprint Cup champion is crowned. The global economic crisis acted like a giant wet blanket thrown on top of NASCAR's phenomenal explosion in popularity and sponsorship money. Without Dale Sr. or some other star emerging to really fill his shoes on and off the track, the sport as a whole stumbled.

NASCAR also faces a tremendous generational challenge. Historically, rabid fans went in groups via RVs or campers to weekend races far away from home. The camping tradition necessitated that they bring everything from home or buy supplies at the track or campground, thus getting money into local economies. Races also provided the opportunity for fans to meet and maintain face-to-face relationships, even if only that one weekend per year.

The jury is still out on whether or not Generation X and Millennial blue-collar fans will mirror their predecessors. In an unofficial "State of NASCAR" speech 11 races into the 2011 season, chairman and chief executive France discussed the association's goal to "satisfy the core fan in every way we possibly can," but also "be appealing . . . to new fans." Explaining the differences between past fans and new ones, France concludes, "We're reacting to how young people in particular are taking in with their favorite sports or learning about their favorite sports. It's very different than it was say 10 years ago, say five years ago. You just can't have your head down when all those things are going on while you are trying to grow your fan base" (Pennell "NASCAR CEO").

Dale Jr. is central in building the next generation of fans, beyond those who currently follow him or NASCAR because of his father's legacy. The challenge, though, is that this push cannot be forced or seem too contrived. NASCAR and Junior's sponsors can continue to throw him up as the face of the sport, but there will need to be results on the track that justify the endorsement. Sometimes, ironically, it seems as if the younger Earnhardt himself is caught in this notion. He admitted in 2010 to the *New York Times Magazine*: "People think I'm always pickin' my next move. Hell, I have no marketing savvy. I just do what I'm told. It's frustrating to hear I should decide whether I want to be a race-car driver or a marketing tool. In Nascar I have to be both" (qtd. in Jordan).

Whether it is fair or not, Dale Earnhardt Jr. must continue to wear the mantle for his father's fans, grow his own base, and find a way to deliver wins on the track. He is NASCAR's golden (yet, seemingly conflicted) boy and his success will determine how the sport itself transitions through its current challenges. Undoubtedly, he understands the challenges. In a 2008 interview, he both acknowledged his father's fans, while humbly placing himself within the larger picture, saying:

> My daddy made a name for our family, and he created a mentality. He created a perception that we were very strong and very tough and dedicated people. The large majority of the American public is blue-collar and really relates to that type of mentality. . . . I got very lucky to get a bunch of his fans, and a bunch of his fans want to see me keep the name out there and keep winning races and keep doing well. ("Q&A" 62)

Yet the distance from himself to his father is evident in the statement, particularly when he refers to him as "my daddy," rather than simply "daddy." Furthermore, the reader senses the gap between reality and the public persona when Junior explains that his father "created a perception" purposely to engage with the blue-collar "type of mentality."

Many competing interests have a stake in Dale Jr.'s success, but it seems that many of them are merely held together by the sheer determination of his fans to stick by him through thick and (mostly year after year of) thin. One estimate has him accounting for about 25 percent of revenue NASCAR generates from licensed products. Race fan Tommy Blalock from Cumming, Georgia, sums up the determination of "Junior Nation" saying, "It gets annoying the lack of wins. But we still love him. If he never wins again, we would still love him." Dale Jr. himself takes a more existential position about his lack of victories, explaining, "We've struggled the last couple of years trying to do what we did the first several years. I don't get as bent out of shape as everybody else because that's life and there is no use griping about it; it doesn't move you forward" (qtd. in Glier).

As racing fans' numbers dwindle overall, NASCAR officials must lie awake at night worrying that Junior is one scandal away from sending the sport into an utter tailspin. For an example, they need to look over to how Tiger Woods's series of crises sent the golf world spiraling. PGA Tour officials and players can talk about the health of the game with or without Tiger, but the simple fact is that when he's in contention, ratings soar. If he's not playing, generally, people are not watching.

It may be difficult for fans to imagine, but NASCAR, despite being labeled in a 2005 cover story in *Fortune* magazine as the "fastest-growing, best-run sports business in America," is experiencing significant growing pains as it tries on being essentially a $2 billion corporation. There are countless moving parts and unknown challenges ahead to build on its first 60 years in existence (O'Keefe and Schlosser 51).

For more than 30 of those years, there has been an Earnhardt in racing. The family dominates the sport, even though Richard Petty, the patriarch of the other elite family, is known as "The King." Dale Jr.'s role is critical in whether or not NASCAR gets back on the fast track or simply maintains the status quo until its next Dale Sr. emerges from the pack.

Works Cited

Bartlett, Jeff. "Picking Up the Pieces." *Dale Earnhardt Memorial: Gold Collector's Series* April 2001: 22–29.

Diaz, George. "Dale Earnhardt Jr. Continues to Be NASCAR's Biggest Enigma." *Orlando Sentinel* 18 May 2011. http://articles.orlandosentinel.com/2011–05–18/sports/os-auto-racing-insider-0518–20110518_1_nascar-debut-steve-letarte-dale-earnhardt (accessed 18 May 2011).

France, Brian, and Marty Smith. "'The Whole Package.'" *ESPN: The Magazine.* Dale Earnhardt, The Legend Lives. Hall of Fame Collector's Issue (June 2010): 30–31.

Frank, Martin. "Slow Times for Dover International Speedway." *The News Journal* 15 May 2011. http://www.delawareonline.com/article/20110515/SPORTS06/105150378/Slow-times-speedway?odyssey=nav|head (accessed 15 May 2011).

Glier, Ray. "Lacking Victories, Earnhardt Maintains a Devoted Following." *New York Times* 27 April 2009. http://www.nytimes.com/2009/04/27/sports/auto racing/27nascar.html (accessed 1 December 2010).

Jordan, Pat. "In the Name of the Father." *New York Times Magazine* 5 August 2010. http://www.nytimes.com/2010/08/08/magazine/08Earnhardt-t.html (accessed 15 November 2010).

Montville, Leigh. *At the Altar of Speed: The Fast Life and Tragic Death of Dale Earnhardt.* New York: Doubleday, 2001.

Neumeier, Marty. *The Brand Gap: How to Bridge the Distance between Business Strategy and Design.* Berkeley, CA: New Riders, 2006.

O'Keefe, Brian, and Julie Schlosser. "America's Fastest Growing Sport." *Fortune* (September 2005): 48–64.

Pennell, Jay W. "NASCAR CEO Brian France Addresses State of the Sport Prior to All-Star Qualifying." *SBNation.com* 20 May 2011. http://www.sbnation.

com/nascar/2011/5/20/2181762/nascar-brian-france-state-of-sport-2011 (accessed 20 May 2011).

"Q&A with Dale Earnhardt Jr." *Sporting News* 232.45 (2008): 62. *Academic Search Complete.* EBSCO (accessed 29 August 2010).

Wilde, Jason. "A Modern Day Hero." *Dale Earnhardt Memorial: Gold Collector's Series* April 2001: 31–35.

Woody, Larry. "NASCAR Is Rooting for Junior." *RacinToday.com* 7 May 2011. http://www.racintoday.com/archives/26734 (accessed 7 May 2011).

Chapter 20

Natural Bad Boys: The Rise of Mixed Martial Arts and the New Class of Combat Sport

Eoin F. Cannon

Mixed martial arts (MMA) is supplanting boxing as the definitive combat sport in America and the world. After just 10 years of legal legitimacy in the United States, its arena and television revenues have come to rival boxing's.[1] More important, MMA has become the cultural form through which a rising generation understands and imagines fighting. MMA promoters seized this role in the first decade of the twenty-first century by standardizing its rules sufficiently to earn legal sanction and commercial viability, while aggressively advancing its claim to be the truest arbiter of individual physical dominance in its approximation of "real" or unstructured fighting. This is a significant moment in the cultural history of hand-to-hand combat, a pronounced shift in the creation of meaning through socially acceptable, commercially consumable violence. Boxing supplied influential tropes of race, ethnicity, gender, and class in popular culture in the twentieth century. It was a product of the industrial-age social order, and it projected, across all these other identity categories, working-class experience and values. In the careers of fighters and in fictional representations, more important than pure individual dominance were the ways boxers enacted both the exploitation and the resilience of the workingman and his familial networks.[2] Boxing's decline has coincided with the fragmentation of its stable social base in working-class neighborhoods. MMA's rise presents a new and harder-to-cipher class dynamic in the culture of fighting.

MMA, as both practice and product, is dispersed across the global, postindustrial social order. The serious training that produces its most popular fighters takes place everywhere from Rust Belt warehouses, to beach resort fitness clubs, to college town martial arts dojos. Many of its most successful participants have college degrees, but many also come from broken homes and poverty. If it has a social center of gravity, it is in an emerging zone where the working and middle classes are hard to distinguish, both culturally and economically. This social landscape has become more visible in America since the beginning of the 2008 recession, driven by the spread of disorienting uncertainty throughout the middle classes. The ideals of a stable job base and avenues of mobility for the working class remain unfulfilled, while the fragmentation and sheer unreliability of educational pathways and white-collar labor markets have taken the reality and the idea of security out of middle-class identity.[3] The economic structure of MMA is part of this new labor terrain, where the vast majority of professional fighters work outside stable institutions, for very low pay and with very little control over the terms of their employment. Not surprisingly, the messaging and imagery of commercial MMA appears sharply reactionary. It emphasizes pure individualism and aggressive dominance, reveling in the language of social Darwinism rather than craft tradition or community of practice. These traditions and communities exist, but they have not been made visible in the popular imagery of the sport. Looking within them, one finds the skills and values required to survive and thrive in MMA are more complex than its promotional narratives suggest. In the lives of fighters, and indeed in the formal techniques of the fighting itself, MMA conveys the brutal insecurity of the new economic order for most workers. But its practitioners also exemplify the new and paradoxical combinations of submission and independence, resilience and flexibility, and creativity and fatalism that men and women have developed to survive this world.

The End of Fighting History

MMA's participants and marketers describe it as the evolutionary horizon of all combat sport. This claim is based on the twin ideas that MMA determines which martial arts techniques are the most effective, and which men are the toughest, in some real sense that transcends sports. As is so often the case, this language of ultimate truth is the product of multiple historical processes of economically and socially conditioned construction. What follows will work backward into the various strands of this history, starting from the formal patterns that actual fights take today. Under the Unified Rules approved by several key state athletic commissions in 2000, professional MMA bouts can take place in a ring or (as is now more common) in a cage, and consist of three five-minute rounds, or five rounds for championship bouts. As a result of the effort to win legal and social legitimacy, nine different weight classes have been introduced, and more than two dozen of the most injurious actions have been banned, ranging from nineteenth-century horrors like fishhooking (mouth-tearing) and eye-gouging, to what were until recently common techniques in no-holds-barred events, such as kneeing to the head and stamping a downed fighter (NJSACB). As a result, fights primarily consist of the established techniques of the amateur disciplines that have proven most effective: kickboxing, wrestling, and submission grappling. The only extra-disciplinary or street technique that remains legal and common is the striking attack from a grappling position, known as ground-and-pound.

An MMA fight can go in many different directions, but under the Unified Rules and weight classes, and with most fighters training in each of the major disciplines, a standard progression has emerged to replace the often-incoherent collisions that filled the first commercial tournaments. Almost all fights begin with a period of stand-up striking, which is effectively kickboxing modified by the need to defend against wrestling takedowns. Fighters may circle each other with boxing-like spacing, or come together in a clinch, using the Thai techniques of knee- and elbow-strikes. The fighter whose advantage lies in the "ground game" typically will try to "shoot" his opponent, taking him down by the legs or midsection using the techniques of scholastic, freestyle, and Greco-Roman wrestling. (Judo throws are less common because of the absence of the *gi*, or robe, to grasp onto.) Once on the ground, wrestling techniques continue in the battle for preferred position. However, because MMA does not recognize wrestling pins, grappling and ground-and-pound predominate.

The first decisive lesson about interdisciplinary fighting that MMA taught was the indispensability of submission grappling, which entered in the form of a Brazilian jiu-jitsu derived from early twentieth-century Japanese judo. Submission grappling involves the effort to induce an opponent to "tap out" or quit under the pressure of a hold, such as an arm-lock or a choke. In most MMA contests, one fighter will assume the grappling "guard" position, lying on his back and controlling his opponent from his hips. The upper fighter will try to "pass" this guard, by getting over the opponent's legs to gain full control of the upper body, and very often he will aim punches and elbows down during this struggle, in the fierce ground-and-pound action that MMA fighting is best known for. If ground fighting results in a stalemate, the referee will instruct the fighters to stand and restart, often initiating a similar sequence of events. MMA fights end by knockout, defined by the first moment that a fighter cannot "intelligently defend" himself; or by submission, when a fighter taps out, signaling to the referee that he is conceding defeat. MMA defenders point to the "intelligent defense" rule, and to tapping out, as key safety advantages over boxing, in which 8- and 10-counts permit multiple concussions. Judges score each round to decide a winner in the event that the fight goes the distance.

The development of these patterns in contemporary MMA tell a story about the globalization of fighting culture in the twentieth century, both through the international exchange of combat techniques, and through the legal and commercial exigencies of marketing fighting as spectacular entertainment. These two motives can be found interwoven in each of the major contributing strands of the modern sport. Brazilian jiu-jitsu, for example, originated after the arrival of itinerant judo master and professional wrestler Mitsuyo Maeda in Brazil in 1914. Maeda had been teaching judo and fighting professionally against boxers, wrestlers, and all comers across the West for 10 years. During his first years in Brazil, he was hired by businessman Gastao Gracie to train his adolescent sons. These and two subsequent generations of Gracies developed their own, more expansive grappling form, taught it to others, and advertised it heavily in an open call to fight professionally that became known as the "Gracie challenge" (Green and Svinth 62, 69). The Gracies were also a driving force behind the spread of Brazil's *vale tudo* or "anything goes" fight spectacles, from circus sideshows to modern sporting events. The Ultimate Fighting Championship (UFC), the promoter that has led the commercial rise of the contemporary sport, was cofounded in 1993 by Rorion Gracie, who had recently come to the United States seeking new markets for the family's methods, including its famous challenge. Gracie fighters won several of these early tournaments, and by the late 1990s, American MMA practitioners were seeking out their seminars in "BJJ" before entering the ring or cage.

The most successful of these American students were former college and even Olympic wrestlers looking for professional avenues for their abilities. One of the most lucrative outlets they found was an organization called Pride Fighting Championships, founded in Japan in 1997. Pride was an enterprise in the tradition of Japanese "shoot wrestling," in which professional wrestlers set aside scripts to fight competitively in special events. Pride invited fighters from various disciplines around the world, primarily Brazilian grapplers and American wrestlers, to fight against each other and Japanese professionals in single-night tournament spectacles. These globally watched events promoted the idea, essential to the martial arts in popular culture, of finding the single greatest fighter in the world. Between 1997 and 2007, when Pride was bought out by the UFC, champions came from each of these three primary backgrounds, as well as one notable addition: heavyweight Fedor Emilianenko was a product of the Russian Army's *Sambo,* a judo-based hybrid form designed for combat situations. With no single discipline emerging as dominant, a hybridizing process ensued: fighters returned in consecutive years having trained in how to defend against and even attack in, the rival disciplines. Every top American MMA champion has been a product of scholastic wrestling who then fought in Pride, or in similarly interdisciplinary events that demanded cross-training. This exchange has had a mutually legitimizing effect, proving wrestling's worth against other martial arts, and bringing MMA into the respectable world of high school and college sports ("Popularity"). This, in turn, is one of the main avenues through which MMA is taking over fighting in the American cultural imaginary. High school wrestling is the socially admired, publically funded venue where young people fight. And its participants, more than a quarter of a million strong, look to MMA as the popular arena where their scholastic forerunners have thrived and their own types of skills have proven indispensable.[4]

The striking arts' contributions to MMA are often attributed to Western boxing and to formal Asian traditions such as karate and taekwondo, but they owe more directly to the preexisting fusion sport of kickboxing. Professional circuits emerged in Japan in the 1960s and America in the 1970s, and more recently, Thailand's professional *Muy thai* culture has been a major influence. Japan's K1 kickboxing promotion has produced several top MMA contenders from various nationalities, while *Muy thai* schools draw fighters from around the world on training pilgrimages (Sheridan 8–9). Kickboxing in the United States was a product of the Asian martial arts boom begun in the 1960s, which, especially through the influence of Hong Kong action films, produced thriving networks of Okinawan karate, Chinese kung fu and kenpo, Japanese judo, and Korean taekwondo. It was from this kind of popular platform, for example, that Bruce Lee advocated a proto-MMA philosophy of interdisciplinary, "realistic" fighting, *jeet kune do.*

This history, like MMA itself, is a useful antidote to the mystifying discourse surrounding Asian martial arts (also attributable to the karate phenomenon) as occupying a spiritual-philosophical plane that stands above aggressive fighting or commercial spectacle. It is true that "way of life" teachings are prominent in various Asian traditions; but it is also the case that all but the most academic of martial arts schools have been influenced by what full-contact, interdisciplinary competition has revealed about effective technique. From at least the late nineteenth century, when the Kodokan judo institute sent Maeda and others around the globe to spread their teachings by engaging with other fighters and fight traditions, the martial arts have been immersed in cultural exchange and commercial enterprise, including scripted professional wrestling (Green and Svinth xi–xiii). And for its most serious practitioners, MMA is nothing if not a way of life.

Fighting as Business and Labor

The rise of the MMA in popular culture has produced a tension between commercial incentives to create spectacular entertainment, and the athletic ideals of skill, fairness, and good community citizenship. These are values that come from MMA's contributing disciplines, but which also have emerged in unique forms in the culture of MMA gyms in their own rights. And when fighting values run up against marketing interests, this tension manifests in a labor dynamic. The exceptionally energetic promotional efforts of the Ultimate Fighting Championship have driven MMA's success in American popular culture since 2000. The UFC's role in standardizing the rules, the success of its marketing style, and its hardboiled labor tactics have had ripple effects throughout the MMA world. They affect the way smaller promotions and amateur competitions are put together, shaping the pathways into professional fighting and the fighting styles used along the way. They influence the motives and expectations people have for undertaking martial arts training, by inspiring fans to become participants and in the process turning many martial arts dojos into MMA gyms. This is the top-down influence by which the economic structure at the highest commercial level affects the entire social world of the sport and, ultimately, the nature of fighting in the popular imagination.

MMA is strongly identified with the UFC brand by casual fans, and not without some justice, due to the organization's efforts in legitimizing the sport and creating its entertainment format. MMA found itself under legal attack as the 1990s progressed, for the reputed, and often quite real, brutality of its pay-per-view spectacles. Senator John McCain, in particular, led a campaign first to prevent states from legalizing the events, and then to pressure cable systems to spurn pay-per-view feeds of events held abroad. McCain drew a clear line between boxing's longstanding customs for containing the violence of fighting, and what he memorably called the "human cockfighting" of MMA. Despite MMA's legal recognition by the influential state of New Jersey in 2000, the FCC's pressure on cable companies to drop the events had a serious financial impact. With pay-per-view buys dwindling, and no major advertising sponsorship in sight, the New York–based UFC began to falter badly in the late 1990s, despite having had some success at identifying its brand name with the emerging sport. MMA's chroniclers credit Internet-based fan networks for keeping enough interest alive to prevent the sport from disappearing altogether (Wertheim 101–2, 110, 134).

In 2001, the political dynamics changed, in part, some speculate, because legislators' attention turned to terrorism and war, and no-holds-barred fighting itself suddenly seemed less atavistic than it did contemporary. That year, the UFC was bought by brothers Frank and Lorenzo Fertitta, who had inherited and expanded the then-profitable Station Casino in Las Vegas. With Lorenzo Fertitta having recently occupied a seat on the influential Nevada State Athletic Commission, the sport's prospects of legitimacy increased greatly. In addition to working with state athletic commissions and legislatures to develop acceptable rules, their company (named Zuffa, Italian for "scuffle") aggressively sought to drive down or buy out rival organizations, including eventually Pride, in 2007. It invested heavily in live and televised production values, borrowing bombastic styles and customer-friendly techniques from professional wrestling, intentionally aiming to provide the unbroken pace and loud, multimedia spectacle that younger audiences found lacking in boxing (Wertheim 147–48). And in all its marketing, the UFC sought to project the meritocratic "major league" ideal prized by every monopoly institution in professional sports, arguing that its contestants were the best in the world.

The new company named as its president and minority owner Dana White, a high school friend of the Fertittas who was managing MMA fighters, and who had helped convince them to buy the UFC (Wertheim 143–44). White, as both the public face and the backroom power broker of the organization, is a polarizing figure in the MMA world. Most concede to some degree the White-led UFC's role in the sport's commercial success. But several constituencies consider the UFC to be an equally negative force, especially in its treatment of fighters. Unlike boxing promoters, who sign boxers to single fights against specific opponents, the UFC signs its fighters for multifight sequences against unspecified opponents, maintaining control over matchmaking and, to a large degree, over fighters' career opportunities and public images. Several former UFC champions, after gaining enough personal brand-power or at least distance from the UFC, describe the UFC as deceptive and exploitative in its dealings with fighters. In several accounts, the promotion aggressively deters new signees from employing agents, and plays on their aspirations by promising them better terms when they reach the championship level. Unlike sports with collective bargaining or a strong agent presence, the UFC claims exclusive rights to its athletes' images while under contract, in some cases even trying to claim them "in perpetuity" (Ortiz 147, Couture 151–2, 281, Wertheim 190–91). In the face of these criticisms, White is more candid than most executives in sports, or any business, in defending the UFC's actions. He concedes many of the charges, but argues that fight promoters are unfairly singled out for denunciation over labor dynamics and product values that go unquestioned in many other industries (Wertheim 150, Davidson).

The main way that the issue of fighter treatment is discussed in the MMA business, as in so many other industries, is by subsuming it under questions of audience demand. White's primary defense of the UFC is that it acts always on behalf of the fans, and ultimately of the sport itself, by both ramping up the spectacle and by building into fighter contracts as much incentive as possible to fight well and fight entertainingly (Wertheim 148). Very often half of a UFC fighter's paycheck depends upon his winning the match. These amounts range from a few thousand dollars for new fighters, to the mid-six-figure range for established stars, figures that must cover at least two months of training, and most expenses, including medical care. The UFC pays bonuses after its events for "knockout of the night," "submission of the night," and "fight of the night" honors.[5] These incentives equate performance standards with entertainment value in a way that is largely accepted among MMA fans and fighters. It is fair to say that in MMA, much more so than in boxing, a judge's decision, especially if it is close, is felt to be an inadequate outcome to a fight. It fails to prove which man truly exhibited his dominance by incapacitating the other. Stoppages are in the sport's DNA and, the UFC believes, they are what fans want.

One of the difficulties in attracting and pleasing such audiences—that is, in turning MMA into arena- and television-quality entertainment—has been that its key contributing disciplines are not, by nature, spectacular. Brazilian jiu-jitsu has presented a challenge to commercial MMA since its modern-day inception. It was designed not strictly as self-defense, but certainly as a way for smaller fighters to efficiently neutralize aggressive attacks from larger opponents. Jiu-jitsu artists have thrived commercially only by virtue of their success in no-holds-barred events, rather than through victory on the sport's own competition circuits. The sport by itself does not present a compelling narrative to the untrained eye. It is often very difficult for inexperienced observers to recognize what is happening in a jiu-jitsu match, or even to tell which fighter is gaining an advantage, because its physical positions do not correspond to ordinary perceptions of aggression and dominance. The drive to be spectacular also has been a challenge for American wrestlers, whose overwhelmingly amateur culture in schools, the armed forces, and on national squads places team over self, results over style, and humility over bombast.

Because of MMA's claim to arbitrate pure dominance, there is a case to be made that spectacular aggression is, in fact, essential to its understanding of fighting: impressing the people watching is, at a primal level, necessary to the establishment of physical dominance in a social setting. And because MMA fighters and fans alike accept an obligation to "grow the sport," the question of style versus substance is more openly debated as a matter of commercial appeal than in most other sports (Wertheim 151–52). Even participants who reject the UFC's claim to supremacy largely accept the idea that building and keeping a general audience is necessary for the sport's survival. And while fighters object to deception and to the most egregious concessions their contracts demand, they tend to endorse the ideals of meritocracy and audience growth that the UFC argues are its main motivations in controlling matchmaking and maintaining a steeply graduated pay scale.

But what these goals amount to in practice is extraordinary pressure on young fighters to be more than just good at winning contests; instead, they must fight entertainingly and develop a marketable personal brand identity. Most fighters began their training in disciplines that place a high value on defense before attack, intelligence over aggression, sportsmanship over dominance displays, and humility over self-aggrandizement. To counter these inbred tendencies toward craft and caution, it is routine for promoters to remind fighters urgently before a show that their sport depends on fights being entertaining more than it does on their strategic wisdom and technical excellence. In one such message, an executive of the Strikeforce promotion addressed the assembled fighters in the hours before an event in Everett, Washington, that was televised on Showtime in the summer of 2010:

Why are Showtime and CBS involved in a sport like this? Because we have great, great capacity to grow a huge audience. Now how do we do that? Let me tell you something, I gotta just say straight up: winning is not enough. Effort to be spectacular is what launches a sport. Sports do not grow on a straight-line curve, they grow in plateaus. Events, certain bouts, and we've seen it already, launch the sport from where it is, to the next level. The question is, do you want to be a person who participates in that launch? So what I'm telling you is, to advance your position in the industry, to help advance Strikeforce, to advance the sport, it's not about just coming out here and fighting, it's about trying to be spectacular. Because that's what people are going to remember, that's what's going to draw in more fans. So I encourage you to do that for the sport, for Strikeforce, and to advance your own career. (Leydon 2, 7:09–8:02)

MMA is based on the claim that it arbitrates pure physical dominance, and its most successful promotions, such as the UFC and, in this case, Strike-force, claim to have the best fighters in the world. But the message delivered to fighters, in both pay structures and explicit instruction, is that their professional survival depends not only on skill inside the ring, but also on their own role in developing market growth outside of it.

Fictional MMA narrative is built around this tension between internal values and external demands. While boxing has an extensive body of literary writing devoted to it, and many of its films are class-themed works of social realism, MMA's home in fictional representation is in the Hollywood action film, usually centering around an alienated warrior who is drawn back into the fray by a compelling moral obligation. Western heirs to Bruce Lee such as Chuck Norris, Steven Segal, and Jean Claude Van Damme were essentially performing stagy versions of MMA in the fight scenes through which these plots played out. Even earlier, the classical martial arts film could be called proto-MMA, in its battles between rival schools. More recently, MMA champions have appeared in all manner of violent B-movies, and as themselves in professional wrestling shows and TV comedies. Fictional MMA narrative from more highbrow sources is not much different in themes and plots. David Mamet's 2008 film *Redbelt* was built around the conflict between commercial greed and martial ideals. A labor of love for writer and director Mamet, a student of Brazilian jiu-jitsu, the film is about a hardboiled but idealistic jiu-jitsu teacher who emphasizes the form's lessons for navigating a hard life ("I don't teach people to fight; I teach people to prevail"). When circumstances force him into the cage, of course, his killer instincts come out. Few representations of MMA, no matter how serious or well written, have shown interest in demystifying the spectacle of fighting. One exception is the 2002 John Hyams documentary *The Smashing Machine*, which chronicled NCAA wrestling champion Mark Kerr's career in UFC and Pride, revealing the brutal physical toll that no-holds-barred fighting took on his body, and his near-death due to an associated opiate addiction.

Fictionalizing MMA is redundant: its promotion is dedicated to narrative and performance, and under the UFC's control, every match made is "worked," in wrestling parlance, to produce maximal drama. So it makes sense that "reality television" is the screen genre that has done the most to popularize MMA: it is ostensibly documentary, but artfully manipulated by its owners. The UFC and MMA made a decisive leap into American homes in 2005 with the successful launch of *The Ultimate Fighter,* a series on the young-male-oriented cable channel Spike TV. "*TUF*" covered a weeks-long tournament among a stable of young fighters living and training together in two teams, under one roof. Using all the arts of the reality show genre, the producers stoked social tensions, documented drinking sessions and personal crises, and spun out plot lines that enhanced the drama of the episode-ending MMA fights, several of which have gone down as turning points in various MMA weight divisions. Tellingly, a key moment of drama in the first season was the UFC's effective suppression of a labor action by the fighters. Having heard that contestants on a similar boxing show were earning $25,000 for each fight, compared to mere living and training expenses for themselves, the *TUF* fighters threatened to strike. The UFC, which was still financially vulnerable and without an established television presence, responded in two ways. Behind the scenes, it introduced four-figure, incentive paychecks for knockouts and submissions. Publically, on the show, it aired a scene in which White appeared unannounced, and assailed the contestants in a curse-laden tirade for the lack of gratitude and lack of self-belief implied in their threat. In it White repeats the same question over and over: "Do you want to be a fucking fighter?" (Wertheim 184–85). The fighters acquiesced, cowed by the challenge to their competitive spirit. Fighters and audience alike appeared to accept, as a natural "reality" of the fight world, this corollary to success-myth ideology: that giving away one's present labor is a necessary sign of belief in one's eventual rise to the top.

Fighter Images, Fighting Lives

The outcome of these tensions is that fighters' identities have two valences, which sometimes coincide and sometimes conflict: the elements that are used to sell MMA as popular culture versus the elements that go into producing a successful athlete in the cage. In both promotional material and in self-presentation, fighters are pitched to audiences as aggressive, dangerous warriors, the ultimate survivors of a dog-eat-dog world. But when called on to defend the legitimacy of MMA or the character of particular fighters, its promoters and fans will point with pride to these same men's college degrees, small business enterprises, families, and other marks of bourgeois respectability. Institutionalized fighting produces a particularly transparent version of a tension that has run through the history of American masculinity, between the ideals of the heroic loner versus the virtuous, socially embedded citizen. Both of these ideals in MMA identity can be understood through the values fighters develop to build careers on a highly unreliable labor terrain.

The first half of this split personality has a more obvious presence in the imagery of MMA events, as promotional messaging and cage theatrics emphasize individualism and amoral dominance. MMA fighters physically appear more aggressive and self-absorbed than athletes in other contact sports. They have more upper-body bulk than boxers do, and they sport more elaborate tattoos. They have a roster of their own sponsors adorning their trunks, postfight hats and T-shirts, in part to supplement relatively slim base paychecks. Upon entering the cage, and especially in their behavior upon winning, MMA fighters are brash and demonstrative, posturing, strutting, and, in effect, chest-thumping. This personal style may seem unexceptional in a combat sport, but it contrasts sharply with boxing, in which ancillary ring behavior speaks primarily to being situated in a craft tradition and a training family. If the image of the boxer is that of the apprentice, the dutiful son, or the skilled artisan, the image of the MMA fighter is that of a morally ambiguous, tragically fated, utterly alone warrior. The fashion brands that have attached to MMA center on tattoo-influenced T-shirts with legends in blackletter script such as "Affliction" and "Redemption." Fighter nicknames convey the stagy individualism more in line with professional wrestling personae than social backgrounds or fighting styles. Randy Couture was "the Natural" or "Captain America." Tito Ortiz was "the Huntington Beach Bad Boy."

This imagery is not invented whole cloth, but is tied to the public life stories of fighters, in their themes of overcoming hardships, enduring betrayals, and indulging in bad behavior (Beardmore). Again, if the boxer is the good son, very often with a father or uncle or other surrogate patriarch in his corner training him, MMA masculinity reads as an agonized, even self-destructive, struggle to fill the void left by an absent father. MMA fighters more often have training partners, rather than father figures, in their corners, and several ex-champions' life stories attest to the loss of fathers early due to death, drugs, or apathy. Ken and Frank Shamrock were adopted by the man who ran their group home for juvenile offenders in rural Northern California. Tito Ortiz's Huntington Beach, California, childhood was scarred by his parents' heroin addiction, and he attributes his early criminality, long-time drug use, and man-child personality to his father's absence. Even Randy Couture, a clean-cut product of suburban Seattle, Oklahoma State University, and U.S. Army wrestling teams, spends much of his autobiography discussing his poor relationship with an absent father, and confessing his own insecurities about being a good husband and father.

These agonistic elements in fighter identity help to serve event promotion and personal branding, but they can be resituated in the social world that produces and sustains MMA. As such, they fit ordinary patterns of working- and middle-class struggle, especially in the Midwest and West Coast, where the majority of American MMA fighters come from. Unstable fatherhood is but one theme among the trials of individuals, families, and communities in an age of economic insecurity. Other themes in fighters' early family lives include burdensome medical bills, shifting family structures and homes, and, occasionally, drug abuse. But these same fighters describe childhoods shaped by the middle-class pathways of extensively scheduled, multiple youth sports, combined with college aspirations. Very often they are the first in their families to go to college, while these same family lives are shot through with constant financial insecurity.

Sport as salvation is a common theme in athletes' life stories, and wrestling plays this role prominently in MMA biography. Several fighters claim that high school wrestling provided them with the structure needed to survive adolescence and enter adulthood. In these stories, wrestling culture provides role models, peer groups, trustworthy relationships, and secure ground upon which to meet new people. In short, it is a stable social institution within a less secure society. Unfortunately, scholastic wrestling comes to an end before the first paycheck is ever cut. Fighters pursue MMA careers by leaving the dense structures of this amateur world, to gain access to the multiple, interlinked networks of teachers, practitioners, and promoters that make up the MMA economy.

In the grassroots of MMA, between the raw amateur and the paid professional, training and competing practices represent the range of homegrown methods of labor survival among the working and middle classes in the contemporary economy. Accordingly, MMA values are not only those predicted by commercial incentives at the most lucrative level: they are those that serve the needs and aspirations of the workers in its trenches. These include the free exchange of knowledge among disciplines and individuals, a communal effort to build hybrid forms, and flexible and pragmatic structures (including full-contact sparring) that allow the most useful such knowledge to emerge. These values are on display in the culture of MMA gyms, and in the fighting that takes place in its cages, too.

Even the toughest MMA gyms are described as "remarkably egalitarian" places, where, in place of authoritative masters bestowing knowledge, everyone shares advice with everyone else. It is what participant-observer Sam Sheridan calls "the democracy" of MMA, where, with no fixed ranking system, "knowledge is shared" and fighters strong in one discipline seek out those experienced in other forms, to learn and teach (54–55). Greg

Downey expands this kind of observation into a theory of the pedagogy of MMA rings and cages. Downey argues that by deregulating fighting while still maintaining a basic safety structure, the sport as a community has developed extensive new knowledge about the human body's limits and potentials, and furthermore has transmitted that knowledge to the wider, nonparticipating society via its electronic media (109–10). In this view, MMA fighters and their supporters have created something that is of more than commercial value, in a kind of open-source toolkit for defending against bodily assaults and weathering physical trauma. Some former MMA fighters have developed side careers as self-defense teachers, for police, military, youth, and general population audiences.

Gyms often develop communal and even familial dynamics, especially when anchored by pioneering fighters who have proven effective teachers or role models. Ken Shamrock's Lion's Den originated in California in 1994, and developed a reputation for a draconian, confrontational ethos Shamrock associated with his survival of childhood abuse and neglect (Shamrock, Hanner, and Romias). Pat Miletich's Miletich Fighting Systems gym in Quad Cities, Iowa, attracted a variety of aspirants to its combination of Midwestern wrestling work ethic and familial loyalty. Though sparring at the gym is notoriously hard, "MFS" fighters by policy do not fight one another professionally. Brazilian Top Team grew around Gracie family protégés and subsequent Pride champions such as Mario Sperry and Antonio Rodrigo Nogueira, in Rio, in an upper-middle-class jiu-jitsu subculture combining elements of machismo and folk-stoic philosophy. West Coast friends and wrestling champions turned MMA pioneers Randy Couture, Dan Henderson, and Matt Lindland founded Team Quest in Oregon in 1999, in a collaborative, entrepreneurial venture.

The success of these gyms and their resulting reputations prompted their founders (and imitators) to commodify their identities and spread their training methods, by opening franchises in other locations, turning the original communal atmosphere toward a more commercial enterprise. The tension inherent in this undertaking is endemic in MMA culture, as, with paychecks coming only infrequently, entrepreneurial efforts to turn personal skills and traits into steady income are common. Very often fighters undertake these businesses in close social networks, in partnerships and groups that have been training together since before earning their first paychecks. In addition to commercial gyms, they include websites for personal promotion, and lines of athletic and casual wear with MMA themes. In the life stories of fighters, the failure of such enterprises is often experienced as a betrayal of close social bonds developed in the gym (Couture 217–18).

These modes of work are expressed in values that balance strong rhetorics of entrepreneurial self-reliance with commitments to communal support and the idea of a shared fate. This tension speaks to the two sides of labor values in the new economy. Workers not only accept the demands of employers for maximal flexibility, they also internalize values that justify these requirements. At the same time, they seek out and build systems of mutual support as bulwarks against the kinds of social fragmentation that such flexibility can require. In MMA, the first tendency is manifested in the sometimes cartoonish lone warrior imagery, but it also takes more poignant shape in the way even young and inexperienced fighters are urged to accept responsibility for their fates in the cage and to take losses as learning experiences. This ethos can extend to a fighter's whole life, as Pat Miletich, for example, teaches the young fighters who come to him bearing the scars of family trauma a philosophy that bans self-pity but encourages mutual support as well as continual self-improvement (Wertheim 125).

Self-reliance is on obvious display in the cage during a contest; but the values of free exchange of knowledge, lifelong learning, mutual emotional support, and local family and community building all are being put into action, too. Despite the oppositional nature of the contest, a mutual process of learning takes place in fights, especially those between fighters whose styles are complementary. In the cage these values are expressed in the evidence of knowledge-exchange and formal hybridization. Techniques emerge in MMA fighting that can be described as conversations between different disciplines and their traditions. Transitions from the techniques of one discipline to another are especially important, as these are the moments when an advantageous position in one discipline can instantly turn into a liability in another (Sheridan 49). As in the wider labor terrain, survival requires not only the development of multiple skills, but the ability to pivot from one to another on the fly.

Even ground-and-pound, which to the layperson looks like a one-sided schoolyard assault can be understood as a meaningful negotiation of seemingly meager resources and vulnerable position. It is brutal: the aggressor straddles his supine opponent and rains punches and elbows down at his face. But in MMA, the recipient of these blows is in the guard position of the grappling disciplines, a potentially advantageous position from which various submission holds can be attempted. Further, without planted feet, the puncher is unable to generate great force without rearing his arm back, an unboxinglike motion that gives a competent opponent time to slip, block, or deflect the blow. Defending the ground-and-pound is an adequate metaphor for the life and labors of an unheralded MMA fighter. What looks like (and indeed often is) a grim, submissive position, at the same time, is a struggle for survival that requires great heights of composure, resilience, and creativity—traits that in MMA culture, more than in their applications to other kinds of labor, are publically valued, even ennobled.

Hard Lessons

As entertainment spectacle MMA seems to depend to a considerable degree on the mystification of its own economic relations. The UFC works ferociously to present itself as the meritocratic pinnacle of the sport, while exercising as much control as it can over fighters and their images. Its fighter identities and promotional narratives project images of self-made, nihilistic warriors, disowning shared identity and social significance. But at the same time its core audience, as well as its participants, are quite aware of what those relations are. More important, for this insider community, it exists not merely as spectacle but as a grassroots cultural practice closely related to contemporary modes of work.

MMA reflects the experiences of people who have been deprived of, or have rejected, the ideal of stability in their chosen labor market, and instead have embraced values suited to survival in an uncertain world. The particular array of upbringings, educations, and professional labors in MMA makes sense in a society in which the boundaries between the middle classes and the working class are becoming increasingly permeable, and indeed unstable. The uncertainty and flexibility of their work patterns resemble everything from the grasping at hours in a low-paid retail job to the "boundaryless careers" expected of, and often sought by, workers in information industries (Montgomery 43). They are people who, as former champion Chuck Liddell ambiguously puts it, "appreciate risk" (15). Covering a wide range of educational and employment backgrounds, often pulled in several different directions by work and family, MMA fighters submit to exploitation by large companies that dictate the terms of individual achievement exclusively on the principle of what can be sold to the public. At the same time, the fighters greatly prize their own autonomy and the nonmaterial values of the sport, in collectively constructed codes of self-reliance, personal honor, and mutual support. If they have one thing in common, it is that they understand their fighting in the ring unambiguously as an extension of the values it takes to live in the contemporary world.

The ability to work multiple jobs, to change jobs and roles frequently, to be as flexible an employee as possible, and simultaneously to study toward college degrees and professional credentials—all these have become expectations urged on members of the middle and working class alike. In management-speak, in self-help, and in the career advice industry, the rhetoric of flexibility and social Darwinism have become increasingly prevalent, while collective institutions, from unions to government programs to social clubs, have become more ad hoc and less permanent. MMA fighters embrace the stated values of the new era—indeed, some are vocal political conservatives—but in their fighting culture their individualism is moderated by a commitment to mutual support and knowledge-exchange. Issues of loyalty and fair play loom large in discussions of their career trajectories.

Two fighters involved in the aforementioned Strikeforce Challengers event on Showtime illustrate the range of paths MMA athletes have taken, and the kinds of traits they have exhibited, in their efforts to thrive personally and professionally. Showtime's color commentator, Pat Miletich, helped to create the contemporary sport. A former scholastic wrestler, prolific street brawler, sometime boxer, and advanced student of both karate and Brazilian jiu-jitsu, in the 1990s Miletich pioneered the kind of cross-training that has become indispensible to MMA fighters; eventually, he became the first UFC welterweight champion. He then became a legendary teacher of MMA, not just because of his success, but because he was thoughtful about interdisciplinarity, coming to believe that the transitions between forms are where MMA contests are won and lost. Miletich "could box, he could wrestle, he had submissions, and he understood how to put them all together— especially the transitions between them," Sam Sheridan writes. "He could find a weak link in any fighter he met. And coming up at a time when MMA in America was in its infancy, he was a self-made fighter. He had to bring the elements together on his own, mixing up in his own 'laboratory' the stand-up and ground fighting he liked" (Sheridan 49). No writer spends time at Miletich's camp, or studies his fights from his prime, without coming to the conclusion that he embodies all that is pure of motive and culturally creative about MMA.

Miletich's fighting, training, and teaching styles describe not just the traits required for survival in an unforgiving world, but a foundation of zealously protected values necessary for doing so on one's own terms. They echo the struggles of workers to forge meaning as well as eke out livings in industries, like farming and manufacturing, that maintain a kind of gritty cultural cachet similar to that of combat sport but that feature brutal labor economics.[6] Wrestling didn't save Miletich from a difficult adolescence, as it did for some fighters, but MMA gave him his adulthood. Miletich grew up in Bettendorf, Iowa, in a working-class home that broke apart when he was a child. His father was an abusive drinker, two of his brothers died in drug- and drinking-related incidents, and the third did a lengthy stretch in prison. Miletich was a star football player and wrestler in high school, but left community college before completing his freshman year, returning home to help pay his mother's medical bills. He continued fighting, though, becoming a feared street brawler in Bettendorf and the adjacent Quad Cities, a western outpost of the Rust Belt. After several years of menial job drift, depression, and financial struggle, he discovered a local karate gym, where he channeled his talents and his frustrations into the pursuit of more formal fighting knowledge. After winning some small no-holds-barred events, he sought out a jiu-jitsu seminar held by Renzo Gracie and undertook to add the form to his repertoire. Eventually he came to the attention of the UFC and became the top small fighter of his era.

At the peak of this career, Miletich began to attract ex-wrestlers to the small gym he had opened not far from where he grew up. "Like the Iowans engaged in tilling or detasseling corn or working the assembly line at the John Deere or Oscar Meyer plants, the Miletich team engaged in similar honest drudgery, learning and repeating moves until they became as burned in muscle memory as walking," recounts John Wertheim in his biography of Miletich. "Just as Miletich trained like a manual laborer, the fighters followed suit. You show integrity in your workout. You look suspiciously at risk-taking. You prepare meticulously. You enter the cage or ring with a well-conceived fight plan, but you reserve the right to adjust it midfight" (Wertheim 106–7). Without MMA, it seems unlikely that this particular blend of hard experience, natural abilities, voracious autodidacticism, and punishing work ethic could have found the rich cultural and professional expression that it did.

While Miletich performed his duties as a television announcer, Roxanne Modafferi represented a different pathway into the MMA world that night in the 10,000-seat Comcast Arena. A consensus top 10 women's middle-weight since 2007, Modafferi grew up in middle-class comfort in suburban Delaware and western Massachusetts. Inspired by the Power Rangers and Japanese anime cartoons, she followed the path of many middle-class children into martial arts classes, studying tae kwon do, karate, and judo. While attending the University of Massachusetts, she took Brazilian jiu-jitsu seminars, and discovered an MMA gym in Amherst, where she worked on putting these different techniques together. During this time she traveled the circuits of amateur competition, helping to set up mats and rings, and seeking out teachers in other disciplines to broaden her skill base. She also pursued an intense interest in Japanese culture, majoring in Japanese language and literature, and spending a year of her college career studying abroad there. After graduating, she moved to Japan to train in MMA while teaching English to support herself. She represents the middle-class experience of MMA, in which young people turn an affinity for the sport into something akin to an addiction to "testing themselves" with increasingly difficult techniques and increasingly full-contact competition. Modafferi is geographically mobile, and an earnest self-improver, friend-maker, and optimist, traits embodied in the "Happy Warrior" anime-inspired fighting persona she adopted upon a fan's suggestion (Krause). She keeps a quirky, personal blog chronicling her experiences training, teaching, traveling, and learning about Japanese language and culture (Modafferi).

Modafferi, like Miletich, has developed her own ideas about the value and meaning of MMA interdisciplinarity, but she articulates hers in the language of self-discovery rather than labor. Fighting, she says, is "exciting, the ultimate challenge of your physical strength, your mental strength, your emotional strength, your spiritual strength, your intellect, your ability to change your game plan, your adaptability." It is culture as play, but with high stakes. "I can tell a lot about a person from rolling with them, from grappling with them," she notes. "I do it for fun, but a really serious fun. I'm not just playing games, but I see it as playing. Like grappling, you know, I just want to jump on somebody and see if I can choke them out. It's just fun for me. I just love it" (Leydon 1, 0:03–0:54). Women in professional MMA are a small and struggling band of fighters—while Strikeforce and some other small companies promote their fights, the UFC will not countenance women's competition, arguing that there is no audience for it. Modafferi's positive attitude is reflected both in a physical joy, perceivable even during the toughest moments of her fights, and in relationships all across the globe she has developed in the sport.

At Strikeforce, Modafferi was matched against another top-ranked woman, Sarah Kaufman, a former dancer and medical student at the University of Victoria in British Columbia. The first two rounds were closely fought, with Kaufman's harder striking and Modafferi's sophisticated grappling neutralizing one another. In the third round, Modafferi was working methodically from the guard to secure an arm-bar, when the stronger Kaufman used their mutual grip to lift Modafferi up bodily into the air, before slamming her head and upper body down onto the canvas, knocking Modafferi unconscious to end the fight in supremely dramatic fashion. Modafferi said later that she knew she was being slammed, but didn't expect the impact to be as severe as it was, and so allowed it to happen in the hopes of using the momentum to gain a submission hold. Video of Kaufman's slam was turned into short clips and circulated widely on the Internet in the days that followed. It was the kind of moment that the Strikeforce executive had been urging on the fighters in his preshow speech. Strikeforce subsequently dropped Modafferi from its roster, and Kaufman's star looked to be on the rise; until, that is, the men-only UFC bought Strikeforce in early 2011, and the prospects for all of its women fighters looked highly uncertain.

Ever the optimist, the Happy Warrior continued to get fights under other promotions, in the fragmented, countercultural world of women's MMA. Before she could get off the mat, though, Miletich had a lecture for her from the announcing table, exhibiting his sterner and more fatalistic brand of self-improvement. Agreeing with his announcing partner that Modafferi was "a world-class grappler" who had given Kaufman "a lot of problems," nevertheless Miletich intoned in his Iowa drawl about the need for cage-awareness and cutting your losses, as labor values essential to survival in MMA. "You've got to bail on your submission attempt when somebody lifts you up," he urged. "It's your job to do that, you've got to know that you're in trouble and bail on it. She didn't do that, and got slammed and paid the price for it. Out cold" ("Strikeforce Challengers"). Modafferi had fixated on completing her jiu-jitsu technique, resting inside the form in which she was most comfortably superior; she had not recognized the stakes of the transition that was taking place. With a wry satisfaction characteristic of the MMA teacher, Miletich interpreted the violence of the moment as an unambiguous lesson learned, one of great value for both fighter and observers, for future work in combat and in life.[7]

Notes

1. Boxing aficionados object that the two sports' fates are not as inversely bound as these kinds of comparisons suggest. Fighting entertainment as a whole has declined relative to the major team sports, and boxing has hastened its own demise through chaotic and corrupt promotion. Boxing's audience has become older and increasingly divided by ethnic and national affiliation, while much of MMA's growth has occurred in the niche occupied by professional wrestling, where the spectacle of aggression and dominance is consumed primarily by young men (Hauser 156–57). But this age difference suggests a future in which MMA increasingly crowds out boxing. As much as fight fans would like to believe there is room for both, MMA is a perennial topic when questions arise about boxing's struggles to sustain audiences and attract new participants (see Wagenheim, Timmerman, Meltzer, e.g.).

2. For a good account of boxing's relationship to industrial employment and its social order, see Carlo Rotella, *Good with Their Hands* (U of Calif. P, 2002), notably pp. 22–24. In literature, especially beginning in the Depression, when the industrial growth machine stalled and class conflict surfaced, the humble journey-man boxer became a figure that embodied working-class victimization and perse-verance. See, for example, Clifford Odets's play *Golden Boy* (1937); Irwin Shaw's short story, "Return to Kansas City" (1939); Nelson Algren's novel, *Never Come Morning* (1942); and, more recently, David Russell's 2010 film, *The Fighter*.

3. This zone is the latest among what Robert Weir describes as the evolving, multiple meanings of the term *new middle class* (575). The combinations of nar-ratives in the New York Times collection *Class in America* suggest the varying tra-jectories it contains, such as David Leonhardt's "The College Dropout Boom," and Timothy Egan's "No Degree, and No Way Back to the Middle."

4. In the National Federation of State High School Associations' *2009–10 High School Athletics Participation Survey,* wrestling had the sixth-highest total partici-pation, coming next behind soccer and ahead of cross-country running, tennis, golf, and swimming.

5. State athletic commissions release base pay amounts for each fighter after an event. These numbers do not include royalties and other side deals sometimes offered to top fighters. See, for example, the reports on recent UFC event pay scales at *mmajunkie.com.*

6. For an ethnographic study of this kind of struggle in a region not far from Miletich's industrial/agricultural Iowa, see Tom Fricke's "Working Selves, Moral Selves: Crafting the Good Person in the Northern Plains."

7. Renzo Gracie, who taught Miletich's first Brazilian jiu-jitsu seminar, offered the most famous example of this pain pedagogy in MMA. In a Pride match in 2000, Gracie allowed Japanese professional wrestler Kazushi Sakuraba to fully dislocate his elbow, rather than tap out in submission to an arm-bar. He did this, he said later, because he wanted to embrace the moment as punishment for the mistake he had made (Schorn).

Works Cited

Beardmore, Matt. "Dead Man Fighting: Court McGee Was Headed for the Morgue; Now His MMA Career Is Alive and Well." *ESPN The Magazine,* 22 Sept 2010. Web .

Couture, Randy, with Loretta Hunt. *Becoming the Natural: My Life in and out of the Cage.* New York: Simon Spotlight Entertainment, 2008.

Davidson, Neil. "UFC President Defends Salary Structure." *Canadian Press,* 30 Aug 2006. Web. 14 Feb 2011.

Downey, Greg. "The Information Economy in No-Holds-Barred Fighting." In *Frontiers of Capital: Ethnographic Reflections on the New Economy.* Eds. Melissa S. Fisher and Greg Downey. Durham, NC: Duke UP, 2006. 108–30.

Egan, Timothy. "No Degree, and No Way Back to the Middle." In *Class Matters.* Ed. Bill Keller. New York: New York Times, 2005. 105–33.

Fricke, Tom. "Working Selves, Moral Selves: Crafting the Good Person in the Northern Plains." In *The Changing Landscape of Work and Family in the American Middle Class.* Eds. Elizabeth Rudd and Lara Descartes. Lanham, MD.: Lexington Books, 2008. 17–39.

Green, Thomas A., and Joseph R. Svinth. "The Circle and the Octagon: Maeda's Judo and Gracie's Jiu-Jitsu." In *Martial Arts in the Modern World.* Ed. Thomas A. Green and Joseph R. Svinth. Westport, CT: Praeger, 2003. 61–70.

Hauser, Thomas. *The Boxing Scene.* Philadelphia, PA: Temple UP, 2009.

Krause, Alexia. "Interview with MMA Fighter Roxanne Modafferi." *Women Talk Sports,* 9 Dec 2010. Web. 6 Jan 2011.

Leonhardt, David. "The College Dropout Boom." In *Class Matters.* Ed. Bill Keller. New York: New York Times, 2005. 87–104.

Leydon, E. Casey. "Sarah Kaufman vs. Roxanne Modafferi Fight Journal: Part 1." *Mmafighting.com,* 22 July 2010. Web. 15 Jan 2011.

Leydon, E. Casey. "Sarah Kaufman vs. Roxanne Modafferi Fight Journal: Part 2." *Mmafighting.com,* 23 July 2010. Web. 15 Jan 2011.

Liddell, Chuck, with Chad Millman. *Iceman: My Fighting Life.* New York: Dutton, 2008.

Meltzer, Dave. "Boxing vs. MMA: A Contrast of Styles." *Yahoo Sports,* 7 Dec 2008. Web. 25 Feb 2011.

Modafferi, Roxanne. *Roxanne's Blog.* Myspace.com.

Montgomery, Alesia F. "Kitchen Conferences and Garage Cubicles: The Merger of Home and Work in a 24–7 Global Economy." In *The Changing Landscape of Work and Family in the American Middle Class.* Eds. Elizabeth Rudd and Lara Descartes. Lanham, Md.: Lexington Books, 2008. 41–60.

National Federation of State High School Associations (NFHS). *2009–10 High School Athletics Participation Survey.* Web. 24 Feb 2011.

New Jersey State Athletic Control Board (NJSACB). "Mixed Martial Arts Unified Rules of Conduct and Additional Mixed Martial Arts Rules." N.J.A.C. 13: 46–24A, 24B, and 4.25. 2003. Web. 28 Feb 2011.

Ortiz, Tito, with Marc Shapiro. *This Is Gonna Hurt: The Life of a Mixed Martial Arts Champion.* New York: Simon Spotlight Entertainment, 2008.

"Popularity of MMA Has Increased Numbers in Prep, College Wrestling." *The Northwestern.com,* 21 Feb 2011. Web. 4 March 2011.

Redbelt. Dir. David Mamet. Sony, 2008. DVD.

Rudd, Elizabeth, and Lara Descartes. *The Changing Landscape of Work and Family in the American Middle Class.* Lanham, Md.: Lexington Books, 2008.

Schorn, Daniel. "Mixed Martial Arts: A New Kind of Fight." *CBS News.com: 60 Minutes.* 23 July 2007. Web. 27 Feb 2011.

Shamrock, Ken, Richard Hanner, and Calixtro Romias. *Inside the Lion's Den.* Boston, MA: Tuttle Publishing, 1998.

Sheridan, Sam. *A Fighter's Heart: One Man's Journey through the World of Fighting.* New York: Atlantic Monthly P, 2007.

"Strikeforce Challengers: del Rosario vs. Mahe." *ShoMMA: Strikeforce Challengers.* Showtime. 23 July 2010.

Timmerman, Tom. "Boxing Here Takes Hits, but Still Swinging." *St. Louis Post-Dispatch*, 24 April 2009. Web. 14 Jan 2011.

Wagenheim, Jeff. "Beaten up and Choked out, Toney and Boxing Know Their Place (Not in a UFC Cage)." *The Faster Times*, 4 Sept 2010. Web. 15 Dec 2010.

Weir, Robert E. "New Middle Class." In *Class in America: An Encyclopedia*. Ed. Robert E. Weir. Westport, CT: Greenwood, 2007. 574–76.

Wertheim, Jon L. *Blood in the Cage: MMA, Pat Miletich, and the Furious Rise of the UFC*. Boston: Houghton Mifflin Harcourt, 2009.

Index

About the Contributors

KATIE SULLIVAN BARAK is pursuing her doctorate in American culture studies at Bowling Green State University. Her focus thus far has been examining different kinds of representation in visual media.

BOB BATCHELOR is an assistant professor in the School of Journalism and Mass Communication at Kent State University and director of the online master's degree program concentrated in public relations. He earned his doctorate in English literature at the University of South Florida. Batchelor is the author or editor of 10 books, including *The 1980s; The 2000s;* and *American Pop: Popular Culture Decade by Decade* (four volumes). He has published in *Radical History Review, Journal of American Culture, Mailer Review, American Prospect Online,* and *Public Relations Review.* He serves on the editorial advisory board of the *Journal of Popular Culture.*

M. KEITH BOOKER is the James E. and Ellen Wadley Roper Professor of English and director of the Program in Comparative Literature and Cultural Studies at the University of Arkansas. In addition to being the editor of *Blue-Collar Pop Culture,* he has authored or edited a total of more than 40 books on literature, literary theory, and popular culture. Some of his publications include *Strange TV: Innovative Television Series from* The Twilight Zone *to* The X-Files (2003), *Science Fiction Television* (2004), *Alternate Americas: Science Fiction Film and American Culture* (2006), *Drawn to Television: Prime-Time Animated Series from* The Flintstones *to* Family Guy (2006), *From Box Office to Ballot Box: The American Political Film* (2007), *Postmodern Hollywood: What's New in Film and Why It Makes Us Feel So Strange* (2007), *May Contain Graphic Material: Comic Books, Graphic Novels, and Film* (2007), and *Disney, Pixar, and the Hidden Messages in Children's Films* (2009).

EOIN F. CANNON is a lecturer and assistant director of studies for the degree program in history and literature at Harvard University. His book *The Politics of Redemption: Addiction and Conversion in Modern American Culture* is forthcoming from the University of Massachusetts Press in 2012. His research focuses on the cultural histories of drugs and alcohol, sports, religion, and literature.

CATHERINE CHAPUT is an assistant professor at the University of Nevada Reno, where she teaches courses in rhetoric, writing, and critical theory. Her research focuses on the relationship between rhetoric and political economy as it manifests within particular social, cultural, and political texts. Her monograph, *Inside the Teaching Machine,* was published with the University of Alabama Press's series in Rhetoric, Culture, and Social Critique and her edited collection, *Entertaining Fear,* was published by Peter Lang's Frontiers in Political Communication series. She is currently working on a book project, titled *Affect and Our Capitalist Investments.*

MARY CHRISTIANAKIS is an associate professor of critical theory and social justice at Occidental College. Having received her PhD in language, literacy, and culture from University of California Berkeley, she studies literacy development and children's texts from a critical sociocultural perspective, primarily in urban and multilingual school contexts. Dr. Christianakis is also interested in literacy development in out-of-school settings, such as community and cultural centers. Her scholarly writing has focused on curriculum and instruction for culturally and linguistically diverse children. Dr. Christianakis teaches courses on children's literature and popular texts, immigration and education, ethnographic methods, and the interplay between prisons, schools, and the popular media.

SANDRA TRUDGEN DAWSON teaches at Northern Illinois University in the History Department and Women's Studies Program. She is the author of *Holiday Camps in Twentieth Century Britain: Packaging Pleasure,* published by Manchester University Press in 2011 as part of its Popular Culture series as well as articles in peer-reviewed journals about the circus, women's leisure in World War II, and the growth of British tourism. Dawson is currently researching immigration and the establishment of the British National Health Service.

WILLIAM DEGENARO is associate professor at the University of Michigan Dearborn, Department of Language, Culture, and Communication.

Areas of expertise include working-class culture, open-access education, service learning, and the teaching of writing. DeGenaro's research has appeared in journals including *Rhetoric Review, College English,* and the *International Journal of Critical Pedagogy.* During academic year 2010–2011, DeGenaro was a Fulbright Scholar in Lebanon.

JENNIFER R. DUTCH is a PhD candidate in American studies at Pennsylvania State University, Harrisburg. She received her master's of arts degree in English: Writing from the University of New Hampshire and a dual bachelor of arts degree in history and English from Keene State College. Today, the main focus of her research is on foodways, particularly the role of tradition in twenty-first-century home cooking practices.

LORIE WATKINS FULTON received her PhD from the University of Southern Mississippi. An associate professor of English at William Carey University, Fulton is the author of *William Faulkner, Gavin Stevens, and the Cavalier Tradition.* She has published several essays on southern literature and culture and is a former William Faulkner Society Faulkner and Yoknapatawpha Conference student fellow.

JAN GOGGANS is an associate professor of literature and culture at University of California Merced. She has published two articles on John Steinbeck's *The Grapes of Wrath,* and her book, *California on the Breadlines: Dorothea Lange, Paul Taylor, and the Making of a New Deal Narrative* (UC Press, 2010), analyzes the narrative work of Lange's and Taylor's photographic work in the Great Depression. Professor Goggans is currently at work on a second book, tentatively titled "'Working' Class: Fashion as Class Transgression in Literature and Film of the 1930s."

BRIAN GRANGER is a musical theater writer-composer and PhD candidate in theater at the University of California Santa Barbara. His dissertation-in-progress, under the direction of Professors Christina S. McMahon (chair), W. Davies King, and Stephanie Batiste, is titled "Employing Africa on Broadway" and examines the history of African-themed Broadway musicals in light of the symbolic and literal labors these shows require. Granger is a proud graduate of Kenyon College (BA in English and dance/drama), Ohio State University (MFA in creative writing), and New York University/Tisch School of the Arts (MFA in musical theater writing).

LISA HINRICHSEN is assistant professor of English at the University of Arkansas. She teaches widely in the history of twentieth-century American literature, but her research and more specialized courses focus on the literature of the U.S. South, psychoanalytic theory, and autobiographical literature. She has published articles on William Faulkner, Robert Frost, Bobbie Ann Mason, and Elizabeth Madox Roberts, and has work forthcoming on Lan Cao, Worth Tuttle Hedden, and James Weldon Johnson.

ANDY JOHNSON is a PhD candidate in the Department of English at the University of Kentucky where he has taught courses in film and writing. His research and writing usually focuses on twentieth-century stories of war in American literature and film, but he was eager to write his chapter on trucker films in honor of his family members who drive the 18-wheelers and to remind himself of the fun of riding the open highways with his dad in a long-nose conventional Kenworth.

DEREK C. MAUS is associate professor of English at the State University of New York at Potsdam, where he teaches courses on global contemporary literature. He is the author of *Unvarnishing Reality: Subversive Russian and American Cold War Satire* and co-editor (with Owen E. Brady) of *Finding a Way Home: A Critical Assessment of Walter Mosley's Fiction*. He is fairly sure his next book is on either Colson Whitehead or Nikolai Gogol, but it might somehow end up involving both of them.

RICHARD MORA is an assistant professor of sociology at Occidental College. Having received his PhD in sociology and social policy from Harvard University, he investigates youth cultures, media, youth violence, gender, and education. Dr. Mora teaches courses in youth cultures, sociology of education, and social inequality.

JUSTIN PHILPOT is a PhD candidate in the American Culture Studies Program at Bowling Green State University. Despite numerous interventions, he is still interested in nearly everything.

RYAN POLL teaches in the English Department at Northeastern Illinois University. His research focuses on twentieth- and twenty-first-century American literature and culture; scales of space (local, national, regional, and global) and scales of time (in particular planetary time and the temporal patterns of trauma); narratives of globalization; ecocriticism; and subnational and transnational working-class imaginaries. He is the author of *Main Street and Empire* (forthcoming from Rutgers University Press), an examination of how the ideological small town is used in literary, cultural, and political texts to stage and reproduce the nation throughout the twentieth- and into the twenty-first century.

MARCUS SCHULZKE is a PhD candidate in political science at the State University of New York at Albany. His primary research interests are political theory, comparative politics, political violence, applied ethics, and digital media. He is currently working on a dissertation about how soldiers make moral decision in combat.

IRIS G. SHEPARD is a fourth-year English literature PhD student at the University of Arkansas. Her area of specialization includes children's culture with a focus on community literacy and the marginalization of children. In addition to her graduate work, she is the activities director for Razorback Writers, an after-school literacy project designed to help underserved middle school students in northwest Arkansas develop a love of writing and reading. She also is a full-time instructor at Spring International Language School, an intensive English-language program for nonnative speakers. She just completed her first novel, and has published both scholarly work and short fiction.

REBECCA TOLLEY-STOKES is an associate professor and librarian at East Tennessee State University. "Around and Around She Goes: Roller Derby in Appalachia" appeared in *Now & Then*. She co-edited *Generation X Librarian: Essays on Leadership, Technology, Pop Culture, Social Responsibility and Professional Identity* (2011). Her professional interests include organizational culture, servant leadership, emerging technology, the digital divide, and scholarly communication and publishing. Outside of library and information technology her research interests include women's history, class issues, food, photography, Southern Appalachia, and popular culture. She was Fresh Meat with the Little City Roller Girls in 2010 before an injury ended her roller derby dreams.

TERRENCE T. TUCKER is an assistant professor of English at the University of Arkansas, specializing in studies of African American culture.

DANIEL CROSS TURNER is an assistant professor of English at Coastal Carolina University. His published scholarship, including numerous articles and interviews about contemporary writers and filmmakers, focuses on regional definition in national and global contexts, and on aesthetic forms' potential to record historical transitions. His first book, on poetry and memory in modern southern culture, is under contract with the University of Tennessee Press. His current book project explores conjunctions and conflicts between primitivism (aesthetic, philosophical, ethnographic, ecological) and modernity in the literature and cinema of the transforming U.S. South from 1919 to the present. He is co-editor of the southern literature listserv on H-Net (H-Southern-Lit).